W9-AXG-257

STUDIES IN HONOR OF T. W. BALDWIN

STUDIES IN HONOR OF T. W. BALDWIN

edited by Don Cameron Allen

UNIVERSITY OF ILLINOIS PRESS

Urbana, 1958

Manufactured in the United States of America
Library of Congress Catalog Card No. 58-6992

CONTENTS

INTRODUCTION

Don Cameron Allen

In the fall of 1925, the undergraduates learned that a new assistant professor of English had arrived in Urbana and was offering courses in Mediaeval and Elizabethan Drama. The more venturesome of them promptly signed his register to be greeted by a genial and enthusiastic young man, who looked almost avid when he talked about the problems in his subject and how he hoped to solve them. The scholarly approach was something new in undergraduate courses in English Literature, which were usually attended because of their restfulness. But it was shortly discovered that there was no rest under Professor Baldwin, who expected his protégés to read play texts in heaps and not just English texts alone. Actually, his courses began with the Romans and could not end until his students, like himself, had mastered all that could be known and seen to it that more was known than before.

It is now a generation later and Professor Baldwin in obedience to university regulation is leaving his chair. No professor has ever retired in greater vigor; few professors have added so much to our knowledge and kept a contagious delight in knowledge for itself. It is, likewise, hard to think of many professors who welcome, as Professor Baldwin does, the competition of his students and colleagues. His first question has always been: "What are you doing now?" *You* had better be prepared not to say, "Nothing." It was a dull colleague or student, indeed, who did not take fire from him.

This is, of course, not the place to summarize Professor Baldwin's achievements or describe his gifts as a scholar. They are too well known to demand description, too large to admit summary. In 1916 when he left Princeton, our knowledge of the drama and stagecraft of the age of Shakespeare was truly limited. We had, for instance, not yet learned the need for understanding the Elizabethan intellectual background. We knew almost nothing about Elizabethan education or dramatic theory and practice. We had no realization of the process of artistic metamorphosis that brought a poetic figure to

Shakespeare from Ovid via a dozen shapening hands. Many of these matters are now plainer for us, clearer because Professor Baldwin showed us the way.

But learned debts can only be repaid in kind. The scholar knows, or ought to know if he is a scholar, that his name and nature are written on the wind. His visible monument is a fading listing in a library catalogue or a continuing footnote that the expunging editors have failed to erase. His consolation is that what he found out produced other findings, that the intellectual process kept on partly because of him. For this reason those of us who are so much in debt to Professor Baldwin have brought this volume of essays together in his honor, so that in a way we can revise Dante's phrase to read: "Gran favilla poco fiamma seconda."

Johns Hopkins University

CRITICISM OF ELIZABETHAN DRAMATIC TEXTS

Hardin Craig

I don't know that anybody has called attention to the special importance of the new epistemology in humanistic scholarship. Lord Russell asked this question: If the axioms of mathematics must be accepted as true, why may not axioms in other areas of recognition be also so accepted? If it is answered that they may be, they need no argument to support them, but stand in the position of the obvious. This position affords a basis of hope in its doctrine that truth is a matter of complete comprehension and is immediately perceived, having no need of analysis in its final aspect. As Whitehead says, reality is just itself. This is also summarized in these terms: the development of a proposition is at no point a matter for argument; the student merely is or is not able to comprehend. Every proposition rests on the acceptance of an axiom, a postulate, or another proposition. No part by itself is adequate. The truth is a totality that embraces both method and proof. The use of argument is of another sort. Its function is to assist in determining whether the criteria of an abstraction are actual or illusory and whether, if established as fact, they are adequate in extension. The new way seems to be that of total comprehension — complete clarity and probability in general conception and complete concinnity in all the parts. For example, T. W. Baldwin in *William Shakspere's Small Latine and Lesse Greeke* (Urbana, 1944) devoted himself to Shakespeare's education. Back of the subject lay an erroneous belief, widely accepted, that Shakespeare had no formal education. When Baldwin got through, there were no more records of Shakespeare's schooling, at Stratford or elsewhere, than there had been before, but the totality of the investigation, the soundness of the general concept, and the agreement of its parts with one another and with the basal proposition left no room for reasonable doubt that Shakespeare was educated in an Elizabethan grammar school. Not even the most barren skeptic could doubt the truth of Baldwin's conclusion or find in it, aside from details, any occasion for argument or debate.

This change in the concept of the search for truth was long in coming and was no entirely new thing. It is in agreement with Baconian induction held tenaciously by the Scottish school as late as the nineteenth century. It comes back to us, however, so reinforced and developed as to be unrecognizable. It tells us there is no partition between the so-called material and the so-called spiritual, so that we are now in the same situation as the thinkers of the pre-Cartesian world. We are of course far better off in our knowledge than were the educated men of the Renaissance and far less hampered by superstition and dogmatism than they were, but they held the emancipatory doctrine of the unity of nature, and it has come back. With better powers of definition we again think of ourselves as in the midst of an indivisible continuum of varied but not totally separable elements. The greater natural scientists have renounced materialism, and it is strange that we who have opposed the doctrine that nothing exists except matter should still be bound by the fetters of the scientific method and should accept its formalities as sole tests of truth. The effect of the new epistemology is, however, not to abandon the scientific method but to supplement it. The concept of absolute truth according to which an eternal and indestructible house of truth was to be built has given way to a relativistic concept. The proven hypothesis is now regarded as a fragment and scientific principles themselves as working hypotheses.

We have also been provided with a theory of cognition appropriate to the universality of a space-time continuum both as regards comprehension and discovery, into which we need not enter at this time. We shall, however, select for consideration somewhat arbitrarily two controlling aspects of the new epistemology. One is the aspect of completeness, and the other the aspect of consistency. The former is inherent in the new philosophy and brings with it the demand that the criteria of abstraction shall be complete. The latter is a matter of logic, which is of course the operative aspect of the new epistemology. We may content ourselves in this connection with calling attention to the doctrine of the formation of classes as advanced by the symbolic logicians. According to this the context of abstraction must be pure, that is, admit into the class no member that does not belong there. It must also be as complete as possible, for incomplete contexts give rise to partial truth or outright error. This, it may be said in passing, is an unfortunate legacy from the sciences to the humanities. We shall draw our illustrations from the field of the textual criticism of Elizabethan dramatic texts.

Emendation, or the attempt to correct or improve texts, is no doubt an ancient practice, often an effort to restore what an author had written. It had in it from the beginning until its latest formulation an element of choice in which the emendator became for the nonce an author. For ages the texts of ancient secular and religious works passed from one copyist to another and now and then industrious scholars made efforts to produce editorially better texts. The most conspicuous name among students of the interrelations of texts is that of Karl Lachmann, who, in his edition of the New Testament in 1842, discovered the significance of common errors and laid down others of the principles of textual criticism. He thus founded a new science with which, by and large, there is little fault to be found, but note that the formal textual criticism of the classics operates by means of groups or families toward an archetype or supposedly perfect original from the hand of an author. Such a system, correct as it is, does not and cannot apply without adaptation to many dramatic texts. Mystery plays when traced back to their origins simply disappear in tropes or tiny Latin *ordines*. What we have before us is an aggregate of the work of many hands at many times, or, at best, some extensive redaction by an unknown reviser. We may sometimes be able to tear the composition apart and show the stages of its amplification, but the difficulties of describing textual relations still continue, and in order to understand the interrelation of versions we are forced to introduce other considerations besides mere variants.

A milder form of the same uncertainty appears in versions of Elizabethan plays such as those of Shakespeare. There is, first of all, the matter of Shakespeare's revision of his works. Some scholars have anachronistically rejected the idea that Shakespeare revised his plays, having inherited, perhaps from some academic ancestor, a wrong interpretation of the statement of Heminges and Condell that they found no blot in his papers. It is preposterous to hold such a view, for the evidences of revision are many, widespread, and convincing. If there exist, as is often the case, two or more versions of the same play, or scene, both obviously the work of Shakespeare, which shall we say is the original?

There is nothing rigid or unintelligent about textual criticism as developed by classical scholars for the determination of the interrelations of classical texts. It makes ample allowance for every sort of exigency that might appear in the experience of a transmitted text, such as problems of collation, accidental resemblances among texts, intermixture or conflation, the influence of non-extant manuscripts, the nature of *testimonia,* and so on. It provides for the use of every sort of subsidiary aid that it needs — translation into other languages, casual quotations, imitations, and ancient commentaries. It studies causes of corruption, not only emendation, but errors of eye, hand, and mind; also misreadings, haplography, dittography, phonetic confusion, metrical dislocation, and wrong words. Classical textual criticism is adapted to its needs and serves them well. The trouble comes when it is applied mechanically to Elizabethan dramatic texts and so poorly understood that textual criticism becomes merely a matter of variants. The fact remains that the texts with which we deal were not transmitted from copyist to copyist through centuries but came about in other circumstances.

No obligation therefore rests upon us to ignore the special conditions that existed in Elizabethan times or the customs and influences that were then at work. Let us consider, as a case in point, the customary ways of supplying manuscripts to the stage, which seem to have brought into existence two versions of a new play — the author's original manuscript and a new version of the same. The author's original may be reasonably supposed often to have been in a relatively disordered state. The problem would be simpler if the author's original had been destroyed or thrown away, but such copies seem sometimes to have found their way into the hands of publishers. Moreover, in the making of a clean copy for submission to the censor and for the use of the company, especially, one would think, if the author made it himself, changes might be introduced. The clean copy became the authorized playbook of the theater, and, when it got into the hands of the actors, new and worse troubles began. Plays became subject to what we might call stage degeneration, a force that operated inevitably to a degree proportional to the amount of their use on the stage and to the competency of the actors who played them. But the early vicissitudes of plays are not over, for such plays might be cut down for acting, and stage versions may, for all we know, have been acted in London theaters, but, in any case, they were used by traveling companies in the provinces, where acting was on a low level because of ignorance, want of skill, poverty, and lack of enough members of the troupe. Such plays got into print, and the textual results are often somewhat appalling; yet these bad texts are often respectable in origin and not infrequently tell us what the dramatist said. All of these special circumstances need to be taken into consideration in the textual history of Elizabethan plays, and formal textual criticism is inadequate unless this is done. We sometimes have to reckon with such things as multiple versions and how and why they came into existence, revisions, the relative disregard of an author's original words if the copyist, the printer, or especially the actor decided to change them, abridge them, or omit them. This is merely a way of saying that nothing short of the completest possible knowledge will serve our turn. We have space for only two illustrations. The first is from *Hamlet.*

The relation of the text of Q1 (1603) to that of Q2 (1604-5), on the one hand, and to that of F (1623), on the other, is a problem of importance, but one about which there has been no agreement. The ways in which dramatic texts came into existence seem, however, to afford a simple solution with some interesting implications. The title page of Q2 says, "Newly imprinted and enlarged to almost as much againe as it was, according to the true and perfect Coppie." If this means anything, it means that Q2 was a revision, and internal evidence, into which we need not go, supports that view. The folio text in normal practice would have been based on a clean copy of that revision, but, if that is true, why does the text of Q1 agree in original readings sometimes with Q2 against F and sometimes with F against Q2? That is the problem. Q1 was printed from a stage version. It is full of the marks of a prompter. It has also almost certainly been shortened and so changed as to require fewer actors for its performance. Its title page tells us that it had been acted "in the two Vniversities of Cambridge and Oxford, and elsewhere," and its degenerations by actors show that it had been played by a provincial company. If it is a shortened stage version, of what text is it a condensation? Not of Q2 or of F. There is only one other possibility, and that is the lost play that has been revised into the form of Q2. The great amount of speculation and debate about this and other similar problems seems to have come about through failure to take into consideration all the factors necessary for the formulation of a correct conclusion.

An examination of the areas of the plot where there are no Q1 variants suggests that the revision was mainly amplificatory and devoted to the enrichment of the play in poetic beauty and dramatic interest. That there was such an unrevised original at the basis of Q1 is made certain by the balanced relation of the text of Q1 between the texts of Q2 and F. Thus placed, Q1 would be in position to arbitrate between the two better texts. When there are errors and misreadings in Q2 and not in F, Q1 ought, unless it itself is in error, to agree with F, and when there are errors and actor changes in F that do not appear in Q2, Q1 ought to agree with Q2. Q1 does these things in an overwhelming number of cases. Out of seventy-eight major variants, i.e., those that affect the meaning of the text, in which the quartos agree with each other against the folio version, there are sixty-four in which Q1 seems unquestionably to support Q2 and only fourteen about which there may be even a slight doubt. Out of sixty-six of such variants in which Q1 and F agree against Q2 there are about fifty-nine cases in which Q1 supports an original reading in F and only seven that might be open to question. These determinations are of course based on individual judgments, but I am by no means sure that the doubtful cases are not fewer than stated. There is only one possible explanation of this situation. Unless Q1 retains original readings from a version basal to both Q2 and F, such as the play revised into the form of Q2, it could not possibly arbitrate as it does between the two other texts.

My second illustration, which I shall not work out in detail, comes from *Richard II* and *1 Henry IV*. These plays were entered in the Stationers' Register to Andrew Wise, the former on August 29, 1597, and the latter on February 25, 1598. Quarto editions of *Richard II* were published by Wise in 1597 and twice in 1598; quarto editions of *1 Henry IV* in 1598 and 1599. All of the texts published by Wise are bad and show no disposition to grow better. Then, in a full court held on June 25, 1603, the ownership of both plays was set over from Andrew Wise to Matthew Law. Law had a good printer and the quality of the texts issued by him is immediately and continuously better — Q3 (1604), Q4 (1608), and Q5 (1613) of *1 Henry IV* and Q4 (1608) and Q5 (1615) of *Richard II*. The corrections of the texts are for the most part simple matters. There are some additional errors, but, in general, the intelligent common sense of Law's printer makes itself felt. In so doing it restores original readings that appear in the folio text of 1623.

It is reasonable to believe that these original readings had remained in the playbook undisturbed and that they appeared in the folio in due course when the playbooks were set up by Jaggard and Blount. A literal application of the theory of textual variants, however, suggested to scholars that the folio version was set from a quarto with which it agreed in certain correct readings, although because of other differences it became necessary to invent many processes, such as the collation of quartos with playhouse manuscripts, the use of quartos as promptbooks, and various sorts of contamination, all of which seem both costly and unnecessary. It is true that in the case of *1 Henry IV,* except in its relation to the Dering version, the conventional view has not been severely held and that in the case of *Richard II* opinion has wavered, as it naturally would, as to whether the folio was set up from Q3 or Q5. Possibly back of the desire to supply the printers of the First Folio with printed instead of handwritten copy is the very natural feeling on the part of scholars that, if they themselves had the work of composition to do, they would prefer print to the Elizabethan secretary hand. It might be said, however, that that chirography probably did not have the difficulty for Elizabethan printers that it has for us. My main point, however, is that, in the textual history of the two plays, agreements, as well no doubt as differences, may have come about in another way than transcription.

University of Missouri

OLD-SPELLING EDITIONS OF DRAMATIC TEXTS

Fredson Bowers

Read before the English Drama Section of the Modern Language Association of America, at the University of Wisconsin, September 10, 1957.

The rationale of a critical old-spelling edition of an Elizabethan play — or of any text for that matter — is not to be summed up under any single heading. But if we isolate the one unique reason for its existence, surely we must say: The critical old-spelling edition seeks to establish the text and thereby to become a definitive edition.

Let us break this statement down to its various parts.

A critical edition. This has three senses. An edition may be called critical if it is a critic's edition, that is, if it is designed to satisfy the standards for accuracy and completeness that a critic should require of any text on which he proposes to base his investigations. In the second sense, an edition is critical if its text has been edited on critical principles. I take it that the proper application of the critical editorial process is to produce a text that recovers the author's final intentions more faithfully than any preserved transmitted document. Third, in a subordinate sense, the edition (as distinct from the text) may be called critical if it endeavors in its introduction, apparatus, and commentary to provide a critic with all necessary information about the text and the circumstances of its composition and transmission.

The critic addressed is not necessarily of the "total values" school, one whose insensitivity to the details of a text often makes him impatient with the standards and methods of textual criticism.[1] Rather, the edition is designed for the whole republic of serious readers, ranging from the student

[1] As the critic I once heard argue in a public discussion that it made no difference whether in *Hamlet* Shakespeare wrote *sallied* or *solid flesh,* since the "total values" of the play were not in the least affected by the choice of reading.

anxious to evaluate the literary merit of the play, through every shade of endeavor from the investigator of dramatic technique to the metrist, and even including the philologist concerned with Elizabethan idiom and orthographic habits. In short, anyone dealing with the work as a literary, ideological, or linguistic document, and therefore anyone who is concerned to read the text in its most carefully established form.

An established text. Much confusion inheres to this phrase. There are two levels at which a text becomes established. At the first level the editor seeks the document containing the text in its most authoritative preserved form; that is, by collation of readings, aided by any other internal or external evidence, he establishes from among the various documents in which the text may be preserved that one that has the most immediate transcriptional link to the author's holograph manuscript. This is a substantive text. If all later texts derive from this without reference to fresh authority, the editor has established the sole authoritative documentary form of the text. Except for whatever evidence is available within this document, no other known authority for the text can exist.

Of course, the case is not always so simple. More than one text may claim authority. A second document may have been inscribed from an independent manuscript, or the text may be partly derived from the initial substantive authority but altered by consultation of some other authoritative document now lost. It is clear in these complex cases occurring within the Elizabethan drama that, in plays where multiple substantive authority exists, even though one text may be much inferior to that in the main substantive document, no one document can be established as representing in every detail the text in its most authoritative known form.

However, we cannot deny that it is usually possible to discover which one or more documents contain the text in any state of authority. The question then arises — if we take the simplest case, in which only a single authoritative document exists, and we can demonstrate that fact, why have we not established the text if we reprint it exactly as found in that document? The first objection, though more than a quibble, is not so peremptory as to dispose of the question. It is legitimate to ask, however, which form of the text and in what concrete example of the document? Are we to accept *any* example without regard for its mixture of uncorrected and corrected states of the type? Shall we accept the uncorrected states exclusively, or the corrected states exclusively even in cases in which the editor admits that the proofreader sophisticated the text?[2] Some editorial discretion is inevitable; and

[2] See the Malone Society Reprint of Chettle's *Hoffman*. I don't know what a conservative reprint editor would do if most of the press-corrected formes were

even here it is obvious that we must move away from the strict reprint concept.

More important, however, is the objection that the establishment of the most authoritative documentary form (ordinarily the first edition) does not in any sense provide the critic with a text that is, in Greg's words, "so far as the available evidence permits, in the form in which we may suppose that it would have stood in a fair copy made by the author himself, of the work as he finally intended it."[3] Until the errors of the printing process, at the very least, are weeded out, it is certainly anomalous to speak of establishing a text. Thus we must distinguish between establishing the documentary form, and establishing the text itself. A photographic or type facsimile, or a diplomatic reprint, of the document remains, therefore, a specialist's tool that presents the text only in its raw and inevitably corrupt state. To invite the literary critic to make his own decisions about the nature and extent of these errors as he reads for quite other purposes is not to furnish him with anything that can be called a critic's edition. And in complex cases, when multiple authority is present, the reprint theory would require a literary critic to face a parallel text of three editions of *Hamlet* from which it would be his privilege to select what he fancied were Shakespeare's intentions.

To establish the text the editor must himself treat it critically. That is, he must attempt to recover what the author actually wrote — in his final intentions — as closely as bibliographical techniques, linguistic analysis, and critical intelligence can guide him. In complex cases he must separate the authority of the substantives (the author's final words) from the authority of the accidentals (the texture of spelling, punctuation, capitalization) that clothe these substantives;[4] and by any necessary eclectic selection contrive that form of the text that in all its details most closely corresponds to what

---

unauthoritative, but one or more exhibited authoritative alteration. I think it demonstrable, for instance, that Dekker himself corrected one forme of *The Magnificent Entertainment.* Grounds exist for believing that the second stage of the proof correction of one forme of Dekker's *Match Me in London* was ordered by the proofreader referring back to copy so that the alterations are authoritative; and I believe that Dekker himself corrected proof for the first stage of press-alteration of another forme in this play, but not the second stage of the same forme. For various problems connected with the reprinting of the most authoritative readings in a press-variant text, see my "The Problem of the Variant Forme in a Facsimile Edition," *The Library,* 5th Series, VII (1952), 262-72.

[3] W. W. Greg, *The Editorial Problem in Shakespeare,* 2nd ed. (Oxford, 1951), p. x.

[4] See W. W. Greg, "The Rationale of Copy-Text," *Studies in Bibliography,* III (1950), 19-36.

would have been the authorial intentions in print;[5] in other words, presents the words of an author in their most authoritative recoverable form. Only an edition made up by the most advanced methods of textual criticism is properly a critical edition, of sufficient trustworthiness for general critical use.

Old Spelling. Such an edition must be in old spelling. If the words of an author are to be presented in their most authoritative recovered form, the form cannot be distinguished from the word. Since the Elizabethan forms of words are an essential part of Elizabethan English, any interference with these forms places the critical reader at an arbitrary remove from the author's characteristics so far as these may be determined, and certainly from the linguistic characteristics of the period. It matters nothing that at the present stage of our knowledge we cannot often be sure what are authorial and what compositorial characteristics in the orthography of dramatic texts. Generalizations are difficult because different compositors certainly treated their copy in very different ways. Yet this is beside the point. As Greg remarks: "For the critic modernization has no attraction in itself. So long as there is any chance of an edition preserving some trace, however faint, of the author's individuality, the critic will wish to follow it: and even when there is none, he will still prefer an orthography that has a period resemblance with the author's to one that reflects the linguistic habits of a later date."[6]

No system of modernization can be contrived that does not do violence to the Elizabethan English of a play.[7] The only consistent form of modernization is the complete and absolute normalizing of all Elizabethan variant forms that do not reflect different meanings. This sounds easier than it is. On the other hand, the school of partial modernizers, as represented by the New Arden and the New Yale editors, save something, but not enough to make their efforts worthwhile. And in the process of attempting to distinguish words in which variant spelling reflects authentic forms (Arden) or different pronunciations (Yale), the editors involve themselves in such logical (and linguistic) contradictions as in fact to do more damage by their commissions than the total modernizers by their omissions. For there is no partially modernizing edition extant that does not retain as significant variation what is actually a mishmash of compositorial misprints, orthographical vari-

[5] See my "Current Theories of Copy-Text, with an illustration from Dryden," *MP,* XLVIII (1950), 12-20.

[6] Greg, *Editorial Problem,* pp. li-lii.

[7] *Ibid.,* p. li: "To print *banquet* for *banket, fathom* for *fadom, lantern* for *lanthorn, murder* for *murther, mushroom* for *mushrump, orphan* for *orphant, perfect* for *parfit, portcullis* for *perculace, tattered* for *tottered, vile* for *vild, wreck* for *wrack,* and so on, and so on, is sheer perversion."

ants demonstrably *not* reflecting pronunciation differences in the text in question and demonstrable compositorial usages mixed with inferential authorial characteristics, while all the time concealing by modernization about as much true evidence as has been inconsistently emphasized (along with the false) by special treatment.[8] In such a matter it is better to be ignorant than to be misled. By its nature, no modernized text of an Elizabethan play can be trustworthy enough to satisfy the requirements of a serious critic.

A definitive edition is only a comparative term, since we must always believe that from time to time the accumulation of scholarship will enable an editor to improve on the work of his predecessors. But in its own day an edition may be called definitive if — on the positive side — by stretching the limits of contemporary scholarship it has recovered what appears to be the most authoritative form of the dramatist's text. This recovery must always extend beyond the form of the text in any single authoritative document, and only in this extended sense may the text be called truly established and therefore definitive. Thus no facsimile or conservative reprint of an authoritative document can qualify as a definitive edition, except as an edition of that document. Since the printed document represents a trans-

[8] See Alice Walker, "Compositor Determination and Other Problems in Shakespearian Texts," *Studies in Bibliography,* VII (1955), 4: "Among textual critics, though wiser heads have never supposed that the spelling of printed books was the author's (the Old Cambridge editors, for instance, rejected the idea of an old spelling Shakespeare on this account), there is even yet a great deal of muddled thinking. Spellings of one writer are compared with those of another on the evidence of printed texts of different dates from different printing houses [f.n.1: H. T. Price, for instance, in *English Institute Essays 1947* (1948), 143-58] and the vagaries of compositors are being erratically introduced into modernised texts of Shakespeare [f.n.2: I have remarked on this in a recent review of the New Arden *Titus Andronicus.* It is the general policy of the new series 'to preserve all older forms that are more than variant spellings' — a policy which has not, I suspect, been seen in relation to its logical linguistic conclusions. When Muir, for instance, in the New Arden *Lear,* followed the Folio's 'murther', what was he reproducing — the compositor's spelling or a scribal alteration of the Q1 spelling on the authority of the *Lear* prompt-book? If it was the prompt-book spelling, was it Shakespeare's? Further, if consonant variants, like 'murther' and 'vild', are preserved, why not the vowel variants in 'show' and 'shew', 'blood' and 'bloud'? Why not the common 'alablastar' or 'abhominable' and (contrariwise), in early texts, 'clime' for 'climb' or 'limmes' for 'limbs'? Muir went so far as to reproduce Compositor B's arbitrary distinctions between — 'd and — ed of weak preterites and past participles in prose. But what will happen in the New Arden *As You Like It* where there are two compositors favouring different conventions? Modern English is one thing; the habits of the compositors of Shakespearian texts are quite another, and the arbitrary preservation of a selection of the latter has no linguistic principles behind it.]" See also Greg's review of the New Arden *Titus Andronicus* in *MLR,* XLIX (1954), 362, and Arthur Brown's comments in "Editorial Problems in Shakespeare: Semi-Popular Editions," *Studies in Bibliography,* VIII (1956), 19.

mitted form of the author's holograph, the critical editor's attempt to go in back of the document to recover as much as he can of the purity of its source must always transcend the value of the conservative editor's labors.

On the negative side, a definitive critical edition — though admitting editorial correction, emendation, and even the conflation of authorities — should not unnecessarily interpose the editor between the original and the reader. Unnecessary interposition may be regarded as (1) any interference with the author's final intentions so far as these may be ascertained; (2) any interference with the transmitting agent's intentions when these do not appear to differ significantly from what we may suppose to represent the author's intentions; and (3) any interference with the general linguistic habits of the period contemporary with the documentary form of the copy-text when these do not appear to differ from (1) or (2) above.

Under these conditions, the modernized text (though sometimes qualifying as critically edited) must be rejected as nondefinitive, since it unquestionably interferes (no matter what its form) with the linguistic and orthographic habits of author, of compositor, and of the period.

The critical old-spelling edition seeks to establish the text and thereby to become a definitive edition. This is its rationale.

It would appear, therefore, that a need exists for a class of text aimed at an audience somewhere in between the bibliographer and the school child, or the drugstore trade. I suggest that this need may be filled by properly constructed critical old-spelling editions. At the upper level these editions should be qualified to serve as a trustworthy basis for advanced critical inquiry; at the lower level they should not be beyond the ability of a literate undergraduate to handle.

Let us not be too solemn about this critical old-spelling edition. It should be a reading text first, and a reference text only secondarily. And the editor should make every effort to appeal to the maximum group of users so long as this catholicity is not achieved at the expense of critically dangerous modifications. Briefly, these old-spelling editions can and should be made more attractive to the general user, first by removing all but the most immediately pertinent of the apparatus to appendices in the rear, thus freeing the text page from all information that is only of reference value and so of no immediate concern to the reader.[9]

Second, at the risk of offending some conservatives, I strongly advocate that an old-spelling editor should modernize the *u:v* and *i:j* conventions, just as he now customarily normalizes the old long *s* in the interests of the

[9] See the treatment of the apparatus advocated in the prefatory remarks to my *Dramatic Works of Thomas Dekker,* Vol. I (Cambridge, Eng., 1953).

present-day reader. The period of the Elizabethan drama is not itself consistent in this usage;[10] and we shall do ourselves a good turn by removing what is probably the most serious bar to the use of old-spelling texts by general readers.

It is a shameful thing that we are bringing up a generation of undergraduates who are scarcely conscious that the language of the past differed in its forms from that of the present, that Shakespeare did not write in logically punctuated Johnsonian periods, and that the speech of characters in Elizabethan plays was not almost entirely a series of exclamations starting with "Good Morrow!" Yet it is our fault, and not the undergraduates'. If we deliberately alienate them by associating an old-spelling text with specialized scholarship over their heads, instead of offering it as the normal means of reading the literature of an earlier period — and a means that can be materially eased by a few typographical reforms — we alone, and our pedantry, are to blame. The methods by which we can contrive that textual good money should drive out the bad are so obvious and so sane as to reflect seriously on our competence as teachers and as scholars if we reject this offered good and do not shape the editing of texts to our purposes instead of to the purposes of the publishers of textbooks and the laziness or timidity, but often only the inexperience, of our academic textbook editors.

[10] For two excellent examples, both from the year 1604, see the practices of the different compositors within each first edition of Dekker's *Magnificent Entertainment* and *The Honest Whore,* Part I.

University of Virginia

HUMOR AND SATIRE IN HEYWOOD'S EPIGRAMS

Burton A. Milligan

There is more humor than satire in the six hundred epigrams of John Heywood, and both the humor and the satire follow to a large extent conventions established in fabliaux, jestbooks, colloquies like Erasmus's, Latin *facetiae,* animal fables, medieval *exempla,* and medieval and early Renaissance satire generally.

Heywood saw himself accurately as an epigrammatist who was primarily a jester: "Ye sir, I take mery mirth a golden gift"; "Art thou Heywood that hath made men mery long? / Ye: and will, if I be made mery amonge."[1] Most of his epigrams that are primarily humorous, rather than primarily satirical, fall into the following categories: epigrams dependent upon puns and other verbal quibbles; narrative epigrams treating ridiculous or extravagant situations like those of jestbooks and animal fables; and epigrams whose humor arises from flitings, ingenious invective, and the exchange of witty insults.

Epigrams based upon puns and verbal quibbles are numerous; indeed, sixty-eight of the six hundred epigrams are of this sort, and many others employ wordplay incidentally. The "false wit" upon which this group of epigrams depends has interesting predecessors and successors: a good deal

[1] "Of Heywood," Epigram 100 of *The fifth hundred of Epygrams,* in *John Heywood's "Works" and Miscellaneous Short Poems,* ed. Burton A. Milligan (Urbana, 1956), p. 224. In subsequent footnotes, for the sake of simplification, the full titles of the four collections of epigrams will be abbreviated as follows, and the number following the abbreviation will be that of the epigram concerned; all page references will be to the edition cited above:

The fyrste hundred of Epigrammes — 100
Three hundred Epigrammes, vpon three hundred prouerbes — 300
The fifth hundred of Epygrams — 500
A sixt hundred of Epigrammes — 600.

of the wit of Sir Thomas More and his group, the more strained verbal humor of Shakespeare and his age, and much of the elaborate punning of John Donne and other metaphysical poets. Within the general framework of the pun and the quibble, Heywood employed several stock devices: puns on verbs and common nouns; puns on proper names, especially place names; elaborate anecdotes based upon wordplay and pun. Some examples of Heywood's puns or quibbles on verbs and common nouns are the following:

Iacke and his father.

Iacke (quoth his father) how shall I ease take?
If I stand, my legges ake, and if I kneele,
My knees ake, If I goe, then my feete ake,
If I lie, my backe akthe, If I sit I feele
My hyps ake: and leane I neuer so weele,
My elbowes ake: Sir (quoth Iacke) peyn to exile,
Sens all these ease not, best ye hang a while.[2]

Of store.

Store is no sore, yes, store may be a sore.
I thinke it a sore, of sores to haue store.[3]

Of a butler and a hors.

The butler and the beere horse both be like one.
They drawe beere both: that is truth to bide one.
Both drawe beere in deede, but yet they differ lone:
The butler drawth and drinkth beere, the horse drinkth none.[4]

Among numerous examples of puns on proper names, the following are representative:

Of Newgate wyndowes.

All Newgate wyndowes bay wyndowes they bee.
All lookers out there stand at bay we see.[5]

Seekyng for a dwellyng place.

Still thou seekest for a quiet dwellyng place.
What place for quietnes hast thou now in chase?
London bridge. Thats ill for thee for the water.
Queen hyth. thats more ill for an other mater.[6]

[2] *100:* 25, pp. 115-16. In my edition of Heywood's *Works,* p. 286, I have called attention in a note to the similarity between this epigram and Donne's epigram "A lame beggar," *Poems,* ed. Sir Herbert Grierson, 2 vols. (Oxford, 1912), I, 76:

I am unable, yonder begger cries,
To stand, or move; ife he say true, hee *lies.*

[3] *300:* 59, p. 155. [4] *500:* 7, p. 204. [5] *600:* 20, p. 232.

[6] The allusion is probably to the stews nearby. Cf. John Stow, *The Survey of London* (London, 1618), p. 683: "Next adioyning to this Queene Hithe, on the West side thereof, is Salt Wharffe, named of Salt taken vp, measured and sold there. The next is Stew lane, of a Stew, or Hot-house, there kept."

Smartes Key. thats most ill for feare of smartyng smart.
Carter lane. nay, nay, that soundth all on the cart.
Powles cheine. nay in no wise dwell not neere the cheine.
Wood street: why wilt thou be wood yet once againe?
Bread streete. thats to drie by drought thou shalt be dead.
Philpot lane. that breedth moist humours in thy head.
Siluer streete: Coper smithes in Siluer streete: fie.[7]
Newgate streete. ware that man. Newgate is hard bie.
Faster lane: thou wilt as soone be tide fast: as fast.
Crooked lane: nay crooke no more, be streight at last.
Creede lane: they fall out there, brother against brother.
Aue mary lane: thats as ill as the tother.
Pater noster row: Pater noster row?
Agreede: thats the quietest place that I know.[8]

Of Powles.

Thankes to god and good people, Powles goth vp well:
Powles goth vp, but when goth poolyng downe: that tell.[9]

Good examples of anecdotes based upon, or built up for the sake of, verbal wit are the following:

A saiyng of Patche my lord cardinals foole.

Master Sexten, a parson of knowne wit,
As he at my lord Cardinals boord did sit,
Greedily raught at a goblet of wyne:
Drinke none (said my lord) for that sore leg of thine.
I warrant your grace (quoth Sexten) I prouide
For my leg: For I drinke on the tother side.[10]

Mistakyng an errand.

Feastyng a freend, the feaster (whose man did waite)
Bad him at the last course, fetche the clouted conceite.
What bringst thou here knaue (quoth he) what hast yͧ doone?
I haue (quoth his man) brought here your clouted shoone.
Clouted shoone carterly knaue, what dost thou dreame?
Eate thou the clouted shoone, fetche vs the clouted creame.[11]

[7] This allusion is almost certainly to the debasement of silver coins by the addition of copper. A number of Heywood's satirical epigrams, considered later in this paper, dealt with this abuse.

[8] *600:* 51, pp. 237-38.

[9] *600:* 62, p. 240. The reference to Paul's going up well is to the reconstruction of St. Paul's after the fire of June 4, 1561. The great spire was struck by lightning, and the roof of the church was burned. According to Stow, p. 623, the Queen, citizens of London, and the clergy promptly donated funds for repairs; and "such expedition was vsed, that within one Moneth next following the burning thereof, the Church was couered with boords and lead, in manner of a false roofe against the weather, and before the end of the said yeere, all the sayd Iles of the Church were framed out of new timber, couered with lead and fully finished."

[10] *100:* 44, pp. 123-24. Sexten, Cardinal Wolsey's fool, was nicknamed Patch.

[11] *100:* 77, p. 133. A conceit was "a fancy trifle for the table."

A hearer of a sermon.

What bringst thou from the sermon Iacke? declare that.
Forsooth maister (quoth he) your cloke and your hat.
I can thee good thanke Iacke. for thou art yet sped,
Of somewhat in thy hande, though nought in thy hed.[12]

Narrative epigrams employing and often combining elements of the fabliau and the jestbook are fairly numerous. One of the most tasteless of these, although undeniably one of the most popular in its own time, as its having been published in a separate ballad sheet indicates, is the epigram "Of a number of rattes mistaken for diuelles in a mans sloppes,"[13] which recounts the misadventures of a man who put cheese in his hose and was beset with rats, which he mistook for devils. "Of the foole and the gentlemans nose," interesting because of its relationship to the More circle, is an example of Heywood's ability to achieve wit as well as broad farce in this type of epigram:

One gentilman hauyng an other at meate,
That guest hauyng a nose deformd foule and great.
The foole of that house, at this tyme standyng by,
Fell thus in hand with that nose sodeinly.
Nose *autem,* a great nose as euer I sawe.
His master was wroth, & cride hense with that dawe.
One saide: talke no more of great noses ye foole,
Lest ye be talkt[14] withall in the whippyng schoole.
The foole warnd of great noses no more to speake,
To mend that faut, this way these woords did breake.
Saide I, this is a foule great spittell nose?
Byr lady I lyed, it is a fayre littell nose.
Will not that foole be had hence (quoth the master?)
Thou wilt foole (quoth one) be walkt with a waster,[15]
If thou speake of any nose great or small.
The foole at thyrd warnyng, mindyng to mend all,
Stept to the boord againe criyng as he gose,
Before god and man, that man hath no nose.
The foole was feakt for this: but what of that?
The great faute here to note, he amended nat.
Whiche is this: not the wise, but the foole ye see,
In clokyng of one faute, makth fautes two or three.[16]

[12] *100:* 62, p. 129.

[13] *600:* 100, p. 247. This epigram, together with Epigram 9 of *The fifth hundred of Epygrams,* was published in a black-letter broadsheet printed in London by Rouland Hall for James Rowbothum (n.d.).

[14] *talkt* 'beaten.'

[15] *walkt with a waster* 'beaten with a cudgel.'

[16] *100:* 86, p. 135. "Ellis Heywood, in his *Il Moro,* tells of a guest at More's home who had a very long nose, which brought forth an ejaculation concerning it from a member of the household, in the gentleman's hearing. More gave a glance

Several of the little narratives suggestive of fabliaux also exhibit a little more wit than mere contrivance; for example, the two following:

A question to a childe.

Who is thy father childe, axt his mothers husband.
Axe my mother (quoth he) that to vnderstand.
The boy dalieth with you sir: for verily
He knowth who is his father as well as I.
The man, of this childes wit, was wrapt in such ioy.
That he knew not what he might make of the boy.[17]

An account of a mans children.

Wyfe, of ten babes betwene vs by encrease growne,
Thou saist I haue but nyne. no mo of your owne.
Of all thynges encresyng, as my conscience lythe,
The parson must needes haue the tenth for the tythe.[18]

Among all the humorous epigrams of Heywood no other kind is found as frequently as the epigram that is a witty insult or a contest in insults. The epigrams of this type are characterized by ingenuity, zest, considerable wit, and a great deal of good humor. Some of them suggest flitings, others the less inspired invectives of Hal and Falstaff, still others Nashe's knack for witty abuse, but only a few the sharper acid and more satirical quality of some of Jonson's similar epigrams. Elaborate classification of these particular epigrams is pointless, but there are several favorite subjects or targets: shrewish wives, delinquent husbands, dolts, ugly and ill-favored persons, rogues, and criminals. Whether humor or conventional satire against women is more involved in the epigrams about shrewish wives might be debated; but with Heywood, as so often with Chaucer, one feels that humor was the main intent. Out of a multitude of examples of this sort of humor, the following are fairly representative:

Of the wyues and hir husbandes waste.

Where am I least husband? quoth he, in the wast:
Which comth of this, thou art vengeable streit laste.
Where am I biggest wife? in the waste (quoth shee)
For all is waste in you, as far as I see.[19]

A wiues defence of hir beetill brow.

Were I to wed againe wife, I make a vow,
I would not wed a wife with a beetill brow.

---

of rebuke, whereupon the confused man said that the guest had a really handsome nose, in fact hardly any nose at all. Another rebuke followed, and then came the assertion that the gentleman had no nose whatsoever! This incident is also told in Cresacre More's *Life of Sir Thomas More,* and in Erasmus' *Apothegms.*" Robert W. Bolwell, *Life and Works of John Heywood* (New York, 1921), pp. 135-36.

[17] *600:* 50, p. 237. [18] *500:* 27, p. 210. [19] *100:* 35, p. 121.

And I (quoth she) rather would a husband wed
With a beetill brow, than with a beetell hed.[20]

Weddyng and hanging.

Weddyng and hangyng are desteny I see.
Weddyng or hangyng, which is best, sir (quoth shee?)
Forsooth good wife, hangyng I thinke best (quoth hee)
So helpe me god, good husband, so thinketh mee.
Oh how like lambes, man and wyfe here agree.[21]

Of a yeres fayre.

The fayre lastth all the yere, but wyfe I tell thee,
In this yeres fayre, for fayre I can not sell thee.
I have woorse lucke (quoth she) and began to scoule,
I can not sell thee there, for faire nor for foule.[22]

Of liyng and true saiyng.

Wyfe, the people are disposed all to lye:
For thou are commended vniuersallye.
Nay syr: the people to tell truth, are all bolde,
For you are discommended of younge and olde.[23]

The fool, the dolt, the daw were Heywood's natural targets, and these he attacked with homely humor and straining wit, rather than with anything more subtle or malicious:

Of feedyng and teaching.

Thou art better fed then taught, I vndertake:
And yet art thou skyn and bone, leane as a rake.[24]

Hap and wit.

Better be happy then wyse, here art thou hit,
Thy hap hath euer ben better, then thy wit.[25]

Promise of lycence.

I wyll say no more, tyll the dayes be longer
No no, say no more tyll thy wyt be stronger.[26]

Taunts about ill favor — red noses, ugly faces, blackened teeth — are fairly numerous and uninspired. There are no swollen parcels of dropsies, huge bombards of sack, stuffed cloak-bags of guts, roasted Manningtree oxes here, or anything else half so ingenious. The wit is hardly better or worse than that in Donne's second elegy "The Anagram" about Flavia, who,

though her eyes be small, her mouth is great,
Though they be Ivory, yet her teeth be jeat,
Though they be dimme, yet she is light enough,
And though her harsh haire fall, her skinne is rough;

[20] *100:* 79, p. 133. [21] *300:* 6, p. 148. [22] *300:* 63, p. 155.
[23] *500:* 50, p. 214. [24] *300:* 42, p. 152. [25] *300:* 123, p. 166.
[26] *300:* 168, p. 176.

What though her cheeks be yellow, her haire's red,
Give her thine, and she hath a maydenhead.[27]

In harmless good nature Heywood probably wins this contest.

Of Pepper.

Thou takst pepper in the nose, and yet thy nose,
Lookth not blacke like pepper, but red like the rose.[28]

Of a good face.

I did set a good face on the matter Ione,
Thou didst borow it then Bes, for thou hast none.[29]

Of a woman dekt in two coloures.

My honny bes, blacke and white set the out nette.
Thy here whyte as perle, thy teeth blacke as iette.[30]

Of the high way and a maydes face.

The more the highway is washt, the fouler it is.
Mayde, the high way and thy face, are lyke in this.[31]

Taunts to criminals and rogues incorporating jests about cropped ears, prisons, purse cutting, etc., and frequently involving puns on the names of London prisons, are not uncommon:

Of flotyng and fleetyng.

Thou art a flote thou weenst, beyng in the fleete:
But flotyng and fleetyng agree not there meete.[32]

A man at an ebbe.

Thou art at an ebbe in Newgate, thou hast wrong.
But thou shalt be a flote at Tyburne ere long.[33]

Of eares glowyng.

Thyne eares may glowe, lets see whether they glow Iohn.
I lye: thyne eares can not glowe for thou hast non.[34]

Of a cutter of purslane.

This herbe purslane thou cutst pretily I see:
But to cut a purse in a lane, none lyke thee.[35]

Satire, where it is found in the epigrams, is the kind that Joseph Hall was to call toothless. "In all my simple writyng," claimed Heywood, "neuer ment I, / To touche any priuate person displeasantly"[36]— a claim supported by the epigrams themselves. Follies, not the individuals committing them, were the object of his satire.

[27] *Poems,* ed. Grierson, I, 80. [28] *300:* 212, p. 184. [29] *300:* 108, p. 163.
[30] *500:* 23, p. 209. [31] *600:* 6, p. 230. [32] *300:* 55, p. 154.
[33] *300:* 56, p. 154. [34] *300:* 250, p. 190. [35] *500:* 30, p. 210.
[36] "To the reader," *The fifth hundred of Epygrams,* p. 200.

Those folies, beyng sercht in reasons boundcs.
Reason maie be surgion saluyng those woundes.
Turning those sores to salues.[37]

To compare Heywood's minor achievement as a satirist with the great achievements of Chaucer or Fielding would be grotesque, but to compare his theory of satire, his tolerance, moderation, and good humor, his temper and humanity, with theirs is not absurd.

In subject, the satire in Heywood's epigrams is mainly conventional and of the sort found in many other medieval, early Renaissance, and middle Renaissance works — in Chaucer, in *Cocke Lorelle's Bote,*[38] in *The Ship of Fools,* in *The Steel Glass,* for instance. Heywood satirized the rogueries of tradesmen, craftsmen, and laborers; the law's delays; eternal human failings such as lack of love and charity, gossip and slander, hypocrisy, and pride. Little of his satire is topical, although what there is — on such subjects as the Catholic-Protestant controversies, coinage problems, and current fashions — is interesting. Moreover, in one respect Heywood was a most original satirist, original in employing his satirical wit against the half-truths, whole lies, and stale truisms of some proverbs. That many of the epigrams upon proverbs are not what I have in mind here, must be made plain. In the epigrams, as well as in the *Dialogue* on marriage, Heywood often showed respect for the distilled worldly wisdom of some proverbs as well as amused contempt for the platitudes and pseudo-wisdom of others. Also in many instances the epigrams upon proverbs have no connection with either approval or disapproval of the proverbs; in these instances the proverbs serve merely as an axis for a turn of wit, verbal or otherwise, directed not at the proverb but at a subject or a person.

The satire on roguery in trades and crafts is little more than a reiteration of the conventional charges of medieval and early Renaissance satirists. The thievery of millers is satirized,[39] the complicity of brokers with thieves,[40] the tricks of shoemakers,[41] the cheats of ale sellers and vintners,[42] the unreasonable fees of barbers,[43] the use of false measures,[44] the tricks of watermen.[45] Heywood was more interested, in the epigrams of this group, in neat turns of wit than in satire on roguery, as the following examples show:

[37] "To the reader," *The firste hundred of Epigrammes,* ll. 18-20, p. 104.
[38] *Cock Lorelle's Bote* is the only work alluded to by title in all of the epigrams; see *300:* 189, p. 180.
[39] *100:* 91, p. 136. [40] *300:* 52, p. 154.
[41] *100:* 56, p. 128 and *300:* 144, p. 172.
[42] *500:* 14, p. 207 and *500:* 21, p. 209.
[43] *500:* 86, p. 221. [44] *300:* 66, p. 156. [45] *600:* 32, p. 234.

Of the Milner and the Sexten.

The milner tolth corne, the sexten tolth the bell,
In whiche tollyng, tollers thriue not a lyke well.
Thone tolth with the clapper, thother in the hopper.
Thone sauerth of syluer, thother soundeth of copper.

Of a wyne drawer.

Drawer, thy wyne is euen with thee now I see:
Thou persyste the wine, and the wyne perseth thee.[46]

The satire on abuses of the law is no less conventional:

The suertie of some seale.

As sure as it were sealde with butter, for sooth:
Sum butter seale lastth, as longe as some waxe dooth.[47]

Of long sutes.

Sutes hange halfe a yere at Westminster hall,
At Tyburne, halfe an houres hangyng endeth all.[48]

Heywood's satirical epigrams on such universal human failings as lack of kindness and charity, gossip and slander, hypocrisy, and pride are conventional in subject matter, but usually not conventional in treatment and tone. In intensity, seriousness, sometimes bitterness, they are set apart from the merely witty satirical epigrams. They tell us, as Heywood's other writings do, that Heywood was the real enemy of unkindness and affectation. Among a number of epigrams commenting upon men's lack of brotherhood and kindness are the following:

Of spite.

If there be any, as I hope there be none,
That would leese both his eies, to leese his foe one,
Than feare I, there be many as the world gothe,
That would leese one eie, to leese their foes bothe.[49]

How god will not do for vs.

Euery man for him selfe, and god for vs all:
God will not seale that writing, write it who shall.[50]

Of falshed.

There is falshed in felowship, there is so
The felowshyp is small els as the worlde doth go.[51]

The hatred of invidious language and slander expressed in several of the epigrams probably sprang directly from Heywood's general good will toward men, but possibly also from his resentment at having been the victim of what

[46] *500:* 21, p. 209. [47] *300:* 120, p. 165. [48] *500:* 12, p. 207.
[49] *100:* 58, p. 129. [50] *300:* 96, p. 161. [51] *300:* 208, p. 183.

he regarded as slanderous anti-Catholic attacks. Certainly Heywood's bitter "Ballad against Slander and Detraction"[52] comes to mind when one reads some of these epigrams, particularly the following one:

Of tunges and pinsons.

One difference this is, on which our tunges may carpe,
Betweene pinching pinsons, and taunting tunges sharpe.
Where these twoo nippers nip any where or when.
These pinsons nip dead thinges, those tunges nip quick men.[53]

The point is made more subtly in the following animal fable and exemplum about a wren and her young:

The wrenne, and hir birdes.

Of a nest of wrens late bred in a hedge,
Whiche the dam forsakyng, when they were fledge,
One saide: Alas mother what is the why,
That ye draw from vs vnnaturally?
Child (quoth the dam) I dooe now vnto thee,
As my dam in my youth did vnto me.
Wherby I am blamlesse in that I do,
Sens I do but as I haue bene done to.
Mother (quoth he) to deale as ye be delt with,
Is not alwaie meete: but this is the pith:
As ye would your dam should haue delt with yow,
So should ye our dam deale with your birdes now.
Why sonne (quoth she) thinkst thou me such a foole?
That my childe shall set his mother to scoole?
Nay adieu (quoth she) and away she is flowne:
This childe for this checke refusyng for hir owne.
Whiche done, the wren calth his brothers and sisters,
And vnto them this lesson he whisters.
I see and ye may see (quoth he) by this case,
The triall of tauntes out of tyme and place.
Where faire woordes haply my mother might haue won,
This taunt makth hir refuse me for hir son.
Whiche may teach vs all, where euer we becum,
Rather by silence alway to be mum,

[52] *Works,* pp. 263-67. I am inclined to agree with Bolwell's comment, pp. 126-27, concerning this ballad: "This piece, signed by Heywood, seems too hot for unprovoked composition. If we search about for some incident in his life which might have called forth this wrathful utterance, there is nothing more appropriate and fitting to suggest than his imprisonment in connection with the Cranmer affair, against which he may have circulated, as a broadside, this indignant outburst." In 1544, Heywood, John More, and William Roper were indicted for treason because of charges they had made against Cranmer.

[53] *500:* 99, p. 224.

Than in ought at libertee, or forbydden,
To taunt our betters, openly or hidden.[54]

Numerous epigrams attack pride, not in the medieval manner, as the personified abstraction of one of the seven deadly sins, but in a more secular and somewhat less conventional manner. Heywood's own strong feelings about egotism and arrogance seem to be involved at least as much as are conventional satirical protests against pride:

Of the proude cocke.

Euery cocke is proude on his owne dunghyll,
The hen is proud inough there marke who wyll.[55]

Of pryde.

If thou wylt needes be proud, marke this freend myne:
Of good deedes be not proude: they are not thyne.
But when thou plaiest the knaue in yll deedes growne,
Be proud of those yll deedes: they are thyne owne.[56]

Of Peter.

Peter the proude, and Peter the poore, in whiche,
Poore Peter oft as proude, as Peter the riche.[57]

Heywood would have agreed with a later and far superior satirist that affectation is the source of the true ridiculous. Heywood was the enemy of such hypocrites as the fool pretending wisdom; the poor man, wealth; the bad man, virtue. He ridiculed particularly the religious hypocrite, as in the following epigrams:

Of saiyng grace.

To say grace fayre and to say grace oft Iohn,
From Gracechurch to Grantam, thy lyke thers non.
At breackfast, at diner, at supper, at all,
At syttyng, at rysyng, haue grace we shall.
Thers no man a lyue, in house, streete, or feelde,
That saith grace so ofte, and showth grace so seelde.[58]

A keper of the commaundementes.

If it be (as it is) muche commendable,
To kepe Gods preceptes, geuen Moyses in table:
In kepyng the same (as thou hast pretended)
Thou maist well be marueylously commended.
First for thy hauyng any mo gods but one,
Thou kepest within that bound. For God thou hast none.

[54] *100:* 22, p. 114. Cf. also "An aduise against mockyng," *500:* 3, p. 204; and "Of toung, mouth, teeth, and wisdome," *600:* 2, p. 229.
[55] *300:* 242, p. 189. [56] *500:* 42, p. 212.
[57] *600:* 85, p. 244. Cf. also *300:* 233, p. 188; *500:* 74, p. 219; and *600:* 84, p. 244.
[58] *600:* 12, p. 231.

Hauyng or worshippyng of god false or true,
Thou hast nor worshippest God olde nor newe.
  And as for the committyng of Idolatrie,
By grauyng to thy selfe any Imagerie,
This twenty yeres daie in weather hot or coole,
Thou handledst no caruyng nor woorkyng toole.
  The name of God in vayne thou consentst not till,
Thou neuer swerst but for some purpose good or yll.
  And as for the holy daie, thou doest breake none,
For thou wilt rather make twentie then breake one.
  Father and mother not dishonoured by thee:
For thou neuer comst where any of them bee.
  And where thou shalt not kyll, to cleere the of that,
Thou neuer durst abyde to fyght with a gnat.
  Than all adultery of fornicacion
Chastitee dischargeth, by this approbacion.
All women hardly can beare the their fauour,
To abyde thy sight: and in no wyse thy sauour.
  For stealyng or theft, what euer thou hast beene,
Thy handes at this daie are knowen to be cleene.
How canst thou steale ought in house, feeld, or streete?
Thou sittest in Newgate fast bound handes and feete.
  By false witnesse thou neuer hurtest man, for why,
Eury woord thou speakest, eury man thinkth a lie.
  Now, to couet in mynde thy neighbours asse,
Or his house, when bondage will not let the passe.
To ride to the tone, or go to the tother,
Or in consented thought one waie or other.
For to couet thy neighbours maide or his wyfe,
Or of thy neighbours thinges to couet any thyng,
Whan couetousnes can no way bryng winnyng,
But that lacke of credite, libertee, or loue,
Kepth the from that couetyng can moue.
Thou hast to shrewde a wit in desyre to dwell,
To haue thinges, from whiche dispeyre doth the expell.
Thus in gods precepts, except thou cleere appeere,
I know not who the diuell can say he is cleere.[59]

Many of Heywood's most witty and distinctive satirical epigrams are aimed directly at the falsity, sententiousness, or absurd logic of some proverbs and indirectly, one cannot help feeling, at gullible and unthinking mouthers of the same proverbs. In these epigrams, Heywood's wit and good sense are brought together, rather than parted as they usually are in the epigrams whose humor depends upon puns and quibbles. Heywood has often been called one of the first collectors of English proverbs, but he has not received

[59] *100:* 30, pp. 118-19.

proper credit for exposing their vulgar errors. Among many good examples of Heywood's satire in this original and attractive vein are the following:

Of an akyng eye.

Better eye out, then alway ake:
In rage of ache, true as I spake:
But in meane ache, meanely to mone,
Better an akyng eye then none.[60]

Of a cattes looke.

A cat may looke on a kyng, and what of that.
When a cat so lookth: a cat is but a cat.[61]

Of wrestlyng.

The weaker hath the woorse, in wrestlyng alway,
Best for the weake to leaue wrestlyng then I say.[62]

Of enough and a feast.

As good ynough as a feast: ye god saue it.
Inough were euen as good, if we might haue it.[63]

Of great clarkes.

The greatest clarkes be not the wisest men
Be smaule learnd or vnlernd fooles wysest then.[64]

Of striuyng.

He strIueth agaynst the streme, by custums scoole
That striuer is either a fishe or a foole.[65]

One naturally looks closely at the epigrams of Heywood — the author *of The Spider and the Flie,* of the well-known laudatory verses to the young Princess Mary, and of the ballad celebrating the marriage of Queen Mary and Philip II of Spain; the man whose Catholic sympathies led him into trouble and finally into exile — for allusions to Catholic-Anglican controversies and expressions of his reactions to these controversies. What one finds is meager, partly perhaps because Heywood knew that caution in these matters was imperative to him except during Mary's reign, partly no doubt because he was not by nature an extremist or agitator. At any rate, the only epigram in which his Catholic sympathies are expressed openly and unequivocally is No. 274 of *Three hundred Epigrammes, vpon three hundred prouerbes,* published early in Mary's reign:

Of Roome.

Roome was not bylt on one day, that is well knowne,
Nor in one day Rome wyll not be ouerthrowne.

[60] *300:* 17, p. 149. [61] *300:* 117, p. 165. [62] *300:* 156, p. 174.
[63] *300:* 200, p. 182. [64] *300:* 206, p. 183. [65] *300:* 203, p. 183.

For where Rome semd puld downe in one day brother,
There is Roome set vp agayne in an other.[66]

Behind the obvious exultation over the restoration of Catholic power in England there is, one may feel, Heywood's personal devotion to the new Catholic queen. The contrast is striking between the tone of the epigram on Rome and that of the epigram "Of Rebellion," the opening epigram of *The syxt hundred of Epigrammes,* written several years after Elizabeth's accession to the throne and not long before Heywood became an exile:

Of Rebellion.

Against god I dayly offend by frailte:
But against my prince, or natiue countre,
With as much as bodkin, when I rebell,
The next daie after hang me vp faire and well.
The next daie after? naie the next daie before
Wishe thou thy selfe hangd, in that case euermore.
Before, thou hangst honestly vnwoorthyly.
After, thou hangst, woorthyly vnhonestly.
But ho? at our fyrst dyshe in our mery feast,
Why talke we of hangyng our myrth to molest.
Be our cheese no better than our pottage is,
Better fast then feast at such feastes as is this.
But beyng true to god, queene, countre, and crowne,
We shall at all feastes, not hang vp, but syt downe.

Otherwyse.

Wylt thou be taken for a true Englyshe man?
Ye: be true to god, thy queene, and countre than.
Stand fast by thy countre, who euer wold wyn it,
Better stand fast by it, then hang fast in it.[67]

Heywood's failure to play the sycophant to Elizabeth added weight to his protests of loyalty to her and to his country.

Other somewhat more veiled epigrams deal with religious turncoats, both Catholic and Anglican. The following, from *Three hundred Epigrammes, vpon three hundred prouerbes,* refer to trimmers who returned to Catholicism under Queen Mary. The tone of these epigrams suggests fervent indignation and even the possibility that Heywood had in mind specific trimmers:

Turnyng of typettes.

He hath turnd his tippet, that turne showth playne,
Our typpets haue ben turnd and turnd agayne.

[66] *300:* 274, p. 194. [67] *600:* p. 229.

Otherwyse.

He hath turnd his typpet dyed it and drest it,
Vpon the right syde and feyre and playne prest it.

Otherwyse.

He hath turnd his typet and prest it so close,
That for a turnd typpet it hath a fayre glose.

Otherwise.

He hath turnd his typpet, lord how he prouydes,
Typpetts turnd, dyed, shorne, and worne bare on both sydes.

Otherwise.

He hath turnd his typpet, twyse in my sight:
Fyrst on the wronge syde and last on the right.

Otherwyse.

He hath turned his typpet an honest turnyng,
To turne his typpet and turne round for burnyng.

Otherwyse.

He hath turned his typpet shorne agaynst the wull ful,
And more against his will then against the wul.

Otherwyse.

He hath turnd his typpet, that haue we turnd all.
Sum halfe turne, sum hole turne, turnd round as a ball.

Otherwyse.

He hath turnd his typpet, ye for a whyle:
But might he turne agayne, lord how he wold smyle.

Otherwyse.

He hath turned his typpet, yet mo turns ye mocke,
But who doth weare his typpet a weathercocke?

Otherwyse.

He hath turnd his typpet, now for a noueltee,
And for a noueltee wolde turne streyght ageyne he.

Otherwyse.

He hath turnd his typpet, or his typpet turnth hym,
But which turnth which, I see not by sweete saint Sym.

Otherwyse.

He hath turnd his typpet,
For symony a syppet.

Otherwyse.

He turnth his typpet, if that turnyng turne hym
Into the pulpyt, that turnyng is turnd trym.[68]

[68] *300:* 68, pp. 156-57.

Epigram 67 of *The fifth hundred of Epygrams* is bitter on the subject of Catholic turncoats early in Elizabeth's reign:

Of turnyng.

Wilt thou use turners craft still? ye by my trouth.
Much thrift and most suretie in turners craft growth.
Halfe turne or whole turne, where turners be turning,
Turnyng keepes turners from hangyng and burning.[69]

The epigram "Of Reedes and Okes" may allude to the position that Heywood tried to take and to encourage in the storms of religious controversy — a position of moderation, conciliation, and acquiescence to the authority of the crown. The symbol of the obdurate oak and the bending reed in this epigram may have a broader application than to overzealous and moderate Catholics during Elizabeth's reign, but it may well have them in mind. At least partly corroborative of the latter possibility is Heywood's attitude toward Catholic zealotry and moderation, toward violent methods and peaceful, in *The Spider and the Flie*. Also the nature of the allegorical symbolism suggests *The Spider and the Flie:*

Of Reedes and Okes.

Wyll you reedes at the windes will stil make lowe beckes?
Wyll you Okes stand stiffe stil while wind breke your neckes?
Wyll you reedes, like apes, still tucke & bowe eche ioynt?
Wyll you okes, like asses, still stand stiffe at one point?
Wyll you reedes be still bendyng bowyng bodies?
Wyll you okes be still stoute stiffe necked nodies?
Wyll you reedes be staggeryng still for vayne auayles?
Will you okes be stern still till your tops kisse your tayles?
Will you reedes shrinke still to all windes towardly?
Wyll you okes swell still at all windes frowardly?
Wyll you reedes crouch still to be the windes footestooles?
Wyll you okes crake still to be the windes hed fooles?
Okes wyll do as we haue doone. so wyll we reedes.
Wherin for our purpose marke what ende proceedes.
In eche one storme a thousand okes downe are blowne
In a thousand stormes not one reede ouerthrowne.[70]

Debasement of English coinage is the subject of some of the topical satire. Of six epigrams in *The fifth hundred* that are satirical concerning the increasing debasement of silver coins by the addition of copper, the following are good examples:

Of testons.

Testons be gone to Oxforde, god be their speede:
To study in Brasenose there to proceede.[71]

[69] *500:* 67, p. 217. [70] *500:* 95, pp. 222-23. [71] *500:* 63, p. 216.

Of redde Testons.

These Testons looke redde: how like you the same?
Tis a tooken of grace: they blushe for shame.[72]

The timeliness of these satirical jests and the point of the Brasenose pun are indicated by a passage in Camden:

King Henry the eyght, who had infinite wealth left by his prudent and sparing Father, and so enriched himselfe by the spoyles of Abbayes, by first fruits, tenths, exactions, and absenties in Ireland, was yet so impouerished by his pompous profusion, that in his later dayes he first corrupted the rich coyn of this flourishing Kingdome with Copper, to his great dishonour, the dammage of Successors, and the people, although for his aduantage for the present. Vpon which occasion, that we may insert a tale, when we purpose nothing serious here: Sir Iohn Rainsford meeting Parson Brocke, the principall deuiser of the Copper Coyne, threatned him to breake his head, for that he had made his Soueraigne Lord the most beautifull Prince King Henry with a redde and copper nose. So base and corrupted with copper was his money, as also of King Edward the 6, that some of them which was then called Testons because the Kings head was theron figured, conteined but two pence farthing in siluer; and other foure pence half penny.[73]

There is also, in *The sixt hundred,* an epigram about the defective and clipped coins that were then in circulation:

Of syluer to be borowed.

Hast thou any bowde syluer to lend me Ione?
Nay: hast thou any broken syluer for me? none.
Hast thou any clypt syluer? I had, but tis gone.
Hast thou any crakt grote? crakt grote? nay not one.
No syluer, bowde, broken, clypt, crakt, nor cut,
Hers a freend for freendshyp, not woorth a crakt nut.[74]

Finally, three of the topical epigrams give interesting satirical views of fashions in dress current in Heywood's time. Fashion seems not to have blinded Heywood's eyes to the absurd or the extravagant: the hooped skirts and petticoats, the enormous ruffs worn by men, the feathered hats, perfumed gloves, shoes designed for show rather than fit, and other similar fineries:

When certaine thinges came fyrst.

Whens came great breeches? from little wittam.
Whens come great ruffes? from small brainfoorth they cam.
Whens come these round verdingales? from square thrift.
Whens come deepe copped hattes? from shallow shift.
Whens come braudered gardes? from the towne of euill.
Whens come vncomde staryng heades? from the deuill.
Whens come these womans scarfs? from folly Iohn.

[72] *500:* 64, p. 216. [73] *Remains* (1614), pp. 208-9. [74] *600:* 3, p. 230.

Whens come their glitteryng spanges? from much wanton.
Whens come perfumde gloues? from curiositee.
Whens come fyne trapt moyles? from superfluitee.
Whens come cornde crooked toes? from short shapen shoone.
Whens come wylde hie lookers? from midsomer moone.
Whens come fayre painted faces? from peinters tooles.
Whens come all these? from the vicar of sainct fooles.[75]

Of verdingales.

Alas poore verdingales must lie in the streete:
To house them, no doore in the citee made meete.
Syns at our narow doores they in can not win.
Send them to Oxforde, at Brodegates to get in.[76]

Of sauyng of shooes.

Thou wearst (to weare thy wyt and thrift together)
Moyles of veluet to saue thy shooes of lether.
Oft haue we seene moyle men ryde vpon assys:
But to see assys go on moyles: that passys.[77]

The humor and satire of Heywood's epigrams owe much to conventions of popular medieval literature. Topical allusions are rare, although the epigrams give occasional glimpses of the England of the 1550's and 1560's. The source of the almost unique quality of the epigrams is the poet's distinct and likable personality. His simplicity, arising in his best work from sources superior to naivete, rudeness, or near-doggerel verses, his good humor, tolerance, and shrewdness set him apart from other English epigrammatists, most of whom wrote in the tradition of Martial or affected to do so. No appraisal of the essential quality of Heywood as a writer has been more acute than Gabriel Harvey's, which placed him among "the sonnes of the Inglish Muses" but rightly regarded him as one of the lesser sons:

Amongst the sonnes of the Inglish Muses; Gower, Lidgate, Heywood, Phaer, & a few other of famous memory, ar meethinkes, good in manie kindes: but abooue all other Chawcer in mie conceit, is excellent in euery veine, & humour. . . . [78]

[75] *500:* 19, p. 208. [76] *500:* 55, p. 215. [77] *600:* 87, p. 244.
[78] *Gabriel Harvey's Marginalia,* ed. G. C. Moore Smith (Stratford-on-Avon, 1913), p. 226.

University of Illinois

THE BLATANT BEAST

Leslie Hotson

To say that *blătant* or *blattant,* the epithet introduced by Spenser to characterize his frightful monster, has in later ages been strangely altered in meaning is, I believe, wide of the mark. I think it would be truer to say that our *blātant* has nothing whatever in common with Spenser's *blătant.* For there is nothing even remotely dreadful or fiendish in the modern adjective, which we employ for "noisy, offensively clamorous or obtrusive" and the like. And if one thing is certain, it is that the monster Calumny, begotten of Cerberus and Chimæra, stirred no such trivial notions either in Spenser's mind or in the minds of his Elizabethan readers.

Consider again his view of the Beast:

> [Envie and Detraction] gotten had
> A monster which the blatant beast men call,
> A dreadful feend of gods and men ydrad.
>
> No wound . . . so sore doth light
> As doth the poysnous sting, which Infamy
> Infixeth in the name of noble wight . . .
> Such were the wounds the which that *Blatant Beast*
> Made in the bodies of that Squire and Dame.
>
> That monstrous Beast . . .
> In which [*i.e.*, in the Clergy] such spoile, such havocke, and such theft
> He wrought . . .
>
> [He]
> Spake licentious words and hatefull things
> Of good and bad alike, of low and hie,
> Ne Kesars spared he a whit nor Kings,
> But either blotted them with infamie,
> Or bit them with his banefull teeth of injury.

Spenser's dread monster does not bellow; neither does he vulgarly obtrude himself. What he *does* do is to inflict poisoned wounds. He works havoc; he blackens with infamous lies; he bites deadly. The Beast in brief shares the poetical character of Envy, Detraction, Calumny: *wounding* or *tongue-wounding, injurious, black-mouth'd, biting.* It is definite sense of this sort — of the hurt, the harm, the injury his bite inflicts, and not the clamor he may or may not incidentally produce — which the poet must have meant to convey by the epithet. Further, it was precisely this meaning which contemporaries took when adopting Spenser's term. In *2 Return from Parnassus,* acted at Cambridge about 1601, "the blattant beast" rules the Isle of Dogs, "Renting [i.e., rending, tearing] the credit of whom ere he please." And in verses to Folkingham's *Art of Survey* (1610) we find "Couch rabid Blatants"[1] — that is, detractors pictured as deadly-biting mad dogs.

Yet despite all these unmistakable pointers to the exact thought behind Spenser's use of the word, the only efforts I have seen to trace its origin seek it in terms of meaningless noise. For example, *The Century Dictionary* comments:

Also written *blattant;* one of Spenser's words, in *blatant beast,* perhaps a mere alliterative invention; otherwise intended for **blatand,* Sc. *blaitand,* archaic ppr. of *blate,*[3] var. of bleat.

Webster's New International Dictionary asserts flatly that the Beast in the *Faerie Queene* is "A bellowing monster." And of *blatant* it adds,

Appar. coined by Spenser, perh. fr. archaic pres. part. of BLATE, to bleat.

The *Oxford English Dictionary* is somewhat fuller, but in the same sense:

Apparently invented by Spenser, and used by him as an epithet of the thousand-tongued monster begotten of Cerberus and Chimæra, the "blatant" or "blattant beast," by which he symbolized calumny. It has been suggested that he intended it as an archaic form of *bleating* (of which the 16th c. Sc. was *blaitand*), but this seems rather remote from the sense in which he used it. The L. *blatīre* to babble may also be compared. (The *a* was probably short with Spenser: it is now always made long).

"Rather remote" is putting it mildly. Any respectable etymologist must have felt the worm of conscience on finding himself representing Spenser's dread and fiendish Beast as "bleating." To offer an etymon so sheepish verges on treachery to the Prince of Poets. Possibly it was a proper unease of this kind which moved J. B. Leishman to his note: "The phrase 'blatant beast' was perhaps suggested to Spenser by Malory's 'questing beast.' "[2] *Questing* means "opening," "giving tongue on finding the scent," as a hunting dog or hound. This at least draws our minds away from bleating to

[1] Qu. *OED* in v. Blatant. To the examples it prints may be added Fletcher, *The Wild Goose Chase,* IV. iii: 'Thou art a beast, a monster, A blatant beast!'

[2] *Pilgrimage to Parnassus* (London, 1949), 360 n.

yelping, which is some relief; but the non-Spenserian fixation on "noisiness" is still there.

No students would have been baffled by Spenser's *blătant* or *blattant* had they recalled that Elizabethan university men read Greek, or had they consulted his fellow-Cantabrigian Joseph Wibarne. For a passage on "Vaine Titles of Heroycall Vertue" in Wibarne's *The New Age of Old Names* (1609) provides the long-forgotten derivation:

> Cicero Offic. 1
>
> Vertue according to the Stoickes, was diuided into *Cathecon* and *Catorthoma,* that is, into Vertue meane and possible, or Vertue transcendent and heroycall, such as the Scriptures ascribe to *Sampson,* the Poets their Apes to *Hercules,* and our writers to Prince *Arthur.* This vertue hath beene three wayes assaulted, First, by calumniation, for actions done by diuine instinct, haue euer found some *Zoylus, Momus,* Mastix, or tongue of blattant beast, so called of βλαττω, to hurt.[3]

Wibarne finds Spenser's coining from the Greek, to symbolize Calumny, both happy and acceptable.

But what could it have been, one asks, which has blinded all latter-day scholars familiar with Greek (of which I am not one) to this evident source? Was it the slight euphonic change to *tt* of the usual *pt* of *blapto?* But Littleton gives

> Blatta, æ. f. à βλαπτω, *noceo,* qu. blapta. A kind of moth or fly, that eats books or cloths.

And manifestly this Greek borrowing was not in the least far-fetched. Its naturalness and aptness for Calumny appear by a locution quoted in Robert Constantin's *Lexicon Græco-latinum* (1592): "βλαπτειν και διαβάλλειν, *lædere & infamare*"—precisely the action of the wounding, black-mouth'd Beast Spenser sought to characterize. For the adjective, Constantin has βλαπτικὸς: *noxius, lædens, nocuus.* The word was not an unfamiliar one in the university man's Greek vocabulary. For *nocens* the *Vocabulorum . . . commentarij* of G. Morelius (London, 1583) gives ὁ βλάπτων, and adduces "Planud. ex Ouid. . . . *nocens ferrum* . . . βλαπτων σίδηρος . . . hurtfull iron. . . ." And Scene 2 of John Christopherson's Cambridge play Ϊεφθάε (about 1544) includes the line: "κακουργῖα βλαπτει κακούργους πολλάκις."[4]

About Spenser's *blătant* or *blattant,* then, nothing puzzling or difficult remains. So far from being a "mere alliterative invention" or a dialectical curiosity dredged up from archaic Scots, it was a familiar bit of Greek anglicized: one so natural to Elizabethan readers of the classics that it was promptly approved and adopted.

[3] Sec. I, Ch. 15, p. 72.

[4] F. S. Boas, *University Drama in the Tudor Age* (Oxford, 1914), p. 52.

For us, the moral is plain. Never neglect the obvious sources, and for the educated Elizabethan, Greek and Latin are obvious. Remember Bullen's experience with the *Oncaymœon* of Marlowe's Faustus. The abiding puzzle is where and how our *blătant* arose, foreign as it is to Spenser's Greek importation both in sound and in sense.

Northford, Connecticut

THE ORIGIN OF THE EUPHUISTIC NOVEL AND ITS SIGNIFICANCE FOR SHAKESPEARE

Ludwig Borinski

The "euphuistic novel" is a clearly defined type of literature not only in style, but also in structure and contents, even in its philosophy of life. It is not yet generally realized that this entire tradition in all its aspects is not the creation of John Lyly, but of George Pettie. His unpretentious collection of stories[1] has so far received less than justice at the hands of literary historians. Indeed, R. W. Bond in his edition of Lyly's works (I, 139 ff.) has traced the *style* of *Euphues* back to this source, but the dependence goes much further and includes the contents as well. Even the Italian casuistry of love, the *dubbio d'amore,* which according to Violet M. Jeffery[2] plays such a prominent part in Lyly, exists already in Pettie, e.g., at the end of *Sinorix and Camma,* and at the beginning of *Icilius and Virginia.* That Greene is a direct imitator of Pettie was proved by Emil Koeppel as early as 1892.[3] Pettie created the euphuistic style of narrative, where the narration proper is reduced to a minimum, and half the story consists of long reflective speeches, letters, and semidramatic dialogue, all swelled by euphuistic comparisons in repeated variations. The main explanation of this curious form is, of course, the taste of the epoch. The later sixteenth century is everywhere an age of dialectics. Rhetoric of a highly argumentative kind becomes the fashion,[4] and this is not confined to textbooks and school exercises. Tasso

[1] *A Petite Pallace of Pettie his Pleasure, 1576.* I quote from I. Gollancz's edition (London, 1908).

[2] *John Lyly and the Italian Renaissance* (Paris, 1928).

[3] *Studien zur Geschichte der italienischen Novelle in der englischen Literatur des 16. Jahrhunderts* (Strassburg, 1892), pp. 27 f.

[4] See T. W. Baldwin, *William Shakspere's Small Latine and Lesse Greeke* (Urbana, 1944), Vol. II, Ch. 32.

dramatizes the epic as Pettie dramatizes the novel. His *Gerusalemme Liberata* is full of speeches of a strongly political and dialectic kind — Satan's speech in hell in Canto IV, Godfrey of Boulogne's speech in Canto I, Alete's diplomatic harangue in Canto II. When, in 1567, Thomas Paynell translated parts of Des Essarts' version of "Amadis de Gaula," he confined himself to a collection of extracts, consisting of "eloquent orations, pithy epistles, learned letters, and fervent complaints."[5] This was before Pettie, and shows what the novel-reading public was then mainly interested in. The Italian Renaissance comedy had few long speeches, but when Gascoigne translated Ariosto's *Suppositi,* almost his only addition was a long soliloquy of the moralizing sort (Damon on parents and children in III.iii; this is also a common theme of Pettie's speeches). Early English tragedy of the type of *Gorboduc* also consists of such long harangues, in imitation of Seneca.

But Pettie was also following more specific models, of which the most obvious one, pointed out by Bush,[6] is of course Belleforest, who had remolded the novels of Bandello to suit the new taste. He interlarded Bandello's fine straightforward tales with long turgid speeches, letters, and interminable moralizings. That he was Pettie's model (in the translations of Painter and Fenton) is clear even from the title of the *Petite Pallace,* which is a variation of Painter's, and from numerous allusions.[7] He imitated Belleforest's moralizing prologues and many specific rhetorical devices, such as the exclamation "no, no!" in the middle of a soliloquy (e.g., Fenton, I, 92, 109).[8] But Belleforest does not explain everything. He is much less dramatic than Pettie. His harangues and soliloquies are inorganic later additions to stories originally conceived as factual narratives. His speeches are in the tradition of textbook rhetoric, mainly laments with the usual commonplaces inherited from Seneca,[9] with the instability of fortune as the main theme, the conventional *suasoria* (e.g., Fenton, II, 269), and the curse (II, 299).

Despite his strong debt to Belleforest, Pettie's art bears a closer resemblance to Aeneas Sylvius Piccolomini's masterpiece *Opusculum de duobus amantibus Eurialo et Lucrecia,* which with twenty-eight editions and eight translations in the fifteenth century alone, was among the most popular literary creations of the Renaissance. Before Pettie's time it had already four times

[5] E. A. Baker, *The History of the English Novel,* I, 251.

[6] Douglas Bush, "The Petite Pallace of Pettie His Pleasure," JEGP, XXVII, (1928), 162-69.

[7] Koeppel, p. 23.

[8] *Certain Tragical Discourses of Bandello Translated into English by Geoffrey Fenton,* the Tudor Translations, XIX (London, 1898).

[9] A very exhaustive treatment of this form is given in Wolfgang Clemen, *Die Tragödie vor Shakespeare* (Heidelberg, 1955), pp. 187-256.

appeared in an English version.[10] With its preponderance of long soliloquies and other speeches, letters, dramatic dialogue, and reflections by the author over mere narrative,[11] it was a "dramatic novel" long before Belleforest's time, and surpasses him immensely by its marvelous, truly lifelike psychology, which is probably superior to anything written between Chaucer and Shakespeare. With its two editions of 1550 and 1560 it was widely known in England before the work of the Frenchman, and apparently created the fashion of the dramatic novel which Painter, Fenton, Paynell, etc., tried to satisfy with their translations.[12] Actually it may have been Belleforest's model in his remodeling of Bandello, since it was as popular in France as it was in other countries.[13] It recommended itself to Pettie, because it is truly dramatic, and speeches, letters, and dialogue are not inorganic ornaments but are functionally integrated in the whole. But there are much more specific resemblances. All euphuistic novels are dominated by the *soliloquy of conflict.* The hero or heroine is confronted with the temptation of unlawful love. They begin by resisting it with moral arguments. This is followed by a sudden and unprepared turn to the opposite, not introduced by any comment of the author; the power of love proves irresistible and is again justified by all sorts of arguments, this time of a strongly sophistical kind —

[10] *Ca.* 1515 at Antwerp, *ca.* 1550, 1560, and 1567 in London. I quote from the 1567 edition "The goodli History of the most noble & beautifull Ladye Lucres of Scene in Tuskan, and of her louer Eurialus . . . ," *The History of Plasidas* (London, 1873). The 1560 edition has the same title. The popularity of this novel in England is further attested by several later translations. Painter had only three editions, Fenton, two.

[11] In the first nineteen pages (out of a total of forty-eight) I count at least thirteen pages of such material. Later on, the narration becomes more important, but it is still strongly intermixed with speeches and letters. George B. Parks, *Before Euphues,* Joseph Quincy Adams Memorial Studies (Washington, 1948), pp. 475-93, who studies the percentages of "subjective expression" in early Elizabethan fiction, states, curiously enough (p. 484), that Aeneas Sylvius' story "does not contain much psychological material," and "remains on the whole objective." It has been pointed out by H. J. Savage as a possible source of the "letter device" in "The Beginning of Italian Influence in English Prose Fiction," *PMLA,* XXXII (1917), 1-21.

[12] Closer investigation would probably show that both Painter and Fenton knew it. Painter's title *The Goodly History of the True and Constant Love between Romeus and Julietta* is clearly an imitation of the title of the English translation of Aeneas Sylvius. Fenton (I, 235) has a marginal note: "A woman more readye of witt than a man in extremities"; Aeneas Sylvius, p. 138, says: "as woman's wit is more ready than man's in sudden perils." In both cases, there is a practically identical situation involving a surprised adulteress.

[13] For Aeneas Sylvius' popularity in France, see Charles E. Kany, *The Beginnings of the Epistolary Novel in France, Italy, and Spain,* Univ. of California Pubs. in Modern Philology, XXI, 1. Even the poetic insertions in Belleforest may be an imitation of the French translation of Aeneas Sylvius' novel, in which songs, etc., are added by the translator.

the right of nature, of freedom, and especially of passion against reason. In most cases this is repeated several times, as reason regains the upper hand, but only for a time, because passion grows stronger and in the end prevails. Only rarely is reason the victor (sometimes in the case of heroines of the Lucretia type who have to resist seduction). This type of soliloquy is ubiquitous in Pettie as well as in Lyly and Greene. It is the central piece (often there are several of them) in all euphuistic novels and plays. Its form is extremely stereotyped. Parallels in Belleforest are rare and remote; the nearest case is Fenton, I, 40, but in this instance there is only one sudden turn, no protracted wavering, and it is conscience which prevails over passion.[14] A quotation of an example from Aeneas Sylvius will show how much closer he is to Pettie and his followers, p. 116 f.:

I wot not what letteth me that I can no more company with my husband. Nothing deliteth me his embracings, nothing pleaseth me his kissings, his words annoy me, so standeth always afore mine eyen the image of the stranger that today was next unto the Emperor. Cast alas, oh unhappy, out of my chaste breast that conceived flames, if thou may. If I might, alas, I should not be, as I am, evil at ease. A new kind of strength against my will draweth me. My desire and my reason moveth me diversely. I know the best and the worst I follow. O noble citizen, what hast thou to do with an unknown man, why brennest thou in stranger's love? why seekest thou thy lust in a strange country? If thy husband loveth thee thine own country may give thee what thou lovest. Oh, but what a manner of face hath he? what woman would not be moved with his beauty, youth, nobleness, and virtue? Surely I am, and without his help I despair, God grant us better. Shall I betray, alas, the chaste spousals, and betake me to a stranger, I wot not whence? which when he hath abused me, shall depart, and shall be anothers and so leave me behind. But by his countenance it is not like to be so, and the nobleness of his mind seemeth not to be such, nor so pretendeth not the grace of his beauty that I should fear deceit or his forgetting of love. And he shall promise aforehand assured, why do I dread? I shall apply it without further abroad; parde, I am so fair that he will no less desire me than I him; he shall be mine forever, if once I may receive him to my kisses. How many do woo me wheresoever I go? how many rivals do watch afore my door? I shall intend to love, either he shall tarry here, or at his departing carry me with him. Shall I than forsake my mother, my husband, and my country? My mother is forward and always against my appetites, my husband I rather want, than have, my country is there as I delight to dwell. But shall I so lease my fame? Why not? What have I to do with men's words which I shall not hear? Nothing shall he dare that feareth the threatening of fame, many others have done the same. Helena would be ravished. Paris carried

[14] What is more, often in Belleforest there is no such soliloquy where there is an occasion for it, e.g., Fenton II, 161: "Here love and pity seemed to quarrel within the heart of Luchyn; the one, putting the prey into his hands, provoked him to crop the fruits of long desire; the other, defending the cause of the wretched captive. . . ." In this case, too, conscience is the victor; this is normal in Belleforest and differs from both Aeneas Sylvius and the euphuists.

her not away against her will. What shall I tell of Diana and Medea? No man blameth the faulter that faulteth with many.

Other examples in Aeneas Sylvius are on pages 121-22 and page 141. There are particularly close parallels in Pettie, where even the arguments of the heroine, especially that between patriotism and filial duty and love of a stranger, resemble Aeneas Sylvius (Pettie, II, 21 ff.; II, 45 f.; II, 93 ff.). Aeneas Sylvius got the soliloquy of conflict from his literary model, Boccaccio's *Filostrato,* from whom he also borrowed the figure of the procurer Pandarus in the form of Pandalus; he mentions also Cressida and Emilia in the *Teseide.* The clearest instance is Criseyde's long soliloquy, II, stanzas 68-77 (Chaucer II, 703 ff.). Here reason is the winner, although only for a time. Boccaccio does not fail to add that love remained in her heart, only to break out later on. But otherwise the pattern is identical with those of Aeneas Sylvius and the euphuistic novel, marked by strongly argumentative and sometimes sophistical reasoning and especially by the sudden, unprepared break, as in stanza 75:

> E stando alquando, poi si rivolgea
> Nell altra parte: misera, dicendo
> Che vuoi tu far? . . .

Boccaccio used the device again in his novel of *Tito e Gisippo* (Giornata X, 8), this time with the victory of passion over reason, backed with the usual sophistical arguments: Tito had first resisted his unlawful passion, appealing to reason, and, concluding: Che dunque farai, Tito? Lascerai lo sconvenevole amore, se quello vorrai fare, che si conviene. E poi di Sofronia ricordandosi, in contrario volgendo [note the almost identical expression], ogni cosa detta dannava, dicendo: Le leggi d'amore sono di maggior potenza, che alcune altre: elle rompono, non che quelle dell' amistà, ma le divine. . . .[15] Boccaccio's novel may ultimately derive from a Byzantine or Greek source.[16] In fact, I have found *one* analogue to this soliloquy of conflict in a Greek novel, Achilles Tatius' *Clitophon and Leucippe* V, cap. 25 ff. (Melitta's speech). But the resemblance is rather remote, different from the pattern of Aeneas Sylvius and Pettie, and thus no possible source of the device in the euphuistic novel.

[15] Boccaccio still advertises the "break"; so does Aeneas Sylvius in one instance in the Latin original, in clear imitation of Boccaccio, p. xli: "En Euriale, quid sit amoris imperium nostri! Longi luctus, breves risus, parva gaudia, magni metus; semper moritur et nunquam mortuus est qui amat. Quid tu his nugis immisceas iterum? *ac cum se frustra niti videret,* "quid tandem," ait "incassum miser amori repugno? num me licebit quod Iulium licuit, quod Alexandrum, quod Hannibalem? . . . " But this was dropped by the English translator who thus created the stereotyped form in the euphuistic novel.

[16] S. L. Wolff, *The Greek Romances in Elizabethan Prose Fiction* (New York, 1912), pp. 248 ff.

The strong note of sophistry is not confined to the soliloquy of conflict, but pervades all speeches, letters, and especially the dialogue of Aeneas Sylvius' novel. In Belleforest it is not nearly as conspicuous. But the same sophistry is perhaps the most characteristic feature of the euphuistic novel, and, what is more, its symptoms are identical. It is always the sophistry of love and the justification of the irresistibility of passion: "Nothing is better when love is crept into the bones than to give place to the rage, for whose striveth against the tempest, oft times suffereth wrack and who driveth with the storm escapeth" (Aeneas Sylvius, pp. 148, 150). One of many instances of such sophistry in Pettie (*Sinorix and Camma,* I, 14) is: ". . . Why am I so blindly bold, beastly to blaspheme against that which proceeds altogether of nature, which nature hath implanted in all men, and which I ought to follow without repining and resisting?" Aeneas Sylvius is also fond of naturalistic arguments taken from animal life, another commonplace of the euphuistic novel, differing from the "natural science" imagery of euphuism, although somewhat related to it: "It is a natural passion. Birds are burnt with this fire. The turtle and the dove doth love. What shall I say of beasts? The horse moveth battle for love. The fearful hart seeketh to fight, and by believing showeth his furour. The fierce tiger etc." (p. 122). Compare, e.g., Scilla's justification of female wooing in Pettie: "And if it be lawful to follow the example of creatures without reason, doth not the cow low to the bull, doth not the mare neigh to the horse, doth not the ewe bleat to the ram etc. . . ." (II, 10). As in the euphuistic novel, this all-pervading dialectical tone is advertised by the author, e.g., in Euryalus' letter to Lucres: ". . . if thou wouldst have swaged my love, thou shouldst not have shewed thine *eloquence* . . ." (p. 129). See Pettie: "You must use great eloquence to yourself to persuade you to such an impossibility," and the answer: "There is an orator [viz. love] which of late hath taken up his dwelling within me, who hath eloquence to persuade me to a far greater matter than this" (I, 73), or the remarks on "sophistry" and "fallacies" (II, 163).

The well-known fondness of the euphuistic novel for examples from classical mythology and history has only a vague parallel in Belleforest, who prefers Roman and modern history, whereas Aeneas Sylvius uses more or less identical patterns and shows the same preference for legend and mythology as Pettie, e.g., Pyramus and Thisbe (p. 115; Pettie I, 168), Phyllis, Sapho, (p. 128), Candaules (p. 142; Pettie I, 130), Antonius and Cleopatra (p. 130; Pettie I, 197; II, 38). An example may also show the strong stylistic resemblance with euphuism: Lucres writes to Euryalus: "Many examples do move to refuse a stranger's love. Iason that won the golden fleece by Medea's counsel, forsook her. Theseus had been cast to the Minotaur had not the counsel of Ariadna helped him, yet did he leave her behind in an island. What became of the unhappy Dido that received the wandering Aeneas? Was not her love her death?" (p. 128).

This example may also illustrate the most widespread of these patterns, which concerns unfaithfulness in love. Most conspicuous among the many speeches and letters are two long parallel letters written by Lucretia and Euryalus, where both argue the habitual unfaithfulness of the opposite sex. Lucretia mentions the examples just quoted, and Euryalus replies: "But more are to be brought, my Lucres, whom women hath deceived: Troilus by Cresyde,[17] Deiphobus by Helena, and Circe by her enchantments deceived her lovers." These two lists of unfaithful men and women are constantly reproduced in the euphuistic novels, with slight variations (e.g., Pettie, II, 23, 71; Greene, *Mamillia* 26, 51, 66, 225, 235; *Arbasto,* 205, 225, 242). Aeneas Sylvius is thus certainly partly responsible for the main interest of these novelists, which is unfaithfulness and dissembling in love. Pettie is already full of it in *Cephalus and Procris, Minos and Pasiphae,* and *Pygmalion's Friend,* and it becomes a stereotyped cliché in Lyly and Greene. Belleforest had not been specially concerned with it; in fact, many of his tales even tell of shining examples of loyalty and generosity. It can be strictly proved that the English had a special interest in this theme of treason and dissembling. In Fenton's translation of Belleforest, where the original has: "mais en matiere d'aymer, il me semble si volage, et inconstant . . ." (II, 261), he paraphrases: "But for his *faith,* or care of promise where *loyalty* should most appear, I accompt him . . . so apt to *dissemble* and inconstant by nature," and similarly expands a speech on page 263.

One of the strongest proofs of Aeneas Sylvius' influence on Pettie is provided by the plot of his first tale, *Sinorix and Camma.* In all his three possible sources — Plutarch's *De claris mulieribus,* Guevara's *Reloj de los Príncipes,* and the third book of Castiglione's *Cortegiano* (according to Bush,

[17] Called "Crisis" in the Latin original. Chaucer and Lydgate have Criseyde, Caxton, Briseyde. "Cresyde" looks like a contamination of Aeneas Sylvius' Latin form and Henryson's Cresseid, made popular by Thynne's edition of 1532. It is the accepted form in Gascoigne, who constantly mentions "Cressid," and in all euphuistic novels, which might be a further proof of their dependence on Aeneas Sylvius. From there it got into general literature and Shakespeare, whose "Cressida" would thus ultimately derive from Aeneas Sylvius. The question deserves further investigation. Pettie probably first coined the phrase "kites of Cressid's kind" (II, 113) for the sake of euphuistic alliteration. This phrase is taken over by Greene (*Mamillia,* p. 16, *Card of Fancy,* p. 132) and Shakespeare (*Henry V,* II.i.78). This is symptomatic of the popularity and influence of the euphuistic novel. Greene's works are always quoted from Grosart's edition, The Huth Library.

loc. cit., Castiglione is the only possible source) — the earlier parts of the story, as told by Pettie, viz. the details of the attempted seduction of the heroine, are not mentioned. These details are apparently filled in from Aeneas Sylvius, although sometimes in a slightly modified form, to suit the exigencies of the story: The seducer writes a letter and tries to present a jewel to the heroine, using a procuress for these purposes; the conversation of the procuress with the heroine is related, and the heroine dismisses the procuress with terms of abuse, but still seriously considers her offer afterwards; a servant tries to withhold his master (his mistress in Aeneas Sylvius) from his sinister plans, using identical arguments of respect for public opinion and reputation. The scene is laid in Siena, the scene of Aeneas Sylvius' novel, whereas in the source no particular city is mentioned; Bush is puzzled by this. Siena is spelt Scienna; in the English translation of Aeneas Sylvius the spelling is Scene; Fenton, on the other hand, has Syenna in his novel of Angelica. It may be of interest that Aeneas Sylvius' novel contains a very effective comic scene in the servants' quarter (p. 145), which is somewhat reminiscent of Lyly's and Shakespeare's clown scenes. One of the servants is called Dromo after Terence's Andria.

The renewed interest of the later sixteenth century in this old masterpiece of the early *quattrocento* is easily explained. The more strictly narrative and less psychological art of the Italian Renaissance novella could not satisfy the new demand for drama and psychology.[18] But exactly this semidramatic, psychological type of "problem-tale" had existed once before in European literature, in the highly sophisticated *versetale* of the later Middle Ages created by Boccaccio and perfected by Chaucer. Like Pettie's tales, it had consisted mainly or largely of long speeches and letters full of subtle psychological analysis, complicated and sophistical reasoning, and philosophical reflection. A late and over-refined offshoot of medieval dialectics, the "soliloquy of conflict" is clearly related to the medieval *débat* and scholastic *quaestio.* It is significant that the later sixteenth century everywhere sees a revival of all forms of medieval dialectics: the casuistry of love, the *débat* also in its pure form (in Pettie's *Germanicus and Agrippina,* and often in Greene), scholasticism in the universities. Aeneas Sylvius, the imitator of Boccaccio, had been the last representative of this late medieval tradition. He combined it with the new Renaissance feeling for real life and strong and immediate experience; hence his unique greatness. Even his style is

[18] How little the intervening period had cared for dramatic and psychological devices, may be gathered from the fact that Sir Thomas Elyot in his version of *Tito e Gisippo* (*The Governour,* II, 12) drops Boccaccio's soliloquy of conflict, confining himself to a few conventional sentences about the lover's anguish of mind.

not the Ciceronian period of the Renaissance; his use of short and pointed antithesis, clear and crisp, is somehow akin to the new fashion of prose which arose after 1550, much more so than Belleforest's and Fenton's clumsy periods.

Boccaccio had another and even greater pupil, Chaucer. In Chaucer's *Troilus and Criseyde* and, to some extent, in his Knight's Tale, the age found another precedent for what it wanted. The euphuistic novel, including the works of Pettie, is also full of reminiscences of Chaucer. They would demand a special study. But it is essential to remember that the tradition initiated by Boccaccio reached the Elizabethan age by two parallel channels which confirmed and reinforced each other. Chaucer may have strengthened the interest in the inconstancy of lovers. Pettie and his followers developed a further pattern of psychological and sophistical speech, the *seduction speech;* this had a brilliant model in Pandarus' and Diomedes' seduction speeches. "Destiny" is a commonplace repeated *ad nauseam* in the euphuistic novel, especially in Greene. It is one of the clichés of all Renaissance literature; Aeneas Sylvius, too, has it, but Chaucer was particularly fond of it. Chaucer also considerably expanded the conventional picture of the melancholy of love, although even this is not absent in Boccaccio and Aeneas Sylvius. Chaucer and Boccaccio had a common source which is the ultimate starting point of this entire tradition: The *Roman de la Rose.* Here we have already all the main elements which eventually were to be made up into the euphuistic novel: the *débat* between reason and passion with the victory of passion, the dialectical and sophistical style, the semidramatic form with dialogues and endless speeches, especially long soliloquies, the friend who advises the lover, the conventional symptoms of Petrarcan love with special emphasis on the lover's melancholy, even such details as the idea that the cruel mistress is guilty of murder (Aeneas Sylvius, p. 127), that intellectual education and eminence is a charm equal or superior to beauty (Aeneas Sylvius, p. 127; Pettie, *passim*), and the bribing of servants (Pettie, II, 97). The *Roman de la Rose* is a sort of final codification of the courtly literature of the High Middle Ages. Its elements can be traced back to the twelfth century. The lover's soliloquy between conscience and passion exists already in the *Lai d'Eliduc* of Marie de France (462 ff.), although not yet in the stereotyped form of Boccaccio and Aeneas Sylvius. In Chrétien's *Lancelot* it appears already as the *débat* between Reason and Love, with the victory of Love, allegorizing the inner conflict of the hero.[19] In Aeneas Sylvius we once find a true "Alba" in the Provençal style (p. 156), which had also been imitated by Petrarca (Sestina I). The *dubbio*

[19] Cp. C. S. Lewis, *The Allegory of Love,* (Oxford, 1936), p. 30.

d'amore also dates from the twelfth century, and so do many articles of faith in the religion of love, e.g., that refined and well-born souls are specially prone to love, a notion which was frequently expressed in Belleforest and adopted by Pettie and Greene. It has to be emphasized in this connection that love in the narrative literature of the Renaissance, in Aeneas Sylvius as well as in Belleforest and in the euphuists, is always of the Petrarcan, not of the Platonic, variety. These two traditions of the Renaissance are sometimes confused. Platonic love is a source of intellectual enjoyment; Petrarcan love causes "sweet pain" and similar cases of oxymoron, is a "tyrant," or a "prison" (Aeneas Sylvius, p. 119), is akin to death (Aeneas Sylvius, pp. 121, 155), but is nevertheless desired. The euphuists kept the two varieties clearly separate: e.g., Greene (*Mamillia*, p. 80) knows two kinds of love, "the desire of that which is good," which is rooted in "the intellectual part of the mind," and "what the common people call love," which is then defined in Petrarcan terms.

Yet the euphuistic novel is not only a restatement of medieval traditions. We may point out at least a few of the "new" elements in Pettie. The first is the demand for pure tragedy. Even the translator of Aeneas Sylvius gave his novel a strictly tragic ending; in Aeneas Sylvius the hero had to survive and marry another lady, because he wrote a "true tale" and had to conform to the facts of the case. Belleforest and Fenton are confirmed atrocity mongers; Pettie's tales are mostly "tragical histories" of the gloomiest kind. It was the age of Seneca. The revenge motif frequent in Pettie may actually derive from Seneca; Fenton, too, is fond of it; however, the revenge of Lucretia is mentioned also by Aeneas Sylvius (p. 120). Aeneas Sylvius gives the long description of the heroine's beauty (pp. 1-2), which is a standing feature of the Italian novella. There is nothing similar in Pettie, who, in this respect, set the fashion for his imitators. When Greene comes under the influence of the Greek novel, he never imitates its *ekphrasis,* with the one exception of the description of Europa in *Morando* (pp. 56-57). The English clearly had less esthetic and more psychological interest. Pettie's main addition consists in a strong dose of philistinism. This is common to all early Elizabethans. Even the writings of Belleforest in France are full of the French type of family discipline. But this is nothing compared with his English contemporaries. Ascham, Gascoigne, Barnaby Googe, Fenton, Lyly, even Sidney and Spenser, and countless minor writers exhibit a deadly uniformity in this respect. They all teem with warnings against women and love, the breeder of effeminacy and the deadly enemy of martial virtues. Apparently all this had something to do with the Spanish menace, so that all these writers reflect the outlook of what may be called the Elizabethan war party; hence Lyly's pronounced misogynist tendency, which has so far puzzled students.[20] In itself the diatribe on women was a commonplace of Renaissance literature. Baptista Mantuanus, often mentioned by our authors, and Guevara were rich sources of these attacks. But this denouncing of women had always been balanced by the cult of love. Now love as such is denounced, mainly for the reason just mentioned. In Pettie's *Admetus and Alcest* we read that love is unworthy of a warrior, and this is followed by the conventional denunciation of the lascivious knight and the carpet captain. In Lyly's *Campaspe* this is the main theme. Patriotism is everywhere rather prominent. There are other symptoms of a pronouncedly "middle-class" outlook. The questions of parental authority, money, and social equality in marriage are in the center of many of Pettie's tales, and the education of children and choice of a profession are much discussed, both by Pettie and Lyly. Even a strong element of sexual asceticism is general in the age, whereas it is conspicuously absent in Aeneas Sylvius. The loathing of illegitimate sexuality, which is compared to hell (Pettie, II, 120) is expressed in the ubiquitous formula of "love-lust." Pettie in *Pygmalion's Friend* defends the possibility of innocent friendships between men and women (and is imitated in this by Greene in *Mamillia*), and he goes on to state:

> Yea; I am persuaded that the wanton lover himself is as well satisfied with the good countenance, loving looks, and perfect agreement of his mistress's mind with his, as with the use of her body. Which, although he oftentimes earnestly desire, yet I think it be as much to know thereby her unfeigned good-will towards him, to confirm it with a natural bond, and to procure her contentment, as for that he reposeth the fulness of his felicity therein.

In such master strokes of fine psychological insight, Pettie is definitely a forerunner of the age of Shakespeare. This sexual asceticism has no religious background. Its reasons are again utilitarian, based on maintaining professional efficiency. In Pettie's version of the old legend of Alexius, the hero finally relinquishes marriage, because "I perceive by this pleasure of the body my mind to be molested . . . my wit dulled, my understanding blinded, my memory weakened, my senses sotted. . . ." Similar arguments are used in *Marginalia* by Gabriel Harvey, who is professedly antireligious. The tone of the euphuistic novel is distinctly pagan. Its outlook on life centers round the two notions of "nature" and "destiny" which appear on nearly every page.[21] Pettie in *Alexius* discusses the uses of the various learned professions

[20] E. C. Pettet, *Shakespeare and the Romance Tradition* (London, 1949), p. 201. Pettet also quotes E. C. Lewis.

[21] Even these two notions are already prominent in medieval courtly literature, which was also pagan in a way.

for the officer, and in the end mentions also "Divinity," which may serve "to dehort his soldiers from swearing, from blasphemy, from drinking, from whoring, and in the hour of death from despairing." This is definitely the lowest form reached by the Anglo-Saxon religious genius up to that time; after 1870 it appeared again. For the rest, divinity is called "contemptuous." Lastly, the euphuistic novel is full of the theory of the "gentleman," again like practically all the literature of the age. Even this tradition ultimately goes back to the *Roman de la Rose,* which is a textbook of good manners for the ideal knight, although it was of course strengthened and modified by the educational enthusiasm of the Renaissance.

The euphuistic novel thus created by Pettie became one of the main starting points of Shakespeare's work. Shakespeare knew Pettie,[22] but he also knew Aeneas Sylvius, borrowing the latter's psychological master stroke for the letter device in the first act of the *Two Gentlemen of Verona.*[23] Aeneas Sylvius may have furnished further suggestions. In his novel we read of the procuress, after the heroine has torn up the love letter (p. 124): "Another would have been afraid, but she well acquainted with the manners of women, thought of herself: Now wouldst thou most, when thou showest most the contrary." Compare *Two Gentlemen* III.i.93: "A woman sometimes scorns what best contents her." Quite apart from these direct borrowings from Aeneas Sylvius, the *Two Gentlemen of Verona* has all the characteristics of the euphuistic novel. It is a tale of unfaithfulness in love with a plot partly derived from Lyly's *Euphues,*[24] in which we find typical soliloquies of conflict (II.iv at the end, and II.vi), where passion prevails over reason with the usual sophistical arguments. Act III, scene ii contains a seduction speech, in the form of a dialogue, like Pandarus' seduction of Criseyde and Iago's seduction of Othello. Parental authority in marriage is a central theme in the play and is much discussed (I.iii.48 ff.; II.iv.174). Love is altogether conceived in the Petrarcan and courtly tradition, in which the lover is the "servant" of his "mistress" (II.iv.1 f.). He does "penance for contemning love" (II.iv.129). This is another cliché of the euphuistic novel (e.g., in Greene's *Mamillia* and *Arbasto*), which is also prominent in Chaucer's *Troilus and Criseyde* and may again be traced back to the courtly

[22] Koeppel, p. 28.

[23] John A. Guinn, *The Letter Device in the First Act of the Two Gentlemen of Verona,* Univ. of Texas Studies in English (Austin, 1940).

[24] *Two Gentlemen of Verona,* ed. R. Warwick Bond, *Arden Shakespeare* (London, 1906), pp. xxi f.

authors of the twelfth century, who had it from Ovid.[25] In IV.iv.172 f. we hear of Ariadne and Theseus as an example of unfaithfulness in love. Love is called a chameleon (II.i.168), as it was often in Greene's *Mamillia.* The play is also full of the theory of the "gentleman" and of courtly life.

But the influence of the euphuistic novel is strongest in Shakespeare's two longer poems.[26] Their type of narrative is identical with it, typified by endless speeches (and even a letter) written in the stereotyped pattern of the soliloquy of conflict (*Lucrece,* ll. 190 ff., 1156 ff., and, in a modified form, *Venus,* ll. 931 ff.), with several sudden "breaks" (e.g., *Lucrece,* l. 239), a minimum of action, and, mostly, the victory of passion over reason, strongly argumentative and dialectical passages, and arguments of a pronouncedly sophistical nature. This argumentative character is again repeatedly advertised in *Lucrece,* l. 268 and in ten more similar passages.[27] In *Lucrece* there is a *débat* between the seducer and his victim; *Venus and Adonis* is one long *débat* — on line 609 we even read: "Her pleading hath deserved a greater fee." Equally prominent is the seduction speech, appearing in *Venus and Adonis* everywhere, in *Lucrece* in the great seduction speech of Tarquin and in the speech of Sinon in the description of the Trojan War, which again foreshadows Iago's seduction of Othello. Sinon is also described as an example of the theme of dissembling which we found was one of the main interests of the euphuists, and it is interesting in this connection that Greene mentions Sinon as the type of the dissembler twice in *Mamillia* (pp. 182, 233). The resemblance to the euphuistic novel is closest in the *Rape of Lucrece,* which in plot and structure has much in common with Pettie's *Sinorix and Camma*: the seduction speech of the tyrannous ruler, the refusal of the heroine after a long soliloquy of conflict, the seducer's soliloquy of conflict, the heroine's long speech urging revenge, the final suicide of the heroine. Long reflections serve to articulate the narration into sections in *Sinorix and Camma* and also in *Venus and Adonis.* This technique is also employed by Aeneas Sylvius with consummate skill. Commonplaces like nature and destiny, time and opportunity (also found in Greene, e.g., *Menaphon,* p. 119), the mingling of love and death, etc., abound also in Shakespeare. It would take a separate study to prove the dependence in details. I confine myself to a few very specific borrowings: Lucrece's and

[25] Wolff, *loc. cit.,* pp. 413 ff. cites Poliziano's *Giostra* as the first European example after the Greek novel. This illustrates the danger of dating such traditions from the Renaissance, whereas mostly they had been commonplaces throughout the Middle Ages.

[26] And in Marlowe's *Hero and Leander,* but not in Lodge's *Glaucus and Scilla.*

[27] See T. W. Baldwin, *On the Literary Genetics of Shakspere's Poems and Sonnets* (Urbana, 1950), pp. 123 ff.

Tarquinius' main argument against the crime is reputation, and this is also practically the only motive of virtue in Aeneas Sylvius' *Lucretia.* In both cases it may illustrate the pagan tone of this sort of literature, although in Shakespeare this epoch is already drawing to a close, for in him we also hear much of conscience and hell. And more specific still: Pettie is fond of rather coarse-grained comparisons taken from the sphere of commerce, e.g., I, 28: "Neither must you think that that which is deferred is taken away, for as yourself or any other that oweth money, though you defer your creditor for a time, yet you defraud him not altogether of his due, so though God take days with you for a time, yet assure yourself he will pay you truly at length, yea, and perchance with large usury beside your debt." Also see Greene, *Mamillia,* pp. 10, 24, 112, 149; *Venus and Adonis,* ll. 210, 511 ff., 768; *Rape of Lucrece,* l. 134 ff. Shakespeare has also the parallels from the animal world (*Venus and Adonis,* l. 875 and the episode of the horses; *Lucrece,* ll. 543, 554, 694). The influence of the euphuistic novel is still considerable in *Love's Labour's Lost*: a soliloquy of conflict opens IV.iii, and in I.ii.61 we read "as it is base for a soldier to love."

Much of Shakespeare's later work is developed out of these inherited formulae, clichés, and conventions of his earliest phase. It would be a fascinating task to show how he filled them with life and reality, remolded and enriched them. A few hints may suffice in this place. The prose parts of his comedies retain much of the character of Lyly's plays. Hence their lack of action and their strongly dialectic character, which in Lyly was a legacy of the euphuistic novel. Lack of action is also conspicuous in the closing acts of many of Shakespeare's comedies. The art of conversation in classical English comedy, its repartee and wit, are thus connected by a slender link with medieval courtly dialectics. Shakespeare's clown dialogue takes its start from Lyly's. But these are relatively unimportant details compared with some of Shakespeare's main motifs which can also be traced back to the euphuistic novel. The tragic period is dominated by the idea of unfaithfulness and ingratitude which had already been the main preoccupation of these earlier writers. In many cases — *Othello, Hamlet, Cymbeline, Winter's Tale* — it is still unfaithfulness in love and marriage. All this is again a link with the medieval world. Loyalty was the base of the code of chivalry; hence its central position in courtly literature from the very start. This includes also loyalty in love and marriage (see Chrétien's *Érec et Enide*). The loathing of illegitimate sexuality also reappears in Shakespeare: in *The Rape of Lucrece* it is compared to hell, just as it was by Pettie. In this early work this horror of "lust," the negation of "love," is already just as prominent as in the sonnets and in the great tragedies. The seduction speech of the euphuists and of Shakespeare's early poems is developed into the great demagogic speeches of *Julius Caesar* and *Coriolanus,* and the masterful insinuations of Iago in the third act of *Othello.* It remained a central feature of English literature throughout the seventeenth century; seduction speeches of the same sophistical and psychological type are in the center of Milton's three great poems and of Dryden's *Absalom and Achitophel.* The melancholy of love in the euphuistic novel with its stereotyped symptoms becomes the melancholy of Antonio, Jacques, and Hamlet. No doubt this was a commonplace of the age; Elizabethan melancholy is not derived from the euphuistic novel, but the novel was the main popularizer of its symptoms. Hamlet's *Weltschmerz* has many features in common with that of Palamon and Troilus, and the novel is among the connecting links: Pettie (I, 144) makes the unhappy lover reproach God in terms strongly reminiscent of Palamon at the end of the first part of the Knight's Tale and of Troilus (III, ll. 1016 ff.). It has to be emphasized that such literary influences do not explain Shakespeare's genius. He filled them with new substance and experience. But they are significant nevertheless. Apart from the Latin classics we may distinguish four literary traditions which became important in Shakespeare's development: Senecan tragedy, the tradition of the Fall of Princes,[28] the euphuistic novel, and the Arcadian novel with its background of Greek romance.[29] Clearly the euphuistic novel is the most important of all four.

[28] See Willard Farnham, *The Medieval Heritage of Elizabethan Tragedy* (Oxford, 1956).

[29] It appears from Wolff's repeatedly quoted study that there is no direct influence of the Greek novel on the euphuistic novel. When Greene comes under this influence in his later works, the euphuistic tradition grows correspondingly weaker, although it never completely disappears.

University of Hamburg

THE EARLIEST(?) PRINTING OF SIR THOMAS MORE'S TWO EPIGRAMS TO JOHN HOLT

Harris Fletcher

In his article entitled "Thomas More, Grammarian and Orator," (*PMLA,* LVIII [1943], 337-52) William Nelson spoke of the large amount of attention then being accorded to Sir Thomas More and dwelt at some length on More's relations with the little-known John Holt or Holte. Nelson printed More's two Latin epigrams addressed to Holt using the texts found in the only two then (1943) known printed editions of Holt's *Lac Puerorum,* or *Mylke for chyldren,* one of 1510(?), the other of 1520, both listed in *STC,* that have constituted the only ancient texts we have had for these two epigrams. In 1949, A. W. Reed published an essay entitled "The Young More," in the papers of the Thomas More Society using a few documentary details concerning More and mentioning Holt now and then. The latest edition of More's epigrams by Bradner and Lynch (Chicago, 1953, pp. 117-19, 238-40), mainly follows Nelson's work for the text of these two poems, but is a less trustworthy text. With Reed's additions, we seem to have about all we shall ever know about Holt and the two epigrams.

It is notable that the most pertinent facts come from Anthony Wood (*Athenae,* 1691, col. 7-8), who wrote a short account of Holt and also mentioned him in a few accounts of other men. The articles in *DNB,* that on Holt (Holte) by Gordon Goodwin, that on More by Sir Sidney Lee, and that on John Morton (1420?-1500), are still valuable, as only the Holt article has been superseded. Reed's industrious account of probably everything that can ever be known of the onetime London schoolmaster, John Holt, hints that Holt taught not only John Colet, but William Lily as well.

Lac puerorum. M. holti.
Anglice Mylke for chyldren.

This Nicholas Holt was Schoolemaster of St Anthonies Schoole in London, whose Scholler (amongst others) was Sr Thomas More that sometime famous & learned Lo Chancellor of England, whose Latine Epigrams upon this his Masters Grammar you have here at the beginning & end of the Booke; That he was the author of those Epigrams wch he wrote being a youth there is no doubt he being Scholler to Mr Holt at that time, being from thence preferred to Archb. Morton who died Ao 1500 Sr Tho More then being but 20 y. old

see Sr Tho: Mores Life written by T More his Kinsman publ. in 4to

Plate I

It is certain that More and Holt knew each other in grammar school and also through their mutual indebtedness to John Morton who became Archbishop of Canterbury in 1486 under Henry VII and who served as patron of sorts to both young More and Holt. The epigram by Holt addressed to Morton, and the two by More addressed to Holt, each in its own way points toward some such connection between More and Holt effected through Morton.

Our concern herein, however, is chiefly confined to the two epigrams, and we may leave the biographical implications to Wood, Nelson, and Reed.

Recently, the University of Illinois Library acquired a copy of Holt's little *Lac Puerorum* in an edition that has escaped all bibliographers, as there seems to be no listing or notice of it anywhere since Wood (1691). In Wood's account of John Holt, attention was called to a copy of an edition of the *Lac* that had been offered for sale in the sale catalogue (Wing S-4, 151) of the books of Richard Smith or Smythe (1590-1675). The catalogue was entitled *Bibliotheca Smithiana, sive catalogue, 15 May 1682.* In that sale catalogue, p. 188, under English Books in Quarto, the entry reads: "310. *Holt,* Master to Sir Thomas More (Nic.) his Accic. & Gram. (with *R.S.* Acct. of the Au. MS.) *Ant.*" As is so frequently the case, Wing was confused, and identified the author of this entry, Richard Smith or Smythe, the book collector, with another Richard Smith (1566-1655), Bishop of Chalcedon. The Bishop wrote all the entries in Wing listed under the name Richard Smith except the one in which we are interested. Our Richard Smith was later noted for his *Obituary,* not published until 1849. Wood identified this particular copy of Holt's little book once owned by Smith by stating that on its title page it had a penned attribution of the *Lac* to Nicholas Holt as author. He guessed that this attribution was an error, mistaking Nicholas Holt for John Holt, although he surmised that Nicholas, also a schoolmaster in London, may have been John's father. The copy now at the University of Illinois seems to be the one cited by Wood and described in the sale catalogue of 1682.

The title page itself (see Plate I) is made up of two lines of type and a woodcut that is approximately four inches high and three and one-half inches wide. In the center of the engraved plate are the letters that symbolize the Christ, IHS. At the upper left is the eagle, St. John, with the bull, St. Luke, at the upper right. At the lower left is the lion, St. Mark, and the angel, St. Matthew, is in the circle at the lower right. The two lines of type read:

Lac puerorum. MR. holti./ Anglice Mylke for chyldren./

Below the woodcut is the following in penned, almost drawn, characters:

[in margin
at left]
see/
Sr Th:Mores/
Life written/
by T. More/
his kinsman/
publ. in 4to/

This Nicholas Holt was Schoolemaster of St/
Anthonies Schoole in London whose Scholler (amongst/
others) was Sr Thomas More that sometime famous &/
learned Lo. Chancellor of England, whose Latine Epigrams/
vpon this his Masters Grammar you have here at the/
beginning & end of the Booke; That he was the author of/
those Epigrams wch he wrote being a youth there is no doubt/
he being scholler to Mr Holt at that time being from thence prefered/
to Archb. Morton who died A° 1500 Sr Mr More then being but 20 y. old/

The book itself identifies the author as John Holt, as on the verso of the title page (see Plate II) the heading to the epigram addressed to Archbishop Morton is by John, not Nicholas, Holt:

Ad reuerendissimu dnm suum dnm Iohannem/ [note that in this type font there was no differentiating between *I* and *J* in the capital letters, and in lower case, only in the ligature, *-ij,* does any form of *j* appear] morton Cantuarien archipresule. totiusque Anglie pri/matem & titulo sancte anastasie cardinalem Iohan/nis holt Epigramma.

Again on the verso of [g-3] (see Plate III) was printed:

Finis/Finis opusculi Magistri Iohannis holt/ Quod Lac puerorum appelauit/

Thus, there can be no doubt of the authorship of the little book, and also there can be little doubt that this copy is the one once owned by Richard Smith, described in the sale catalogue in 1682 of his books, and referred to by Wood in 1691.

Wood offered a little more information than anyone else who has dealt with any edition of the *Lac* has ever used. He guessed that the book had first been published about 1497, seeming to imply that it first appeared in print in England, "(Printed also the works of *John Stanbridge*) being the first of note, or most fit for use, that ever was printed in *England,*" a slightly different conclusion from that drawn by Goodwin (*DNB*) and one too often uncritically repeated since. The *Lac* is not the earliest Latin grammar known to have been printed in England, and probably is not even the earliest known grammar ever printed in English, for *STC* 15,294 can be dated as 1481 although only two leaves survive. However, the entire bibliography of the *Lac* can be only very imperfect, as but one copy of the London edition by Wynkyn de Worde with a date of [1510?] supplied in *STC,* another by Richard Pynson, [1520], and scraps of an edition done at Antwerp by van Berghen conjecturally dated [1520?] are known at all to bibliographers or scholars.

Ad reuerendissimũ dñm suum dñm Johannem morton Cantuarieñ archipresulē. totiusq; Anglie primatem & titulo sancte anastasie cardinalem Johannis holt Epigramma.

Hoc operis quodcūq; pater dignissime cernis
Holtiades domino dedicat omne suo
Autor ut instituit tantillum opus edere primum
Et tibi non tactas dedere primitias
Incussit validos tanti censura timores
Patris ab incepto me tua pene trahens
Sed tamen in miseros pietas quā suggeris omnes.
Et mihi presentem plus pius ipse facis
Abscidit a pauido uanos mihi corde timores
Quod mihi mentis erat. perfice. perge. iubens
Ergo faue lingue censor venerande latine
Tam cito vix natum ne moriatur opus
Quicquid erit placido supplex precor excipe vultu
Ingenium arbitrio dasq; rapisq; tuo
Hec equidem in varium breuiter collecta moretum.
Ex multis rapui furta pudica locis
Vnde tui causam pater alma dedere nepotes.
In sibi perpetuas vtilitatis opes
Edideram celebri Lamithe pie presul in aula
Digna volens pueris commoda ferre tuis

Thome more diserti adolescentuli in lucubratiunculas Holtiade. Epygramma

Quem legis holtiade tenerū pia furta libellum
Seu vir seu puer es. lac puerile voca
Dulce. sed & meritum liber hic me iudice nomē
Lactea qui pueris dogmata prestat. habet
Vos angli legite hec iuuenes. in maxima quorum
Exiguum q̄uis commoda surgit opus
Que vos in minimum legitis digesta libellum
Precepta in paucos pauca legenda dies.
Holtiades eadem vigili quesita labore
Legit ab innumeris pauca voluminibus
Sedulus ille vagis sese circumtulit agris.
Mellifice officio q̄ bene functus apis
Quicquid ibi in dulces sapidi congessit acervos
Mellis in hunc paruum rettulit aluearium.
Hoc opus anglorum cupienti intrare iuuente.
Prima sit in reliquam ianua grammaticem
Hanc tamen ante forem docti struxere. sed horum
Quisq; suos latio fecerat ore modos
Quid bene fulta penus prodest tibi. quando retentat.
Janua magnificas irreseranda cibos
Angle puer latio quid ages sermone. sapisse
Non potes in primo verba latina die
Te decet altricis tenerum recubare sub alis.
Discereq; ex verbis non tua verba tuis
Structa. sed et verbis iam pridem ianua nostris
Grammatice verum si fateamur erat.
Illa tamen vetus & tunsi lacerata frequenti
Que vix assiduo pulsa labore crepat
Janua nostra noua est. tenereq; facillima turbe
Ad digiti minimum q̄ cito aperta sonum

Plate II

Opusculum

agre with the last. as Vir ⁊ mulier magna ad me ve
nit. Hic illius arma hic currus fuit

But yf the worde that closeth be plurell. thenne it
must agree in gendre ⁊ psone wyth the cheef. as Ego
⁊ uxor amatissimus. in the whiche is silepsis in pson
⁊ gendre. but nat in noumbre

To this fygure may be reduced suche cõstructiõs
Vrbẽ quã statuo. ⁊ Fabulas quas fecisset ⁊c.

When. ij. or more thinges be generally cõpared
in one worde ⁊ afterwarde specyally set oute. as Aqui
le volauerũt vna ab oriẽte. alia ab occidente. then is ẏ
fygure Prolepsis. ⁊c.

Cetera plãtus ⁊ plenius disces ex Sulpitio.

Finis

Finis opusculi Magistri Johannis holt
Quod lac puerorum appellauit

Thome more epygramma

Macte puer gaude lepido quicunqz libello
Delicijsqz tui pastus es holtiade
Nec tibi dat carnes nec acerbos arbuta fructus
Dat tibi que dulci pocula lacte fluunt.
Carnis in inualida massa grauis incubat aluo
Arbuta non sapide sunt leuis humor aque
At lac ⁊ infantem sine pondere nutrit alumnũ.
Lactis ⁊ infanti dulcis in ore sapor
Pastus es hoc igitur. visum est decuisse nequibat
Grandia tam tenerum pondera ferre iecur

nunc vbi deleteris lactere. alimenta mouentur
Non mellita minus fortia sume magis
Ergo aut Sulpitij placida lepidissime mensa
Vtilibus Phoce vel satur esto cibis
Aut Sepontini bibito noua musta Perotti.
Aut Diomedeis condita mulsa cadis
Aut alium quẽcunqz velis imitari exopta
Dulcia qui caute misceat vtilibus
Precipue sed Sulpitij documenta capesses
Holti consilijs vsc vel vse meis
Discenda holtiades heteroclyta liquit ab illo
Et quodcunqz tenent nomina queqz genus
Recta leges illic que sit constructio post hoc
Preterita ⁊ verbis iuncta supina suis
Sedulus ⁊ tandem longe pulcherrima disces.
Carmina limitibus continuisse suis
Ergo musarum chorum ingressa iuuentus
Quum per Sulpicium plectra lyramqz geres
Dic modo. ferre lyrã quũ dextra nequiuerat holt?
Admouit labiis vbera chara meis

Hac opus hoc pressit menda vacat iste libellus
Non nisi correctas imprimit ille notas
Antwerpie.

Plate III

As the book at hand has been unknown to bibliographers since 1682-91, it can herein be only described; it cannot be more than identified with the Richard Smith copy. It is a small book measuring about 4¾ inches by 6¼ inches, with some headlines trimmed, because at some time or other the book was carelessly trimmed so that when it is closed as now bound, the top and bottom edges slope from left to right. This careless trimming has eliminated some running heads after about the middle of the book. The book is mostly in 8's, the title page being [a], and the book continues through [a8], [b8], [c8], [d8], [e4], [f8], and the half sheet, g, [g4]. Today it is bound in an inexpensive recent morocco binding with pencil scribblings on the inside of front and back covers, the one on the inside of the back cover reading "collated and perfect" with some illegible initials following. Except that the signatures count correctly, this statement is nonsense, as no other copy is known, and there is literally nothing with which to collate this book bibliographically. The text is identical in length with the texts of [1510?] and [1520] although there are printing variants throughout.

On the recto of the final leaf (see Plate III) is a colophon of sorts indicating the book was printed by Bac or Back at Antwerp but supplying no date, which reads:

> Bac opus hoc pressit menda vacatiste libellus/
> Non nisi correctas imprimit ille notas/
> Antwerpie./

If Wood was right about an edition of 1497, then this copy may be one of a pirated(?) edition done for some schoolmaster at Antwerp, perhaps between 1497 and 1500, the latter date being the latest possible one for the first edition of the book anywhere because John Morton, to whom the book was addressed, seems to be still alive, and it is known that he died in 1500. All available evidence points toward the printing of this book before 1500, but there is not a scrap of proof. Some hints of the date come from the type, and some come from the few facts known about the printer. It is unfortunate that so little is known of him as a printer of cheap English books, for the scanty accounts of him have little enough to say of his lesser publications. Godfrey Back, as he signed himself at least once, or Gevaert Bac or Back as his name appears elsewhere, according to P. D. Vander Meersch ("Godofredus Back, imprimeur a Anvers, de 1494-1511," *Le Bibliophile Belge,* II [1845], 247-48), had been a bookbinder, but on November 19, 1492, he married the widow of the printer Van der Goes and became a printer, continuing the printing business left by Van der Goes. He is said to have occupied a house in Antwerp named *Tvogelhuys* (birdhouse) throughout his entire printing career. Probably the house bore a birdcage as its sign, and Back adopted the device of a birdcage as his own. This device is found in the copy at hand on the verso of the last leaf (see Plate IV). As Back continued to print, the device changed, but the earliest known device of the birdcage in Back's books is the one in this one. Back died in 1516 but seems to have stopped printing about 1510 or 1511. Hain, probably following Wood, listed an edition of the *Lac,* dating it *ca.* 1497, but neither Copinger nor any other bibliographer following Hain added anything to Hain's meager description of this 1497(?) printing. We can say with certainty, now that the book before us has actually appeared, that Gevaert Bac or Back printed at least one edition at Antwerp of Holt's *Lac,* perhaps sometime between 1497 and 1500. The book at hand is printed in type that appears in every fifteenth-century book known to have been printed by Back. The font has the peculiarity of rarely using the *j* character, as already noted. Only two leaves of any gathering have signature letters, as a-iij, a-iiij; b,b-iij; c-i, c-iij; d-i, d-iij; e-i, e-iiij; f-i, -iij; g-i; [c-5] is cropped at the bottom by the careless trimming which affects some letters in the bottom line of both sides of the leaf. These are printing characteristics that seldom appear after 1500.

Wood stated that Holt's *Lac* was sometimes printed or published with grammatical works by another Englishman, John Stanbridge (1463-1510), and *STC* 23,1555, n.d., by Godfrey Back at Antwerp is suggestive. *STC* has dated this edition as [1510?], which is obviously as conjectural as the [1510?] for the edition by Wynkyn de Worde. This type is the same as in the Holt book before us, but if Enschede and others are correct in their claim that Back used only fifteenth-century type in all his printings, the type in the Stanbridge books points no more to a definite date than does the type in the Holt book at hand. This fact only points to the probability of this Holt book having been printed before 1500; it scarcely proves it. Thus the copy at hand may be, and perhaps is, a hitherto unknown incunabulum by an English author, first printed in English at Antwerp about or slightly before 1500. I think this is about as far bibliographically as we can go with any certainty with what is known to date about the book.

Leaving the flats and shallows of these bibliographical facts and perhaps fancies, let us turn to the text proper of the two epigrams by More as found in this Smith copy of the *Lac.* These texts have never before been either recorded or collated, for they have been unknown. In the Back printing, they offer a few variations from those in the texts that have been collated by Nelson and by Bradner and Lynch. Because of the ready availability of the two recent printings of the two epigrams, I present here only the texts as found in this Back printing, but collate with [1510?] as *A* and

Plate IV

[1520] as *B*. An effort was first made to collate the Back text with Nelson and Bradner and Lynch. The Nelson text is a good one, but was discarded for purposes of collation as the Bradner-Lynch text was found so untrustworthy that it seemed pointless to use it. Recourse was then made to the films of the originals as listed in *STC*. *A* herein means *STC* 13,604, therein hesitatingly dated [1510?], the only copy being in the British Museum. *B* is the other edition, *STC* 13,605, [1520], again only the British Museum copy is known. The fragments *STC* 13,606, at Oxford and Cambridge also dated [1520?] have been used, and named herein as *C*. At least once, only the Back copy has a word, as in the first collation, in which case only a blank occurs for the other editions, *A, B,* and *C*.

On the verso of the title page after the epigram by Holt to Archbishop Morton (Wood's Moreton), appears the following (see Plate II):

Thome more diserti adolescentuli in lucubraci[/]
unculas Holtiade. Epygramma
Quem legis holtiade tenerumpia furta libellum
Seu vir seu puer es. lac puerile voca
Dulce. sed & meritum liber hic me iudice nomem
Lactea qui pueris dogmata prestat. habet
Vos angli legite hec iuuenes. in maxima quorum
Exiguum quamuis commoda surgit opus
Que vos in minumum legitis digesta libellum
Precepta in paucos pauva legenda dics.
Holtiades eadem vigili quesita labore
Legit ab innumeris pauca voluminibus
Sedulus ille vagis sese circuntulit agris.
Mellifice officio quam bene functus apis
Quicquid ibi in dulces sapidi congessit aceruos
Mellis in hunc paruum rettulit alueolum.
Hoc opus anglorum cupienti intrare iuuente.
Prima sit in reliquam ianua grammaticem
Hanc tamen ante forem docti struxere. sed horum
Quisque suos lacio fecerat ore modos
Quid bene fulta penus prodest tibi. quando retentat.
Ianua magnificas irreseranda cibos
Angle puer lacio quid ages sermone. sapisse
Non potes in primo verba latina die
Te decet altricis tenerum recubare sub alis.
Discereque ex verbis non tua verba tuis
Structa. sed et verbis iam pridem ianua nostris
Grammatice verum si fateamur erat.
Illa tamen vetus & tunsi lacerata frequenti
Que vix assiduo pulsa labore crepat
Ianua nostra noua est. tenereque facillima turbe
Ad digiti minimum quam cito aperta sonum

Title page 2 **Anglice**] —
Title 1 **more**] more/ (A & B) 2 **Epygramma**] Epigramma (A & B)
1 **holtiade**] Holtiade 2 **es.**] es/ 3 **Dulce.**] Dulce/ &] et 4 **Prestat.**] prestat/ 5 **iuuenes.**] iuuvenes/ 8 **dies.**] dies 11 **Sedulus**] Sedulis 14 **alueolum.**] alueolum 15 **iuuente.**] iuuente 16 **grammaticem**] grammaticam 17 **Struxere.**] struxere/ 18 **lacio** or **latio**] (the seeming **c** may be foul case for **t** or it may be intentional; but see 2:28) latio/ 19 **tibi.**] tibi 20 **magnificas**] magnificos 21 **lacio or latio** (see line 18)] latio (unmistakably) **sermone.**] sermone/ 23 **alis.**] alis 25 **Structa.**] Structa/ 26 **Grammatice**] Grammatice/ **erat.**] erat/ 27 **tunsi**] tunsu 28 **vix**] xix (A) vix (B) 29 **est.**] est/

On the verso of leaf [g3] (see Plate III) appears:

Thome more epygramma

Macte puer gaude lepido quicunque libello
  Delicijsque tui pastus es holtiade
Nec tibi dat carnes nec acerbos arbuta fructus
  Dat tibi que dulci pocula lacte fluunt.
Carnis in inualida massa grauis incubat aluo
  Arbuta non sapide sunt leuis humor aque
Ac lac & infantem sine pondere nutrit alumnum
  Lactis & infanti dulcis in ore sapor
Pastus es hoc igitur. visum est decuisse nequibat
  Grandia tam tenerum pondera ferre iecur
[N]unc vbi desieris lactere. alimenta monemu[s]
  Non mellita minus fortia sume magis
Ergo aut sulpitij placida lepidissime mensa
  Vtilibus Phoce vel satur esto cibis
Aut Sepontini bibito noua musta Perotti.
  Aut dyomedeis condita mulsa cadis
Aut alium quecunque velis imitariex [*sic*] opta
  Dulcia qui caute misceat vtilibus
Precipue sed Sulpitij documenta capesses
  Holti concilijs vse vel vse meis
Discenda holtiades heteroclyta liquit ab illo
  Et quodcunque tenent nomina queque genus
Recta leges illic que sit constructio post hoc
  Preterita & verbis iuncta supina suis
Sedulus & tandem longe pulcherrima disces.
  Carmina limitibus continuisse suis
Ergo musarum chorum ingressa iuuentus
  Quum per Sulpicium plectra lyramque geres
Dic modo. ferre lyramquum dextra nequiuerat holtus
  Admouit labris vbera chara meis.

Title **epygramma**] epygramma. (B)
2 **Delicijsque**] Delicus (A & B) Delicijs (C) 4 **fluunt.**] fluunt 8 **sapor**] sapor. 9 **igitur.**] igitur/ 11 **lactere.**] lactare/ 12 **minus**] nimis **magis**] magis. 13 **sulpitij**] Sulpitii 14 **cibis**] cibis. (A) cibus. (B) 15 **Perotti.**] Perotti 16 **dyomedeis**] diomedeis 17 **imitariex** (foul case for **r**)] imitarier **opta**] opta/ 19 **Sulpitij**] Sulpitii 20 **consilijs**] consiliis **meis**] meis. 21 **heteroclyta**] heteroclita

22 **genus**] genus. 23 **constructio**] constructio/ **post hoc**] sed post 24 **suis**] suis. 25 **disces.**] disces 26 **suis**] suis. 27 **chorum**] choreas 28 **Sulpicium**] Sulpitium (see 1:18) 29 **modo.**] mode/ **holtus**] Holtus. 30 **meis.**] meis.

As is usual with texts of this period, no claims can be made for the authenticity or validity or lack of either for the Back texts of these two epigrams. It is obvious from several of the variants from Nelson and Bradner and Lynch that the printer, Back, was responsible for some, such as the repeated **-cunque** (2:1, 17) where the two other texts have **-cumque.** Users of printed texts from this and even later periods, and from the beginnings of printing until well into the nineteenth century are aware of the capricious nature of such texts as these. So far as I know, there are no manuscripts extant anywhere of these two epigrams; hence we really have only printed texts, which, in a way, are no texts at all, yet in other ways must be accepted and cannot be emended at will, except, as in today's printing, to correct obvious errors of omission or commission. Even such emendation for the kind of Latin displayed in these two epigrams can be most treacherous for the emender.

These two epigrams addressed by More to Holt in themselves are really addressing grammar school boys about the study of grammar. In the first one, More admonishes the boys to read Holt's book carefully, telling them that though the book is small, if they heed what they find in it, they will benefit greatly. Master Holt has arranged in brief compass what he has culled from much reading of many volumes. More then exclaims on how well Holt has succeeded, working like the bee gathering honey in many journeys through the fields. The little book is the gateway or introduction for all English boys to enter the realm of grammar. They need the protection of a book or teacher who will induct them by means of their native tongue into the intricacies of the Latin language. More admits that such an entrance into the study of Latin has existed before, indeed, was made a long time ago. But that entrance (did he refer to Stanbridge?) is old and opens only with difficulty. Holt's little book or gate is not only new, it also opens easily, almost at the tapping of a finger on it.

The second little poem, also in elegiacs, is even more figurative in its appeal to boys to make use of Holt's easy steps to Latin. This time, instead of the book being a gate or entrance to the Latin tongue, it is dealt with as an excellent, healthful form of food for the very young, the food itself being Latin grammar, of course. The food is offered in the form of milk, and, unlike stronger viands, will never upset the boy who drinks of it, for even a child is nourished, not upset, by sweet milk. Holt intended this, knowing full well that the child could not digest heavier food. However, the boy should not stop with Holt, who actually weaned the lad from his native tongue. The boy must now turn to stronger viands, and especially to some of the older and standard Latin grammarians who wrote in Latin, such as Sulpitius, Phocas, Perotti of Siponto, and Diomedes, or any other of like authority. All who take Holt's advice or More's will avidly seek out Sulpitius above all, finding that Master Holt has omitted various complex phases of Latin grammar that are unnecessary as a boy begins its study, but soon become vital. As the boy progresses, he will find that Sulpitius actually contains the most beautiful of poems. Therefore, when any of you later become poets, thanks to Sulpitius, you will say: "ferre lyram quum dextra nequiuerat holtus/ Admouit labris vbera chara meis" or, quite literally, "before my right hand could even hold a lyre, Holt offered a fare most welcome to my lips."

The point about Sulpitius containing the most beautiful of poems needs one or more of the old editions of his grammar to explain it. In such an edition as *Grammatice Sulpitiana cum textu Ascensiano recognito et aucto* (Iehan Petit: Paris, [1505]), in 6's for the most part, the grammatical statements by Sulpitius are printed in metrical form, the commentary on them being in a smaller type and in prose. Thus More meant that when the boy could appreciate Sulpitius' learning, he would find his metrical lines most beautiful because most useful.

The other and more ancient grammarians, Phocas, Diomedes, and Perotti, are so well known that they need no more comment than that afforded them by Bradner and Lynch.

These two little Latin epigrams by More are perhaps more personal than they are great poetic efforts, showing his relations with Holt and his great interest in the education of boys in particular and learning in general. Probably Bradner and Lynch have published the final form of the collected Latin poems by More, consequently the above texts should be available to all who care for More's poetical efforts.

University of Illinois

SPENSER'S SCHOLARLY SCRIPT AND "RIGHT WRITING"

Roland M. Smith

> "The right writing of our English . . . is a certain reasonable course, to direct the pen by such rules as are most conformable, to the proprietie of *sound,* the consideration of *reason,* and the smoothing of *custom* ioyntlie."
>
> —Mulcaster's *Elementarie* (1582)

Ben Jonson appears to have summed up popular opinion when he defended the burial of Shakespeare in Stratford Church rather than in Westminster Abbey:

> My Shakespeare, rise! I will not lodge thee by
> Chaucer, or Spenser, or bid Beaumont[1] lie
> A little further to make thee a room.
> Thou art a monument without a tomb.

After the turn of our own century, Sir Sidney Lee wrote of the author of these lines that he is "the only literary contemporary of Shakespeare, of whose handwriting the surviving specimens exceed a few scraps."[2] Recent researches, however, have done something to invalidate Sir Sidney's observation. Shakespeare, it is true, remains in a very real sense "a monument without a tomb"; he is also essentially a monument without a hand. Yet for Spenser, and perhaps for his "maister deere" Chaucer,[3] we now possess "the touch of a vanish'd hand" in a considerable body of holograph manuscript.

[1] Not Francis Beaumont, Master of Charterhouse and acclaimer of Spenser. See T. W. Baldwin, "The Three Francis Beaumonts," *MLN,* XXXIX (1924), 505-7.

[2] *A Life of William Shakespeare* (London, 1915), p. 518. The earlier editions are even more in error.

[3] Despite the admirably cautious analysis of R. M. Wilson, some critics are already proceeding on the assumption that the recently discovered MS of *The Equatorie of the Planetis,* ed. Derek J. Price (Cambridge, 1955), is in Chaucer's hand. (See F. N. Robinson, *The Works of Geoffrey Chaucer,* 2nd ed. [Boston, 1957], pp. viii f.)

Thirty-five years ago little or nothing was known or established concerning Spenser's handwriting.[4] Collier and Grosart and Gollancz had all accepted as Spenser's certain documents which can no longer be considered his, or had branded as forgeries other documents which can now be labeled authentic. Not until 1923[5] did Henry Plomer make the first series of important identifications of papers — sixteen in all — in Spenser's hand. Some fifteen years later Raymond Jenkins published the results of a search for further documents; in addition to those listed by Plomer, he identified thirty written in Spenser's secretary hand between 1580 and 1582 while Spenser was serving as Grey's secretary, and four more written between 1585 and 1589.[6] Thus, by 1940 more than fifty documents, eleven of them from the later period, had been attributed to Spenser's pen.

Until now, identifications have been based entirely upon palaeographical evidence. To Plomer's list of idiosyncrasies, "the sloped writing, the long-drawn-out *f*'s and *s*'s, the truncated *p* looking like an overgrown *x*, the pump-handle filial *o*, the capitals *B*, *I*, and *E*, and many other letters," Jenkins added Spenser's cramped way of writing "for."[7] Detailed examination reveals other peculiarities which separate Spenser's secretary hand from that of other writers. His Italian hand is even more strikingly distinctive. But it is inevitable that among thousands of documents like those in the Public Record Office, there are to be found some hands so markedly similar that it is almost impossible to distinguish them.

Not all critics have been agreed that certain letters were written by

---

They may be right. But it cannot be denied, as Wilson (p. 162) remarks, that there are still no undisputed "holograph or autograph Chaucer documents known, in spite of the very considerable labor that has gone into the assembling of all relevant life records."

[4] In the later expanded editions of his *Life of Shakespeare,* Lee could still write confidently: "Of the voluminous fruits of Edmund Spenser's pen, nothing remains in his handwriting save one holograph business note, and eight autograph signatures . . ." (New York, 1916), p. 516. On some of the problems presented by the identification of Spenser MSS, see Hilary Jenkinson, "On Autographs," *History,* n.s. VIII (1923), 98-108, and "Elizabethan Handwritings," *The Library,* 4th Series, III (1922), 33-34. Jenkinson does not consider the possibility of investigating a writer's spelling habits, which should, incidentally, make it clear that Spenser did not "copy" the Waterford depositions of March 16, 1581 (*Calendar of State Papers for Ireland, 1574-85* [hereafter cited as SP], 81.36.II).

[5] "Edmund Spenser's Handwriting," *MP,* XXI (1923), 201-7.

[6] See "Spenser with Lord Grey in Ireland," *PMLA,* LII (1937), 338-53, and "Spenser: The Uncertain Years 1584-89," LIII (1938), 350-62. In addition, Jenkins lists (*PMLA,* LII, 345) thirty-six letters which were addressed, though not written, by Spenser.

[7] Other secretary hands, like that of Grey's letters SP 80.10 and 80.32, written in January, 1581, ran *f*'s and *o*'s together in this fashion, but not with Spenser's consistency.

Spenser.[8] For example, in his edition of Spenser's *View,* Renwick rightly claimed (p. 285) that Grey's letter of November 12, 1580, to the Queen survives in "Spenser's most careful and beautiful Italian hand." Elsewhere the same editor's views are less acceptable, for it can be shown that Grey's letter dated January 15, 1581, is not, as Renwick states, "in Spenser's hand."[9] Again, Gollancz's assertion that an early version of Sonnet I of the *Amoretti* was written by Spenser has been adequately refuted by A. C. Judson.[10] In each instance it is demonstrable that Spenser was not the writer on grounds entirely apart from those already advanced. For even though the hands resemble Spenser's hand, Spenser's spelling is too distinctive and too consistent to permit attributing these documents to him.[11]

In discussing "the tangled subject of this poet's handwriting," Jenkinson observed in 1923, "palaeography of the current hands has been too much neglected."[12] True, but palaeography alone will not provide the key to unlock the heart of the problems which still confront us. The personalities of writers like Grey and Spenser, who were "rugged individuals" in different ways, are partially revealed by their penmanship, which to the practiced eye becomes unmistakable, but their individuality is even more strikingly marked by what Mulcaster would have called the "autoritie" of their "ortografie." It will be well, then, for future investigators to take both script and spelling into account.

Despite Jenkins' belief that the first document in Spenser's secretary hand which has survived is the Smerwick letter of November 28, 1580, there are two pieces, not noticed until now, that antedate it by almost three months. These, the earliest specimens we have from Spenser's pen, are copies of letters written to Grey, the first from Hugh Magennis on August 29, not long after the Lord Deputy's arrival in Ireland, and the second from Nicholas Bagenal bearing no date but calendared under September 2. Both copies,

[8] For this "pioneer history" the best summary is that of W. W. Greg (*English Literary Autographs, 1550-1650* [1932], Part II, XXXIX), who first recognized as Spenser's three distinct hands, two for English (Italian and secretary) and a third for Latin.

[9] *A View of the Present State of Ireland,* ed. William L. Renwick (London, 1934). Renwick (p. 281) quotes from the letter (SP 80.10), p. 1, lines 26-32. Such spellings as *Neyther, onlye, dowbte, heavie, smale* (2x), *beesydes, throwghlie* (and elsewhere in the letter *sondrie, poaste, supplie,* etc.) are not Spenser's. Jenkins is right (*PMLA,* LII, 344, note 22) in observing that, except for the "Copie of my priuat" (SP 79.24.I), "nothing in Spenser's autograph" for December, 1580, or the two following months has been preserved in the Irish State Papers.

[10] "Amoretti, Sonnet I," *MLN,* LVIII (1943), 548-50. See the Variorum edition of Spenser's *Minor Poems* (Baltimore, 1943-47), II, 419-20.

[11] Spenser was not in the habit of writing *hir* (for *their*), *eies, dieng, harts,* or *shee,* as did the scribe who wrote the *Amoretti* copy.

[12] *The Library, op. cit.,* pp. 33-34.

probably written in Dublin after Grey's unhappy return from Glenmalure but before Pelham invested him with the sword of state, are indisputably Spenser's, in handwriting and in spelling.

In all, at least fifty-nine documents are extant in Spenser's own hand, requiring 115 large sheets of the poet's "allowaunce of paper . . . and parchment."[13] All but nine of these are letters, either originals or copies. Of these originals thirty-five, from 1580 to 1582, bear the signature of Lord Grey, five, in 1585, bear the signature of Sir John Norris as president of Munster, and two, in 1588-89, the signature of Sir Thomas Norris as vice-president of Munster. Since no convenient record of Spenser's writings is available, they are listed below in their chronological order. In each instance the palaeographical evidence, so ably presented by Plomer and Jenkins, has been corroborated through a study of the spelling, which reveals more consistency than is usual in an Elizabethan writer. Thus the handwriting of all the following documents may be confidently assigned to Spenser.

TABLE I

1580

1. SP 75.75. Sir Hugh Magennis to Grey, from Narrow Water (near Newry), Aug. 29. 1 p. Copy.
2. SP 76.1. Sir Nicholas Bagenal to Grey (from Newry), Sept. 2? 1 p. Copy.
3. SP 78.29. Grey to the Queen. Smerwick, Nov. 12. 7 pp.
4. BM Addit. Grey to Burghley. Limerick, Nov. 28. 2 pp.
   Reproduced by Jenkins, *PMLA,* LII (1937), 338-39.
5. SP 78.68. Grey to Walsingham. Clonmel, Nov. 30. 1 p.
6. SP 79.24.I. Grey to the Queen. Dublin, Dec. 22. 3 pp. Copy.
   Last two pages reproduced by Plomer, *MP,* XXI (1923), 205, Fig. 3.

1581

7. SP 81.15. Malby-Burke Articles. Togher (Ir. *An Tóchar*), Mayo, March 7. 3 pp. Copy.
8. SP 81.20. Miler Magrath to Sir Lucas Dillon, from Toom (i.e., Toomyvara [Ir. *Túaim uí Mheadhra*] in Tipperary, erroneously calendared "Turin"), March 11. 3 pp. Copy.
   In Latin. Grosart believed this copy to be "wholly in the handwriting of Spenser," but Plomer (p. 207) observed, "it is difficult to understand what

[13] According to the "Booke of Concordatums" (SP 92.20.I), p. 10, Spenser and Reynoldes were paid at the rate of £15 per year. The record shows that Reynoldes was paid to the end of 1581. If his services actually ended Dec. 31, he may not be the scribe of the letters attributed to Hand D: see below under Table II, no. 18. The nine letters ascribed (under no. 6) to Hand B, however, were all written before 1582. In the same "Booke" Nathaniell Dillon is twice named as being paid for "attendinge the Lo: Deputie in sondrye iorneyes" but not as one of his secretaries.

TABLE I (Continued)

authority Grosart had for speaking so confidently." Since Plomer wrote, enough evidence has become available to show that Grosart was right. I shall discuss Spenser's Latin hand elsewhere.

9. SP 81.36.I. Ormond to Grey, from Cork, March 13. 2 pp. Copy.
   This copy is adequate refutation of Plomer's claim (p. 207), "None of the other letters which bear Spenser's attestation as 'copia vera' are in his handwriting."
10. SP 81.39. Burke's submission to Malby. March 20. 2 pp. Copy.
11. SP 82.54. Grey to the Queen. Dublin, April 26. 4 pp.
12. SP 83.47. Grey to Walsingham. Wexford, June 10. 1 p.
13. SP 84.13. Grey to the Privy Council. Dublin, July 10. 2 pp.
14. SP 84.14. Grey to Walsingham. Dublin, July 10. 1 p.
   Reproduced by Plomer, Figs. 1, 2, and by Greg (XL, a, b).
15. SP 84.28. Grey to Walsingham. Dublin, July 18. 1 p.
16. SP 85.5. Grey to the Queen. Dublin, Aug. 10. 6 pp.
17. SP 86.50. Grey to the Queen. Dublin, Nov. 6. 4 pp.
18. Cecil, 12.16 (no. 1078). Grey to Burghley. Dublin, Nov. 28. 1 p.
19. Cecil, 12.19 (no. 1081). Grey to Burghley. Dublin, Dec. 10. 2 pp.
20. SP 87.64. Grey to Walsingham. Dublin, Dec. 29. 1 p.

1582

21. SP 88.2. Grey to the Privy Council. Dublin, Jan. 3. 2 pp.
22. SP 88.12. Grey to Burghley. Dublin, Jan. 12. 2 pp.
23. SP 88.39. Grey to the Queen. Dublin, Jan. 25. 2 pp.
24. SP 89.18. John Nugent's Confession. Dublin, Feb. 5. 6 pp. Copy.
   First page reproduced by Plomer, Fig. 4: cf. Greg (XL, c, d).
25. SP 89.30. Grey to the Privy Council. Dublin, Feb. 13. 1 p.
26. SP 89.35. Grey to the Privy Council. Dublin, Feb. 18. 1 p.
27. SP 90.1. Grey to Walsingham. Dublin, March 1. 1 p.
28. BM Cotton Titus. "Newes out of Munster." March 23. 1 p. Copy.
   Reproduced by Jenkins, *Stud. Philol.*, XXXII (1935), 126. Apparently the original inclosure with SP 91.17, from Grey to Walsingham, whose clerk substituted in its place the now calendared copy, SP 91.17.I.
29. SP 90.31. Sir Edward Butler to Waterhouse. March 24. 2 pp. Copy.
30. SP 90.48. Grey to the Privy Council. Dublin, March 27. 1 p.
31. SP 90.52. Grey and Council to Privy Council. Dublin, March 28. 1 p.
32. SP 91.11. Grey to Walsingham. Trim, April 4. 1 p.
33. SP 91.26. Note of letters to Walsingham. 1 p.
   Reproduced by Plomer, Fig. 5.
34. SP 91.38. Grey and Council to Privy Council. Dublin, April 19. 1 p.
35. SP 91.52. Grey to Burghley. Dublin, April 30. 1 p.
36. SP 91.53. Grey to Walsingham. Dublin, April 30. 1 p.
37. SP 92.9. Grey to the Privy Council. Dublin, May 7. 1 p.
38. SP 92.10. Grey to Walsingham. Dublin, May 7. 2 pp.
39. SP 92.11.I. Grey and Council to the Queen. Dublin, May 9. 7 pp. Copy.
40. SP 92.30. Grey and Council to Privy Council. Dublin, May 11. 1 p.

41. SP 92.46. Grey to Walsingham. Dublin, May 16. 1 p.
42. SP 93.64.I. Thomas Meagh to James Meagh. May 17-June 29. 3 pp. Copy.
43. SP 92.85. Grey to the Privy Council. Dublin, May 28. 1 p.
44. SP 93.64. Grey to Walsingham. Dublin, June 29. 1 p.
45. SP 94.28. Grey to Walsingham. Dublin, July 16. 1 p.
    Reproduced by Plomer, Fig. 6.
46. SP 94.46. Grey to Walsingham. Kilmainham (Dublin), July 28. 1 p.
47. SP 94.47. Grey to Walsingham. Dublin, July 28. 1 p.
48. SP 94.61. Grey to the Privy Council. Kilmainham, July 31. 1 p.

1585

49. SP 115.13. J. Norris to the Privy Council. Dublin, March 7. 1 p.
    Reproduced by Plomer, Fig. 7.
50. SP 115.14. J. Norris to the Privy Council. Dublin, March 7. 1 p.
51. SP 115.15. J. Norris to Burghley. Dublin, March 7. 1 p.
52. SP 115.16. J. Norris to Walsingham. Dublin, March 7. 1 p.
53. SP 115.41. J. Norris to Burghley. Clonmel, March 31. 4 pp.
54. SP 115.42. Note of Desmond lands. 1 p.

1588

55. SP 135.66. T. Norris to Walsingham. Limerick, July 1. 5 pp.
    First page reproduced by Jenkins, *PMLA,* LIII (1938), 350.

1589

56. SP 140.37. T. Norris to the Privy Council. Shandon Castle, Jan. 22. 3 pp.
57. SP 144.70. Spenser's answer to the Articles. [May.] 1 p.
    Last 8 lines reproduced by Jenkinson, *The Library,* 4th Series, III, Plate XI (A); all but secs. 2 and 3 reproduced by Greg, XXXIX (a, b).
58. SP 147.16. Spenser's bill against the Lord Roche. Oct. 12. 2 pp.

Undated [1589?]

59. The British Museum grant to McHenry. 1 p.
    As early as 1832, a writer in *Gentleman's Magazine,* CII, 305, stated: "The signature alone is Spenser's autograph." Both Collier (1862) and Grosart (1884) branded the piece a forgery, and as late as 1909 Stronach rejected it as Spenser's: "the document is in the handwriting of a clerk." See Warner's clear reproduction and his convincing argument that Spenser wrote it. In both hand and spelling it is in striking agreement with the other documents from Spenser's pen. (Cf. Carpenter, *Reference Guide,* pp. 286-88.)

These documents which have survived in Spenser's hand must, of course, represent a small part of the output of his secretarial pen. Other extant pieces may have gone unnoticed, but it is too much to hope that more than a few will come to light. Nor may one assume that Spenser was the writer of any one of these lost documents, including the original of "Newes out of Munster" (SP 91.17.I above) or of the letter to the Queen (14c below). Three extant "collections of extracts" (SP 84.52.I, 86.17, and 96.6) contain twenty-eight marginal references to letters of Grey of which only nine appear to be in existence; a fourth collection, listing Grey's services to April 26, 1581, has been labeled "missing" by a recent hand (cf. SP 96.6, endorsement). An uncalendared letter from Grey to the Privy Council, written on Jan. 14, 1581, is cited in all three collections; other missing letters are drawn upon in more than one of these:

(a) Grey to the Queen, Aug. 28, 1580.
(b) Dublin Council to the Privy Council, Sept. 28, 1580.
(c) Grey to the Privy Council, April 26, 1582.

There are furthermore a number of single references to letters written by Grey on the eve of his recall, in July and August, 1582. If we may judge by these collections, about a third of Grey's letters have survived. Among those missing are letters to the Queen as early as August 28, 1580, and as late as August 10, 1582.

I. The Italian Hand

Little has been written or known concerning Spenser's Italian hand. Its stately script fully justifies Renwick's phrase "careful and beautiful." As one might expect, the poet employed the same characteristic spelling whether he used the Italian or the secretary hand, or for that matter, the bastard hand in which he copied the Magrath letter. To his spelling habits I shall return later.

In 1937 Jenkins (*PMLA,* LII, 338) maintained that "only one of Grey's secretaries besides Spenser wrote an Italian hand," and added: "Further investigation of Spenser's Italian hand may therefore prove that most of the significant letters of Grey to the Queen are in Spenser's Italian hand." Eighteen letters to the Queen, all but the first in the Public Record Office, have survived from Grey's administration, written between August 12, 1580, and May 10, 1582, of which thirteen were from Grey alone and five were sent jointly by Grey and the Dublin Council. The following table shows that these letters, extant in twenty-two forms, include five written and addressed in Spenser's Italian hand and subscribed and signed by Grey (nos. 3, 8, 10, 12, and 15).

Table II

1. BM Cotton Titus B.xiii, p. 305. Grey's first letter to the Queen, Dublin, Aug. 12, 1580, "reporting the state in which he found Ireland."
   Printed by Egerton in Grey's *Commentary of the Services and Charges of William Lord Grey* (Camden Soc., 1847), vol. 40, pp. 77-78.
2. SP 77.12. Grey to the Queen. Dublin, Oct. 5, 1580. 2 pp.

In Grey's hand, and addressed by Grey.[14] Except nos. 3 and 9, the letters below are also from Dublin.

3. SP 78.29. Grey to the Queen. Smerwick, Nov. 12, 1580. 7pp.
   (Table I, no. 3.) Written and addressed "To her Ma^ty^ yeue this." In Spenser's ITALIAN hand. Subscribed in Grey's hand: "Y^r^ Hyg. most [*sic*] & faythefull subiect & seruant." Jenkins' assumption (p. 343), "It is indeed probable that Spenser penned this letter," no longer involves the least doubt.

4. SP 79.25. Grey to the Queen. Dec. 22, 1580. 3 pp.
   Written and addressed (as in no. 2), "Too her Matie yeeue this," in Grey's hand.

4c. SP 79.24.I. Copy of the same without signature. Without date. 3 pp.
   The body is in Spenser's secretary hand. It is difficult to understand Plomer's statement (p. 205) that this letter is "known only from the copy which Lord Grey had made of it at the time," since the original (no. 4 above) in Grey's hand has been preserved and calendared along with it. Plomer failed to note that this copy is not entirely in Spenser's secretary hand, the marginal "Post script" being in Spenser's Italian hand (see Plomer, Fig. 3) and the words "Copie of my priuat" being subscribed in Grey's hand. The indorsement "Copie of my pryuate [*sic*] to her Matie" is likewise in Grey's hand.

5. SP 79.26. Grey and Council to the Queen. Dec. 23, 1580. 1 p.
   In Hand A. The address "To the Quenes most excellent Matie" is, contrary to the usual practice, in Spenser's secretary hand. Also in Hand A are Grey's letter to Burghley and Geoffrey Fenton's to Walsingham, both written from Smerwick, Nov. 14, 1580 (SP 78.37 and 78.38), five days after the fort had surrendered. This scribe, who had thus been at Smerwick with Spenser, also wrote toward the end of Grey's administration the letter (SP 92.73) from Grey and the Dublin Council to the Privy Council in London, extolling Capt. Thomas Clinton's services at Smerwick.
   The subscription "Yr Ma^tes^ most humble and faithfull subiectes and servants" is in Geoffrey Fenton's hand; compare Fenton's later letter to Leicester from Dunstable (SP 85.26), Aug. 26, 1581.

6. SP 80.38. Grey to the Queen. Jan. 28, 1581. 1 p.
   Written and addressed in Hand B. The frequency with which this secretary hand recurs raises the possibility that it may be that of Timothy Reynoldes. If, as Pauline Henley (*Spenser in Ireland* [Dublin and Cork, 1928], p. 24) conjectures, Reynoldes had been in office since 1572 or 1573, there is little evidence that he acted as Sidney's secretary, or as Pelham's, whose secretary was Morgan Colman. And if a "Secretarye to the Lo: Deputie" (SP 92.20.I, p. 10) might be expected to write an Italian hand, only Hand D (13 and 16 below) seems likely to be Reynoldes'. See comment under no. 18 below.
   Also in Hand B are letters 9 and 11 below, and six letters from Grey to the Privy Council (SP 83.45, 84.12, 85.13 and 85.37, 86.51 and 86.81) among others.

7. SP 80.39. Grey and Council to the Queen. Jan. 28, 1581. 2 pp.
   In Hand C, with seventeen leading words written in Italian script.

[14] All of the letters to the Queen appear to have been addressed by their writers except nos. 5, 11, 17, and 18 (addressed in Spenser's secretary hand) and 13 (addressed in his Italian hand).

TABLE II (Continued)

8. SP 82.54. Grey to the Queen. April 26, 1581. 4 pp.
   (Table I, no. 11.) Written and addressed in Spenser's ITALIAN hand. Subscribed in Grey's hand: "Y^r^ hyg. most humble seruant & faythefull subiect," with signature.
9. SP 83.44. Grey to the Queen. Wexford, June 10, 1581. 1 p.
   In Hand B (see no. 6 above). Subscribed and signed by Grey.
10. SP 85.5. Grey to the Queen. Aug. 10, 1581. 6 pp.
   Written and addressed in Spenser's ITALIAN hand. Subscribed in Grey's hand: "Y^r^ Hyg. moste humble seruant & faythefull subiect," with signature.
11. SP 85.6. Grey to the Queen. Aug. 10, 1581. 2 pp.
   Bearing the same date as no. 10, this letter, like nos. 6 and 9, is in Hand B. Subscribed and signed by Grey.
12. SP 86.50. Grey to the Queen. Nov. 6, 1581. 4 pp.
   Written and addressed in Spenser's ITALIAN hand. Subscribed in Grey's hand: "Y^r^ hyg. most faythefull subiect & humble seruant," with signature.

12c. SP 86.53.I. Copy of the same, without signature. 5 pp.
   The first of Grey's letters to the Queen in Hand D. This writer, like Spenser, employed his Italian hand for originals and his secretary hand for copies, with a single exception: see no. 18 below. At first glance, this copy, written with blunt pen or thick ink, does not resemble the other work of D. But that we have here the same hand as that of no. 13c below may be seen by comparing the capital letters, especially *E, H, M, N, T, Y*. The convincing evidence, however, lies in the spelling. In this same secretary hand are seven letters before June, 1582, to the Privy Council (SP 87.19, 87.30, 87.32, 87.52; 92.74, 92.77, 92.86) and others.

13. SP 87.29. Grey to the Queen. Dec. 10, 1581. 5 pp.
   In Italian Hand D, like no. 16 below. At the bottom of the last page Grey has added a postscript of five short lines, in addition to his subscription "Y^r^ Hyg. moast humble seruant & faythefull subiect" and signature. But here again, as in no. 5, the address is not by the writer, but in Spenser's ITALIAN hand.

13c. SP 87.18.I. Copy of the same, without signature. 8 pp.
   By the same writer as the original (SP 87.29), but in his secretary hand. This is the only extant letter of Grey's to the Queen of which both original and copy are by the same writer.

14c. SP 88.13. Grey and Council to the Queen. Jan. 12, 1582. 4 pp.
   Copy without signature, in secretary Hand D. No original (written by Spenser?) appears to be preserved. Again, any palaeographical doubts may be dispelled by an examination of the spelling, which is clearly D's.

15. SP 88.39. Grey to the Queen. Jan. 25, 1582. 2 pp.
   (Table I, no. 23.) Written and addressed in Spenser's ITALIAN hand. Subscribed in Grey's hand: "Y^r^ Hyg. most humble seruant & faythefull subiect," with signature.
16. SP 92.8. Grey to the Queen. May 6, 1582. 2 pp.
   In Italian Hand D, like no. 13. Addressed in same Italian hand; compare SP 89.29: "The Examinacion of Iames Nugentes."

17. SP 92.20. Grey and Council to the Queen. May 9, 1582. 4 pp.
    In secretary Hand E. In the same hand are Grey's letters (SP 86.52, 87.38, 91.22) to the Privy Council between Nov. 6, 1581, and April 12, 1582.

17c. SP 92.11.I. Copy of the same, without signature. 7 pp.
    In Spenser's secretary hand, with address (as in no. 5).

18. SP 92.25. Grey and Council to the Queen. May 10, 1582. 6 pp.
    The last of the extant letters to the Queen, in Hand D. In the same hand are two later valuable documents, SP 95.82 and 106.62, which recount Grey's services in Ireland. Although there is no certain evidence, Hand D would appear more likely to be that of Reynoldes than Hand B (secretary hand only).

Thus, including Grey and Spenser, seven writers penned these letters to the Queen.[15] Even if there are not as many letters in Spenser's Italian hand as Jenkins supposed, these five are of sufficient length, consisting of twenty-three large sheets, to give us an adequate impression. The first, until now believed to be the earliest letter we have from Spenser's pen, was written at Smerwick on Nov. 12, 1580, exactly three months after Spenser's arrival in Ireland (if we assume that he sailed with Grey on the "Handmaid"), and sixteen days before the Limerick letter of Nov. 28 in secretary hand reproduced by Jenkins.[16] The next three were written later in the following year, April 26, Aug. 10, and Nov. 6, 1581, and the fifth is dated Jan. 25, 1582. In both hand and spelling they show distinctive divergences from the two letters written in Italian hand, possibly by Timothy Reynoldes.[17]

Plomer's identification of Spenser's Italian hand in 1923 was the more remarkable in that he had so little evidence to work with. As he observed with respect to the "Italian" script of Miler Magrath's Latin letter to Sir

[15] Jenkins (*PMLA,* LII, 338) ascribed Grey's letters in the P.R.O. to "seven or eight different hands," of which "approximately one fourth, or forty, are in the hand of the deputy himself." Of the letters to the Queen, Grey wrote only three, all before Christmas, 1580; all but two of the remaining originals were penned by Spenser (5, all in Italian hand), D (3, two in Italian), and B (3, none in Italian). Of the extant copies, all in secretary hand, two are by Spenser and three in Hand D. The original of no. 14 appears to be lost.

[16] *PMLA,* LII, 338-39. Spenser's earlier letters to Harvey, written well within the year preceding the poet's arrival in Dublin, were, like the other printed works, not permitted to appear in Spenser's own spelling. Was the compositor, or perhaps Harvey, responsible for the alterations?

[17] Nos. 13 and 16. Distinctive spellings in this Italian hand are: *boathe, chardge, dowghte, duetie, eny, hoame, oother(s), owane, perceaue, reguarde, sheowed, tootcheth, whoaly,* etc. These forms suggest a faithful, even servile, copying from an original written by Grey, whose spelling is strikingly similar. *Humblenes,* a favorite hybrid (or as Mulcaster would have termed it, a "mungrell compound") of Grey's, appears even in the *Faerie Queene,* though the poet shows a strong preference for *humility* (7x) and *humblesse* (7x). Cf. *ablenes, oldnes, syncerenes,* forms which Spenser seems to have used only when copying Grey's drafts, and *vrgentnes,* in Thomas Norris' letter of 1588.

Lucas Dillon, there was "no document with which this can be compared, only a few scraps, such as the words written on the back of Grey's letter of July 10, 1581." Jenkins' later studies amply confirm Plomer's palaeographical findings. Plomer's logical assumption that "Lord Grey would not have employed two secretaries to write one letter" can be readily supported by further examination of the addresses of originals and the indorsements of copies. And his argument for a single scribe would have been even more convincing had he noted that the marginal word "Post script" on the last page (Fig. 3) of Letter 4c, obviously in the same hand as the rest of the "copie," is in Italian — not secretary — hand. It is as obviously in the same Italian hand as the four lines, the "few scraps," of Plomer's Fig. 2, with which it offers comparison, especially in the ligatured *st* and the small *p*. Both "scraps" may be further compared with the Italian hand here reproduced (Fig. A), in such features as the phrase "for lyfe,"[18] the *st*, as in "requested" and "hostages," and individual characters.

As letters were ordinarily addressed by their writers, it is not surprising to discover that all five letters to the Queen were not only written but addressed by Spenser in the same dignified Italian script:

(3) To her Ma^{ty}: yeue this./
(8) To her most excellent Matie:
(12) To the Queenes most excellent Matie: /
(10 and 15) To the Queenes most excellent Ma^{ty}:/[19]

Further authentication of Spenser's hand may be found by comparing these with other addresses or with Spenser's indorsements of copies (e.g., Table I, nos. 9, 29, or 42).[20] In those rare instances where Spenser furnished a secretary-hand letter with his Italian indorsement,[21] his holograph is unques-

[18] Spenser almost invariably spells "lyfe" (Grey's "lyeff"), though "life" does occur. But I have found no variants for the frequently recurring word "tyme" (Fig. A, line 9); cf. also "tymely," vntymely," etc. In transcribing, Renwick (*View,* p. 285, and Variorum *Prose Works* [hereafter cited as *Var.Pr.W.*], p. 524) misreads *farre* [*faire?*] (Fig. A, line 1) as *sawe;* for *surcease* read *surceasse* (line 7).

[19] Compare the more economical if less modern spelling of the salutation of Barnaby Rich's MS "Looking[-Glass] for Her Maiesty, Wherein to View Ireland," which begins: "To the quens most excelent ma^{ti}. Most excelent & gratyous pryncesse, vij yeares are allredy expyred syth I delyuered such informatyons for your ma^{tis} servyce in Ireland . . ." The "vij yeares" (1592-99) lead us to the small book, "no copy of which is known" according to Thomas H. Cranfill and Dorothy H. Bruce, *Barnaby Rich* (Austin, Tex., 1953), p. 56. Rich's holograph MS (SP 205.72), unknown to his most recent biographers, is of considerable orthographical interest.

[20] Jenkins (*PMLA,* LII, 345) erroneously described the indorsement of no. 9 (SP 81.36.I) as "undoubtedly in Spenser's Italian hand." It is rather in the same bastard hand as the heading of Plomer's Fig. 5 or his indorsement of the Magrath letter (Table I, no. 8).

[21] Spenser's undated copy of the letter calendared as of "9 May 1582" (SP 92.11.I)

in wonder; theyr fault therefore farre to bee aggrauated by ye vilenesse of
their Commaunder, & yt at my handes no condition of composition they were to 2
expecte, other then yt simply they sholde render me ye forte, & yield theyr
selues to my will for lyfe or death: wt this answere he departed; after which 4
there was one or two courses two and fro more, to haue gotten a certeinty for some
of their liues, but fynding that yt would not bee, ye Coronell him self about 6
Sunne setting come forth, & requested respitt wt surceasse of armes till ye nexte
morning, & then he would giue a resolute answere; fynding yt to bee but a 8
gayne of tyme for them & losse of the same for my self, I definitely answered
I would not graunt yt, & therefore presently either yt he tooke my offer or elles 10
retourne & I would fall to my busines. He then embraced my knees, simply
putting him self to my mercy, onely he prayed yt for yt might hee might abyde in 12
ye Forte, and yt in ye morning all should be putt into my handes: I asked hostages for ye performance; they were giuen. Morning come I presented my com- 14
panies in battaile before ye Forte: ye Coronell comes forth wt x or xij of his chiefe

Fig. A. The first Smerwick letter, Nov. 12, 1580. (SP 78.29, page 4, lines 13-27.)

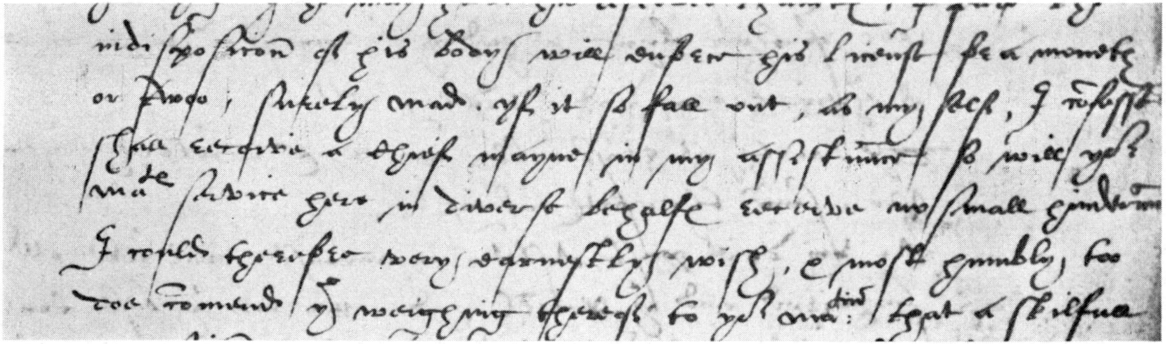

Fig. B. Spenser's secretary hand. Dec. 22, 1580. (SP 79.24.I, page 1, lines 12-17.)

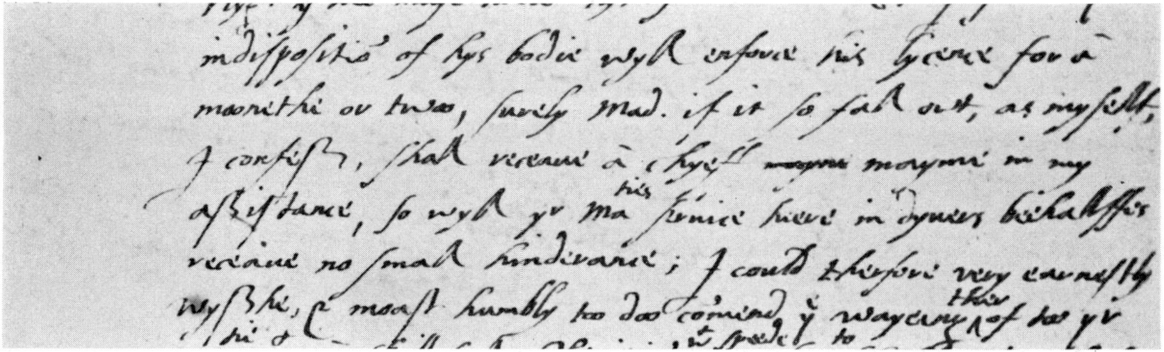

Fig. C. Grey's hand. Original letter, Dec. 22, 1580. (SP 79.25, page 1, lines 14-19.)

tioned; even when original letters to the Queen, written by neither Grey nor Spenser, appear in secretary hand (e.g., SP 80.38 and 80.39, both of Jan. 28, 1581), the address is normally written by the same scribe.

How far, we have a right to ask, does the spelling corroborate the fact of Spenser's penmanship? Much evidence is available, but a few examples should suffice. To begin with, the spellings in the five addresses listed above, including the variants "Ma(ies)tie" and "Ma(ies)ty" and even the unexpected imperative "yeue," are all to be found elsewhere in Spenser's secretary hand. In the copy of Grey's letter of Dec. 22, 1580, printed below (cf. Plomer, Fig. 3 and p. 205), "Matie:" appears five times, but the more usual "Ma^{ty}:" may be found, for example, in the Limerick letter of July 1, 1588, printed by Jenkins in *PMLA*, LIII, 350 (lines 2 and 13). In Plomer's Fig. 3, all is in Spenser's hand except the last line, where Grey has added the words, "Copie of my priuat." Grey's likewise is the indorsement, not noted by Plomer, 'Copie of my pryuate to her Matie./" If the difference between these hands were to be overlooked, the knowledge that Spenser's spelling was normally "copy" (cf. note 21) and "priuate" would suggest the work of another scribe. Except for "yeue," the remaining words in these five Italian addresses show Spenser's regular spellings.

The formula "yeue this" appears in a number of Spenser's addresses in secretary hand, for instance, Cecil Papers, 11.114 and 12.16 in 1581, and SP 89.30; 89.35; 90.48; 91.38; 91.52, all in 1582. Here Spenser spells "yeue" with complete consistency; other secretaries write "geve this" (81.35), "yeve these" (82.53), etc. Grey, less consistent than Spenser, wrote both "yeeue this," as in 79.5 (Dec. 9, 1580) and "guyue this," as in 92.11 (May 7, 1582). That Spenser may have been conscious of a need for "improved orthography" (and of the shortcomings of Grey's old-school spelling) is strongly hinted in his statement concerning the name "MacCarthy" in the P.R.O. MS of the *View:* "Carthaye beeinge almoste verie Carthage: for *y:* and *g:* ar in moste languages Changable letters, as in Englyshe *yeue* and *geeue. yate* and *gate: foryett* and *forgett.*"[22] The forms *yeue, yate, foryet,* which Spenser knew, if only from his reading of Chaucer, were not yet entirely obsolete; both *yate* and the participle *yeven* had appeared in the *Shepheardes Calender.* After 1579, of course, such *y* forms are hardly to be

---

is indorsed (and dated) in Italian hand: "Copy from my L: Dep^{ty} & Councell to her Matie/x Maij." Here Spenser's two capital *M*'s are found together. The first is identical with that seen in "Morning" (Fig. A, line 14); the second is that of the first line of Plomer's Fig. 2.

[22] *Var.Pr.W.*, p. 92.

expected, but as late as the *View*,[23] among some forty occurrences of the verb *give*, the Ellesmere *geue* (3887) and *geven* (4692) may perhaps represent survivals from Spenser's own manuscript. Were the poet living today, he might illustrate the palatalized *g* by comparing not Carthy and Carthage, but surnames like Yeats and Gates, or Churchyate and Churchgate.

The importance of identifying what Spenser wrote, whether in Italian or secretary hand, extends far beyond the "philological" in the narrow sense of that term. For example, there is the question of the poet's relations with Grey and Raleigh. M. St. Clare Byrne was quite right in assuming, "When [Churchyard] writes such forms as Rawley . . . he is probably being perfectly accurate."[24] That Spenser was also being accurate in writing "Rawley" in 1581 and 1582 is to be gathered from Raleigh's own signature at the time (e.g., in SP 80.82). In connection with Spenser's later friendship with Raleigh and his still later defense of Grey, it is worthy of note that he himself copied Ormond's letter to Grey (SP 81.36.I) of March 31, 1581, concerning David Barry's (and Ormond's) complaint against Raleigh and that he later penned Grey's letter to Burghley (SP 88.12) of Jan. 12, 1582 on the "very plausible shewe of thrifte" in Raleigh's "plott," as well as Grey's unvarnished pronouncement to Walsingham (SP 92.10): "As for Capt. Rawleyes assignem^t . . . I haue no łre wch specifieth any such thing to me; and for myne owne part I must bee playne I nether lyke his carriage nor Company, and therefore other then by direccion & commaundem^t & what his right can require, he is not to expect at my handes." Clearly, Spenser, like Grey, formed his own opinions and made his own decisions. Seven years later, when Colin Clout came home again, Raleigh was spelling his name in many different ways, including "Rauleigh" and "Ralegh." The spelling most familiar today, "Raleigh," appears to be one that the Shepherd of the Ocean himself never used. Was this form, which appears in the *Colin Clout* dedication and again in the *Faerie Queene* "Letter," the result of Spenser's "accuracy" or of the all-too-common compositor's caprice?

To return to the Munster MacCarthys, or the Clann Charrthaigh. What Spenser tells us in the *View* about their name and activities, when supplemented by what he learned about them through copying the letters of Grey and Norris,[25] opens up new social and political vistas of the poet's Kilcolman

[23] The spellings of even this MS, like those of the recent editions by Renwick and Gottfried, based upon the Rawlinson-Caius and Ellesmere MSS, cannot be accepted as those of the poet. Of the other prose writings, the *Axiochus* shows far closer resemblance to Spenser's autograph remains than even the Harvey letters.

[24] *The Library,* 4th Series, V, 248. Sir John Pope Hennessy's spelling of the letters reproduced in his *Sir Walter Ralegh in Ireland* (London, 1883) is quite unreliable.

[25] From March 20, 1581, to July 1, 1588 (Table I, nos. 7-53). On these letters see *PMLA,* LII, 345; LIII, 357-58; and note 20 above.

background. But these revelations would make too long a story to recount here.[26]

II. Spenser's Spelling

Spenser may have "in affecting the Ancients writ no Language," but for an Elizabethan his orthography is strikingly modern and "practical." It has been remarked, "The one thing that it is apparently safe to say about Elizabethan spelling is, that if it were possible for an author to spell a word in two or even three ways in . . . one paragraph, the chances are he would do so."[27] Like most generalizations, this one calls for modification. It holds true for many writers, including Ascham and Elyot. But after Cheke had laid the groundwork, followed by Thomas Smith and John Hart, Elizabethans became more spelling-conscious. By 1570 A. W. Pollard's statement has much validity: "The tragedy of Tudor spelling is not that it had no system, but that it had a bewildering number of rival systems, all of which have left their mark on our poor language, which has been further defaced by countless false analogies."[28]

That Lord Grey and his secretary were members of differing schools may be gathered from a perusal of their "rival systems" as revealed in their versions of the same letter. Grey's original and Spenser's copy are calendared under date of Dec. 22, 1580 (Table II, 4 and 4c above):

Letter from Lord Grey to Queen Elizabeth, Dec. 22, 1580

Original, in Grey's Hand:		*Copy, in Spenser's Hand:*
That thynges concernyng ye descry-		That thinges concerning ye descry-
ing of hollowe & faytheless hartes		ing of hollow & faithlesse hartes
too y^{r} Matie bee reuealed, nothyng		to yor Matie: bee revealed nothing
dislykes mee, but y^{t} ye cryme	4	dislikes mee, but y^{t} ye crime
shulld lyght uppō sum sutche, as		should light vpon some such as
is now tootched, pardoon I craue,		is now touched, pardon I crave
if too sorrowe it, I can not denye.		yf to sorrow yt I cannot deny.

[26] The significant fact about the "Carthage" passage is not Spenser's abandonment of the Carthaginian theory (still perpetuated by Charles O'Connor in 1753) but its revelation that he knew traditions of the early Munster saint who was associated with "Slewlogher," the wild district west of Kilcolman which was a constant source of anxiety for the poet, and with Lismore, where his friend Raleigh was remodeling the castle in 1589. For part of the story, see Patrick Power's edition of the *Life of St. Mochuda of Lismore* (Irish Texts Society, London, 1914), introduction and notes.

[27] M. St. Clare Byrne, "Anthony Munday's Spelling as a Literary Clue," *The Library,* 4th Series, IV, 10.

[28] "Elizabethan Spelling as a Literary and Bibliographical Clue," *ibid.,* IV, 5.

Original, in Grey's Hand:		*Copy, in Spenser's Hand:*
The state of y^{e} cause at sum	8	The state of y^{e} cause at some
lengthe by ā generall łre frō vs		length by a g$\overset{c}{n}$all l$\overset{c}{r}$e from vs
of y^{r} Councell heere is delyuered		of yor Councell here is deliuered
vntoo y^{r} Hyg. w^{t} sutche wryghtynges		vnto yor Hig. w^{t} such writinges
& instructioons by y^{e} bearar as	12	& instruccions by y^{e} berer as
contayne y^{e} growndes of owre pro-		conteyne y^{e} growndes of o^{r} pro-
ceedinges in it. The L. Chanc.		ceedinges in yt. The L. Chauncello^{r}
his greate pollicie & intollerable		his great pollicie & intolerable
trauayle, too ye greate empayring	16	travaile to ye great empairing
of his healthe, & no less perryll		of his health and no lesse perill
of hys lyeff, hathe chieffly, if		of his life hath Chiefly yf
not onely, beaten owte this mat-		not onely beaten out this mat-
ter: I therfore humbly beeseetche	20	ter. I therefore humbly beseeche
yr Hyg. y^{t} hee maye haue hys de-		yor Hig. y^{t} he may have his de-
serued thanckes; I feare ye indis-		served thanckes, I feare the indis-
positiō of hys bodie wyll enforce		posicion of his body will enforce
his lycence for a moonethe or twoo,	24	his license for a moneth or twoo;
surely Mad. if it so fall owt, as		surely Mad. yf it so fall out, as
myselff, I confess, shall receaue		myself, I cōfesse shall receive
ā chyeff mayme in my assistance,		a Chief mayme in my assistaunce
so wyll y^{r} Maties seruice heere	28	so will yor Ma^{tes} service here
in dyuers beehallffes receaue no		in diverse behalfes receive no
small hinderance; I could ther-		small hinderaunce I could there-
fore very earnestly wysshe, &		fore very earnestly wish, &
moast humbly too doo cōmend y^{e}	32	most humbly too doe co$\overset{c}{m}$end y^{e}
wayeing therof too yr Matie, y^{t}		weighing thereof to yor Ma$\overset{tie}{:}$, that
a skillfull Phizitiō were w^{t} speede		a skilfull Physicion were w^{t} speed
sent to Chester, y^{e} lack wherof		sent to Chester, y^{e} lack whereof
is his vndooyng, & not possyblie	36	is his vndooing, and not possibly
can hee contynew thus heere w^{t}owte		can he contynew thus here w^{t}out
seeking remedie by better skill,		seeking remedy by better skill;
too yr Maties gracius care I ther-		to yor Ma$\overset{tes}{:}$ gratious care there-
fore beequeathe it.	40	fore I bequeath yt.
The Biss. of Dublin lykewyze hathe		The Bish. of Dublin likewise hath
sheowed no small trowthe & con-		shewed no small trouth and Con-
stancie in thys seruyce, hauyng not		stancy in this service having not
a lyttle endangered hymsellf by	44	a litle endangered him self by
auowtchyng hys chardge agaynst y^{e}		avouching his Charge against y^{e}
Earle. Delluin surely hathe been		Earle. Delvin surely hath bene
ye cariar of ye Earle intoo this		ye Carrier of ye Earle into this
mischieff; whowse obstinate af-	48	mischief, whose obstinate af-
fectiō too poperie hathe now ap-		feccion to Poperie hath now ap-
prooued hym vnsaffe too hymsellf,		proved him vnsafe to him self,
vnsownde too freende, disloyall		vnsownd to ffrende disloiall
too Prince, & fallss too God;	52	to Prince & false to god:
sutche is ye yeelde of sutche seede,		such is the yield of such seede,

Original, in Grey's Hand:		*Copy, in Spenser's Hand:*
whytche, woold too God, were not so		w^{ch}, would to god, were not so
plentie in this lande: y^{r} Matie		plenty in this land: yor Ma:^{tie}
must bee carefull therfore too	56	must be carefull therefore to
roote it owte, ootherwyze w^{t}owte		roote yt out, otherwise w^{t}out
heapes of care, mass of treazure,		heapes of Care, masse of threasure
& contynuall warre neuer account		& continuall warre neuer accoumpt
too swaye this goouernment. Yr	60	to sway this goucrncment. Yo^{r}
Hyg: at my leaue taking, guaue mee		Hig. at my leave taking gave me
ā warnyng, for beeyng strict in		a warning for being strict in
dealyng w^{t} religiō, I haue ob-		dealing w^{t} religion, I have ob-
serued it, how obcdicntly so euer,	64	served yt, how obediently soeuer,
yet moste vnwyllingly, I must con-		yett most vnwillingly I cōfesse,
fess, & I dowght as harmefully too		and I doubt as harmefully to
yr & Gods seruyce, ā cancker neuer		yor & gods service, a Canker neuer
receauyng cure w^{t}owte corisiue	68	receiving Cure w^{t}out corrosiue
[*sic*] medcines.		medicines.

The rest of Grey's letter, given below, may be compared with Spenser's copy, of which the concluding pages are reproduced by Plomer, Fig. 3.

I haue not been able too doo any thyng vppō ye rebells 70
heere sincc my coōmyng owt of ye west, for entending too
this cause: but God not lettyng, im̄eediatly after ye xij
dayes I wyll abroad agayne, neyther in ye meane seasoon
shall sum bandes bee Idle, neyther haue they been all this 74
whyle, for this last weeke w^{t} 200. footmen, & 80. horss.,
Capt Russell & Sr Hen. Harrington leading ye horssmen, &
s^{r} Wyll. Standley ye foot., wee tooke frō vnder theyr
fastnes 1000. of theyr kyne & had ye kylling of ā doozen 78
or twentie of theyr kearne & galliglass.
The Northe is reazonable quyett, & Tyrlaghe ā ientle callme
Pr. since the fortes taking. /
An eyght dayes past Asckettin in Munster was attempted too 82
bee surpryzed & ye rebells had gotten intoo ye base courte
& cutt of one of ye watche, & reatched ye Castle gate,
forced ye lockes therof, & were entring, when Parcker y^{e}
Cunstable w^{t} hys warde onely runnyng too ye place stoode it 86
& by force & greate value repullsed them. Desmonde hyssellf
hathe in manner no force. Ihō hys broother scullckes vp &
downe ye wooddes w^{t} ā 300. swoordes, & now is sd too bee on
hys retourne intoo these partes. / 90
Connaghe is in greatiest [sic] stur now of any prouince of
this lande ClanRiccardes soonnes & Orourck beeyng ye heads
therof. Yr Matie in my opinion myght doo well too vse sum
threates too ye father, in case by ā daye hee cause them not 94
too desist frō theyr rebellius actioons & cōome in. But I
hoape in God, y^{t} Sr Nich. Mallbie w^{t} ye forcies y^{t} by this

hee hathe wyll make shortt woorck amongst them.
This beeyng all y^{t} at this tyme I haue too trooble yr Hyg. 98
w^{t}, sauyng y^{t} it maye pleaze ye same, too remember y^{r} powre
soldiores w^{t} a thowroghe paye, & vittayles frō tyme too
tyme, w^{ce} is owre oother kylling want, I take humble leaue
w^{t} contynuall prayer too ye Allmyghtie God too guyue yr 102
Matie length. . . . lyeff, euer healthe & direction of his
spiright. . . . Dub. this xxijth of Decemb^{r}. A^{o} 1580.
marg.] postscript.
As I was cloazing vp heerof I was aduertized fro. . . . S^{r}
Edw. Moore & Capt. Mackwoorthe, whowme . . . . had sent too 106
take ye Earles soonnes, that ye L. Garratt was escaped,
in what manner ye letter it sellf shall sheowe, I hauyng
heerw^{t} sent yr Hyg. the same. The Earle takes this in
merueylus greeuus sorte & prayed earnestly y^{t} hee myght 110
bee suffered too wryte too my La. his wyeff for y^{e}
recoouerie of hym, w^{ce} I grawnted.
Yr Matie hathe heere of Sr Lucus Dyllon ā merueylus good
& faythefull seruant, ā rare Iewewell [sic] of this 114
countrie birthe, I beeseetche yr Hyg., y^{t} hee maye knowe
hys desert to haue been recōmended.

If Spenser sought to steer a moderate course between an orthographical Scylla and Charybdis, or between the Perissa of excess and the Elissa of deficiency, he must have reckoned Lord Grey among the retainers of Perissa. In any event, he made shorter work than Grey of such often-recurring words as "arre," "soonnes" (92), "shortt woorck" (97), "Allmyghtie" (102), "cloazing" (105), "lyeff" and "wyeff" (103, 111), and "beeseetche" (115). In the Elissa camp were writers like Barnaby Rich, who wrote "ther" for both "their" and "there," "wer," "prof," "lyf," "mad" (for verb forms, but for the adjective, "madde"!), "in ded," "ned" for "need," etc.[29] If Thomas Churchyard, who acknowledged a long friendship with Rich and possessed autograph notes which Rich wrote down as early as 1572, felt the inadequacies of Rich's spelling, the fact may explain his efforts at reform. Instead of "mad," "prof," "lyf," the 1575 edition of *Churchyard's Chippes* indicated vowel length by "maed," "proeff," "lyeff." Such "straining of *custom,*" as Mulcaster would have termed it, was not destined to long survival.[30]

[29] On the other hand, Rich's writings abound in curious spellings. Among those occurring more than once are *feyght, physytyan, polytytyan, prevyleadge, strenkthyn,* and favorite improprieties like *contemptyous* and *perlyous.* Rich's *extreamytyes* is already spelled *extremities* by Mulcaster, Spenser, and even Grey!

[30] See Byrne, "Thomas Churchyard's Spelling," *The Library,* 4th Series, V, 243-48. Marshe, reprinting the *Chippes* in 1578, permitted fewer of Churchyard's forms to survive than in 1575; but in 1593, perhaps for the prestige of his printing house, eliminated the "eccentric" spellings printed earlier. Wolfe had less reason in 1590 to alter Spenser's characteristic forms, as he (or his compositor) unquestionably did. (See Variorum ed., *The Faerie Queene* [hereafter cited as *Var.F.Q.*], I, 522 ff.)

In studying Spenser's spelling from copied letters rather than original documents, we are at a disadvantage because the poet sometimes inadvertently copied down Grey's own spelling. Grey's influence is no doubt to be found, for example, when Spenser writes "chardge" for his usual "charge," "coald" for "cold," and on one occasion "doothe" for "doth." As such spellings are, however, relatively rare, it may be asserted that Spenser's spelling shows on the whole the same sturdy, almost courageous, independence which characterized his relations with Burghley and others. For obvious reasons, such original documents as the British Museum "grant" to McHenry, the "Note of lettres" (Plomer's Fig. 5), and Spenser's 1589 "Reply to the commissioners" are more likely than the letters to give us the author's normal spelling.[31]

If in many respects Spenser seems more "modern" than Mulcaster, it is in part because he is less the reformer. He yields even more than Mulcaster to "the force of common use"— to "consent" and "prerogative" and "custom," which he honors more in the observance than in the breach. Where Mulcaster is led to write "natur," "gide," "fantsie," or "mokt," Spenser bows to majority usage. Among the more prominent features contributing to the modern appearance of Spenser's orthography are the *-y* endings, (as in *day, -ly, -(i)ty; body, easy, envy, very,* etc.); *-ing* and *-ed* endings (compare Mulcaster's "participles contract," like *cald, performd*); *-ue* (where Mulcaster has *dew, trew, vertew*); *should* and *would* (Mulcaster's *wold*); modern *-ea-* (Mulcaster's *helth* and *heuie*), *-ie-* (Mulcaster's *chefe* and *pece*); *-oa-* (Mulcaster's *boste, coste*), *-oo-* (Mulcaster's *prouf* and *roum*); *debt* and *doubt* (Mulcaster's *det* and *dout*), and such common words as *are* (Mulcaster's *ar,* Grey's *arre*), *too* (Mulcaster's *to*), *you* and *they.* With the notable exception of *litle,* Spenser is modern in the doubling of consonants, where Mulcaster prefers to write *aple* "with the *a* short," (p. 143), *setle, tikle; rable* "not daring to duble the *b*" (p. 141), *midle; carie, mariage,* etc. The following representative list (p. 84) permits comparison of Spenser's spelling with that of his two "masters."

But no Elizabethan, including Spenser, achieved anything like a standardized spelling. Even Mulcaster, despite the vigor with which he advocates reform, is far from consistent; on every page of his *Elementarie* one finds

[31] There are all too frequently, of course, those human lapses of which anyone can be guilty; see, for example, Fig. A, line 5, where Spenser wrote carelessly "one or twoo coouses two and fro." When he wrote "he might a written" (SP 93.64.I, p. 2, l. 26), the solecism was doubtless his, not Meagh's. But whatever his source, his spelling was remarkably consistent.

TABLE III

Grey	*Mulcaster*	*Spenser*
aduertiss	aduertis	aduertize
allreadie	al(l)redie	already
alltoogeather	al(l)togither	altogether
arre	ar	are
authoritie	autoritie	authority
awaye, daye	awaie, daie	away, day
beeseetche	beseche	beseech
brieff; chieff	brefe; chefe	brief; chief
cariadge; mariadge	cariage; mariage	carriage; marriage
carie	carie	carry
challendge	chalenge	challenge
coomme, camme	com, cam	come (comme), came (cam lx)
coomforte	cumfort	comfort
coompanie	cumpanie	company
delyght	delite	delight
dowght(e)	dout	doubt
field; yeeld, yeald	feild; yeild	field; yield
guyde	gide	guide
meazure, pleazure	measur, pleasur	measure, pleasure
neede; in deede	nede; in dede	need; indeed
onece (attonece)	once, ones	once
peeople	peple	people
piecies	peces	pieces
prouff, prooff	prouf	proof(e)
quyck, syck	quik, sik	quick, sick
recknynges	reknings	reckonings
sum, soom	som	some
they, theyr	theie, their	they, their (theyr)
tootched	tuched, tucht *Contract*	touched
trooble, trowble	truble; duble	trouble; double
trew, true; valew	trew; valew	true; value
wayed	weied	weighed
wyzedoome	wisedom	wis(e)dome
zelus	zelous	zealous

spellings which are at variance with those set up in his "Generall Table."[32]

[32] Mulcaster's *Elementarie,* ed. E. T. Campagnac (Oxford, 1925), pp. 190-245. Almost at the outset (p. 1, l. 5), *persuades* (as often) is printed although the Table calls for *perswades,* despite what Mulcaster terms "the latin enfranchisement." For *childern* (1, 7) Mulcaster has three alternative spellings, which he discusses on p. 125. Again, *any* (1, 20) clearly violates his rule (pp. 126, 147), as against *anie* (2, 13). Though he refers (p. 291) to "both mine own and the printers errors, which will not be auoided," Mulcaster lists very few errata.

The alternate forms which appear in Figs. A and B may be considered fairly representative, the first form listed being the one more frequently written by Spenser: *bee—be, chief—chiefe, he—hee, that—y^t^, the—y^e^, their—theyr, to—too.* Many of his variants involve the final vowel or diphthong and what he called "changeable letters." But while *i* and *y* seem often interchangeable (*said, sayd; alwayes, alwaies*), like *u* and *v* (for instance, *have* occurs about as often as *haue*), one may discern a Hamlet-like method in his aberration. The extent to which accentuation enters into Spenser's "rival system" will be discussed later. The following groupings according to present-day spelling,[33] exemplify only in small part some of the poet's more representative or striking habits, as compared with those found in the *Elementarie,* which is cited as *M.*

A. Forms which are modern in Spenser only.

(a) Vowels and diphthongs.

Medial *au.* assault, default, fault (*M*: -alt), but malt; cause, bycause (see *M* 131, 143).

Medial *ie.* field, yield (*M*: ei, cf. sheild); chief(e), grief, grievous, piece, relief(e), relieved (*M*: e); siege (*M*: se(i)dge). But beleefe, beleeve. Cf. sherief (*M*: shirif).

Medial *igh.* delight, plight (*M*: -lite); spright — spirite (*M*: spir(i)t). Grey writes spyryght (spiright).

Medial *o.* come, some (*M*: cum, com p. 16, l. 14; som, but see p. 159, ll. 3-6); comfort, company, compas(se), forth (*M*: cum-, furth).

Medial *oo.* stood — stode; wood — woodd — wodde (*M*: wod).

Medial *ou.* nourish (*M*: nur(r)ish); touch (*M*: tuch, p. 25, l. 2: cf. much, such); trouble (*M*: truble); troupe (*M*: troup; Grey: troopes — trowpes). Cf. proof (*M*: prouf); soldier — souldier, so(u)ld, to(u)ld.

Medial *u.* church (*M*: chirch). Cf. *M*: chirn, but churle (Spenser).

Medial *ui.* build, building (*M*: bild, p. 80, l. 17; p. 85, l. 5).

Final *ay, ey.* away, day, may, payment, say, etc.; they, obey, survey.

Final *ise.* Promise, purpose (*M*: -is), but practize (noun). Verbs: cf. aduertize, temporize.

Final *ould.* could, should (so *M*); would (*M*: wold).

Final *ue.* Spenser is far more modern than Mulcaster (p. 129: "*nv, trv, vertv* or *nu, tru, vertu,* to be written *new, trew, vertew*"). Cf. due, residue, pursue (*M*: -dew, pursew/persew), reskued, true — trew, value — valewe, vertue, but viewe.

-gue. league (*M*: leag), tongue (*M*: tung).

Final *ure.* censure, coniecture; nature; measure, pleasure (*M*: -ur); cf. threasure (*M*: treasur; see pp. 168-69).

Final *uy.* buy (*M*: by, byer, bying: p. 130).

[33] In the verbal ending *-ize* (*advertize, temporize*: Mulcaster's *-ise*), Spenser accords with current American usage; but in the ending *-our* (*favour,* but *favored, favorable; honour,* but *honorable*) he anticipates British usage, again differing from Mulcaster's *fauor, honor,* etc.

(b) Consonants.

Initial *wh*. whole (*M*: hole, "manifest greke": see p. 174). Cf. who, whome, whose (Kökeritz, *Shakespeare's Pronunciation* [New Haven, 1953], p. 231).

Medial *b*. debt, doubt (*M*: det, dout, but dowt, p. 280).

Medial *k*. sclacknes, tickle (*M*: slak-, tik-).

Medial *qu*. exchequer (*M*: exchekker), banqueting (cf. Shakespeare's banket).

Medial *r*. carriage, mar(r)iage (*M*: -ariage).

Medial *th*. authority (*M*: autoritie). It is to be presumed, by analogy, that Spenser would have spelled Mulcaster's *ortografie* as we spell it today (as in Harvey's letter [Variorum *Prose Works*, p. 475, four times]).

Final *d*. indeed (as one word; *M*: in dede, p. 2, line 21, etc.).

Final *k*. quick, sick, stick (*M*: quik, sik, stik).

B. Forms which are modern in neither Mulcaster nor Spenser.

(a) Vowels and diphthongs.

Medial *e/i*. al)together, hether(to, thether, wether — weather, whether (*M*: -gether -gither; hither, thither, weather, whither). Cf. ether — either, nether — neither.

Medial *ee*. bene, betwene (*M*); deeme, heede, keepe (*M*: deme, etc.) but shepe (*M*); beseech(e) but speache (*M*: speche). Cf. eache — ech (*M*: ech), reach (*M*: rea(t)ch; teach).

Medial *eo*. people (*M* prints both *peple* and *people*: see p. 132). Cf. beof — beoffe (*M*: befe).

Medial *ie*. frend, frendly, -ship(pe), etc. (*M*: frind, see p. 162).

Medial *o, ou*. co(o)sen, doozen (*M*: -osen); com(m)e; sommer (*M*: somer).

Medial *oa*. abrode; reproche; co(a)ld, ho(a)ld, but so(u)ld, to(u)ld (cf. A above); boast, coast (*M*: -oste). *M* 131 sees no need for an *oa* diphthong. Cf. othe (*M*).

Medial *u*. begonne (*M*: -gon). Cf. wonne. running — renning (as in *Shepheardes Calender,* cited hereafter as *SC*).

Final *air*. despeire. This form occurs only 4 times (out of 34) in Spenser's printed poetry. (*M*: despare, dispare.)

Final *eign*. forreyne (*M*: foren). See below, p. 94.

Final *-ealth*. welth, but health (*M* p. 4, 11. 20-21: health, helth), stealth — stelth.

Final *-en* (strong past participle). doen — donne (*M*: don) but gone; loaden (*M*: loden); lyen. Spenser's poetry shows *lyen* 6 times and *lain* only twice. Cf. shewne, sworne.

Final voiceless stops. bishop (*M*: bisshop); hot (so *M*; often spelled whott); flock (*M*: flok), quick (quik), etc.

(b) Consonants.

Initial *g*. gard (cf. regard), but guyde — guide; guift(e). *M* does not recognize *gu-*: gard(ian), gesse, gide, gise, etc. But cf. guerdon.

Initial *s*. sclender (*M*: sklender). Cf. Spenser's sclacknes, schedule (Shakespeare's cedule, sedule, shedule, etc.).

Initial *th*. threasure (*M*: treasur). The initial English *t* sound, as in Hotspur's pun on *throne* (see Kökeritz, pp. 150, 320-21), is not to be confused with the *th* commonly heard in Irish and Anglo-Irish speakers today.

Medial *ch* (*k*). retchlesse (*M*: rechlesse). Cf. *Mother Hubberds Tale* 950. Spenser's poetry offers no Northern form.

Medial *s*. hazard (*M*: hasard); cf. the "zeddish sound" in *M*'s *lasie* (the *laesy* of Spenser's verse). Mulcaster is quick to point out that intervocalic *s* is "a maruellous deputie" for *z* ("a consonant much heard amongst vs, and seldom sene").

Final voiceless stops.

Following short vowels: back(e), lacke (*M*: -ak); clocke; antique (accented on first syllable), politique, publique (*M*: -ik), reliques (*M*: reliks).

Following long vowels or diphthongs: deepe, keepe; seeke (*M*: seke), etc. See under "Medial *ee*," above. frute (*M*), brute — bruit (noun).

Final voiced stops.

Following short vowels: ebbe (*M*: eb); adde (*M*: ad), spred (*M*).

Following long vowels: heede, exceede, proceed(e), etc. (*M*: -ede).

Final *f*. cutt of, farre of (so *M*). Cf. beoffe — beof (*M*: befe), stuffe (*M*: stuf).

Final *m, mb*. lymmes — lymbes (*M*: lims; cf. p. 151, s.v. thumming). deeme, esteeme, seeme (*M*: -eme).

Final *n*. begonne, past part. (*M*: begon).

C. Forms which are modern in Mulcaster only.

(a) Vowels and diphthongs.

Initial *e*. æmulate, æqually, præcise, præparation, præsentnes, præuent, tædious (*M*: -e-). The Latinism *cærule* (*Virgils Gnat*) no doubt reflects Spenser's own spelling. Spenser writes *emong, emongst* more often than *among(st)*.

Initial *i*. yf, yt, ytself, yssue (*M*: ishew) outnumber the *i* spellings. yron (*M*: iron): see Harvey's comment (Variorum *Prose Works*, p. 475, line 482).

Medial *i*. bynd, fynd, fyre (cf. Harvey, *ibid*., p. 476), mynd, myne, etc.

Medial *o*. affoord; so(o)ne. Cf. poore, tooke. This doubling of *o* is not common in Spenser, who silently emends Grey (other, word(e), work(e), etc.). The past participle *vnderstoond* appears in his copy of Nugent's confession.

Medial *u*. retourne(d); gonner, nomber, sondry (*M*: sundrie); tombled. Cf. amboishment.

Final *en* (strong past participle). growen (*M*: grown, but growen, p. 262, 1. 4), knowen, vnknowen, throwen, ouerthrowen. But cf. owne (Grey's owane).

Final *o*. adoe, doe; goe, forgoe. Spenser regularly writes *so*, but *soe* and *soo* occur once each.

Final *or*. demeanure, valure (as in *Richard II*: cf. Kökeritz, p. 271).

Final *ow*. shewe (showe 2x), shewed, shewes (*M*: show).

(b) Consonants.

Initial *h*. hable, -nes, dishabled, inhable, vnhable. Spenser writes both *hostages* and *ostages*. Initial *h* was apparently not pronounced in *an hundreth* (3x in SP 78.29) and *an humble*. With Spenser's *might a written* (note 31 above) compare the *Hamlet* Quarto *would a thought*.

Intervocalic *c*. gratious, malitious, pretious, spatious, suspition (*M*); cf. ambition, ambitious.

Intervocalic *ph.* prophete, but nephew (*M*: neuew). Mulcaster laments the continuing use of "Grecian" *ph* and suggests replacing it with "the latin f, as why not?" But if in his Table he usually accepts custom (cf. orphan, prophane, diphthong — difthong, but cifer, graf: see pp. 210, 228, 230), he often breaks with tradition in his text, where he writes *philosofers* and even *filosofie, pamflet,* etc.

Intervocalic *r.* Spenser shows no preference between *thorough, -ly* and *through, -ly* (cf. Grey: *thow(gh)roghe* and *throwghe*), adj., prep., and adv.

Final voiceless stops.

Following short vowels: entrap, step; hap — happe; ship — shipp; toppe. admitt, gett (to gette, lx), knitt(e), knott. drinck, thancks, thinck(e), winck.

Following long vowels or diphthongs: wayt (cf. ayd below); exploytt (noun, accented on second syllable).

Final voiced stops.

Following short vowels: curbe, disturbe; ebbe, glibbe (noun). bidde, ridde, ledde (infin.) but bid, rid, led (past part.). Cf. hundreth (*M*: hundred). bragge (noun). (There are no instances in Spenser's hand of *bog, leg* (as in *View*) or *hag, egg(s)* (as in his poetry).

Following long vowels or diphthongs: ayd, ayde; thred [tre:d]. (In *FQ* IV *thrid* rimes with *did, hid, mid.*) I am assuming a long vowel here in view of Spenser's pun (*Axiochus* 156, 185, 199) *trade of life — thred of life.* Cf. initial *th,* under B (b) above. (There are no examples of Spenser's spelling of *brogue* "Irish shoe" (Grey: *broage,* usually *broges*).

Final *-pt.* conceipt.

Final *age, e(d)ge, udge.* advauntage; alleage (*M*: alle(d)ge); iudg, ac)knowledg (*M*: knowle(d)ge); personage, vicaredg — vicarege (*cf. Rich*: parson, but "personages & vycarages," p. 5, 1. 34).

Final *l.* mele; raile (v.), saile (noun pl.); spoile (spoyle lx), toile (toyle lx). *M*: toil but spoyl!

Final *m.* scumme; cf. Trymme.

Final *n.* began(ne), sonne, sunne, tenne, wonne.

Final *r.* farre, warre; sturre.

Final *s.* Noun pl.: actes, armes, bandes, etc. But occasionally *-s*: actions, reasons, ships, weapons.

Adverbial: elles — els; eftesoones — eftsoons. But needes (*M*: nedes). towardes.

In the letters penned between 1580 and 1590, there appears to be little perceptible change in Spenser's own habits. Certainly his spelling grows no more "modern";[34] in fact, some forms we know today occur in his earliest writing. For example, there is an increasingly marked tendency to replace

[34] One exception appears to be the word *journey.* In the Grey letters Spenser regularly wrote *iorney,* but in the Norris letters this form occurs only once, the usual spelling being *iourney* (Mulcaster's *iournie;* Grey's *ioorney*). The form *grawnt(ed),* which appears only in the Norris letters, is hardly a modernization over Spenser's usual and frequent spelling *graunt(ed).*

the early -*tion* suffixes (cf. *condition, composition,* Fig. A, 1. 2) with -*cion* (as in *indisposicion,* Fig. B). Despite Harvey's strictures,[35] Spenser continues to write *sithens* — not the *sithence* of the printed poems and the Ellesmere MS. The infinitive form *bee* outnumbers *be* (as in Fig. A) in 1589 as in 1580; conversely, the pronoun forms *he, me, she, we* are consistently preferred over *hee, mee,* etc. The only significant changes in Spenser's spelling are not so much individual or personal as social, and reflect the poet's increasing familiarity with his Irish background. They concern not English but Irish words, such as *kerne* and *Aherloa,* to be discussed later.

Just how "modern" is Spenser's spelling? Let me attempt to answer the question by drawing upon a well-known list of the hundred words most commonly used.[36] By tabulating the spellings of Spenser, Mulcaster, and Grey which are no longer current, we shall be able to arrive at percentages. Among the first ten words in the list (*the, of, and, to, a, in, that, it, is, I,* in order of frequency), there are two deviations from present usage: Grey's regular spelling *too* and Spenser's variant form *yt,* which appears more often (in late documents, 1585-89, as well as the earlier ones) than *it.*

This table will show how close Spenser came to modern spelling. If wc

[35] See p. 93 below. *Sithens* occurs five times in the Grey and Norris letters, thirteen times in Spenser's poetry, and, as late as 1596, twenty-two times in the *View.* Spenser's *eftsoons,* often branded as a poetic archaism, appears in the Meagh copy (1582: *eftesoones*) and in the Norris letter of 1588 (*eftsones*); it continued to be used in reputable prose, Spenser himself using it twelve times in the *View* and even later in the *Brief Note.*

[36] Godfrey Dewey, *Relativ Frequency of English Speech Sounds* (Cambridge, Mass., 1923 = 1950), p. 19.

TABLE IV

	Spenser	*Mulcaster*	*Grey*	*Hand B*	*Hand D*
4			too		
8	yt/it			yt	
12	bee/be		bee		bee
15			yow	16 withe	
17			hee		hee
24		ar	arre		21 nott
25	(wee)		wee	wee	wee
26			hys		
28		theie			
32			wyll	31 whiche	
35			hathe	hathe	hathe
37			owre		
39	bene	bene		bene	beene
41	(theyr)		theyr	theire	theire

TABLE IV (Concluded)

	Spenser	*Mulcaster*	*Grey*	*Hand B*	*Hand D*
42			ther		theere
46	yf/if				
47	(mee)		mee		mee
					48 whatt
49			woold		woolde
50			whow		whoe
52			hym		
54		hir			hir
55	warre		warre	warre	warre
56			yowre		
57		anie		enny	eny
61	tyme		tyme		tyme
				62 vpp	62 vpp
63	doe		doo	doe	doo
64			owte		
66	then	then	then	then	then
67	onely	onelie	onely		onlie
68			shee		shee
70			oother		
71			intoo		
74		peple	peeople		
75			sayed	saied	saide
76		maie	maye		maye
78			abowtt		
80		som	sum/soom	81 thes	81 theis
82			twoo		twoo
83		verie			verie
84			beefore		
85			greate	greate	greate
					86 coolde
87			sutche	soche/suche	suche
88			fyrst		
89			vppon	vppon	vppon
90		euerie	euerie		everie
92		com	coome		91 howe
95			shulld		sho(o)lde
97			lyke		licke
99	litle	litle	lyttle	lytle/litle	
100		saie	saye		saye
101	bycause	bycause	beecause		
	100 — 11	100 — 16	100 — 44	100 — 18	100 — 35
	89%	84%	56%	82%	65%

NOTE. — This modern list contains two words which had not come into current use in Spenser's day: no. 35, *has,* for which I have substituted its equivalent *hath,* and no. 60, *its,* in whose place I have added no. 101, *because.*

accept his minority spellings *be, if, it,* which occur in substantial numbers, his percentage reaches 92. The fact that he copied from Grey's drafts may account for some of his old-fashioned spellings, though not of course for the regular recurrence of such forms as *onely* and *tyme,* from which he never varied. The net result of expanding our list to 200 words (which space will not permit here) would be merely to decrease the percentages almost proportionately: Spenser's to 85 per cent, Mulcaster's to 80.5 per cent, and Grey's to 46.5 per cent. Using the same method of comparison, with holograph letters only, we may note that Spenser's spelling is more modern than that of well-known literary men who were his contemporaries in Ireland. His friend Lodowick Bryskett, whose spelling bears a marked resemblance to Spenser's, is not far behind with 88 per cent; Geoffrey Fenton and Barnaby Rich, surprisingly, are not far apart, with 73 per cent and 70 per cent. Accepting Arber's statement concerning the integrity of the Leyden text of Stanyhurst's *Æneis* (p. xxii), we find Stanyhurst still less modern with 61 per cent.

This table would indicate, among other things, that Mulcaster contributed little to the spelling of Spenser, whose relations with his master are quite obscure. There is no evidence that Spenser came directly under Mulcaster's influence during his formative years, or even that Mulcaster's spelling rules were formulated before Spenser left the Merchant Taylors' School. Renwick thinks that Mulcaster was "teaching on these principles" before 1569. If so, it is surprising that Spenser's actual spelling bears little resemblance to that advocated in the *Elementarie.* In any event, it would appear that any magnetism exerted by "Mast. Wrenoc"[37] came after Spenser had formed his own spelling habits, which he continued to adhere to with striking consistency.[38] The "rules" drawn up in the *Elementarie,* which was not issued in its two

[37] If this is, as Moore Smith once suggested ("Spenser and Mulcaster," *MLR,* VIII [1913], 368), an anagram. Spenser's habit of writing *ow* before a nasal points to the spelling "Mowncaster" rather than "Mouncaster." Mulcaster, according to *DNB,* was "commonly said to have been a native of Carlisle." The earliest recorded spelling of "Muncaster," also in Cumberland, is the twelfth-century "Molecastre," apparently the *castra* of *Múli,* an Old Norse personal name "recorded in the North from the 10th century." Cf. the last *Mul-* spelling in 1389: "Mulcastre vel Moncastre," and later, in 1505: "Moncastre al. Mouncastere." See A. M. Armstrong et al., *Place-Names of Cumberland* (Cambridge, 1950), II, 423-24.

[38] Spenser's consistency is corroborated by the two letters in behalf of James Vaughan written in his own hand — that from Grey to Burghley (SP 91.52) on April 30, 1582, and that eleven days later (May 11), from Grey and the Dublin Council to the Privy Council. Except for salutation and complimentary close, they reveal his characteristic orthography.

printings until Spenser's secretaryship under Grey[39] was virtually over, are completely at variance with the poet's practices.

It is a further feather in Spenser's crowded cap that he out-Mulcastered Mulcaster in anticipating the future of English spelling. Milton's nephew Edward Phillips, who has been often associated and even credited with the final "fixing" of our orthography, bad as it still is, was in 1658 still populating his *New World of English Words* with forms which frequently resemble Mulcaster's or which, when compared with those of the "modern" Spenser, appear (to use Phillips' own word) "antiquitated."

III. "This Sad Hersall of His Heavy Stress"

Among the major problems still confronting the spelling reformers in 1579 was that of vowel (and syllable) length. The *Shepheardes Calender,* which reveals the extent to which its author had become immersed in the poetry of Chaucer, offers no more certainty as to the poet's orthography than do the *Faerie Queene* and the other printed works. One could wish that Spenser's letters to Harvey, begun in the same year, had included, in addition to the comments on the "Quantities of English sillables," Spenser's views on Chaucer's final *-e,* a subject which is still being debated.[40] In his own practice, it is clear, Spenser rejected Churchyard's solution in writing "bene," "nere," "madc," and "lyfe," his frequent "doen" and "vndoen"[41] being exceptions which cannot be laid at the door of Grey, who regularly wrote "doonne." Like Rich and Mulcaster, Spenser stood opposed to the doubling of *o* as practiced fairly consistently by Grey and Munday[42] and Stanyhurst, who could even write, with fine scorn for Latin quantity, "too thee oother eend of thee roume."

On the eve of his service under Grey, Spenser's struggle with syllable quantity and Harvey's rallying on the subject gave him food for thought but no cause for capitulating. The symbol of measurement became Spenser's "carpenter," a word which does not survive in his verse or prose outside the Harvey correspondence: "For the onely, or chiefest hardnesse, whych seemeth, is in the Accente: whyche sometime gapeth . . . and sometime

[39] Queen Elizabeth's revocation of July 12, 1582, had not arrived on July 16, when Grey renewed his appeal to "repayre ouer" in a postscript (SP 94.28, Plomer's Fig. 6) to Walsingham.

[40] James G. Southworth, *Verses of Cadence* (Oxford, 1954), after commenting on his differences with Talbot Donaldson over Chaucer's prosody, concludes (p. 5), "I now think that we were both wrong."

[41] In Spenser's hand the minority form *donne* occurs but seven times. Cf. the strong participial endings listed under B and C above (pp. 86, 87).

[42] Byrne, "Anthony Munday's Spelling as a Literary Clue," pp. 9-23.

exceeding the measure of the Number, as in *Carpenter*, the middle sillable being vsed shorte in speache, when it shall be read long in Verse. . . But it is to be wonne with Custome, and rough words must be subdued with Vse." Here, perhaps, rather than in spelling, lies Mulcaster's influence in "the kingdome of oure owne Language." Harvey's repudiation was unequivocal: "You shal neuer haue my subscription or consent . . . to make your *Carpĕnter* our *Carpĕnter*, an inche longer, or bigger, than God and his Englishe people haue made him." Spenser's duties between 1580 and 1582 may have interfered seriously with the progress of his poesy, so that Grey's recall doubtless produced mixed emotions.[43] The year 1582 saw not only Grey's revocation and Spenser's "retirement" to New Abbey but the publication of two books which revived the quantity argument, Mulcaster's *Elementarie* and Stanyhurst's version of the *Æneid.* In his chapter "Of Distinction" Mulcaster, perhaps recalling the Spenser-Harvey argument, discusses "the long or short pronouncing of syllabs" and distinguishes between the *long time,* as in *repĕnting,* and the *short time,* "to be pronounced short and quik, as *carpĕnter.*" Stanyhurst, in his foreword "Too thee Learned Reader" (Arber ed., p. 12), supports Harvey in maintaining that Latin rules can hardly apply to English "in middle syllables."[44] Precise interpretation is not easy. Yet one point is clear: the controversy leaves its mark on Spenser's spelling in the Grey and Norris letters which have survived from the eighties.

Much of Spenser's deviation from custom, where his orthography seems to us least modern, may be traced to his views on quantity and accent, with allowances for French influence where Mulcaster permits greater "enfranchisement," and to his use of final *-e*. The listing below gives mono-

[43] Not only the "fennes of Allan" passage in Book II but "Envy [on the] ravenous wolfe," as early as Book I, Canto IV, would appear to belong to the New Abbey period. It may even be that Spenser found hints for the three Sarazins, Sansfoy, Sansloy, and Sansjoy, from the Burkes (*View* 4107 ff. and SP 81.15 and 81.39, which he copied), whose motto is inscribed under their armorial bearings in two of the chapels in Kinalekin Old Abbey (cf. Cinel-Fhechin, *Annals of the Four Masters,* A. D. 1601) in Leitrim barony near Loughrea, County Galway: UNE FOY . . . UNE ROY . . . UNE LOY. See John O'Donovan, *Ordnance Survey Letters, Galway* (Bray, 1928), II, 504-10; Richard W. Church, *Spenser* (London, 1879), p. 90 (as quoted by Grosart, *Life,* I, 536).

[44] Meres in 1598 named "but two Iambical Poets, *Gabriel Haruey,* and *Richard Stanyhurst,* bicause I haue seene no mo in this kind." See Don Cameron Allen, *Francis Meres's Treatise "Poetrie"* (Urbana, 1933), pp. 79, 134. A year later appeared the *First Booke of the Preservation of King Henry the VII* (*STC* 13,076) in "english rythmicall Hexameters" by a writer who could — like Harvey in 1592 — "reuerence" both Spenser and Stanyhurst. Spenser's remarks on Stanyhurst in the *View* (1713-19) may have stemmed from literary as well as religious and political differences. It is difficult to measure the degree of Spenser's sarcasm or of his "playfulness" here. But most modern critics underestimate the poet's sense of humor.

syllabic forms (wherever extant in his own hand) and the stressed and unstressed variations. As this is a large subject, my discussion is limited to a few selected key morphemes.

–AIN. Monosyll. gayne, playne, slayne, Spayne, vayne.
Stressed: agayne, complayne, disdayne, remayne (cf. remaynder).
Fr. -tenir. conteyne (contayne lx), enterteyne — interteyne (enterteigne lx), maynteyne (maynteigne lx), obteyne, perteyne, reteyne (retayne lx), susteyne. With the infrequent -teigne compare seign(i)ory.
Fr. -streindre. constrayne (constraint), but restreyne (restreint). Cf. -streynen forms in the Chaucer MSS.
Fr. -taindre. attayne. Cf. attaynders, but attaint.
Unstressed: captein, certein (-ly, -ty), sodein (soddein); but forreyne, mountayne (*M*: foren, mountain), villeinous.
–EAN [ɛ:n]. Monosyll. cleane, meane. Cf. Deanerathes, *View* 2424.
Stressed: demeane (so *View* 4193 but demaynes 4641).
Spelled *demeasne* in Sir Henry Sidney's 1583 *Discourse*.
–AIM. Monosyll. ayme, clayme, mayme.
Stressed: proclayme, reclaymed.
–AIL. Monosyll. fraile, raile (v.), saile (noun pl.).
Stressed: assayle, avayle, preuayle; entrayld, trayling. Cf. countervaile, *View* 1593.
Unstressed: battaile, victaile — vittaile — victell, trauaile — trauell, merveile (merveilous).
–EAL [ɛ:l]. Stressed: appeale, conceale, reveale. Cf. weale, zeale; enterdeale (*View* 1396, 1877; *Brief Note* 83).
–AIR. Monosyll. aire, faire — fayre (native adj.)
Stressed: affaires (Fr.), despeire, impayre, repaire (Fr. -parer) but repayre (BM Grant).
–EAR [ɛ:r]. Monosyll. beare, cleare, deare, feare, heare, neare.
Stressed: appeare, forbeare, forsweare. Compare Spenser's rimes with *there, were,* etc.
–AULT. See medial *au* above (p. 85).
–EGE. Stressed: alleage. Cf. alleageaunce.
Unstressed: knowledg, vicaredg (see under C, p. 88).
–ESS. Stressed: confesse (Fig. B), distresse, neuerthelesse, redresse, successe, vnlesse (*M*: onelesse).
Unstressed: busines (Fig. A), M^{ris}:, goodnes, happines, highnes, wit(t)nes — wit(t)nesse. French: countesse. Irish: galloglas — galloglasse. Compare pentisse (*M*: penthouse).
–OICE. Monosyll. voyce. Stressed: reioysed.
–OIL. See final *l*, under C above (p. 88).
–OIN. Stressed: adioyne, purloyne. Cf. ioyne.
–OINT. Monosyll. ioynt, but point.
Stressed: annoynte (Fr. -oindre), but appoint (Fr. pointer, poncter). The form *appoynt* occurs once.

–OUND. Monosyll. bownd, fownd, grownd, sownd.
Stressed: compownd, expownd, redownd.
–OWN. Monosyll. crowne, downe, towne. Cf. medial *ow* in clowded, fowre, howre, powder.
Stressed: renowne — renowme. Cf. *Brief Note* 31, and note (Variorum *Prose Works,* p. 431).

Here, as in Figs. A and B, the forms are symptomatic of Spenser's spelling. It is clear that *i* and *y* were not used indifferently. The poet's predilections may be summed up as follows:

(a) long *i* in stressed syllables, as vowel or in diphthongs, is written *y* (except before *l* and *v*): *lyfe* (Fig. A, 4) but *liues* (6), *fynding* (6,8), *gayne* (9), *tyme* (9), *prayed, abyde* (12), *mayme* (B 3).
(b) short *i* in stressed syllables is written *i*: *assistaunce* (B 3), *hinderaunce* (4), *skilfull* (6); cf. *litle, victaile,* etc.
(c) *i* in unstressed syllables (except final *-y*): *certeinty* (A 5), as vowel or in diphthongs, *respitt* (7), *battaile* (15), *busines* (11).

I have found no occurrences in Spenser's hand of *time, fire* (singular or plural), *mine,* and only five instances of *life* (never *lyues,* pl.). Before nasals *y* (long) is regular, but before liquids it is less frequent, in both stressed and unstressed syllables: *forreyne* but *battaile.* Spenser seems never to have written *whyle* (Grey: *whyll*) or *myle*: compare *vilenesse* (A 1) and the *-aile, -oile* endings listed above. His variants frequently seem to be the result of an unresolved struggle between his normal inclination and his consciousness of French forms or origins.[45] Unlike *i* and *y,* however, *u* and *v* appear to be used interchangeably.

Spenser's method in employing final *-e* may be accounted for, in large part at least, if we recall his early insistence upon the length of the middle syllable in *carpenter.* We have noted above the forms *ioyne* but *ioynt, constrayne* but *constraint*; compare his frequent spellings *conteyne* but *content.* Without exception, it would seem, a syllable ending in *nt* (long in Latin) merited no final *-e* in Spenser's scheme whether long or short. Other syllables noted by Harvey (*-ern-, -est-,* etc.) received similar treatment except, and this was an important deterrent, when Spenser recalled their French counterparts. Once more the recognition of Romance analogies appears to have caused variation in spelling.

Long after Harvey had written, perhaps with a sly glance at Spenser's

[45] Cf. *inquyre* but *require, desyre — desire* (Fr. *-sirer*), *retyred — retired* (Fr. *-tirer*), *inspire,* and (unstressed) *empire.* Before *u*(*v*) Spenser usually has *i:* (long) *aliue, arrive;* (short) *give, giuen* (cf. Grey: *guyue(n)* but imperative *yeeue;* (in diphthongs) *con-, per-, receive* (Fr. *-cevoir,* OF. *receivre*). He regularly writes the native word *kyne,* like *myne,* but (no doubt for similar reasons) as regularly *line.*

own pen, "Haue wee not *Mooneth,* for *Moonthe: sithence,* for *since: whilest,* for *whilste: phantasie,* for *phansie: euen,* for *evn* . . . and a thousande of the same stampe: wherein the corrupte *Orthography* in the moste, hathe beene the sole, or principall cause of corrupte *Prosodye* in ouer many?", Spenser continued to write *moneth, sithens, whilest, fantasy,* and *euen!* We may conclude that Spenser's spelling was seldom or never capricious, and that like Mulcaster he followed a well-considered "system" which under the Elizabethan circumstances was subject to those "errors which will not be auoided."

IV. The Discomposing Compositor

It is now more than a quarter-century since the first Johns Hopkins Variorum volume appeared with a textual appendix[46] which involved conjectures on the poet's spelling. The editors, Professors Heffner and Strathmann, working largely in the dark, without knowledge of Spenser's spelling habits, followed the 1596 *Faerie Queene,* which in their opinion showed "sufficient alteration for the better to justify the opinion that Spenser was responsible for an incidental revision." This is often less satisfactory than Osgood's procedure in the *Concordance,* which was "based on M[orris] corrected by D[odge], and includes the variants of vocabulary in Oxf." (p. vii). The *Concordance* is closer than *Variorum* in recording such regular Spenser spellings as "hable"; in fact, to follow *1596* is to move away from the poet's own MS spellings. A brief analysis (p. 521) leads the editors to "certain general preferences" such as: "bloody(ie)" in *1590,* "bloudy(ie)" in *1596*; . . . "hable" in *1590,* "able" in *1596.*" In the "Faults Escaped" appended to *1590* one finds "pelf" (*1596* "pelfe") and "contayne" (*1596* "containe"). In all these instances, as in the *1590* catchword "Druncke" (*1596* "Drunke"), the *1590* form is regularly Spenser's.

The Variorum list of examples (pp. 522-24) is necessarily far from complete. The figures below are not the ones given there but instead represent the preponderance of one change over its opposite; for example, "au — a [42]" below indicates the difference between "a — au [4]" and "au — a [46]." The difference between "e *added* [173]" and "e *dropped* [168]" would seem inconclusive; Spenser, as we have seen, wrote both *chief* and *chiefe,* and the printer's changes from *doe, secrete,* and *whome* are modernizations that Spenser cannot claim. Only the more numerous listings are considered here, though some of the more interesting changes fall in the smaller categories (*e.g.,* "o — u [20]," always — be it noted — before a nasal; Spen-

[46] *Var.F.Q.,* I (1932), pp. 516-25.

ser's thancked — *1596* thanked). The asterisk indicates Spenser's preferred, if not his exclusive spelling; the first form entered is that of *1590*.

au — a (42): -aunce* — -ance; chaunge* — change. (French influence)
ee — e (36): bee* — be. (Add Spenser's *shalbee, wilbee,* not noted.)
e — ea (52): welth* — wealth. (In these instances the printed form is usually a modernization not Spenser's.)
oo — ou (69): blood* — bloud.
es — s (75): partes* — parts. (Cf. *dayes, handes,* etc.)
y — i (235): agayne* — againe; sayd — said; theyr — their* (p. 85).
y — ie (162): body* — bodie, vnworthy* — vnworthie.
double consonant > single (73): mett* — met. (Cf. had,* of,* yett.*)

As the editors are careful to point out, their list does not "take into account the many cases in which *1596* agrees with *1590* in the spelling of a word which is changed elsewhere." All too frequently, neither *1590* nor *1596* reflects Spenser's spelling, which is often more modern than that preferred by the printer. For example, such changes as *freend — friend, yeald — yeeld* do not concern Spenser's forms, which were consistently *frend* and *yield*. Compare also the change listed as *suddeine — suddaine*: this word (variously spelled) occurs sixty-four times in *Faerie Queene* but never once as Spenser spelled it (*sod(d)ein*: p. 94 above) in the Grey letters. The Variorum lists are more significant in what they fail to reveal. The word *captein* (Spenser's form: p. 94) appears five times in *1590* — never twice alike![47] This printer's pi — or compositor's comedy of inconsistency — makes it evident that Wolfe in 1590 was appearing, to borrow Spenser's phrase from the *Shepheardes Calender,* in "sheepes clothing" and that Field in 1596 was having a field day.

The comments of the editors on Spenser's seeming archaism and the practice of the printers — whose compositors on occasion followed Spenser's copy much as Spenser sometimes reproduced Grey's spelling — are as much to the point as they are sound. Among "other books printed by Wolfe" (p. 525) was *Churchyard's Challenge* in 1593, the text of which (as Miss Byrne has pointed out: cf. footnote 24 above) "reveals the modernization considered necessary by the ordinary compositor in the 'nineties." Clearly, the "tyranny of the typesetter" and "freedom of the press" flourished long before the phrases were born.

[47] This is but one example of the liberties which the compositor took with Spenser's spelling, whatever may have been his pronunciation; twice both pronunciation and spelling are trisyllabic, at the end of the line (cf. *Macbeth,* I.ii.34). The Ellesmere scribe writes the word (singular and plural) thirty-two times, but only once (*View* 3757) does Spenser's consistently maintained spelling (*captein*) appear.

V. "What Needs This Colourable Word?"

Writers at the turn of our century were prone to believe that words then considered obsolete were, when found in Spenser's poetry, archaisms consciously introduced by the poet. While the criticism of the past forty years has shown an increasingly healthy reaction against such an assumption, the early views are still being perpetuated. What may we learn of this aspect of Spenser's style from the documents which we now know to be from his pen?

It must be remembered that the diction of the letters dictated by, or copied from, Grey and the Norrises was theirs and not Spenser's, even though Spenser often altered their spelling to conform with his own "system." Archaisms in Spenser there undoubtedly are. But when words so labeled crop up in the expository letters of these military men, their archaic or poetic nature must be called into question. They become suspect, in fact, when we find Spenser employing them beyond his poetry in the *View* or his other prose writings.

One critic in 1926[48] rightly observed that many of Spenser's words cited as archaisms are "not really archaisms since they are also found in the writings of his contemporaries." Thus *eftsoons* occurs not only "in Puttenham" but frequently in Bryskett and Geoffrey Fenton, not to mention twelve occurrences in the *View;* on Spenser's own writing of the word, see note 35 above. The form *moe* is found in Spenser's Italian hand (SP 85.5) and in Grey's letters in his own hand; cf. Meres's use of *mo* quoted in note 44. *Tho* (meaning *then*) occurs often in Mulcaster's *Elementarie* (three times on pp. 271-72) and well into the next century. When Miss Pope wrote, "Into Spenser's spelling went vagary and visualization" (p. 616), she was of course discussing not Spenser's spelling but the compositor's. Consequently her observation on *only,* "more frequently spelled *onely* in the *Faerie Queene,*" has little validity, as Spenser himself apparently never used the modern form. Among the verbs discussed, *doen* (also *vndoen*) is Spenser's usual form for the past participle, occurring in his bill against Roche as late as 1589; *comen* (p. 608) appears in his Italian hand (SP 86.50); *layne — laine* occurs but twice in Spenser's poetry as against six instances of *lyen,* which appears in "must haue lyen waste" in Spenser's own hand (SP 92.11.I). The form *bounden* is hardly "poetic," since it is found

[48] Emma Field Pope, "Renaissance Criticism and the Diction of *The Faerie Queene,*" *PMLA,* XLI, 607; cf. especially pp. 604-12. In the *Athenæum* for 1920 (I, 252), R. W. King maintained that "Spenser was an inventive archaist, seeking to give his style and diction an old-world air . . . by cherishing words like 'eftsoons,' 'sithens,' 'ywis,' 'eke,' and 'wight.' . . ."

in Grey's letter (SP 92.30, again in Spenser's hand) as well as in Fenton's regular subscription "Your honours most [*or* whollye] Bownden. . . ." In Spenser's hand we find both *quod he* and *quoth he* (SP 89.18 and *Axiochus* 16; cf. *Axiochus* 48 and *View* 2381). And that *discounsel* (p. 610) is not to be "classed as poetic" may be seen from Sir John Norris' letter (SP 115.13, Plomer's Fig. 3, line 11), written in Spenser's hand.

A more recent writer[49] in a chapter on "Spenser's Poetic Diction" includes comment on words that are written by Spenser in the letters of Grey and the Norrises. She brands as a "neologism" *surceasse* (see Fig. A, line 7, where it is Grey's word), as an "unusual archaism" *fortilage* (also in prose, *View* 5135), and as a "well-established poetic phrase" *put in ure* (p. 187), which occurs (as Grey's phrase) not only in Spenser's hand (SP 78.29, p. 6: "Why should yt not be putt in vre?") but also in Grey's own hand (SP 82.48, p. 2: "ye plott y^t^ is entended . . . too bee putt in vre"). The verb *impeach* is "especially remarked" (p. 227) in the "common Spenserian sense of 'prevent' " — a prose sense in which it was used by Sir Henry Sidney and others, including Spenser, who in the *View* also wrote *impeachful* (41) and *impeachment* (251, 2590). Such a "poetic-archaic word" (p. 196) as *carke,* which is cited from Gascoigne, Warner, and other poets than Spenser, may be found in Sidney's prose and elsewhere as well as in Grey's letters (cf. SP 87.18: *carck,* verb, in Grey's own hand). The verb *bewray,* "little removed from ordinary prose," (p. 203) must be accepted as ordinary prose in *View* 2420 and in Grey's letters, where Spenser copied it twice (*bewray,* SP 88.39, in Italian hand; *bewraied,* SP 94.61). Other words which cannot be attributed to Spenser, where we have no evidence that the poet had a part in phrasing the letters he penned, include the verb *deeme* (pp. 246, 263), found in Grey's letter SP 94.47, and the noun *hap* (pp. 257, 263), which occurs in the prose of Sidney and in letters by both Grey[50] and John Norris (SP 86.50: "the hardnes of his happe," and SP 115.15 and 115.16: "by very hard hap"). The danger of relying upon NED for the earliest occurrence of a word is again seen in the "neologism" ("apparently

[49] Veré L. Rubel, *Poetic Diction in the English Renaissance from Skelton through Spenser* (New York and London, 1941), especially pp. 186-272. Many words listed in the chapter on Spenser are badly classified. The use of *sith* by Rich (as in note 19 above) and other prose writers well into the seventeenth century shows that such a word may not be considered "more poetic than archaic" (Rubel, p. 259).

[50] Grey also uses *hap* as a verb (SP 87.18, p. 9). The name "Hap Hazard" given to Spenser's Kilcolman estate is first cited in NED as the name of the Vice in R. B.'s *Appius and Virginia* (1575). That it was current earlier is indicated by the nonce-word (?) "happ hazarder" in Harvey's *Letterbook* (ed. Edward J. L. Scott, 1884) of 1573. In the *Panoplie* (1576) of Abraham Fleming (cf. *Var.Pr.W.,* p. 477) it is spelled both "hap hazard" and "happe hasarde."

Spenser's own," p. 264) *approvaunce,* which appears not only in the *View* (1712) but as Grey's word in 1582 (ten years before the first citation in NED), in SP 94.61, copied in Spenser's hand.

Harvey's objection to *sithence* (p. 96 above) firmly establishes the currency of this "absurd" form in 1580. The Ellesmere scribe, like Harvey, almost always spells it in this fashion, whereas in Spenser's hand it appears only as *sithens* (note 35). The comparative *lenger* occurs in Grey's letter to the Queen (SP 82.54) in Spenser's Italian hand but nowhere in the Ellesmere *View.* Much could be written concerning Spenser's use of the *-head* suffix, as in *ddrearyhead, drowsyhead, falshedd, hardyhead, livelyhead,* and *lustyhead,*[51] for none of which we know Spenser's actual spelling. It may be noted here that the ending of *widowhed* (twice in *Faerie Queene*) may represent the printer's preference over Spenser's *-head* (as in *The Teares of the Muses* and *Colin Clovts Come Home Againe*), since Spenser wrote *widowhead* in Grey's letter SP 91.38.

A few words in Spenser's hand, many of them military terms and not to be found in his poetry, merit the brief comment which follows.

al(l)gates. Miss Pope (p. 612) rightly notes that this adverbial was not limited "to poetic language" in Spenser's day. It is used by both Spenser (*View* 4919) and Harvey (Letter IV, p. 451).

aqua vitae. In Nugent's confession, p. 3; *View* 2509 (where Spenser is discussing *coynye*). For a full discussion of the use of *aqua vitae* in Ireland, see *Ulster Journ. of Archaeol.,* VI, 283-93.

armada. The early "erroneous form *armado*" is first listed in NED from 1533. Grey's *armata* (SP 78.30) in 1580 is earlier than any *-a* forms cited, antedating Hakluyt's *armada* (1599) by almost twenty years. Drury (SP 58.9) in 1577: *armathoes.*

barricadoase. In Spenser's Italian hand (SP 78.29, p. 3) from Smerwick. This plural form, not in NED, is perhaps one of those occasional spellings copied from Grey. As above in *armada,* the *-o* endings are earlier than the *-a*: cf. Florio, 1598, as cited in NED. NED recognizes no instance of *barricade* before 1642.

cal(l)iver. Twice in Nugent's confession (p. 3). It has been convincingly argued (*Éigse,* II, 44) that Irish *cuilbheir* is derived from this English word, and not as previously thought from *culverin*:

culuerings. In Italian hand, Smerwick letter. Spenser's vivid recollection of the Smerwick massacre may well account for the scene describing the "three great Culuerings" in *F.Q.* V.10.34.

ebbe (noun). In Italian hand, SP 82.54: "in their most ebbe and misery," 1581.

[51] Mulcaster's Table has "widowhood," and many of Spenser's *-head* words are clearly poetic. In the 1590 *Faerie Queene* the *-head* and *-hed* are distributed equally; in the 1596 edition, *-head* outnumbers *-hed* by 11 to 2. Spenser could hardly have coined "headlesse hood" without being conscious of a play on the suffixes.

Cf. "that lowe ebb," *View* 3777. NED (2. b) cites no similar phrase earlier than Shakespeare's *Tempest*.

hackabuse-acroke. See *muskett* below. Cited in NED, *s.v. Hackbut,* 2.

horseboy. In Spenser's hand, SP 92.11.I: "numberes of horses & horseboyes." *View,* 8x: "these rakehellye horsboyes growinge vp in knaverye and villanye," "those kerne, stocaghes and horsboies," etc. (Irish *eachlach.*)

imprest. Of frequent occurrence. In Spenser's hand, SP 88.2: *imprested* and *impresting*.

lorship. Twice in Spenser's hand, SP 81.15 and 39. Form not recorded in NED, but cf. *lorchuppe, s.v. Lordship*.

march (noun). In Italian hand, Smerwick letter: "three causes hindered greatly my marche" (Grey: *martche*). Spelled *march* in Fenton's letter from Smerwick two days later. This is ten years earlier than the first citation in NED sb. 4). *View* 1779, 4112.

muskett. In same letter: "they had not . . . but Muskett & hackabuse-acroke." Seven years earlier than the first citation in NED ("Muskettes and calleevers and holebertes," 1587).

musketiers. In same letter, 1580. First NED entry: 1590, Marlowe's *Tamburlaine* (muscatiers). Modern spelling not given before Scott (1814)!

ouerpestured. SP 88.2 (1582): "so ouerpestured with the claymoures of the Army." The earliest citation in NED (s.v. Overpester) is from Daniel in 1599.

parenthesis. SP 92.10 (1582): "as litle neede of a Parenthesis for my Clearing of any treasonable partes." First citation in NED (2 *transf.*): Ben Jonson, 1599.

parlea (2x), *parley* (noun). Three times in Spenser's hand, 1580, -81, -82. (Grey: *parlea.*) *View* 2398, 2425. With *View* 2391 ("vppon a Rathe or hill theare to parlye") cf. Bishop Lyon's account (SP 207.108) in 1600: "Florence MacCarthy . . . went into Desmond . . . and there on a parley hill had a rod given him by O'Sullivan More, after the Irish custom [*View* 205-16], and so was made MacCarthy More." NED first records Stanyhurst's *parlye,* 1582; see further NED Parley-hill, first cited 1641.

pioneer (noun). In Italian hand, Smerwick letter: "Pioners tooles." Not found elsewhere in Spenser.

rampier. In same letter (p. 3). Cf. Phaer's *rampier banks,* 1555, as cited in NED *s.v. Rampier*.

sticked. In Italian hand, SP 86.50: "they sticked not." Herbert W. Sugden, *The Grammar of Spenser's "Faerie Queene"* (Philadelphia, 1936), p. 116, records only strong forms of this verb in Spenser. Not in *View*. On the survival of the weak preterit, see NED.

vauntmure. In Italian hand, Smerwick letter (p. 3). This already aphetic form (first cited 1562) must have existed earlier than the further reduced *vaumure* (1475).

VI. The Irish Scene

It has been observed above that the orthography of the 1592 *Axiochus* more closely resembles that of Spenser's autograph documents which have survived than any of his other writings. His most substantial prose work, the *View,* which did not appear in printed form until 1633, often bears little similarity in its spelling to what Spenser actually wrote. It is to be expected that a modicum of Irish terms should creep into the correspondence of Grey and the Norrises, the nine discussed below also appearing later in the *View*.[52]

bawne. BM grant to McHenry. *View* 2405: "rounde hills and square bawnes." All four derivations quoted by Gottfried (p. 362) have been long since abandoned (cf. James B. Johnston, *Place-Names of England and Wales* [London, 1914], s.v. Bangor), including that of NED (from O'Clery's *bábhun,* "of unknown derivation"); more recently *Hessens Irisches Lexikon* traces the word to *bó-dún*. Compare *bó-daingen,* "cattlefold" (literally, "cow stronghold"), so glossed in *Ancient Laws of Ireland,* IV, 102.

creat. SP 85.5, p. 2: "a Cowe of the Galloglasses [genitive], whose creat lyeth all on this syde." *View* 7x, 3114 through 3878, spelled *crete;* note, p. 379. NED: s.v. *Creaght,* sb. See further *Ulster Journ. of Archaeol.* (1897), III, 171-72.

galloglas 2x, *galloglasse* 2x (always plural). Cf. *kerne*. *View* 4x; cf. Spenser's brief definition, *View* 2216: "ffor Gallogla[ch] signifies an Englishe servitour or yeoman." See Variorum notes, p. 354. Sir William Drury wrote concerning a troop of thirty horsemen in 1579, "how straunge the vewe of those savadge parsonadges (most of them wearinge glibbes, and armed in maille with pesantses and skulls, and ridinge upon pillions [cf. *View* 2189]) semed" to a party of Austrian tourists.

garron. Spenser's bill against Roche, SP 147.16. *View* 770: "cows and garrons"; 5176: "garrens (?)." Dineley in 1682 called them "guarrent horses."

glenne. Cf. SP 80.10, p. 2: "neare vnto the Glenne" (i.e., Glenmalure). In place-names shortened to *Glen-* (see p. 106 below). *View* 4x: with one exception, *Ellesmere* has *glenne,* which Ware regularly alters to *glynne:* cf. Grey's reports, *Glynn* and *Glyn De Lowre,* and compare Hanmer, p. 21: "*Glan* and *Glyn* are British words, of them have you Glangibbon, . . . Glyndelory, Glynmolowra, &c." NED correctly notes that "the form *glan* represents the [later] Irish pronunciation of *gleann*." (Cf. *Aherloa* below.) Elsewhere I discuss "the Widdowes daughter of the glenne" (*SC, April* 26) as evidence, like *kernes* (also badly glossed by E. K.), that Spenser was in Ireland in the summer of 1577.

kerne 3x (all in Italian hand), *kearne* 2x (both in secretary hand). Used as plural: "their kerne and Galloglasse," "their kerne & churles." On Ir. *ea* (NED) see under *glenne* above; hence Stanyhurst, *Æneis,* II, 8: "what karne of canckred Vlisses . . . ?"

In his brief visit to Ireland in 1577 Spenser had not learned the plural form; hence (*SC, July* 199) the line, "They han fatte kernes, and leany knaues." So Shakespeare formed the plural consistently 7 times, as in *Macbeth* I.ii.13: "kernes and gallow glasses." The word appears, singular and plural, in the *View* 13 times, except for 4620 (an un-Spenserian spelling by the Ellesmere scribe, where Ware and Renwick correctly printed *kerne*).

E.K.'s gloss on "kerne" as "a Churle or Farmer" may be compared with Sidney's phrase (*Discourse,* p. 3), "the tennante, otherwise called the Churle,"

[52] See my list in *JEGP,* XLII (1943), 502-6.

preceding his discussion of "Kerne and Shotte." Calendared under 1580 is a short treatise (SP 79.55) on "two sorts of people . . . the Kerne, the Chorle." See further *Ulster Journ. of Archaeol.*, II, 41-42.

On the loss of *th* in Irish *ceithearn,* see O'Rahilly (under *Aherloa* below), p. 174.

rath. In copying SP 93.64.I in 1582, Spenser twice wrote *Rathangan,* which he doubtless already associated with Stanyhurst. *View* 2391: "Rathe" (better spelling in Renwick, p. 100), the earliest occurrence recorded in NED; 2401: "Rathes." Hanmer, p. 21: *"Rath* a moat or round trench (whereof there are many in Ireland made by the Danes) if *Beda* had not said that it was a Saxon word, I would have said it had been British, and how many names of places are compounded with it in Ireland, were too long to rehearse."

Compare *View* 2424: "Deanerathes" (*varr.* "Danerathes" [so Renwick]); notes, pp. 361-63. Gottfried's conjecture that Spenser coined this compound is refuted by the earlier existence of place-names recorded in Fiants Eliz.: Deanerathe in county Louth, as early as 1566, and Deanrathe in county Dublin (F. 4319), in 1584 the residence of Capt. William Collier. Spenser no doubt knew Collier, "one of the captains," like Lee, who was in Ireland as early as 1569, and lived at "Deanrathe" in Balrothery near Dublin between 1573 and 1584. He was knighted in 1585 and died in 1588. Spenser may well have known his "Deanrathe," if not both.

The *Deane-* and *Dane-* spellings represent no difference in pronunciation, on which see Kökeritz, *Shakespeare's Pronunciation,* pp. 194-209.

tanist. A later spelling of Irish *tánaiste,* the *tánaise* of the early Irish laws. *View:* 9x, generally so spelled; the consistent *tanistih* of *BM Addit.* MS illustrates Renwick's statement (p. 308) that this scribe wrote Irish words and names "in a fashion presumably nearer their pronunciation." The spellings *tawnist, tawnistrie* (cf. below) are similar phonetic attempts by Spenser's fellow-undertaker, Sir William Herbert, at the Irish pronunciation of the first syllable.

tanistry. Here, as in *coshery* and *tanistship,* the suffix is English. *View:* 3x (*-trye,* E.).

The earliest Irish word appearing in Spenser's hand is *Vriaghs,* which occurs twice in his copy of Bagenal's letter, SP 76.1. It does not occur in the *View* or elsewhere in Spenser. This *urragh,* as it is commonly spelled in the Calendars, is presumably the *ārach* (pl. *āirge*) or "covenant" (literally, "binding") of the ancient laws.[53] This exaction, permitted to Shane O'Neill in his 1563 treaty with the Queen,[54] was not one of the "imposicions by the Englishe captaines" (Gerrarde, SP 71.31, in 1580) and therefore not included by Spenser among the "verye wilde exaccions" listed in the *View*

[53] See Rudolf Thurneysen, *Cōic Conara Fugill* (Berlin, 1926), *passim,* and *Die Bürgschaft im Irischen Recht* (Berlin, 1928), p. 83, both in *Abhandl. der preuss. Akad. der Wissensch.* Cf. Turlough's "Petitions" (SP 76.77.I), lines 7-8: "gubernationem illorum, qui vulgariter vocantur Vrracos."

[54] *Calendar of Carew MSS, 1515-74,* p. 352, no. 239: "The said Lord O'Neyll to have all the preeminence, jurisdiction, and dominion . . . over the Lords subject to him, commonly called 'wrrachadh' [*i.e.,* urraghs] and all other."

(Variorum ed., pp. 306-7). Spenser's *i* no doubt represents the aspiration of the liquid, not normally indicated in the spelling, as in modern Irish; compare the similar treatment of the old word *éric* (*Var.Pr.W.*, p. 518: "Ware's considerable knowledge of Irish antiquities undoubtedly led him to alter the spelling of 'Iriach' to 'Eriach'; see further p. 281). Spenser, like his English contemporaries, adds the analogical *s* to form the plural as with *kernes, rathes,* etc.

A number of Irish words, not found in Spenser's hand, appear in documents written by Englishmen during Grey's administration, almost always antedating the first citation in NED. A fuller study of Grey's letters than I have made would probably reveal many in the Deputy's own hand. If more Spenser letters are discovered, they may well contain some of the following:

brogue (noun, "shoe"). NED 1586. See Nicholas White's Diary, 1580, p. 9 (*broges*); Trollope (*broges*) and Wallop (*brogue*) in 1581, etc.

brogue (verb). Not in NED. Grey, in SP 83.6: "so moutche as wyll broage, trowe, and mantell euerie soldior."

coshery. NED 1583 (Stanyhurst). See Sidney's instructions in 1565: "Statute against coin, livery, coshery, &c." Gerrarde's "list of evils" (SP 71.31) in 1580 includes "Cowsherie."

coynye and *livery, cummerick*. See *JEGP,* XLII (1943), 503. On *coynye* (verb), cf. O'Rahilly, p. 370: "Derivatives of *coinneamh* are *coinnmhim,* 'I billet' . . ." anglicized as *coynee, coignye* in the fifteenth and sixteenth centuries.

stocagh. NED 1596 (*View*). In *View* 4x. Chichester (SP 36.31) in 1572: "a stocogh of Feagh mac Hughes." O'Grady, *Catal. of Ir. MSS in British Museum,* I, 501.

trew (verb). NED has only *trews,* sb. pl. (1568 ff.) and *trouse,* sb.[2] Cf. *brogue* (verb) above.

If Spenser's spelling shows any marked advance towards modernized forms, it is in his treatment of proper names, especially place-names. The six letters he wrote or copied before the end of 1580, early in his career as secretary, contain the following in the forms we know today: Ireland, Dublin, Kerry, Kilmallock, Lismore, Lough foyle (two words; *View* Loughfoyle 2x), the Pale, Thomond. All of these show less modern variants in the letters of other writers during Grey's administration (*e.g., Irlande, Dublyn,* Grey's *Kerrie,* Rich's *Paale,* etc.), as well as later in the next century. For the names of the provinces Spenser regularly wrote *Connagh, Leinster* (*Leynster* 1x), *Mounster* (but *Munster* 1x), and *Vlster* (Grey's *Vllster*). The *Connaght* (9x) and *Connaghte* (6x) spellings of the Variorum *View* show that, as far as orthography is concerned, *Ellesmere* and *Caius,*[55]

[55] Cf. Ray Heffner, *MLQ,* III, 510: "as it now stands, [Renwick's edition] is a reproduction of the good text of the Caius College manuscript."

which Gottfried thought "closest to Spenser's completed text" (p. 507), fail to represent Spenser's spelling, whereas *R* — *D*[1] and even more consistently *H*[1] — *Ho* (Gottfried's "mavericks") reproduce Spenser's *Connagh*! The same may be said for many other words. Modern, or virtually so, are the 1580 forms *Corke* (3x: Grey's *Corck*), *Dingle* (4x; *View* 4311 gives the fuller form *Dinglecush* [Ir. *Daingean Uí Chúise*]; NW:[56] *Dengill de Couse*), *Dunganon* (2x; *View* 3543: *Donganon*), and *Dongarvan* 2x. Of more particular interest are the following:[57]

**Aherloa.* From Smerwick, 2x. This form does not occur among the ten variants found in the Fiants; in addition, five others may be seen in the *State Papers,* 1580-82. Spenser was later to use consistently the spelling *Arlo* (3x in the *View* and 9x in his poetry), a more "modern" form than the present-day *Aherloe* — *Aherlow!* Spenser's transition to *Arlo* is seen in his form *Arlogh* ("Newes"), March, 1582. The earliest occurrence of *Arlo* that I know of is in Sentleger's letter of Oct. 19, 1583 (SP 105.25).

On the reduction (as in *Eatharlach* > *Aherloe*) or loss (as in *ceithearn* > *kerne*) of *th,* see O'Rahilly's excellent discussion in *Hermathena,* XLIV (1926), 152-95. Similar is the development of the county name *Carlow,* not found in Spenser's hand. It appears 4 times in the *View*, with many variants, and in the Fiants with 12 variants. But the loss of *th* was anything but rapid, for despite the *Ellesmere* form *Carlo* in *View* 619, 3726, Ware was careful to write *Catherlagh* whenever the word appeared.

On e > ea > a, see *glenne* above. Cf. further *Éigse,* VII (1953), 54; *MLN,* LIX (1944), 1-5.

**Asketen* (Ir. Eas Géiphtine). From Smerwick, 2x. Grey: *Asckettin.* NW: *Asketyn.* Geoffrey Fenton: *Askeyton.* Dymmok (1599): *Aischeton.*

Bentrey (Ir. *Beanntraighe*). In "Newes out of Munster," March, 1582. Cf. *Beintrie,* SP 88.13, Jan., 1582; *Beyntrye,* SP 127.64, in 1586 (neither in Spenser's hand). What Spenser wrote in 1596 (*View* 4256) it is impossible to say;

[56] NW here and below refers to Nicholas White's colorful diary (SP 74.56) of his Munster journey from June 12 to July 22, 1580, over a route which Spenser was to cover four months later. The diary gives evidence of Sir Nicholas's knowledge of Irish; for example: "In the Irishe Ventry is called coon fyntra [= *Cuan finntrágha*]. Which is asmoche to say as whitesande havon bicause the strande is whitesande full of white shells. And Dengill havon is called in the Irishe. Coon. edaf. deryck. [= *Cuan an Daimh deirg*]. which is asmoche to say, as red ox havon." Cf. in 1586 (SP 127.64): "Dengell Covche harberowe."

For those who read modern Irish, there is an almost exhaustive treatment of both Irish and English topographical sources in *Triocha-Céad Chorca Dhuibhne* (Dublin, 1939), by "An Seabhac" (Pádraig Ó Siochfhradha), printed as a supplement to *Béaloideas: The Journal of the Folklore of Ireland Society,* VII-VIII (Dublin, 1937-38). See especially, for Dingle and Ventry, *Cuid a I.,* 3-6, 54-58; for Smerwick and "the Fort," *Cuid a II.,* 99-102.

[57] Forms marked by an asterisk appear in the early (1580) letters. The lists contain significant variants of place-name spellings which shed light on Spenser's increasing familiarity with his Irish background. On the frequent "bad" spellings of the Variorum *Ellesmere MS,* see *JEGP,* XLIX (1950), especially pp. 407-11.

Ellesmere has "Baintree," and no variants are given. (On Ir. *ea* see above under *Aherloa.*)

Breny (Ir. *Breifne*). 2x, in Nugent's confession. A common name for what is today county Leitrim (Fiant 5380: "otherwise Brenyowrark," Ir. *Breifne uí Ruairc*). Later, in the *View* (4222), Spenser wants a garrison between "the Analie and the Brenie [not Spenser's spellings]." This Breny is not to be confused with *Breifne uí Raghallaigh,* today county Cavan ("the Brenny which is O'Reillys Country," Bagenal's 1586 *Description of Ulster, Calendar of the Carew MSS, 1575-88* [London, 1868], p. 435, no. 623).

Carbry, Carbrie (in SP 81.36.I, the second spelling under Grey's influence?), in 1581; later *Carbery* (in SP 92.11.I [1582] and SP 135.66 [1588]). (Ir. *Caiřbre.*) Not in the *View.* Despite the desperate guess in NED, the derivation and meaning of the English verb *Carberry* are still unknown.

**Castlemainge* (Ir. *Caisleán-na-Mainge*). From Smerwick. *View* 4269: *Castlemayne.* NW: *Castell Mayngne,* "bylt in a notable place to rule." White visited this castle on his way to Smerwick and on his return. The strategic position it held probably impressed Spenser later in the same year.

**Clonmeill* (Ir. *Cluain Meala*). In SP 78.68, in 1580. Later *Clonmell,* in Norris' letter (SP 115.41) of 1585. Also (doubtless Spenser's spelling) in *View* 4307, and the "sweet Clonmell" of *F.Q.* IV.

Dengan, Dangan (Ir. *Daingean,* "stronghold"). This was the old name, among others, for Dingle in Kerry, Dungannon (*Dún Geanainn* or *An Daingean Mór*), and Philipstown ("the Dangan in Offaly," *q.v.*). Hogan (*Onom.*) notes that 31 townlands in Ireland bear this name.

Dowalla (Ir. *Dútha ealla*). In SP 135.66, p. 3. The Fiants show three other variants of *Duhallow,* of which the *-allow* (Ir. *Ealla*) is Spenser's "strong *Allo* tombling from Slewlogher steep" in *F.Q.* IV and Mulla's neighbor "Which *Allo* hight, Broadwater called farre" (*CCCHA* 123, 302). NW: *Dowally.*

Dundalk (Ir. *Dún Dealgan*). In SP 85.5. *View* 5x: 530-44, 4307, where the *Ellesmere* spellings are hardly Spenser's.

Fearrmanagh (Ir. *Feara* [or *Fir*] *manach;* cf. SP 56.62 in 1576: "Fermonnock, monachorum portio [*sic!*]"). In SP 89.18 (with marginal note: "Fermanagh in Maguyers cuntrie"). *View* 3x (*E Fer-*, with variants in *ffar-*), *View* 3985 offering one more example of a bad *Ellesmere* spelling.

Fertullagh (Ir. *Feara* [or *Fir*] *tulach,* "men of the hills"). Spenser wrote "ffertullagh" in SP 89.18 in 1582, where it is correctly associated, as the territory of the O'Dooleys, with Westmeath. On the later mystifying "Fertellagh" (*View* 429), connected with Tyrone and the North, see *JEGP,* XLII (1943), 514.

Glenmalure (Ir. *Gleann maoilughra*). Not in Spenser's hand, but see below. As is the case in *View* 3724, where Spenser would shut Feagh mac Hugh out of "his greate glenne," most English writers were content to refer to "the Glenne." But the specific name appears three times in the *View:* 427, 3664, 4201, where the *Ellesmere* form *Glan-* is hardly Spenserian. The corrupt variants offer evidence that the scribes had forgotten Grey's disaster, if, indeed, they had ever heard of it. Only the *A* form suggests familiarity, *Glanmaleeirh* being, like *tanistih* above (p. 41), an effort to represent the Irish pronunciation.

Quite as frequent was the old spelling *Glandaloure:* cf. Clyn's early

"Glandelory" (Variorum ed., p. 289), *State Papers Henry VIII* (V.iii.135), "Glandaloure"; *Carew Cal.*, 1579, p. 177: "Feagh McShane of Glandol[r]," etc.

That Spenser actually wrote "Glenmaloure" seems indicated by his line (*F.Q.* IV.11.44.5), "And balefull Oure, late staind with English blood"—blood which Spenser may have seen and recalled as vividly as Murrough O'Brien's blood (*View* 1939) in 1577. Joyce wrote long ago that Spenser uses " 'baleful' as if it were an equivalent for 'mal'; for the river 'Mal-oure' was baleful . . . even in its very name" (Variorum ed., IV, 271). On the poet's even more elaborate play upon the romance element *mal,* see my discussion of Malfont, probably one of Lord Roche's men (*MLN,* LXI [1946], 30-31).

To be associated with Glenmalure is Feagh's "howsse of Ballinecorre" (probably Spenser's own spelling), *View* 3665, 3723, 4201; in Irish *Baile na cuirre* or *Baile na corra móire,* "the place of the big cone-shaped hill." Here again, the variants show that the copyists knew little whereof they wrote. The proclamation referred to in Russell's *Journal* (*Carew Cal., 1589-1600,* p. 227) under date of Feb. 16, 1595 (*Ballenecor*), is listed in *Proclam. Scot. and Ire.*, II, 143, as "not found."

Leitrim (Ir. *Liatruim*). *View* 4042, -45, -61. See under *Breny* above.

Liffer (Ir. *Leithbhearr, Caisleán Leithbheirr*). In SP 84.13 (postscript) and 4x in Italian hand, SP 85.5, p. 1. Cf. Hand B, in SP 84.53: "Strabane and Leefer." Later (*View* 3979), Spenser wants a garrison "at Strabane and aboute Loghfoile."

The form of "the Liffar deep" (*F.Q.* IV.xi.41.6) may well be the printer's. Joyce has pointed out that "the insertion of the *d* at the end belongs to a class of verbal corruptions very common in anglicised Irish names." Doubtless the analogy of other *ford* endings, as in Carlingford, Waterford, and Wexford, as well as the association with water, hastened the excrescent *-d.*

Lifford, like Slievelougher and Slievemish in the South, had its folklore. But it is not to be confused with other places having similar names, such as Desmond's castle named in SP 58.9 in 1577, "called the forte of thre ennemyes in Englishe & acording the [*sic*] Irishe phrase Porttrenawd because it standeth betwen Kiery, m[c] morishes country, & the mountaines of Slewlogher." It is of the northern "Port of the Three Enemies" (Ir. *Port na dtrí námhad*), on the river Finn opposite Lifford, that Spenser wrote for Grey: "Liffer is a Riuer, that parteth Tyrone & Tirconell: vpon yt are twoo castelles, the one called the Liffer the other Strabane; these Castelles are the onely keyes of Odonnelles countrey towardes Tirloghs." Joyce (I, 264) wrote: "The celebrated castle of Portnatrynod at Lifford, of which the name is now forgotten, and even its very site unknown, is repeatedly mentioned in the Annals, and always called . . . the *port* or bank [or, as translated in the *Annals of Ulster,* "ferry"] of the three enemies; who these three hostile persons were, history does not tell us, though the people of Lifford have a legend about them." Legend, surely, rather than history, is the account in the *Annals of Clonmacnois* (A.D. 1395) of the Connaught princess Cablaigh Mór, "nicknamed the port and haven of the three enemies because she was married to three husbands that were professed enemies to one another."

**Limerick* (Ir. *Luimneach*), 5x; *Limericke* lx. Grey: *Limbrick. View* 3x: 1937,

4273, 4309 (with no Spenserian spellings); the variant *Lymbricke* is regular in *R, D¹, L,* and *N,* on which MSS see Variorum ed., pp. 511-14.

Logh siline "in yᵉ Breny" (Ir. *Loch Sighleann*). In Nugent's confession, p. 1 (Plomer's Fig. 4). *View* 4223: "aboute Lough syllon or some like place of that riuer [the Inny]."

Did Spenser know an Irish legend resembling his account of Bladh (Blomius) and Rheüsa, whose offspring were "the three renowmed brethren" of the *Faerie Queene,* Book IV? See Joyce, Variorum ed., IV, 269-70. In *Turloch Silinde* (ed. Edward Gwynn, *Metrical Dinds.,* III [Dublin, 1913], 376), which Stokes identified with Lough Sheelin, the heroine Silend bears a name which, like the Greek Rheüsa, means "flowing" or "shedding, dropping." See my "Spenser's Irish River Stories," *PMLA,* L (1935), 1048. On the poet's penchant for etymologizing, note the closing lines of Variorum *Faerie Queene,* IV, 271. As for the currency of such legends, it may be remarked that the poem on the river Inny (Ir. *Eithne*) is alluded to in the Life of Hugh Roe O'Donnell (*Beatha Aodha,* Ir. Texts Soc., I, 88-89) under the year 1595: see also Gwynn's note, *Metr. Dinds.,* IV, 381. Even if the Lough Sheelin recorded by Spenser in 1582 and in 1596 is not the subject of the legend, the poet may well have shared the confusion with such recent scholars as Stokes and Gwynn.

Lough roure. In Nugent's confession, p. 5. Ellen Plonkett made search for her child "in yᵉ Breny, & went as farre as Lough roure." This is presumably Lough Ramor (Ir. *Loch Reamhor,* earlier *Loch Muinreamhair*) in county Cavan east of Lough Sheelin (above).

Maryburgh and *Philipstowne.* In SP 88.2, in 1582. *View* 4006: "at Maryborough and Philipstown" [the spellings of a later scribe].

Maryborough, formerly capital of Queens county, is today known as *Portlaoighse,* and Philipstown, former center of Offaly, is now *Daingean Ó bFailghe* (cf. under *Dengan* above); see Butler's notes to Dymmok's *Treatice of Ireland* (Irish Archaeol. Soc., 1842), p. 63. On the often coupled "Leix" (*View* 3x) and "Offaly" (*View* 2x; *BN* 347), see Variorum *View,* p. 405. Compare *State Papers Henry VIII,* p. 443: "[Ochonors] new castell, called the Dengen, which being builded in a grete maresse, by reason whereof, and grete diches and waters aboute the same, was of soche strength, as we have not hitherto seen the lieke in this lande." On this castle, see Curtis, *Hermathena,* XX (1930), p. 317.

Mayo (Ir. *Muigheó*). In SP 81.15. So in *View* 5x: 4043-4107. The English spelling was established early.

Muscry (Ir. *Múscraighe*). In SP 135.66 (1588) also occurs "yᵉ Lo. of Muscries mother." *View* 4277: "on this side of Arlo neare to mvskrie whirke," and 4280: "Arlo and muscrye Whirke." See Variorum variants as well as notes, pp. 407-8. Múscraighe Cuirc is now the barony of Clanwilliam in Tipperary; on its other names, including Múscraighe Breoghain, see *MLN,* LIX, 2-4. Ware altered to *Muskery quirk(e)*; by Pettie's time (1655) it had become modernized to *Muskerry.* NW (p. 9): "The 28th we camped in the edge of Muskry in Sir Cormockes mᶜ Teiges cuntrey"—obviously a reference to another of the Muskerrys, west of Cork city.

Sligoh (Ir. *Sligeach*). In SP 94.28. *View* 4x (*Slygah* 3x, *Sligah*); among the variants listed, the modern *Sligo* occurs only in Ware. It is found, however, in Hand B as early as 1581 (SP 84.53).

**Smerwick* (not Irish). In Italian hand 2x (SP 78.29); in secretary hand (SP 84.28). Grey: *Smerwyck*. NW: *Smerycke*. Bingham: *Smer(r)yck*. The loss of *w in -wick* (O.N. *vík*) is not unusual at this date.

The name is usually explained as a contraction of "St. Mary wick," but if the assumption of NW (below) is accepted, it may derive from Spanish "San Maria," especially since there is no evidence that a St. Mary's church ever existed here. The foreign name has been adopted into Irish as *Smerbhic*.

Ir. *Ard na caithne,* "height of the arbutus trees?" The Inquisition of 1584 has *"Ardnycannye* alias *Smerwick"*; cf. the later Down Survey entry, *"Ardnacanny* alias *Smerwick."* The explanation in NW below seems extremely doubtful.

NW: "The next day being [June] 21th we went to see the forte of Smerycke .v. myles from the Dengill to the westwarde . . . The thing it selfe is but the end of A Rocke shooting oute into the Bay of Smerycke vndr a long cape. Wheron a merchant of the Dengill . . . bylt a prety castell . . . And . . . carying also in his mynde a golden Imagynacoun of the comyng of Spaynards called his bylding *Downe enoyr*. Which is as moche to say as the golden downe. The Auncient name of the bay in the Irishe toung is the havon of *Ard canny* compounded of these words. Ard. and Canny. *Ard,* signifieth *Height*. and *Canny* is deryved of a certen devoute mans name called Canitius, which vpon the height of the Cliffe apering at this day bylt. A litle hermitadge for him selfe to live in contemplacioun there, and so is it as moche to say as Canicius is height and afterwards by the Spaynards it was called Smerycke, by whate reason. I knowe not."

Often referred to in Grey's letters as "the Forte." Cf. *View* 3356: "in that sharp execucion of the Spaniards at the forte of Smerwicke," and 3383. The name of the fort proper, *Fort del Ore* (Ir. *Dún an Óir*), is written by NW as above and by Mayor Water (SP 78.53.I) as *Downeynore*.

Trymme (Ir. *Áth Truim*). In SP 91.11. *View* 4310: *Trim*. On final *m,* see p. 88 above.

**Ventry* (Ir. *Finn tráigh*). This modern form is presumably what Spenser wrote in SP 78.29 at the end of the line, where only "at ye Ven . . ." is clearly decipherable. (See note 56.)

Wexford (like *Smerwick,* not Irish, the Irish name being *Loch Garman*). Grey: both *Waxforde* and *Wexfoorde*. *View*: 7x.

**Youghill* (Ir. *Éochaill*). 2x in *BM Addit.,* from Smerwick. Grey: *Yoghall*. *View* 4313: *Youghall* (but *H*^{2}: *Youghill*).

Spenser's spelling of Irish personal names calls for little comment. Like that of the place-names, it reveals a modern touch (after a somewhat shaky start, perhaps) not shared with Grey and other contemporaries and decidedly more "advanced" than the later *View* manuscripts, including *Ellesmere,* which the Variorum editor considers "the most nearly satisfactory" of the extant copies. Of Spenser's *View* he observed, "we may never know exactly what he wrote," but we now know enough about the poet's orthography to realize how far these copies come from being his. In fact, all too often Spenser's spellings of proper names (or of common words) in the eighties — and we have no reason to think he spelled differently in the nineties — bear little resemblance to those of the Rawlinson MS which was submitted for publication in 1598. The "Magenesse" (lx) and "Magneisse" (2x) of the two earliest documents, which may have been copied exactly from the originals in different hands, show less confidence than "Maguire" (SP 89.18) early in 1582, which suggests that *Ellesmere* "mackguyre" (*View* 3523) is far from being Spenser's form. The name of Turlough Lynagh O'Neill appears early in SP 76.1 for the first and last time as "Turlough Lennogh," and thereafter as "Tirl." (7x), "Tirlagh" (4x), and "Tirlogh" (4x). Spenser's first spelling of the name O'Rourke, in 1580, is "Owrourk" (SP 79.24.I), followed in 1581 (SP 86.50) by "Ororick" and in 1582 (SP 89.18) by ORorick"; on the P.R.O. forms (*View* 1383-1451 n.), see *JEGP,* XLIX (1950), 410. The 1581 forms "Macharty" and "Machartie" (in SP 81.36.I) are replaced by the "MacCarthy" spellings in 1588: the "S[r] Cormock" of the same 1581 letter was Sir Cormac mac Teig MacCarthy, Lord of "Muscry," *q.v.,* who died in 1583. "Pheagh" (SP 82.54) shows Spenser's classical preference for *ph* (cf. p. 88) where other scribes wrote "ffeaghe," etc. The *Ellesmere* "maccachegan" (*View* 4208), revised by Ware to "Mageoghegan," may be compared with Spenser's form "Macgoghegans" in 1582 (SP 89.30), which more closely resembles the spelling of *G* and *P*; in other words, Spenser's 1582 form has a more modern look than forms written some twenty years later. Other names, like the frequently recurring "Burke" ("Burk" lx), offer no spelling difficulties.

If one agrees with the approach of scholars like McKerrow and Greg, one may accept Wrenn's recent *dictum*[58] that "spelling would seem to play a valuable part in reconstructing the history of the text" not only of *Beowulf* but of Spenser. We now have a corrective, or to use Grey's phrase printed above (p. 81), a "corrosive medicine," to scan beneath the surface. We can speak, perhaps, with more authority about what Wrenn calls "true plus" rhymes like Spenser's *arre* and *farre*: "These are rhymes which are true in sound, but whose orthography has been adjusted by poet or printer to make a rhyme to the eye as well as to the ear. In *farre,* Spenser has a correct historical form, if a little archaic. He (or his printer) then adjusts the spelling of *are* to *arre* (which is quite unhistorical) to make an eye-rhyme of that which is already a true sound-rhyme."[59] Did the poet, we may ask,

[58] "The Value of Spelling as Evidence," *Trans. Philol. Soc., 1943,* p. 18.
[59] *Ibid.,* p. 35.

consider even "a little" archaic the spelling *farre,* which he consistently wrote in prose letters, and which, if he copied from Grey's drafts, tacitly corrected Grey's *far*? Did the poet consider *arre* (Grey's spelling which Spenser "corrected" when, frequently and exclusively, he wrote *are* instead) a "quite unhistorical" form?[60]

Not everything that survives in Spenser's hand has been itemized here. There are many addresses and indorsements, like that, in his Italian hand, of the 1580-82 "Booke of Concordatums" (SP 92.20.I), and title pages like that, in his secretary hand, of the later Concordatums (SP 97.23), as well as numerous marginal headings and notations, both Italian and secretary, to documents written by others. A study of them would not add greatly to what we already know from the documents themselves. Although there can be no question that most of what Spenser wrote has perished, including no doubt many letters he wrote as secretary to Lord Grey and perhaps for the Norrises and others, it is devoutly to be hoped that more specimens of his writing may be unearthed. Certainly his autograph remains fail to reveal all the words about which we should like to know. They are adequate, however, to give us a clear idea, orthographically at least, of "the kingdome of his mynd."

[60] While I have made a card concordance of all the words in Spenser's hand, I have indexed only a small number from Grey's letters in his own hand. I have found *ar* (a form championed by Mulcaster along with *far*) twice and *are* but once, in the second letter (SP 75.79) he wrote, as calendared, from Ireland. A study of the State Papers will show that other writers than Grey regularly employed the form *arre*.

University of Illinois

KING LEIR AND *KING LEAR*: AN EXAMINATION OF THE TWO PLAYS

Robert Adger Law

"If we must find an original for *Lear*," wrote the elder Furness seventy-eight years ago, "I think it is in the old drama, and not in Holinshed; and I mean by this that, in reading the old drama, every now and then there comes across us an incident or a phrase that reminds us of Shakespeare's *Lear*, and that this cannot be said of Holinshed's story."[1]

Much more recently Sir Walter W. Greg, the eminent scholar who in 1908 edited the 1605 text of *King Leir* for the Malone Society, has expressed in detail a similar opinion. Greg mentions a large number of close resemblances in incident between the older piece and Shakespeare's *Lear*, and then lists some forty verbal parallels. He concludes:

> Here we have two score parallels between the plays. It will be noted that sometimes a single passage from the old play is echoed in more than one of Shakespeare's; while at other times Shakespeare in a single passage combines reminiscences of more than one of his predecessor's. I do not for a moment suppose that any of these echoes were conscious. Indeed, none of them taken individually would prove any connexion between the two works; while even collectively they might still be put down to coincidence, though less plausibly. But when a similarity of structure and incident has already betrayed Shakespeare's acquaintance with the earlier piece, then the parallels, I conceive, point to his having read it with some care. But in writing *Lear* Shakespeare did not do what he is credited with having done on previous occasions — leave standing whatever he thought good enough to pass muster on the stage; the whole thing has been fused and transmuted in the alembic of his genius. Yet it would seem that as he wrote, ideas, phrases, cadences from the old play still floated below the level of his conscious thought, and that now and then one or another helped to fashion the words that flowed from his pen.[2]

[1] H. H. Furness, New Variorum *King Lear* (Philadelphia, 1880), p. 389.

[2] Walter W. Greg, "The Date of *King Lear* and Shakespeare's Use of Earlier Versions of the Lear Story," *The Library*, 4th Series, XX (1940), 397. Though one

All the evidence that convinced Greg of Shakespeare's careful reading of the old play cannot be repeated here. General similarities in certain characters of the two plays not found in other early versions of the story include those of Perillus with Kent and the Fool, Skalliger and the Messenger with Oswald, and Goneril's husband with Albany. Examples of similar incidents are the youngest daughter's asides as her sisters respond to the love test, the alternate kneeling of father and daughter in the reconciliation scene, the Steward's advice to his mistress to treat the old King harshly, the interchange of messages between the elder daughters, physical punishment offered to a royal representative, and the tearing of an incriminating letter. A few parallel passages follow:[3]

LEIR (*to Perillus*): Vrge this no more, and if thou loue thy life. (l. 569)
LEAR: Kent, on thy life no more. (I.i.156)

LEIR: And think me but the shaddow of my selfe. (l. 1111)
LEAR: Who is it that can tell me who I am?
FOOL: Lear's shadow. (I.iv.250-51)

CORDELLA: Thus ile mock fortune, as she mocketh me. (l. 704)
CORDELIA: Myself could else outfrown false Fortune's frown. (V.iii.6)

PERILLUS (*of Leir*): But he, the myrrour of mild patience,
Puts vp all wrongs and neuer giues reply. (ll. 755-56)
LEAR: No, I will be the pattern of all patience;
I will say nothing. (III.ii.37-38)

CORDELLA: If so the stocke be dryed with disdayne,
Withered and sere the branch must needes remaine. (ll. 1142-43)
ALBANY: She that herself will sliver and disbranch
From her material sap, perforce must wither
And come to deadly use. (IV.ii.34-36)

Though many other parallels, some of them unnoted by Greg, might be given, it will be assumed that Shakespeare, as Greg states, did read the old play with some care. Yet every one admits that similarities between the two dramas are less remarkable than their differences. Since any real source of this great tragedy deserves minute analysis, it seems not out of place to examine the earlier drama in detail that we may determine the nature and the type of the old *King Leir,* and at the same time perceive more clearly the process of Shakespeare's composition.

---

may not be ready to accept all of Sir Walter's positive pronouncements, the entire article is unquestionably the most important study of the relation of the play to its sources that has come since the publication of Perrett's volume.

[3] All quotations from *King Leir* are taken from the Malone Society volume, ed. W. W. Greg (London, 1908). Those from Shakespeare are based on the G. L. Kittredge text (Boston, 1936).

I

So far as known, the fable of King Lear and his three daughters begins with Geoffrey of Monmouth, and his account in the *Historia Regum Britanniae* (*ca.* 1140) represents the core of the story that appears in the old play and in Shakespeare's, though each author was certainly indebted to other versions of the popular legend.[4] Geoffrey's tale follows:[5]

Caput XI

Dato igitur fatis Bladud, erigitur Leir filius eiusdem in regem, qui sexaginta annis patriam viriliter rexit. Aedificauit autem super fluuium Soram ciuitatem, quae Britannice Kaerleir, Saxonice vero Leir-Cestre nuncupatur. Cui negata masculini sexus prole, natae sunt ei tantummodo tres filiae, vocatae, Gonorilla, Regau, Cordeilla. Qui eas miro amore, sed magis natu minimam videlicet Cordeillam diligebat. Cumque in senectutem vergere coepisset cogitauit regnum suum ipsis diuidere easque talibus maritis copulare qui easdem cum regno haberent. Sed vt sciret, quae illarum maiori regni parte dignior esset, adiuit singulas, vt interrogaret quae ipsum magis diligeret. Interrogante ergo illo, Gonorilla prius numina caeli testata est, patrem sibi plus cordi esse quam animam, quae in corpore suo degebat. Cui pater: Quoniam senectutem meam vitae suae praeposuisti, te, karissima filia, maritabo iuueni quemcunque elegeris, cum tertia parte Britanniae. Deinde Regau, quae secunda erat, exemplo sororis suae beniuolentiam patris allicere volens, iureiurando respondit se nullatenus coceptum exprimere aliter posse, nisi quod ipsum super omnes creaturas diligeret. Credulus ergo pater, eadem dignitate quam primogenitae promiserat cum alia parte regni eam maritauit. At Cordeilla vltima, cum intellexisset eum praedictarum adulationibus acquivisse, tentare illum cupiens, aliter respondere perrexit: Est vspiam, mi pater, filia quae patrem suam plusquam patrem diligere praesumat? non reor equidem vllam esse, quae hoc fateri audeat; nisi iocosis verbis veritatem celare nitatur. Nempe ego dilexi te semper vt patrem; & adhuc a proposito meo non divertor. Etsi a me magis extorquere insistis, audi certitudinem amoris, quem adversus te habeo & interrogationibus tuis finem impone. Etenim quantum habes, tantum vales, tantumquete diligo. Porro pater ratus eam ex abundentia cordis dixisse, vehementer indignans, quod responsurus erat manifestare non distulit: Quia in tantum senectutem patris tui spreuisti, vt vel eo amore quo me sorores tuae diligunt dedignata es diligere, & ego dedignabor te, nec usquam in regno meo cum tuis sororibus partem habebis. Non dico tamen, cum filia mea sis, quin te externo alicui (si illum fortuna obtulerit) vtcunque maritem. Illud autem affirmo. quod nunquam eo honore quo sorores tuas te maritare laborabo. Quippe cum te

[4] Wilfrid Perrett, *The Story of King Lear from Geoffrey of Monmouth to Shakespeare,* Palaestra, No. 35 (Berlin, 1904), shows that the chief sources of *King Leir* are Higgins's *The Mirour for Magistrates,* Warner's *Albion's England,* and Spenser's *Faerie Queene,* and that Shakespeare, besides using several English versions of the story, probably read Geoffrey in Latin. Perrett's work is full of valuable material, but is marred by a style frequently repetitive and sometimes obscure.

[5] The text followed is that of Jerome Commelin in *Rerum Britannicarum . . . Scriptores* (Heidelberg, 1587), a contemporary print, pp. 12-15.

hucusque plusquam ceteras dilexerim: tu vero me minus quam ceterae diligas. Nec mora: consilio procerum regni dedit praedictas puellas duas duobus ducibus, Cornubiae videlicet & Albaniae, cum meditate tantum insulae; dum ipse viueret. Post obitum autem eius, totam monarchiam Britanniae eisdem concessit habendam. Contigit deinde quod Aganippus rex Francorum audita fama pulchritudinis Cordeillae, continuo nuncios suos ad regem direxit rogans vt Cordeilla sibi coniugali teda copulanda traderetur. At pater in praedicta adhuc ira perseerans respondit, se illam libenter daturum, sed sine terra & pecunia. Regnum namque suum cum omni auro & argento Gonorillae & Regau, sororibus Cordeillae distribuerat. Cumque id Aganippo nunciatum fuisset, amore virginis inflammatus, misit iterum ad Leirum regem, dicens se satis auri & argenti, aliarumque possessionum habere: quia tertiam partem Galliae possidebat: se vero tantummodo puellam captare, vt ex illa haeredes haberet. Denique confirmato foedere mittitur Cordeilla ad Galliam, & Aganippo maritatur.

Caput XII

Post multum vero temporis, vt Leir torpere coepit senio, insurrexerunt in eum praedicti duces, quibus Britanniam cum duabus filiabus diuiserat, abstuleruntque ei regnum regiamque potestatem, quam usque ad illud temporis viriliter & gloriose tenuerat. Concordia tamen habita retinuit eum aliter generorum Maglaunus, dux Albaniae, cum LX militibus, ne secum ingloriosus maneret. Elapso deinde biennio, moram ipso apud generum faciente, indignata est Gonorilla filia ob multitudinem militum eius, qui conuicia ministris inferebant, quia eis profusior Epinomia non praebebatur. Proinde maritum suum affata, iussit patrem obsequio XXX militum, contentum esse, relictis ceteris, XXX quos habebat. Vnde rex iratus, relicto Maglauno, petiuit Henuinum, ducem Cornubiae, cui alterem natam Regau maritauerat. Et cum a duce honorifice receptus fuisset, non praeteriit annus, quin inter eorum familias discordia orta fuerit, quamobrem Regau in indignationem versa, praecepit patri cunctos socios deserere praeter quinque qui ei obsequium praestarent. Porro pater ultra modum anxius, reversus est iterum ad primogenitam, sperans se posse eam in pietatem commouere, vt cum familia sua retineretur. At illa a coepta indignatione nequaquam reuersa est, sed per numina caeli iurauit, quod nullatenus secum remaneret, nisi postpositis ceteris, solo milite contentus esset. Increpabat etiam eum senem, & nulla re abundantem, velle cum tanta militia incedere. Cumque illa assensum voluntati eius nullatenus praebuisset: paruit ille & relictis caeteris, solo milite contentus remansit. At cum in memoriam pristinae dignitatis reductus fuisset, suam detestando miseriam, in quam redactus erat: cogitare coepit minimam filiam trans Oceanum adire. Sed dubitabat nihil ipsam sibi velle facere, quoniam tam ingloriose (vt dictum est) eam habuisset. Indignans tamen miseriam suam diutius ferre, in Galliam transfretauit. Sed cum se vidisset tertium inter principes, qui simul transfretabat: in haec verba cum fletu & singultu prorupit: O inreuocabilia fatorum decreta, quae solito cursu iter fixum tenditis. Cur vnquam me ad instabilem felicitatem promouere voluistis, cum maior poena sit ipsam amissam recolere quam sequentis infelicitatis praesentia vrgeri: magis enim aggrauat me illius temporis memoria, quo tot centenis milibus militum stipatus & moenia vrbium diruere, & provincias hostium vastare solebam: quam calamitas memoriae meae quae ipsos, qui iam sub pedibus meis iacebant, debilitatem meam deredire coegit. O irata fortuna! venietne dies vnquam qua ipsis vicem reddere potero: qui sic tempora mea sicut paupertatem diffugerunt? O Cordeilla filia, quam vera sunt dicta illa, quae mihi respondisti, quando quaesiui a te, quem amorem adversus me haberes: dixisti enim, Quantum habes, tantum vales, tantumque te diligo. dum igitur habui quod dare potui: visus fui valere eis, qui non mihi sed donis meis amici fuerant. Interim dilexerunt me, sed magis munera mea. Nam abientibus muneribus, & ipsi abierunt. Sed qua fronte, karissima filia, te audebo adire, qui ob praedicta verba iratus putavi te deterius maritare quam sorores tuas, quae post tot beneficia, quae eis impendi, me exulem et pauperem esse patiuntur. Vt tandem haec & his similia dicendo applicuit, venit Karitiam, vbi filia sua erat. Expectans autem extra vrbem, misit ei nuncium suum, qui indicaret in tantam miseriam collapsum, & quia non habebat quod comederet aut indueret, misericordiam illius petebat. Quo indicato commota est Cordeilla, & flevit amare, quaesivitque quot milites secum habuisset: qui respondit ipsum neminem habere, excepto quodam armigero qui foris cum eo expectabat. Tunc illa accepit quantum opus erat auri & argenti, deditque nuncio praecipiens, vt patrem ad aliam ciuitatem duceret, ibique ipsum infirmum fingeret, & balnearet, indueret & foueret. Iussit etiam, vt quadraginta milites bene indutos & paratos retineret, & tunc demum mandaret regi Aganippo & filiae suae sese aduenisse. Nuncius illico reuersus direxit Leirum regem ad aliam ciuitatem absconditque eum ibi, donec omnia quae Cordeilla iusserat perfecisset.

Caput XIII

Mox vt regio apparatu & ornamentis & familia insignatus fuit, mandauit Aganippo et filiae suae, sese a generis suis expulsum esse e regno Britanniae ad ipsos venisse, vt auxilio eorum patriam recuperare valeret. At illi cum consulibus & proceribus obuiam venientes honorifice susceperunt illum, dederuntque ei potestatem totius Galliae, donec eum in pristinam dignitatem restaurassent.

Caput XIIII

Interea misit Aganippus legatos per vniversam Galliam ad colligendum in ea omnem armatum militem, vt auxilio suo regnum Britanniae Leiro socero reddere laboraret. Quo facto, duxit secum Leir filiam suam & collectam multitudinem in Britanniam, pugnauit cum generis & triumpho potitus est. Deinde cum omnes in potestatem suam redigisset: tertio post anno mortuus est. Mortuus est etiam Aganippus. Cordeilla vero regni gubernaculum adepta, sepeliuit patrem in quodam subterraneo quod sub Sora fluuio intra Legestriam fieri praeceperat. Erat autem subterraneum illud conditum in honorem bifronti Iani. Ibi omnes operarii vrbis adueniente solemnitate diei, opera quae per annum acturi erant, percipiebant.

Caput XV

Cum igitur Cordeilla per quinquennium pacifice regnum tractasset, ceperunt eam [inquietare] duo filii sororum suarum, Marganus videlicet & Cunedagius, quae Maglauno & Henuino ducibus coniugatae fuerant. Ambo iuuenes praeclarae probitatis formam habebant: quorum alterum, videlicet Marganum, Maglaunus generauerat, Cunedagium vero Henuinus. Hi itaque, cum post obitum patrum in ducatus eisdem successissent, indignati sunt Britanniam foemineae potestati subditam esse. collectis ergo exercitibus in reginam insurrexerunt, nec a saeuitia sua desistere voluerunt, donec quibuscumque prouinciis vastatis, praelia cum ipsa commiserunt, eamque ad ultimum captam in carcerem posuerunt: ubi ob amissionem regni dolore obducta, sese interfecit.

On analysis, Geoffrey's version of the story may be seen to turn on seven different series of incidents: (1) the love test; (2) courtship and marriages of the three daughters; (3) rebellion of the sons-in-law; (4) mistreatment of their father by the elder daughters and dismissal of all his knights; (5) Cordeilla's kind treatment of her father; (6) Leir's victory over his sons-in-law and restoration to the throne; (7) Cordeilla's later overthrow by her nephews and death in prison. Most of these incidents are followed in both plays, but each author omits the rebellion of the sons-in-law (3), having the King give away his entire kingdom with the love test. The older play modifies (4), neglecting all mention of the knights, and also omits (7), ending happily with defeat of Leir's enemies. Shakespeare's play retains the knights and telescopes with considerable modification (6) and (7). The manner in which each author develops his plot and adds to it will now be examined.

II

A skeleton outline of the anonymous *King Leir* largely resembles that of Geoffrey. Below is a table of scenes in the play, with indications of the successive series of incidents mentioned, and the number of lines in each scene:[6]

[6] Scenes are numbered after the Malone Society text.

TABLE OF SCENES IN *King Leir*

Series	*Scene*	*Topic*	*No. of Lines*
(1)	i.	Leir plans love test in division of kingdom	95
	ii.	Skalliger tells elder daughters of plan	103
	iii.	Test used, Cordella cast out, kingdom divided	143
(2)	iv.	Gallia and Mumford plan visit to Britain	57
	v.	Kings of Cornwall and Cambria meet on way	69
	vi.	Leir welcomes Kings, gives them his daughters	113
	vii.	Gallia meets banished Cordella, woos and wins her	159
(4)	viii.	Perillus bemoans sad plight of Leir with Gonorill	30
	ix.	Skalliger counsels Gonorill to mistreat her father	45
	x.	Gonorill insults Leir, provoking him to leave home	108
	xi.	Ragan soliloquizes on her good fortune	19
	xii.	Gonorill bribes Messenger going to Ragan	117
	xiii.	Cordella rejoices over her happy state	19
	xiv.	Leir and Perillus reach Ragan's palace	63
	xv.	Ragan welcomes Messenger from Gonorill	73

TABLE OF SCENES in *King Leir* (Concluded)

Series	*Scene*	*Topic*	*No. of Lines*
	xvi.	Cordella sends Ambassador to her father	60
	xvii.	Ragan hires Messenger to kill Leir and Perillus	60
	xviii.	Ambassador reaches Cornwall; Leir is missing	17
	xix.	Messenger, starting to kill Leir and Perillus, relents	359
(5)	xx.	Ambassador decides to visit Ragan's court to find Leir	18
	xxi.	Cordella, Gallia, and Mumford plan picnic	71
	xxii.	Ambassador comes to Ragan, who strikes him angrily	111
	xxiii.	Leir and Perillus land penniless in Gallia	100
	xxiv.	Leir meets Cordella; father and daughter forgive each other	265
(6)	xxv.	Ragan, soliloquizing, fears discovery	32
	xxvi.	Gallian army assembles on French coast	45
	xxvii.	British guard deserts post to drink in tavern	30
	xxviii.	Gallian army lands on British coast	12
	xxix.	Gallians overcome British guard	130
	xxx.	Gallian and British leaders exchange taunts	107
	xxxi.	Gallian army puts British to flight	17
	xxxii.	Victory restores Leir to throne	34

A glance at this table will show that Scenes iii, vii, xix, and xxiv, each one the last in its series, are the longest in the play. Furthermore, each one of the four, like the closing Scene xxxii, is climactic to that portion of the plot.

For example, Scene iii in its action follows that of Geoffrey with a few additional speeches, but the entire motivation of the love test is given in preceding scenes. Scene i, which, as Perrett observes, is indebted to *Gorboduc,* tells how the King hits on this test of his daughters. Scene ii explains the reason for Cordella's surprising answer and reveals the jealousy of Gonorill and Ragan of their younger sister, which leads to their conspiracy to incite King Leir against her. During the love test, the motivation is developed further when Cordella in two asides reveals her perception of her sisters' insincerity, and Perillus, like Kent, warns his master of his mistake.

The scenes of the second series deviate widely from Geoffrey. Evidently the playwright wishes to explain Gallia's willingness to wed Cordella without dowry, so he does away with the message sent to King Leir and substitutes a secret visit from Gallia in person after hearing the fame of the three princesses' beauty. With a single courtier the monarch comes in disguise to Britain, meets Cordella by chance after she has been cast off, pretends to court her for his King but wins her for himself. Scenes preceding this one prepare readers for the melodramatic situation through Gallia's determination to test personally the truth of reports that have come concerning Leir's daughters. Another earlier scene introduces the respective two lovers of the elder sisters so that the three weddings may occur on the same day.

As already stated, the third leading incident in Geoffrey's history, that of the sons-in-law's rebellion, is wanting in this play and in Shakespeare's since Leir has already given away his whole kingdom. With this omission in the old play goes another, the gradual reduction of Leir's retinue of knights. In place of their dismissal, the playwright, accepting a hint of Warner, has the daughters co-operate in planning the murder of their old father and his faithful attendant by a paid assassin, who at the last moment declines to carry out his task. Naturally, this scene of attempted murder, the longest scene and the climax of the plot, marks the end of the third series. At least seven scenes clear the way for this action, portraying the daughters taunting and censuring their father, their instructions to the hired murderer, his passing from one to the other, and the false message that he carries. In the culminating scene the assassin finds the old men asleep in a thicket where Ragan has promised to meet them. On their waking he threatens them at length with death by stabbing but changes his mind when frightened by two strokes of thunder accompanied by Leir's apt allusion to hell-fire. Apparently, Shakespeare owes to this scene several hints for his picture of the murder of Clarence in *Richard III*.[7]

The most effective scene in the old *Leir* portrays the pathetic reunion of father and disguised daughter in the open air near the Gallian coast. Three scenes carefully prepare for this meeting, in which Leir and Perillus come ashore, rudely clothed, without money or food, to the spot where Cordella, Gallia, and Mumford, dressed as peasants, are enjoying a picnic.[8] The gradual recognition of each other by father and daughter, the tears shed, and repeated kneelings offered much material to Shakespeare.

The final scene, containing thirty-four lines, is much briefer than any one of the four just discussed. Yet the triumphant victory of Leir's supporters follows six scenes of deliberate preparation. Again the dramatist writes independently of Geoffrey and other versions by imagining a Gallian landing on the enemy coast that surprises the drunken guard and leads to a quick defeat for the British army. The usual conventions of mutual taunts by

[7] Cf. R. A. Law, "*Richard the Third,* Act I, Scene 4," *PMLA,* XXVII (1912), 117-41. The argument for Shakespeare's borrowing has been recently accepted by J. Dover Wilson, *Richard III,* New Cambridge Shakespeare (Cambridge, Eng., 1954), pp. xxvii, 185. Earlier acceptance came from Wilhelm Creizenach, *Geschichte des neueren Dramas* (Halle, 1916), V, 395n.

[8] Perrett plausibly traces the origin of this scene to an incident in Lodge's *Rosalynde* followed by Shakespeare, *As You Like It,* II. vii, where Orlando and old Adam approach the Duke's party at a feast.

rival forces, of single combats, alarums, and excursions make this series of scenes more closely conform to the structure of a typical chronicle play than does any other group.

To sum up, the anonymous playwright has followed the general outline of the narrative presented first by Geoffrey and repeated with slight changes by his followers, but from his own imagination he has added many incidents to motivate the larger action involved. Indeed, only in Scene iii, the love test, has he leaned heavily on the original story. The three longest and most important scenes in the second, fourth, and fifth series, that is, Scenes vii, xix, and xxiv, are all concerned with romantic or melodramatic situations conceived in the author's fancy. Minor scenes prepare for and motivate major action. Moreover, the background chosen is commonly out of doors. Characterization is feeble, the verse pedestrian, but while the play studiously avoids death, there is much action.

III

Shakespeare in handling this material determined to make his play a tragedy ending with the defeat of Cordelia and her death in prison, and to add a subplot borrowed from Sidney's *Arcadia* in which the action frequently parallels that of Leir's ungrateful children. The first change required fundamental differences in character, tone, and emphasis throughout the drama. The second demanded links between persons in plot and subplot, and invention of new incidents to render the analogy of the two stories more distinct. To list all Shakespeare's innovations would be superfluous, but their nature may be discerned if we briefly examine each act of *King Lear*.

The violent rush of the opening scene makes it one of the most remarkable in all Shakespeare. At a single blow the scene provides exposition for both plot and subplot, disposes of the love test and the selection of husbands for the three daughters, and adds the banishment of Kent to that of Cordelia. So at the end of Scene i, we have completed the first and second series of incidents in Geoffrey's account besides having had a vivid portrayal of most of the important figures in the play. Omitting, as did the author of *Leir,* the rebellion of the sons-in-law, the dramatist is able to devote four more scenes in Act I and all of Act II and Act III to the vicious conduct toward their over-generous fathers of the favored children in both plots. Filial ingratitude is the theme pronounced again and again in choric speeches. All stress is on the tremendous suffering endured by the parents.

Though Gloucester twice declares in the third act that Lear's daughters seek his death, no overt act of attempted murder occurs. Instead we have the memorable picture of Lear unbonneted in the storm, to which he is exposed after Goneril and Regan have dismissed his retinue and let him out to the rain and lightning. The climax of the Lear plot falls in the mad scenes of the hovel, a new element in the story, and we meet a similar climax of the second plot in the terrific blinding of Gloucester.

Very little debt to legend or play is to be found in Act III. Contrary to the usual statement that "the original suggestion for the storm" came from two isolated thunderclaps that injure no one in *King Leir,* I believe that its origin lies rather in *Arcadia,* with the opening sentence of the recognized source passage: "It was in the kingdom of *Galacia,* the season being (as in the depth of winter) very cold, and as then sodainely growne to so extreame and foule a storme, that never any winter (I thinke) brought foorth a fowler child: so that the Princes were even compelled by the haile that the pride of the winde blew into their faces, to seeke some shrowding place which a certaine hollow rocke offering it to them, they made it their shield against the tempest's fury."[9] Yet the final scene of this act, in which Gloucester's eyes are torn out, may owe some suggestion to the attempted murder of Leir. For Gloucester, like Leir, declares that the offspring he has so favored may help him in his need, only to learn that the betrayer of his secret was his ungrateful illegitimate son.

With Act IV the structure begins to correspond roughly to the analogous series of scenes in the old play. No longer is the dominant theme filial ingratitude, causing intense suffering, but the tender affection for their aged parents shown by the wronged children in both plots. Every inch a king, Lear disdains to leave his own kingdom and knee the throne of France begging aid, as Geoffrey makes him do. On the contrary, Cordelia seeks him in Britain, using all means in her power to restore his bereaved senses. When she has succeeded in so doing, she reveals herself, to the complete happiness of father and child. Edgar similarly guides and supports his blinded parent, but does not make himself known. To several details echoed from his predecessor, Shakespeare adds an entirely new set of incidents, revealing the adulterous love of both Goneril and Regan for Gloucester's handsome bastard son. Thus plot and subplot are once more closely joined.

In his final act, Shakespeare seems to disregard almost completely the feeble lines of the anonymous play.[10] Telescoping the conflict of Gallian and

[9] *The Complete Works of Sir Philip Sidney,* ed. Albert Feuillerat (Cambridge, Eng., 1922), I, 206-7.

[10] Though "The most famous Chronicle historye of Leire kinge of England and his Three Daughters" was registered for publication on May 14, 1594, and a King Leir play is recorded by Henslowe to have been acted several times in May, 1594,

British armies in Leir's fight for restoration with Cordeilla's defeat and miserable death, as first related by Geoffrey, he substitutes a victory for the forces of evil, tempered by the violent deaths of Regan, Goneril, and Edmund. Then he allows the imprisoned Cordelia to be hanged by hasty order of Edmund, and the aged Lear to rise up and kill her actual hangman just before his own death. So he contradicts all previous assertions of Cordelia's suicide.

No such brief summary could do justice to Shakespeare's moving tragedy or account fully for relations between the two plays. The comparison given may underscore certain structural resemblances and some larger differences as well. While the anonymous playwright sticks fairly well to Geoffrey's main outline, he invents many new incidents to motivate the action. Shakespeare's story follows the skeleton form of lines already drawn, but in creating the body of his work a wide deviation develops. Casual hints and implications from the older play pass into character and action, with an occasional reverse influence, as seen in the contrast between the fiery Kent and the senile Perillus. All this merely confirms Greg's judgment that "the whole thing has been fused and transmuted in the alembic of his [Shakespeare's] genius."

IV

The play of *King Leir* has a simple unity. It has no subplots. Despite varying titles applied in its entry on the Stationers' Register of 1605 as a "tragecall historye," and in the printed text of the same year as a "true chronicle history," it is neither one. It is a typical Elizabethan romantic comedy of the early 1590's, in which all the good are rewarded and all the wicked punished without the shedding of blood. In other words, it belongs to the same category as the comedies of Greene, Lyly, and Dekker, though it is decidedly less realistic than the last named.

The romantic nature of the play does not stop there. Its three longest and most important scenes of new material are full of romantic motifs: love at first sight, proxy wooing, rejection of a proposed royal lover in favor of his agent, acceptance of death as penalty for sin, confidence misplaced in villains, sudden conversion of the wicked on threat of hell-fire, friends

---

Greg doubts its actual publication in that year and sees possibility of revision before 1605. Aside from stylistic evidence, the argument for its early composition is strengthened by the dates of its sources, viz., Warner's *Albion's England* (1586), *The Mirour for Magistrates* (1587), Spenser's *Faerie Queene* (1590), and Lodge's *Rosalynde* (1590). Add to these dates Shakespeare's *Richard III* (*ca.* 1593) and Yarington's *Two Lamentable Tragedies* (probably composed 1594), both of which, I believe, echoed lines from *King Leir*.

coming just in time to prevent starvation. Each of these situations is placed out of doors.

Characters follow conventional patterns. Of the principal figures, obvious attempts are made to picture Leir as an affectionate though misguided father, Cordella as a pious heroine, Gallia as a soldier-king, Gonorill as a blunt-speaking villainess, Ragan as a deeper hypocrite. Of persons added to the original account, Skalliger, courtier attached to Leir and later to Gonorill, is a self-styled parasite. His foil, Perillus, faithful follower of the King in vicissitude, personifies virtue and frequently serves as Chorus. Mumford, the single Gallian courtier, shows a labored wit but is less clever in dialogue than the unnamed Messenger, a "shag-haired villain," ready to commit any crime for reward. Power of vital characterization is certainly beyond the playwright's skill, but each one of those listed offered some hint to Shakespeare.

The large number of scenes results from the careful, even tedious, exposition. No less than five of them are devoted to expository soliloquies by Perillus (Scene viii), by Ragan (Scenes xi and xxv), by Cordella (Scene xiii), and by the Gallian Ambassador (Scene xx). The result is that the motivation is sometimes clearer than in Shakespeare's version. A few touches of realism, such as the Messenger's playing with his victims before proceeding to their murder, and the behavior of the drunken coast guard, reveal genuine humor, and there are several wholly indecent jestings. But the diction, especially of the verse, is pedestrian, naïve to a marked degree. The contrast with *King Lear* in this respect has been most unfortunate for the earlier piece.

What has been noted in this rather minute analysis of the old play has bearing on the unsettled problem of its authorship. In recent years several critics have tended to attribute the drama to Peele, yet the entire absence of real poetry along with the careful attention to narrative structure should rule out this suggestion.[11] Why Kyd's name should be brought into connection with a play in which not a single death occurs is a matter of surprise. The nature of the added material, particularly the open-air scenes, makes more plausible an attribution to Greene or Lodge, though the workmanlike

[11] "Peele had no idea of structure, no common sense of reserve. Reason, order, and consistency simply were not his; but he had in very rare degree some immortal gifts. One was the power of drawing an unearthly beauty out of words, a power that marks him as belonging to a class of poets different from Lyly, Greene, or Kyd." C. F. Tucker Brooke in Baugh's *Literary History of England* (New York, 1948), p. 456. See also A. M. Sampley, "Plot Structure in Peele's Plays as a Test of Authorship," *PMLA,* LI (1936), 689-701.

structure and the lack of genuine inspiration are deterrents. One might hazard the guess that if not done by Greene, it is the work of an imitator. Convincing evidence has not yet been presented. While Shakespeare owes to the play, I believe, a larger debt than is usually recognized, nowhere did he exhibit greater artistic power than in turning this crude romantic comedy into heartrending tragedy.

The University of Texas

SUSANNA AND THE ELDERS IN SIXTEENTH-CENTURY DRAMA

Marvin T. Herrick

I

The story of Susanna and the elders in Daniel 13 has been an unusually durable subject from the fifteenth century to the present time. Plays in Latin, Italian, French, German, Spanish, Dutch, Danish, Czech, and English have appeared from time to time, and sometimes in considerable numbers.[1] The sixteenth century was especially fruitful, but there are records of Susanna plays throughout following centuries, and I have seen one American version written and produced in Urbana in 1955. Susanna was most popular in Germany, where a host of plays has survived, beginning with a vernacular version of the late fifteenth century. Numerous examples are recorded in Italy and France and some of these have survived. There are records of performances by English actors, but only one play by Thomas Garter, published in 1578, has survived from the early English drama.[2]

During the Middle Ages and early Renaissance Susanna shared popularity with two other persecuted wives, patient Griselda and the girl with no hands (the girl who cut off her hands to avoid the shame of marrying her own father). Chaucer, for example, used one version of the latter in the *Man of Law's Tale* and the story of Griselda in the *Clerk's Tale.* In Italy, Susanna was apparently a model of the good woman who refuses any compromise with her virtue; the heroine of the *Rappresentazione di Santa Uliva,* a young princess who cut off her hands when her father proposed marriage,

[1] For a convenient list of early Susanna plays see *Le Mistére du Viel Testament* (Société des Anciens Textes français, Paris, 1885), V, lxvi-cxi.

[2] The story was used by British writers before and after 1578. There was the medieval Scottish poem, the *Pistill of Susan,* and Robert Greene published a prose romance, *The Myrrour of Modestie,* in 1584.

repeatedly compares herself with Susanna. And Susanna outlasted both Griselda and the girl with no hands.

Why was the story of Susanna a perennial favorite with dramatists? For one thing, it is an excellent story in the original biblical version, inherently dramatic rather than narrative. While it lacks the romantic elements of Griselda's martyrdom and the sensational and miraculous misadventures that befall the girl with no hands, it has more verisimilitude, better economy, more restraint, qualities much esteemed during the classical revival, when medieval subjects and techniques were either modified or discarded. Consequently the girl with no hands virtually disappeared in the neoclassical drama of the sixteenth century and the story of Griselda either disappeared or was modified. In England, for example, the Griselda story was combined with the parable of the prodigal son in the *London Prodigal* (1605) and the *Fair Maid of Bristow* (1605). Susanna, however, continued to flourish in both religious and secular drama.

The biblical argument was treated by dramatists in a variety of ways. The religious versions in the vernacular, essentially medieval in form, were histories, often called *istorie* in Italy. After the classical revival struck the popular stage, when the influence of Plautus, Terence, and Seneca became paramount, it was found that the story of Susanna could readily be fitted into the classical mold, that it could be called a comedy, or a tragedy, or a tragicomedy. The writers of the Christian Terence, those clerical schoolmasters who wrote edifying religious plays but tried to compose them in the manner of Terence, found Susanna an eminently fit subject if not quite so congenial as the story of Joseph or the parable of the prodigal son. Some of these Susanna plays in the Christian Terence became popular and at least one of them was an admirable work of dramatic art.

Sixt Birck's *Susanna,* first published in German in 1532, revised and rewritten in Latin five years later, must have been among the favorite plays of the Christian Terence, for there were over a dozen printings between 1537 and 1585. Birck, or his publisher, called the Latin version a "tragical comedy" (*comoedia tragica*), but it remained more history than comedy or tragedy, having a large cast of over forty and retaining much of the loose structure characteristic of medieval drama. Cornelius Schonaeus, in Holland, who contributed seventeen plays to the Christian Terence, followed Birck in his Latin *Susanna* but made the drama more compact, closer to the Terentian pattern. Nikodemus Frischlin, a gifted German poet, combined the liveliness and realism of Birck with a classical economy even stricter than that of Schonaeus in his Latin *Susanna,* first published in 1578 and often reprinted. Frischlin's *Susanna* is an excellent play. The action is well arranged, the characters well drawn, the dialogue natural and lively, and there is a skillful blending throughout of pathos and humor. While moralizing was inevitable in the Christian Terence, Frischlin kept this feature unobtrusive. A nineteenth-century scholar, Robert Pilger,[3] has lamented the fact that Frischlin chose Latin for his best work. Had he chosen his native tongue, the national drama of Germany, in Pilger's opinion, might have developed in competition with that of Elizabethan England.

While I regard Frischlin's Latin *Susanna* as the best play ever written on the subject, I shall illustrate the details of the sixteenth-century Susanna play with two vernacular versions, one in Italian and the other in English. A study of Tibortio Sacco's *Tragedia nova, intitolata Sosanna, raccolta da Daniello Profeta* (Bressa, 1537)[4] and Thomas Garter's *Comedy of the Most Virtuous and Godly Susanna* (1578) will not only show the general characteristics of a sixteenth-century biblical play but also many of the peculiar qualities that distinguish early Italian and early English drama.

II

Sacco was a churchman, Fra Tibortio, with much the same attitude toward the drama as that displayed by the authors of the Christian Terence in Germany and the Low Countries, but he chose to write in the language of the popular *rappresentazioni sacre*. As the prologue stated, the spectator who expected to see a fabulous comedy of Plautus or Terence or some merry fiction was going to be disappointed. "Such a lie is not my wont. You will see a true and worthy ancient history, which I consider more seemly for us friars." Moreover, he added that this was not a pagan history from Livy or Sallust or Herodotus or any other Greek or Latin writer, but one from the prophet Daniel.

Sacco's play offers some similarities and some differences when compared with the popular religious drama that developed in Italy, as did the medieval mysteries in France and England, in the rather free form of histories. The fact that the author was careful to mention Plautus and Terence and other ancients indicates that he had an eye on classical models, and his play bears many classical features. The title page says "new tragedy," which meant in sixteenth-century Italy that it was a serious drama dealing with nonpagan material but composed in classical form. Comic scenes and comic characters were freely introduced in the popular religious plays, but Sacco's comedy recalls Plautus and Terence rather than the native humor of the sacred

[3] *Die Dramatisierungen der Susanna im 16. Jahrhundert* (Halle, 1879).

[4] There is a record of a 1524 printing, but I have not been able to find such a book. The copy at the University of Illinois is dated 1537.

dramatists. Actually *Sosanna* is not a tragedy or a comedy but rather a tragicomedy, but Sacco wrote it before such classical labels had been clarified for the Italian drama by Giraldi Cinthio and Guarini. The play has five acts, as did the plays of Plautus and Terence, and as the *rappresentazioni sacre* did not. The language is also significant. There is no prose, which was often the medium of scholarly dramatists in Italy, like the fifteenth-century humanists and the authors of the learned comedy, the *commedia erudita* of Ariosto, Machiavelli, Dolce, and others. Sacco used three kinds of verse, two of them medieval and the third neoclassical. The usual verse in the play is *ottava rima,* an eight-line stanza of eleven-syllable verses, which was the favorite verse form of the popular sacred drama. In many speeches of his principal comic character, the servant Siro, he used a jogging short-line stanza, similar in rhythm and meter to the stanza often found in English mysteries, e.g. the well-known *Second Shepherds' Play* in the Towneley cycle. For some of the heroine's more serious speeches, however, he used unrhymed verse, the *versi sciolti* of learned tragedies and of many learned comedies, and this verse form was developed expressly in imitation of the ancients.

As might be expected from such an author, a learned Italian friar, *Sosanna* was a mixture of medieval and classical elements with the classical in the ascendant. Sacco's play was not a history, as the prologue suggests, yet a neoclassicist like Giraldi Cinthio would not have called it a tragedy or even a tragedy with a happy ending (*tragedia di lieto fin*), for there was facetious matter in addition to the happy ending, though it could have been called a tragicomedy.

The scene of *Sosanna* is apparently a neutral space outside the house and garden of Joachim and Susanna. There seems to be a shift of scene to within the garden in the second act and then back again. All the events apparently take place between morning and evening. The action falls pretty well into the normal Terentian pattern of *protasis* (exposition), *epitasis* (development), and *catastrophe* (resolution), though the resolution is anticlimactic for a "tragedy."

All of the principal characters save Daniel are introduced in the first act. Susanna opens the play with a short soliloquy; she explains that she has been working on an elaborate altar cloth and now wishes to refresh herself in the garden. Then the two elders, Nacchor and Chaynam, are introduced talking about Susanna, whom they have long admired. Now they devise a stratagem, namely to approach her as she bathes in the garden and to hold over her the charge of adultery if she refuses to comply. Both old men cackle with delight at the promise of their scheme and can hardly wait to test it. Nacchor, the bolder of the two, is made to say, with a nice touch of dramatic irony,

"No more words, let us enter the garden. I believe that we shall be blessed this day." Siro, the leading comic character, a descendant of the Roman *servus,* now enters. He has been sent by his master Joachim to invite the elders to come in the house, but he cannot find them since they have already sneaked into the garden. Siro launches into a grumbling complaint over the hardships of servants: "There is no creature born in this world who is more put upon than we servants. All of us are dubbed gluttons and malaperts in the end." Next Joachim appears, hunting for Siro and complaining about the shiftlessness of servants in general. In the last scene of the first act Susanna reappears on her way to the garden, her maids following.

The garden scene, well conceived and well executed, is in Act II. The elders surprise the young matron as she is undressing, and after some preliminary rhetorical flourishes come to the point. Susanna is firm but modest in her refusal:

Leuatiue de qua, maluaggi mostri.
Non son costumi nostri far tal cose,
Ma in opre virtuose, e grat' a dio,
Mett' ogn'ingegno mio. Vecchi ribaldi,
Spegnete vostri caldi in meggio a l'acque
Dil mar, che sempre spiacque a dio beato,
Un si enorme peccato, e piu ne Vecchi,
Che douerest' esser specchi de virtute,
E procurar salute, alli altri tutti,
E vui piu sete scelerat' e brutti. (II.ii)

(Rise up from here, wicked monsters. It is not our wont to act thus, but rather, thanks be to God, to direct every talent to good works. Lewd old men, quench your heat in the middle of the waters of the sea, for such a heinous sin was always displeasing to blessed God, and more so in old men, who ought above all others to be mirrors of virtue and to seek salvation. And you are most villainous and filthy.)

Nacchor threatens to accuse her of adultery, and Chaynam reminds her that both of them are judges who can have her stoned to death. Susanna fully realizes the tragic dilemma: she must choose either an offense to God or a shameful death. She makes her choice: "Help! Help! Come servants. Alas, I am betrayed." Siro and a fellow servant, Cleante, come running. Although both assure their mistress that they are loyal, it is easy to see that they believe her to be guilty.

Act III is unrelieved gloom. There is no comedy, for even Siro loses his facetiousness and laments the disgrace that has fallen on the whole household. The short-line verses that he commonly uses for his buffooneries now express grief.

Ahime che sbigottito
In casa piange e grida,

E manda l'alte strida
Al ciel stellato.
O caso sfortunato,
O inaudita menzogna,
Quest' e pur gran vergogna
Al mio patrono.
Non so se viuo sono,
Son fuori di me stesso.
O grauissim' eccesso
Di Sosanna. (III.i)

(Alas, what dismay wails and cries in the house, and sends loud shrieks to the starry heaven. O unhappy chance, O unheard lie, this is indeed great shame for my master. I do not know if I am alive; I am beside myself. O most grievous outrage of Susanna.)

Joachim believes that his wife is guilty and is full of self-pity: "Faithless wife, why have you treated me as a base-born peasant?" Susanna's father, who comes to condole with his son-in-law, also believes that his daughter is guilty. Not so the mother, who refuses to come to any conclusion until Susanna has been heard.

The trial scene is in Act IV. The elders make the formal charge of adultery and Susanna denies it: "O false, are you not ashamed to tell such a great lie to the whole family? You found me alone and not with any other." Then she adds, "Wicked old men, I have this faith, that God, who sees all and abides His time, will bring harsh vengeance upon you." The prophet Daniel appears in IV.iv without any previous preparation. With his other characters and situations, Sacco was careful to provide the *paraskeue* or *liaison des scenes* that distinguish the well-knit actions of Terence. Perhaps he thought that Daniel's sudden appearance at the crisis was more dramatic, and it may be that the story was so well known that every one in the audience would be expecting Daniel at this point anyway. Daniel has heard about the case and has already made up his mind that Susanna has been defamed.

Ahi, figli d'Israelle, a questo modo,
Ingiustament' a morte si condanna
Una innocente che non fe mai frodo?
Quanto la vostra cecita ve inganna.
Tornate, che vi voglio sciorr' il nodo
Ch' occupa l'innocentia di Sosanna,
E dimostrarui, e far ciaschun' accorto,
Com' ella e stata condennat' a torto.
E quei dui vecchi perfidi e malegni
Han dett' il falso e han tacciut' il vero. (IV.iv)

(Ah, sons of Israel, is this the way an innocent woman who never wrought deceit is unjustly condemned to death? Come back; I wish to untie the knot for you that binds the innocence of Susanna, and to show you, and make each one perceive, how she has been wrongly condemned. These two treacherous, wicked old men have spoken falsely and have concealed the truth.)

When Nacchor challenges the prophet's right to interfere, Daniel replies that God has sent him to judge the case. Then follows the cross-questioning and the discovery that the elders have been lying. Nacchor testifies that he saw Susanna with her lover under a *cino* tree, Chaynam that the tree was a pine. "This word," cries Daniel, "does not square with the other, and therefore you lie in your throat." Susanna is set at liberty and the elders are arrested. Joachim is thoroughly ashamed of himself and humbly asks forgiveness. Of course Susanna forgives him; she even asks God to be merciful to the elders. Joachim suggests that they all go in the house since the day is drawing to a close.

The last act is anticlimax, but it does provide the satisfaction of seeing the elders get their comeuppance. Although Nacchor and Chaynam whine and beg for mercy, they are dragged off stage to die. Joachim sends Siro out to report on the execution. Then he sends Cleante to find Siro, who dawdles as usual on his errand. The comic tone, absent in the third and fourth acts, has been restored. Finally Joachim himself comes out of the house to find Cleante and Siro. He is naturally impatient for news.

JOACHIM: Answer, Siro, are those elders dead?
SIRO: Pluto has triumphed over their souls.
JOACHIM: Pray speak plainly, and don't poetize to me; I have no wish to jest now.
SIRO: It is even thus; they have just been stoned to death.
JOACHIM: Behold, how God punishes all wrongs.

Joachim returns to the house and Siro announces the end of the play in the Roman manner: "Farewell, and clap your hands."

III

Turning from the earlier Italian play to Thomas Garter's *Comedy of the Most Virtuous and Godly Susanna* (1578),[5] one may at once perceive similarities and differences. The English prologue announces a similar aim and method; that is, this play is a plain one, not in Cicero's elevated style, the matter is true, and the purpose worthy, namely to show how God helps those who are virtuous and trust in him. The verse is typical of early English drama. Most of the dialogue is in fourteeners, but the principal comic character, Ill Repute, a descendant of the medieval Vice and usually called the Vice, often uses short-line stanzas comparable to the speeches of Siro in Sacco's Italian play. There is no division into acts, and the scene changes

[5] Malone Society Reprint (London, 1937).

several times although it never moves outside the city of Babylon. Curiously enough, perhaps, there is a strict economy of time, which is clearly marked; the action begins in the morning, proceeds through the noon dinner hour, and ends in the afternoon.

Garter's play resembles a history in some ways and it also shows classical influence. The author was evidently a learned man and he probably was well acquainted with some of the Susanna plays in the Christian Terence. The medieval features are more prominent than they were in Sacco's play, for Garter's principal model was the morality, which scarcely existed in Italian drama. All of the characters added to the original Old Testament cast are abstract: the Devil has an important role, the Vice is not only the leading comic character but a main cog in the plot, the two elders are named Voluptas and Sensualitas. The play as a whole is a characteristic sixteenth-century mixture of Christian medievalism and pagan classicism. Polonius might have called it a comical-tragical-historical-morality.

Satan opens the play. He has been trying for some time to corrupt Babylon's paragon of virtue, Susanna, but so far has failed. Now he proposes to make one more effort by enlisting the aid of the rascal Ill Repute, who thinks that he may be able to win the lady by means of two lascivious elders, Voluptas and Sensualitas. These elders, who are also called judges, are pillars of the city government, advisers to Joachim, who is here represented as a ruler, a very conscientious but nervous man, continually fretting under his heavy load of responsibility.

Susanna is not introduced until the fifth scene, when she comes to find why her husband is late for the noon dinner. Although Garter made use of the soliloquy, usually to reveal moral character, he generally tried to bring all important actions on stage. This fifth scene, wherein Susanna interrupts Joachim and the two elders at their work, is effective theater. All the while Susanna is talking with her husband the elders are devouring her every feature, her every word and gesture. When Joachim excuses himself and leaves with his wife, the elders close their books and address Venus and Cupid. Wicked characters in the play always call upon pagan deities. Both of the old men are anxious to arrange a meeting with Susanna, but Sensualitas is worried about his reputation:

For God, or for his threatenings, I pass it not a straw,
But for mine honor in this world, is it I stand in awe. (433-34)

He suggests that they employ Ill Repute, who soon appears, and, after some wrangling and a deal of buffoonery, agrees to help them for a price. The Vice is also a pagan, of course, and once echoes a famous line from the *Eunuch* of Terence:

And Venus with[out] Bacchus for wine and Ceres for corn
Is always cold. (449-50)

Just as the clock strikes one the elders enter the garden, where Susanna is preparing to bathe. Two maids, Ancilla and Serva, who are shown grumbling about the hard lot of servants who leave their homes to work for the rich, leave to fetch soap and oil. Then Voluptas, who wastes little time in the preliminary eloquence that Sacco's elders employed, accosts Susanna.

Come lie with us, we love thee well, Susan, be not afraid,
For if thou wilt not, then we shall a testimonal lay
Against thee of a marvelous force, and thus both we will say,
A young man with thee here we found, in very secret sport,
Which caused thee away to send thy maids in such a sort. (748-52)

Susanna tries to persuade them to go away, but soon realizes that she is doomed:

Well better it is without the act, your danger to fall in,
Than to attempt my Lord my God with this so vile a sin. (771-72)

The elders cry help and two male servants, True Report and Servus, break open the gate. Both of these servants are not only loyal to their mistress but refuse to believe her capable of any evil deed or thought.

Following this first crisis in the action are several episodic scenes. Susanna's parents are introduced and Joachim indulges in another soliloquy. Unlike Sacco's Giouacchino, the English Joachim never believes that his wife is guilty. The Vice, bell in hand and spouting his doggerel rhymes, finds a bailey who goes to summon Susanna to her trial.

The trial scene is a good one, lively and very realistic. Susanna is summoned to the bar, the elders are sworn in as witnesses and give their circumstantial evidence, Susanna denies the charge, and the judge sentences her to death. Then "God raiseth the spirit of Daniel." The prophet rebukes the judge and the Israelites for a shameful miscarriage of justice, demands a retrial, and proceeds to show that Voluptas and Sensualitas have been lying. The judge orders the release of Susanna and sentences the elders to death by stoning.[6]

The execution is not off stage, as in the Italian play, but in full view of the audience. Ill Report leads the lynch mob:

Now throw on your stones,
And there is for me,
One as much as three
Shall break all their bones. (1227-30)

The elders beg for a respite in which to ask God for forgiveness and mercy.

[6] The detail of stoning, which appears in most of the Susanna plays, is not in Daniel 13, but it has Old Testament authority.

Then the stage direction: "Here they stone them, and the Vice lets a stone fall on the Bailey's foot, and fall together by the ears, and when the Judges [i.e., elders] are dead, the Vice putteth on one of their gowns." The scene of execution in the English play is thoroughly medieval; there is no classical restraint and no observance of the decorum that forbade the mingling of tragic matter with clownish comedy.

Joachim's servants, True Report and Servus, come looking for the Vice, and they are not deceived by his disguise of the stolen gown.

SERVUS: Why, Sir, is not your name Ill Report?
ILL REPORT: My name is Master Ill Report indeed.
SERVUS: Hearest thou, True Report, this is the man we look for.
TRUE REPORT: Mary, then, is it he that I come for.
ILL REPORT: My good fellow, why what is thy name?
TRUE REPORT: True Report, I am the very same.
ILL REPORT: Gogs wound, Cousin Hugh Report, how the devil met we here?
I think thou sawest not William Report this seven year. (1294-1301)

But the Vice's attempt to pose as cousin Will Report does not work; the servants seize him, the jailer slips a rope around his neck, and he is hanged then and there.

Then follows another stage direction: "Here they have him to hanging, the Devil entereth saying 'Oh, oh, oh!'" Satan is disappointed at losing Susanna, but consoles himself with the Vice, for whom he plans special treatment.

And what there is in Hell to harm or punish him withall,
Or what I may devise anew, his flesh shall feel it all. (1396-97)

Joachim, Susanna, her father and mother, entering for the finale, give thanks to God for the happy outcome of their troubles and for their "most noble Queen" [Elizabeth]. The speaker of the prologue reappears to deliver the epilogue, in which he invites a tolerant reception of the author's efforts to edify his audience.

If any thing hath been amiss, inform him if you please,
If every thing do like you well, to God give all the praise,
To whom I leave you every one, and eke myself withall,
Who grant us all eternal life. Amen now say you all. (1450-53)

This was the conventional type of epilogue for the English morality, comparable to the *licenza* at the close of the Italian sacred play.

IV

Both Sacco's and Garter's plays were representative of sixteenth-century drama, for both combined medieval and classical qualities. The Italian play, although nearly a half century earlier, was further away from the medieval drama than was the English, but it retained several medieval features, such as the biblical subject, the moralizing prologue and epilogue, and two of the three verse forms used. What Sacco did was to impose the form of classical comedy upon the *rappresentazione sacre*. The title "tragedy" was classically inspired, but *Sosanna* was no right tragedy, for it had comic situations, comic characters, jokes, and its style was seldom elevated. Sacco owed little or nothing to Seneca, the principal model for contemporary Italian tragedy; he used no lofty rhetoric, no horror, no ghosts, and no chorus. His play was a tragicomedy although it came too early to bear such a title. Garter's play, dealing with the same argument and following the biblical story about as faithfully as did the Italian, was called a comedy, but it was actually a morality subjected to some modifications inspired by classical comedy. Garter wrote some twenty or more years before Chapman, Shakespeare, and Jonson were active, even some years before the comedies of John Lyly. His *Susanna* belonged to the early Elizabethan drama that Sir Philip Sidney condemned almost without exception, and Sidney would probably have lumped Garter's "comedy" among those "mongrel tragicomedies" that disgraced English letters. Sacco, on the other hand, even if his play was first printed in 1524, wrote at a time when Italian comedy, the *commedia erudita* of Ariosto, Machiavelli, Bibbiena, and others, was well established. In other words, the Italian play was largely neoclassical with some medieval relics clinging to it, and the English play was largely medieval with some neoclassical innovations such as a more economical use of scene and a rather strict economy of time. Both Italian and English plays preserved the unity of action, but this classical quality was inherent in the original biblical story.

Italian drama after Sacco, for the most part, was to draw even closer to classical form although the subject matter was to become freer of biblical and classical sources. English drama after Garter was to borrow more and more from the ancients yet remain a more or less free form.

University of Illinois

MARLOWE AND GREENE: A NOTE ON THEIR RELATIONS AS DRAMATIC ARTISTS

*Una Ellis-Fermor**

Students of the Elizabethan drama are not agreed upon the dating of Marlowe's plays nor always upon their order, and disagreement about the dates and order of Greene's is even stronger. This makes it impossible to set out a sequence of the ten or eleven plays of the two dramatists in a way which would satisfy everyone; *Faustus,* to go no further, dodges to and fro in Marlowe's canon, as we follow now one, now another, biographer, and so does *Orlando Furioso* in Greene's. But if we can seldom say with certainty "This was the year during which this play was written," it follows that we cannot discard with finality any conjectures except those that, in the light of such evidence as we have, are freakish or irresponsible. Thus a student of Marlowe's work is free to argue that the order of the plays is *I Tamburlaine, II Tamburlaine, Faustus, The Jew of Malta, The Massacre at Paris, Edward II.*[1] (*Dido,* which is both of mixed authorship and of double date, gives us little help in considering artistic development.) In the same way, though compassed about by a lesser cloud of witnesses, we may say that the order of Greene's plays is *Alphonsus King of Arragon, Orlando Furioso, Friar Bacon and Friar Bungay, James IV.*[2] (*A Looking Glass for London and England,*

* Professor Ellis-Fermor died March 24, 1958. Because of illness she was unable to see her contribution through the press, and the task of correcting proofs was kindly undertaken by two of her colleagues at Bedford College. — D.C.A.

[1] This order is accepted by many recent students of Marlowe's work, Roy Battenhouse (1941), John Bakeless (1942), Paul Kocher (1946), but F. S. Boas (1940) would assign to *Faustus* the last place in the list of Marlowe's plays.

[2] This order, again, is accepted by many earlier critics, such as Fleay, Ward, Gayley, and Dickinson and by René Pruvost, *Robert Greene et ses romans* (Paris, 1938). But E. K. Chambers, *Elizabethan Stage* (Oxford, 1923), III, 329 would place *Orlando* between *Friar Bacon* and *James IV.*

also the product of collaboration, is also omitted here.) Thus, without trespassing into the territory of doubtful authorship, we have ten plays of which the eight most significant may be arranged in the following order: *I Tamburlaine, II Tamburlaine, Alphonsus, Orlando, Faustus, Friar Bacon, James IV, Edward II.* This involves three hypotheses, one within each of the canons and one at a vital point of intersection. They are (a) that *Faustus* follows *Tamburlaine* immediately, (b) that *Orlando* falls between *Alphonsus* and *Friar Bacon,* and (c) that *Friar Bacon* follows *Faustus.* No evidence that I am aware of squarely contradicts any of these assumptions, and no arguments that I have read appear to invalidate completely those used to support them.

But it is no part of my intention to argue for or against these or other hypotheses, for the cases seem to have been discussed, at least insofar as Marlowe is involved, as fully as is possible on the facts we possess. The time is perhaps not ripe for further discussion and I do not believe it ever will be, unless and until our archivists present us with further facts. All that I ask at present is indulgence to assume what has not been flatly disproved and consider again the relationship that is disclosed if we read the plays in the order I have given. In the limited world of the Elizabethan theater the two young dramatists must have known each other and each other's work; if we had not references to confirm this, common sense would yet make it indisputable. Can we then find evidence of this familiarity in the writings of one or both of the playwrights, whether in imitation, satire, or unconscious response to influence at a deeper level, in the growth of skill or art? It is precisely because I think that the plays, taken in the order I have suggested, disclose a rather interesting phase of mental history that I venture to put forward a reading of their artistic relationship during a brief formative period.

Readers of both dramatists have long been aware that Greene's first play, *Alphonsus,* shows a marked and sometimes a crude response to its successful predecessor, *Tamburlaine,* and that traces of this habit linger on in his drama.[3] This is not in itself strange or unusual. In any age of rapid artistic growth we can trace these responses, often among a group of several writers, and we know that they may vary from the most superficial and flagrant appropriation, the mere imitation and adapting of the success of a movement, to profound and formative influences, which may sometimes, like that

[3] The uncritical imitation of *Tamburlaine* in *Alphonsus* and the satirical parody in *Orlando* have been described with sensitive discrimination by T. H. Dickinson, one of Greene's most sympathetic biographers, in his introduction to the plays in the Mermaid Series (London, 1909).

of Wordsworth and Coleridge, be mutual. In a period like the late sixteenth and early seventeenth century and in a popular art like the Elizabethan and Jacobean drama, one man's discovery in poetry becomes the immediate inspiration of others, one man's advance in craftsmanship the immediate property of his contemporaries. The sign of the major artist is always upon his work, but it is neither safe nor easy to say of any specific habit, still less of any given line or passage, that it cannot have occurred in the work of some other man who had an ear and an eye for language or effects. Were it not that, as Ben Jonson reminds us, imitation falls ever upon the hither side of truth, we should hardly know at times who was teaching and who learning, and the absence of almost all sure dating does but enrich the confusion.

But in the last resort, our knowledge of a man's temperament will often be a governing consideration and a guide. When we have traced Greene's career as a novelist we have learnt something of his habit in imitation, at least to the extent of noting that what appears to begin with the journalist's intention of writing what is popular may well, before he is done, have modulated into the poet's mode, into that Aristotelian imitation to which du Bellay, himself a poet, paid so sane a tribute. Greene was at no time, I think, so sensitive a chameleon as was Peele, but even a chameleon can sometimes be caught venturing upon a tint peculiar to himself; and if we are sufficiently assured that we have traced Greene in his novels passing from imitation in our own popular sense to imitation in Aristotle's and du Bellay's, we may find this an oblique confirmation of a pattern we observe in the plays. At least we shall be prepared to find him submerging himself in an influence and later emancipating himself from it. What will, then, be of primary interest to us is the stages of this process and their further implications.

The subjugation of Greene's genius to Marlowe's seems in this first play to be wholly disastrous, not so much because of his crude attempt to reproduce and outdo a popular figure as because his imagination is itself invaded; because, alongside an almost puerile attempt at superficial imitation, there is a poet's response to the vision of a poet, an imitation in the true sense. And the combination is full of danger. A casual, lighthearted, and almost cynical appropriation of another man's discovery may leave the appropriator unharmed; indeed, if he can thus approach his task, he is probably immune to influence in any case. A sudden irradiation of one poet's mind by another's will almost certainly be wholly beneficent, because the response is itself wholly imaginative; the follower learns from his master only what is already native to him and is carried, it may be, beyond himself to the discovery of a further and greater self. In neither case does an alien genius invade the mind. But when a man deliberately subjects his imagination to another's, especially if that other has stronger passions and more clearly defined thought, and does so in the first instance for the purpose of superficial imitation, the sources of his own poetry may be contaminated. The damage in such a case is done not so much by the actual process of copying (wasteful though that may be of his own gifts) as by the obsession, to which it may lead, with the power of an alien genius. And it is, I think, in some such condition as this that we discover Greene's mind and art in the play of *Alphonsus.*

It is easy to see, from the wreckage Greene has made of Marlowe's poetry and thought, how little affinity there is between the two poets. The absurd figure of Alphonsus, whose pretensions are more like Almanzor's than Tamburlaine's, though beggared equally of Dryden's and of Marlowe's verse; the attempt at a more complex plotting which, at this stage of Greene's development serves only to reveal the purity of Marlowe's simple line; the indistinguishable and undistinguished characters; the verse that labors after Marlowe's exultant rhythm, at best, seldom attaining a workmanlike firmness; the images and descriptions inherited at some removes from Seneca and from what we may perhaps call Marlowe's second-best imagery — all these are familiar to readers of the play. But their importance, for Greene's critics, is that they serve to show the utter incompatibility of the two minds. Greene seldom — one is at first tempted to say never — understands the springs of Marlowe's genius; it is invariably the second-best in Marlowe that obsesses him, in all of Marlowe and not merely in the imagery. So uncritical is his surrender that he reproduces with exaggerated frequency the very tricks that irritate us in Marlowe's early work; the sudden drops into a vulgar or colloquial term, the phrases used to pad out a line, e.g., "the same," "I mean," "and the rest," and the other habits that are but the clumsy accidents of Marlowe's early style. So imperceptive is he that he reduces the range of Marlowe's descriptive terms and images to a few overworked words that rapidly become commonplace; "glittering" serves alike for the "sun-bright" armor of *Tamburlaine,* for skies, thrones, and arms, until at the seventh repetition we perceive that it is no longer serving any purpose at all.[4]

[4] And so it is with the many phrases, like "aspiring mind," that are lifted from *Tamburlaine* to be attached, dead or moribund, to an alien context. Perhaps the most outrageous of these murders is to be found in IV.iii, where Alphonsus proclaims: "I clap up Fortune in a cage of gold,/ To make her turn her wheel as I think best." Seldom does a poet so betray poetry. Numerous as are the instances in which Greene actually reproduces Marlowe's phrasing, the passages in which he molds lines, phrases, and images on Marlowe's are almost beyond reckoning.

For the truth is that Greene, in attempting to reproduce Marlowe's vision, design, aspiration, music, and color, is like a man with a mellow-toned violin attempting to render an angelic choir accompanied by an orchestra of silver trumpets, or a painter in pastel the light of Canaletto. Not only does he fail to reproduce the power and the glory, but, in failing, he forfeits the virtue also of his own instrument; the imitator has ceased to be an artist.

For, if it is easy to see that Greene's art and imagination sink under the burden of imitating Marlowe's, it is equally easy to see the damage they, in turn, have suffered in the attempt. We have premised that Greene's imagination was subjugated to that of a poet utterly unlike himself, and we can, I think, sometimes see the process actually at work. For once or twice in the play he takes over a cadence, a phrase, a thought without bungling, showing that, slender as was the poetic territory the two poets held in common, it had served as the means of communication between mind and mind. In the first scene of the third act, in the middle of the absurd episode in which Alphonsus outdoes Tamburlaine by giving away all the crowns he has won, including his own, there is a sudden echo from a passage that occurs, with totally different tone and placing, in *I Tamburlaine* II.v. Albinus protests at this extravagant gesture of Alphonsus:

> Naples is gone, Milan possessed is,
> And naught is left for you but Arragon. (III.i)[5]

The line by itself has a sufficient similarity in rhythm and syllabic distribution, to its famous antecedent, "And ride in triumph through Persepolis," though the high wind of aspiration that blows through Meander's line is now muted to a cadence of forlorn regret. But Greene immediately gives it to Alphonsus, as Marlowe to Tamburlaine, to echo and in echoing to inform with fresh meaning. To Tamburlaine, Meander's line reveals a vision of triumph and of glory that leads him to lines of passionate exaltation; to Alphonsus, for the duration of one line, it affords the stimulus of a paradox. It matters less that Greene has for once echoed Marlowe's cadence not unworthily, than that he has seen something of the way in which a line can be echoed to serve as a sudden illumination and a pivot of thought. There are not many instances of such sympathy with the poetry of *Tamburlaine,* but that there are any at all reveals the presence of that imaginative imitation which accepts invasion by the thing it imitates. These are slender bridges, but we know something now of how and at what points the invasion may have taken place.

What then of Greene's own genius, of the wreckage made of his own art, of the maiming of his own imagination by the attempt to convert them into

[5] The text followed in quotations from the plays of Greene is, for convenience of reference, that of the Mermaid edition.

Marlowe's? Obviously, few men were ever less suited to turn Marlovian dramatist than Greene, with his peculiar gift for sweetness and for poignancy in cadence and in thought, with his potential quietism, his tenderness, his sure sense of homely values, of pathos and humor lying close together, his instinctive apprehension of the kingly virtues of chivalry, generosity, nobility, and courtesy. Beauty, for such a genius, is not the radiance flung from the "shining palace of the sun," that only an eagle's eye can meet. It is a gentler illumination, often near to sadness, often revealed as a poignant, unaccountable thing, suddenly disclosed and as suddenly withdrawn. In this he may be with Vergil, with Shakespeare, with Dekker, and even with Shelley, but he is certainly not with Marlowe. To the Marlowe of *Tamburlaine,* beauty was a rapture and a sudden glory, the end of man's aspiration; to Greene, a mysterious visitation, mingling tears with joy.

If Greene had been free to choose one from the whole succession of English poets to whom to subdue his imagination, he could hardly have found, unless perhaps in Milton, one more destructive to his native quality. We have seen, in *Alphonsus,* how his verse sinks in the attempt to produce the cadence and rhythms of Marlowe's and this is itself an image of the fate that overtakes his thought, his emotion and each aspect of his dramatic technique. But even as we observe this we are aware that the limpness of his verse, straining at the weight of Marlowe's heroic theme and measure, might in another context be an instrument of some delicacy, capable of its own variety and elasticity:

> Bridle these thoughts, and learn the same of me,
> A quiet life doth pass an empery. (I.i)

The first is as bad a line as the indiscriminate following at once of Marlowe's strength and Marlowe's early clumsiness could make it; the second, in the sweetness alike of its thought and of its cadence, carries us momentarily into a world that is sane, gentle, and secure. And so it is with other moments in the play, where a thought, an emotion disengages itself with pathetic incongruity from the exaggerated hubris and the clamor:

> If ever he had sprung from gentle blood,
> He would not thus misuse his favourer, (II.i)

or a suddenly taut and passionate phrase gives promise of Greene's own later work:

> High Jove be prais'd which hath allotted me
> So fit a time to quite that injury. (IV.ii)[6]

[6] Caught up again later, in the fulness of Greene's dramatic power, as the true climax to a series of passionate speeches and in the context of suspense, by the Prince's words in *Friar Bacon:*

> From Oxford have I posted since I dined.
> To quite a traitor, 'fore that Edward sleep. (III.i)

A flash, again, of fiery chivalry, a hint of that aristocratic dignity which is at its noblest in adversity, which Marlowe seems to have perceived only in his last play, but which, paradoxically, was from the first familiar territory to Greene, already lights up a passage here and there in this preposterous play:

> What, think'st thou, villain, that high Amurack
> Bears such a mind as, for the fear of death,
> He'll yield his daughter . . . ? (V.iii)[7]

Finally, though there is indeed little to be said in commendation of the characters of *Alphonsus,* there is even here one passage at the end which reveals again the presence of qualities, inherent in Greene's mind, that have been overwhelmed and swept away by that genius under which his was "rebuked." When Alphonsus and Iphigena have brought their affairs to a deadlock suggestive rather of that in *The Critic* than of any normal human relationship, the good old man Carinus, the father of Alphonsus, loosens the knot with a few sane speeches, homely and kindly, that carry us forward to the mood of that other father, the King of England, at the end of *James IV.*[8] The character has been imperfectly sketched hitherto, although granted the words on the quiet life that stood out from the context in the first scene. Now he steps into his own, not so much as the father of the triumphant Alphonsus, but as the sole possessor of wisdom, tenderness, sensitiveness, and insight in this graceless play. We turn to him with relief. And the gentle dignity of imagery and music suggests that Greene did too.

Enough has perhaps been said to suggest the nature of Greene's obsession.[9] At the time of writing *Alphonsus,* it would seem that Greene subjected his poetic vision almost wholly to Marlowe's, though it is perfectly clear that his own was of a kind as different as can easily be imagined. We have the evidence of the novels before, and of *Friar Bacon* and *James IV* after, *Alphonsus* to tell us clearly what was the nature of Greene's poetry when it was uncontaminated. But the truth is that we could see this for ourselves from the pages of *Alphonsus* even if no earlier or later writings had survived.

[7] To all who know Greene, it is clear that this is his authentic voice speaking, but again, the echo in *Friar Bacon* confirms us, the framework of the earlier passage serving now to usher in one of the noblest lines Greene ever wrote, one of the great lines of Elizabethan poetry:

> Why, thinks King Henry's son that Margaret's love
> Hangs in the uncertain balance of proud time?

[8] Thou provident kind mother of increase,
Thou must prevail; ah, Nature, thou must rule! (V.vi)

[9] Whether or not this was accompanied by a similar personal relationship is a question outside our scope. We are concerned at the moment with the evident indications of a specific artistic relationship. That evidence would be neither contradicted nor illuminated by taking into account the known habits of both men's lives.

For the most part it is submerged in his limited but complex and contradictory experience of *Tamburlaine,* but enough reaches the surface, in momentary touches of character or direction of plot, in isolated expressions of Greene's own thought and feeling, in lines whose music is still, though faint and evanescent, sweet and gracious, to tell us that this was no beneficent possession.

This state of things could not last. If, again, we had lost all Greene's earlier and later works, and merely known that they had existed, we could still, having followed thus far, have guessed that the next stage would be a revulsion of feeling, a reaction against the dominance of *Tamburlaine,* and that this reaction, though itself healthy, would be peculiarly damaging to any work of art written under its influence and in its mood. This is, I think, precisely what we find in Greene's next play, *Orlando Furioso.*[10]

Putting aside all questions of Greene's debt to Ariosto and the imitation of or satire on the plays of Kyd, and considering only Marlowe's part in the story, it is clear that there are at least three indications of what is happening. Greene is parodying *Tamburlaine,* and principally Tamburlaine himself in the character of Sacripant; he is still imitating Marlowe in some of the ways that we noticed in *Alphonsus;* and his own thought and poetry are finding fuller expression. All this does not prevent the play from being, as a play, an even greater artistic failure than *Alphonsus.* It is a medley,[11] as irresponsible at times as *The Old Wives' Tale* but without the magic or the harmony of mood by which Peele slides from romance to mockery and back to homely gaiety. There is no harmony between any of the three moods Greene reveals in *Orlando.*

The satire on *Tamburlaine* is unmistakable. Sacripant's lines are full of it; the long speeches, especially his death speech at the end of V.i., are often general parodies of Tamburlaine's manner of thought and speech with recognizable phrases from the play imbedded. Sometimes these half-submerged quotations point to the cruder rhetorical passages in Marlowe's play, but sometimes, as in *Alphonsus,* violence is done to his poetry itself:

> Honour, — methinks the title is too base:
> Mighty, glorious, and excellent, — ay, these,
> My glorious genius, sound within my mouth;

[10] *A Looking-Glass for London and England,* which I omit because of the extreme difficulty of disentangling Greene's share from Lodge's, has still, among much that is widely different from Marlowe's work, enough likenesses to both *Tamburlaine* and *Faustus* not only to set up some pretty puzzles of authorship and dating but also to confirm some of our conclusions.

[11] The simultaneous imitation of and satire on *The Spanish Tragedy,* though they do not concern us here, must be given due credit for the variety of tone and texture that they add to the patchwork.

These please the ear, and with a sweet applause,
Make me in terms coequal with the gods. (I.i)[12]

The intention of parody in such passage is, I think, beyond dispute, though it must be admitted that much of such verbal parody in others is recognized as satire principally because it is assigned to Sacripant, whose part as a whole is so evident a satire on Tamburlaine's. But when similar passages occur in the speeches of other characters, we are confronted with a doubt as to where, in this discordant play, the intention of parody gives place to a perhaps unintentional imitation.

For the presence of imitation alongside parody is undeniable and, what is of greater interest, it is often a far better imitation than we found in *Alphonsus.* Throughout the first scene, in speeches which are neither Orlando's nor Sacripant's, imagery and music alike are worthier reproductions of Marlowe's characteristic, if not of his noblest, language. It is as though Greene were achieving now, when we must presume he no longer intends it, what he attempted earlier and could not then achieve. He has to some extent assimilated Marlowe's language and has now, within the limits of his own capacity, arrived at true Aristotelian imitation. This seeming paradox presents no insuperable problem to the student of the artistic process; Greene's mind, now deeply divided, at once repudiates his former obsession and pays it the ultimate homage of learning from it a discipline of language and music that his art might not have reached without it. And so, though what he writes now is in fact a far poorer play than *Alphonsus,* passage after passage (often irrelevant to mood and intention) persuades us that he has received, in the end, not harm but benefit, that what had seemed artistically disastrous in the earlier phase has now, in the moment of repudiation and perhaps because of the repudiation, turned to artistic gain. We cannot, I fancy, trace this in the major aspects of the play's technique; no man could be expected to improve his plotting with some five discrepant sets of material in hand, nor to give depth to all his characters or truth to their relations when torn between divergent purposes. But in the details of technique, as we have suggested, the process can be traced; Greene's verbal music, to go no further, often reaches and even maintains a greater dignity of movement and cadence than was to be found not only in the imitative passages of *Alphonsus* but in those that there seemed most nearly native to him.

This suggestion, that we can trace in *Orlando* a double process of assimilation and rejection, an artistically healthier state than that revealed by

[12] Due allowance must be made for the condition of the text throughout, but this is recognizably Marlowe as we have become accustomed to seeing him in Greene's distorting mirror.

Alphonsus, is confirmed by the continuing emergence of Greene's innate powers. It is obvious that we cannot expect artistic unity from a divided intention, but a play as chaotic as *Orlando* may find room for fragments so irrelevant to its general trend as no work of art would suffer. Angelica is one of those fragments; Marsilius, in his relation to her, is another. In his reading of motive, in his picture of the relationship of father and daughter and of the faithful woman to the man who wrongs her, Greene has come far since his portraits of Iphigena and Carinus. And he certainly did not make that journey under Marlowe's escort. Moreover, even in this unpromising setting, Greene's individual sense of beauty, whether in the English countryside or in human character, finds fuller expression. He understands generosity and magnanimity; Marsilius recognizes that "it fits not for a king / To prize his wrath before his courtesy," and Mandricard responds with an answering gesture that shows us that sudden heights of human feeling and conduct are accessible to Greene. Later, in *Friar Bacon* and *James IV,* these will take their place harmoniously in plays that are attuned to them; here, though unsuited to the emotional context and carelessly woven into the plot, they appear as fragments of Greene's native gift. Lastly, there are, as always in Greene's plays, the exquisite single lines that stay in the memory like fragrance, and they are more frequent than in *Alphonsus.* All in all, Greene, in this impudent and ridiculous play, is emancipating himself very successfully. In the next he is to move with complete freedom.

Friar Bacon and Friar Bungay is familiar to every reader of Elizabethan drama, its quality known and acknowledged. The maturity of tone and mood, the ease with which Greene now controls his plot, his insight into the motives and emotions of his characters, the frank revelation of his faith in plain and homely values, in sweetness and sanity — all these, though the play's technique is sometimes ingenuous — are the mask of a poet in free possession of his native powers. And if we look for signs of its relation to the art of Marlowe, we find the continuation and completion of the process we saw at work in *Orlando;* in spite of and, in part, because of Marlowe's influence, Greene enters now into that possession. We observe, as has just been said, the maturity of Greene's art, the security alike of his humor and of his romance. This is the fulfilment of the growing promise of the two early plays. We see, too, that the achievement here is precisely in line with that early promise, confirming us in the conviction that in those fragmentary passages, irrelevant to the main matter of the play in mood and tone, we were indeed hearing the voice of Greene. Now, through long passages, as in the first scene of the third act, the height of dramatic tension and of emotion is equalled by the movement of the blank verse, the inherent nobility and chivalry of Greene's thought finds expression in that generosity and kingliness of conduct which have now moved to the center of his theme. But perhaps most interesting of all is the relationship to *Faustus,* which many of us still consider to have preceded *Friar Bacon.* If there were no resemblance between the two plays, little would be achieved by setting them side by side; if there were manifest imitations, again we should have to withdraw our claim that Greene was now his own master; if there were signs of satire or bitterness in Greene's gentle mockery, we should have to admit that he was not yet an artist in his own right. But the significant fact is that Friar Bacon is a companion and contrasting figure to Faustus, that the subject matter of *Faustus,* insofar as it touches the practice of magic, is used again by Greene, but that the whole is treated in a mood so different as to make of it a different story, not an imitation, not a parody, but a re-interpretation. We may acknowledge Greene incapable of Marlowe's vision of hell, but we must at least acknowledge also that he does not mock it. Friar Bacon's magic leads to human disaster, but not to the loss of souls. It leads him to a repentance sufficiently serious, but workmanlike and sane, with due promise of amendment of life. There is something matter of fact about the Oxford scholar's attitude, something eminently English in the good-humored and practical emphasis on conduct instead of on thought. Greene is incapable of even a part of Marlowe's understanding, but he has his own interpretation of such legends as that of Friar Bacon and it is that of a man who, knowing this world, values in it the simple virtues of humility and charity that associate it with another. In the last resort, his smile is tolerant. And this is crowning proof that the process of emancipation is complete.

There is no need in this connection to follow him into his last play, *James IV,* since there is, by then, no question of debt to Marlowe, of willing or of unwilling response to an alien genius. His treatment of his sources, the structure of his plot, the grouping of his characters and their self-revelation are as far from Marlowe's in *Edward II* as are by now his language, his cadences, his imagery. If he learnt from Marlowe at all at this stage it was but as every Elizabethan learnt from every other; all trace of a special artistic relationship is gone. And so it is with *Friar Bacon* that the story of Greene's early growth as a dramatic artist ends. His genius had by then prevailed over an influence that, noble in itself, might yet have proved fatal to it, and it had grown to its full power.

But a slight addition may be made to the story and it is perhaps worth making as it, in some sort, sets the seal upon it. The influence of Greene upon the drama of his time was itself wide and has been too generally acknowledged to need description here. His was a pervasive genius; his gift, apart from that "plotting" for which his contemporaries gave him credit, lay in his insight into human motive, his clear sense of certain values in human conduct and in the language and the sweetness of verbal music which were their fitting images. It took nothing by storm, as did Marlowe's, either in thought or in language; but the effects of its influence, though harder to define, were to be found in some surprising places, sometimes, we suspect, among writers who were unconscious of its operation. I think that Marlowe, by one of those paradoxes of the artistic process that delight by their truth no less than their surprise, was himself in the end one of these.

Students of *Tamburlaine* have noticed with interest two characters, Mycetes in the first part and Calyphas in the second, who detach themselves as individuals, utterly unlike the dominant figures. Neither piece of character drawing is strictly necessary to the conduct of the play or to the character grouping. A Persian king could have been deposed to provide the necessary sequence of events without being in himself an interesting sketch of despotic imbecility, and Tamburlaine could have killed an unwarlike son without that son's possessing also the gift of able if cynical justification of his attitude. In fact, we may go further and say that each in his own way momentarily disturbs the plot and the balance of our sympathies by an irrelevant degree of personality. Their characters, slight as they are, are yet drawn with too much individuality for their functions. Marlowe digresses briefly to show an unexpected insight into two minds that question the glory of Tamburlaine's rebellion and to that extent shake our confidence in it. Marlowe's interest is only superficial here and it is no part of his purpose to distract our sympathies from Tamburlaine. If it had been, there are many points in his study where he could have done it more effectively. But the impression remains of his interest in a territory, irrelevant to his intention, that he did not as yet know how to explore.

The characters of the women in his plays, from Zenocrate onwards, confirm the conviction that he knew only imperfectly how to treat the gentler and less clamorous emotions, even when he intended to introduce them. Zenocrate has some exquisite and poignant lines and there are undeniable moments of insight into the nature of her love for Tamburlaine, but he cannot follow her mind as Greene did Margaret of Fressingfield's, and he cannot give her a function in the play. She is there to prompt some of Tamburlaine's noblest speeches, but she does so as a figure and not because of any quality of character in her. The center of Marlowe's interest in the first four plays is the battle of the strong and, despite a certain haunting curiosity, he shows no sign of knowing how to value, much less to assign a dramatic function to, the weak and fragile on one side or the gentle, the tender, and the sensitive on the other.

But in these perceptions lay precisely Greene's virtue and when once he had written *Friar Bacon* he had succeeded in communicating them in a work of art. Indeed, if what we have said so far has been true, he had already made an imperfect and incomplete communication in each of his earlier plays. We assumed at the beginning that his fellow-dramatists knew Marlowe's plays; we may I think assume with equal reason that Marlowe knew whatever else was being written for the Elizabethan stage and that though Greene's two failures may have made relatively little impression, *Friar Bacon,* an evident work of genius, must have made a deeper one. Whatever our views about dating, most of us are agreed that *Edward II* follows *Friar Bacon* and *James IV*. And it is to *Edward II* that this course of reflection leads us.

For in Edward, Marlowe has given the central place in his inner group of characters to a figure weaker than those that immediately surround it and has withdrawn to the periphery the dominant Mortimer, the inheritor of the tradition of titanic rebels against destiny. The Edward of the earlier acts is sensitive and responsive, but tyrannical and imperious, by turns tender and callous, kingly in flashes but irresponsible, an artist, yet self-indulgent and incapable of sustained intention or discipline. Like Richard II, he is destroyed by the simultaneous temptations and demands of his high office and by the pressure of the forces that surround him. His private life is scandalous and his conduct of public life now puerile, now almost insane. Beside him Tamburlaine's is a figure of unflawed purity and purpose, of solid, crystalline integrity, and Barabas is of tough and irreducible metal. Yet he is the focal point of the play, the pivot, albeit insecure, upon which all turns. Marlowe has given him a fragile and intermittent dignity which was all Mycetes lacked to redeem him from the verge of farcical imbecility; and a fine-drawn if self-centered individualism which looks back to Calyphas's cynical clarity and logic. Even more significant than the intent and almost detached accuracy of Marlowe's analysis of Edward's mind is the sureness with which he places him at the center of the play, resting its powerful structure upon his uncertain balance, deriving its events from the interaction of his character with those of the simpler and more powerful characters about it. And in the end, with a fine surprise that reminds us of Greene's sudden moments of insight into the values of conduct, he redeems him by the kingliness of his death, by an instant of magnanimity beyond the reach of Tamburlaine and his peers. It is a strange fulfilment of the uncertain hints in Mycetes and Calyphas; and it may at least be hazarded that Marlowe has here succeeded in exploring hitherto unknown territory and has perceived, by the mediation of Greene's genius, a world of experience which, without it, might have remained hidden and have prompted him to no more than the curiosity that haunted him in *Tamburlaine*.

By what process this assimilation took place it would be vain and even impertinent to conjecture. Marlowe has left us no self-betraying evidence such as Greene's early plays so abundantly afford. But the rich serenity and poetic ease of his last work, *Hero and Leander*, where even the final grace of humor plays its part, reveal a mind at repose in its own strength and assurance. At such a stage of ripe maturity an artist's mind may enter, with a sympathy impossible to its earlier phases, into a world of experience hitherto passed by. Marlowe, as his critics have admitted, called no man father but himself; and those who have recently made the closest study of the processes of his intellect are prepared to look for such paternity as can be discovered in Aristotle, Ramus, Machiavelli, and contemporary science rather than in any of the Elizabethan poets. The suggestion I have here made in no way denies this patent independence of Marlowe's mind, but the seeming paradox of the reciprocal debt may yet complete the story of the artistic relationship between the two poets.

Bedford College, London

SHAKESPEARE'S PROLOGUES AND EPILOGUES

Clifford Leech

Enter Prologue.
For vs, and for our Tragedie,
Heere stooping to your Clemencie:
We begge your hearing Patientlie.

HAM: Is this a Prologue, or the Poesie of a Ring? (III.ii.159-62)

This is one of the four occasions in *Hamlet* where the word "prologue" is used. One of the purposes of this article is to consider why neither this play nor any other of Shakespeare's tragedies written between 1599 and 1608 has either prologue or epilogue despite his familiarity with these devices.

Certainly the practice of beginning and ending a play with a formal address to the audience was common throughout Shakespeare's lifetime. Partly it derived from the prologue and epilogue of Latin comedy, partly from Seneca's use of a monologuizing chorus, partly from the expositors in medieval drama.[1] According to Professor A. N. Wiley, who alone has compiled statistics on this matter, 48 per cent of the plays of the years 1558-1642 have a prologue or an epilogue or both, 16 per cent have only a prologue, 11 per cent only an epilogue.[2] In contrast to this, of Shakespeare's thirty-seven plays, eleven have a prologue or an epilogue or both, one has only a prologue, five have only an epilogue. All such figures must, of course, be regarded with caution. A prologue would constitute the first, an epilogue

[1] E. K. Chambers, *The Elizabethan Stage* (Oxford, 1923), II, 547, n.1; *Rare Prologues and Epilogues 1642-1700,* ed. Autrey Nell Wiley (London, 1940), pp. xxiii-xxiv; Ferdinand Lüders, "Prolog und Epilog bei Shakespeare," *Shakespeare-Jahrbuch,* V (1870), 276.

[2] Wiley, p. xxvii.

the last, page of a manuscript; either might be detached and mislaid.[3] New prologues and epilogues might be written for revivals or for court performances: we know, for example, that Middleton received five shillings for providing prologue and epilogue for the court performance of *Friar Bacon and Friar Bungay* at Christmas, 1602,[4] and Heywood's *Pleasant Dialogues and Dramas* (1637) and Shirley's *Narcissus* (1646) contain numerous prologues and epilogues written for plays by other dramatists or for revivals or special performances. A new prologue or epilogue might be printed along with the original play, as Heywood's were for *The Jew of Malta* in 1634, and as many of the Caroline prologues and epilogues for Beaumont and Fletcher plays appeared in the Folio of 1647. Often the fact that we have these additions to the original text is not indicated in a heading: we can see that the prologue to *The Woman's Prize* is such an addition, because it refers to Fletcher in the past tense, but we cannot be sure that such internal indications will always be found. In the later years of the period, there was a looser connection between a play and its prologue and epilogue than had earlier obtained. This could lead to the use of the same prologue or epilogue for different plays: *Thierry and Theodoret* and *The Noble Gentleman* share a prologue, and *The Woman-Hater* (edition of 1649) and *The Noble Gentleman* an epilogue.[5] Where the relationship with the play was as tenuous as this, we may well believe that a prologue or epilogue might be omitted from the printed book.

Against this, we have to recognize that the vogue of prologues and epilogues became so thoroughly established in the Caroline years that they were then more frequently printed than before; indeed, the reader might well take their inclusion as a guarantee that the play had found its way to the stage. For all these reasons, not only is it difficult to arrive at satisfactory statistics for the incidence of prologues and epilogues, but it is also dangerous in many instances to assume that a particular play either had or did not have these devices at its first performance. Nevertheless, the figures already given for Shakespeare are interesting: only 30 per cent of his plays have an extant prologue or epilogue or both, in contrast to the figure of 48 per cent given by Professor Wiley for the period as a whole.

At this point, however, we need to define the terms. We may take a prologue as being a direct address to the audience, preceding the play, normally spoken by a single actor who is usually but not necessarily alone on the

[3] The Epistle to the Reader prefixed to Aphra Behn's *The Dutch Lover* (1673) says: "The Prologue is by misfortune lost." Quoted by Wiley, p. xxxiii.

[4] *Henslowe's Diary,* ed. W. W. Greg (London, 1908), II, 149.

[5] Other examples are given by Wiley, p. 280, n.l.

stage.[6] The speaker may be an impersonal Prologue or Chorus or may be an abstraction, such as Ate in *Locrine,* and Rumour in *2 Henry IV,*[7] or a person appropriate to the spirit of the action that is to follow (Machiavel in *The Jew of Malta*): it is not the practice to have the prologue spoken in the person of a character in the play.[8] An epilogue is a similar direct address to the audience, again normally spoken by a single actor, but here it is frequent practice for the speaker to remain within the character that he has been acting in the play. The dramatic world and its characters have become fully established in the spectator's mind, and epilogues of this personal type allow that world to linger in a kind of half-existence, so that it comes to terms for a moment with the world outside the play. Often such final addresses to the audience have no separate heading, yet they are clearly epilogues in function and spirit. Thus, in giving the above figures for the incidence of epilogues in Shakespeare, I have included Puck's concluding words in *A Midsummer Night's Dream,* Feste's last song in *Twelfth Night,* and Pandarus's conclusion to *Troilus and Cressida.* With or without the heading, however, it is Shakespeare's normal practice to assign epilogues to characters of the play. In addition to the three instances just mentioned, Rosalind speaks the epilogue to *As You Like It,* the King of France that to *All's Well,* and Prospero that to *The Tempest.* In certain other instances, while not using a character from the play, he still avoids the wholly impersonal address, in both prologue and epilogue: the prologue to *2 Henry IV* is spoken by Rumour, its epilogue by a dancer; in *Pericles* the prologue and epilogue, as well as the inter-act and occasionally inter-scene speeches, are given to Gower; the Prologue to *Troilus,* being "A Prologue arm'd," is given a measure of distinction from the wholly impersonal speaker. Only in *Romeo and Juliet, Henry V,* and *Henry VIII* are prologue and epilogue of the impersonal kind, and special considerations may have operated in each case. It is thus evident that Shakespeare does not normally take advantage of the device to speak to us in his own person. When Marlowe ushers in *1 Tamburlaine* or Jonson *Bartholomew Fair,* we feel that we are hearing the

[6] The Ghost of Don Andrea in *The Spanish Tragedy,* for example, is manifestly a prologue-speaker, though Revenge is present with him.

[7] In this instance the prologue is headed "Induction" in the Folio. The present article is only incidentally concerned with the dramatized prelude, as used in *The Taming of the Shrew* and commonly by Jonson and others, to which the term "induction" is normally applied.

[8] Lüders, pp. 285-86, suggests that the opening speech of *Richard III* has the function of a Euripides prologue, but the use of the dramatic character in this instance separates the speech from the Elizabethan prologue proper. In the printed text, of course, it has no separate heading. In function it resembles the opening speeches of *Hoffman* and *The Revenger's Tragedy.* Don Andrea's Ghost, on the other hand, never takes part in the action of *The Spanish Tragedy.*

tone and emphasis of the writer's own voice, but Shakespeare preserves an indirectness when he could most easily have abandoned it.

If, however, we again look at the incidence of prologue and epilogue in his work, we may notice striking features of distribution. Of his sixteen examples of the two devices, nine come in the group of ten plays extending from *2 Henry IV* (1597-98) to *All's Well* (1602-3);[9] of these ten plays, three have both prologue and epilogue, three have an epilogue alone. Earlier than *2 Henry IV* we find only one prologue, *Romeo and Juliet,* and one epilogue, *A Midsummer Night's Dream,* in fifteen plays. After *All's Well* until *Timon of Athens* (1607-8), we have seven plays with neither prologue nor epilogue. Then, in the remaining five plays, we have two with both prologue and epilogue, and one with an epilogue alone.

We have, indeed, indications, apart from statistics, that there were times of general disfavor for prologues or epilogues. In the prologue to *The Birth of Hercules* (1597, at earliest) we read:

> I am a Prologue, should I not tell y[o]u soe
> You would scarce knowe me; tis soe longe agoe
> Since Prologues were in use; men put behinde
> now, that they were wont to put before.
> Thepilogue is in fashion; prologues no more.[10]

And the prologue to *The Woman-Hater* (*ca.* 1606, edition of 1607) begins:

> Gentlemen, Inductions are out of date, and a Prologue in Verse, is as stale as a black Velvet Cloak, and a Bay Garland.[11]

In 1615 we find the epilogue referred to as customary in J. Cocke's piece of character-writing, *A common Player:* he says, concerning the player's judgment, that he "dares not commend a playes goodnes, till he hath either spoken, or heard the *Epilogue.*"[12] Yet in the dedication to Massinger's *The Unnatural Combat* (*ca.* 1621, printed 1639) the absence of prologue and epilogue in the publication is explained by the fact that the play was "composed at a time . . . when such by-ornaments were not advanced above the fabric of the whole work." Until reliable statistics are compiled, relating to each group of five years within the period and taking into account the possibly varying practices of public and private theaters, it is not easy to assess the weight that should be given to these statements. But a glance at the plays which can be dated from 1590 to 1597 will show a comparative

[9] The dates for Shakespeare's plays here given are those suggested in E. K. Chambers, *William Shakespeare: A Study of Facts and Problems* (Oxford, 1930), I, 270-71. The date of *Timon* is, of course, in dispute, but its placing does not affect the groupings here made.

[10] Quoted by A. N. Wiley, p. xxvii.

[11] Quoted in *The Elizabethan Stage,* II, 547, n.l.

[12] *Ibid.,* IV, 256.

dearth of both prologues and epilogues; then there follows the time in which we have noticed most of Shakespeare's examples as occurring, and here the numbers in general rise sharply. The years 1603-20 show variations in use corresponding to variations in dramatic kind, and must concern us in more detail. Then, for a brief while, there appears to be a dearth again, and this presumably explains Massinger's statement in the dedication to *The Unnatural Combat.* In the Caroline years, however, the practice becomes fully established, in a way clearly anticipatory of that found in the Restoration. We shall see that this represents a change in the function of the prologue and epilogue from that which obtained in the public theaters of Shakespeare's time.

In the earliest Elizabethan years the classical and medieval influences were especially strong. The practice of professional drama on an ambitious level was, too, something of a novelty, and prologue and epilogue could be used to bridge the gap between the worlds of actors and spectators. It appears to have been normal throughout the period for prologues to have been specially written for court performances, and the need which was felt for them on such occasions would be experienced more generally when the London theaters had not fully established themselves as familiar places of resort. Moreover, the tragedies of the earliest years owed much to Senecan example: their strongly "ritual" character would increase the appropriateness of formal address to the audience; their classical handling of the dramatic material would make the prologue useful in conveying information concerning past action. And along with Seneca went the morality inheritance: plays from *Cambises* to *Faustus* did, at least on one level of significance, offer an *exemplum* of a general moral. The prologue could assert the generalization; the play that followed would demonstrate its validity through a single particular; the epilogue, in reminding the audience of the generalization, would complete the framework and preserve the dominance of the moral idea. In these early years we also find the prologues to the two Parts of *Tamburlaine,* which do not assert a moral but which challenge current dramatic practice, explain the writer's purposes, and make prominent mention of the dominant figure in the plays. Here indeed Marlowe is farther from the norm than in *Faustus,* where his employment of prologue and epilogue is thoroughly in tune with medieval practice. Yet it would appear that a tendency to dispense with prologues and epilogues emerged with plays of new, specifically "Elizabethan" kinds. The "romantic" comedies of Greene, *Friar Bacon and Friar Bungay* and *James IV,* do not use the device, and the inductions that we find both with *James IV* and with Peele's *The Old Wives' Tale* may indicate a sense that this new kind of drama might appropriately use a new method of constructing a bridge between play and audience. So, too, the early history plays remarkably avoid prologues and epilogues: this is true of Shakespeare's first "tetralogy" and also of *Edward I, Edward II, Edward III, Woodstock, The Troublesome Reign of King John*[13] and *The Famous Victories of Henry the Fifth.* Marlowe's practice would here seem to be illuminating: he uses prologues for both parts of *Tamburlaine,* prologue and epilogue for *Faustus,* a prologue for *The Jew of Malta,* but neither prologue nor epilogue for *Dido, Edward II,* and *The Massacre at Paris. The Massacre,* indeed, like other late sixteenth-century plays on contemporary French history, may well have been seen in the same light as the plays on English historical themes. Yet, of course, we must not expect complete consistency in the practice, and we find *Titus* without a prologue or epilogue, *Romeo and Juliet* with a prologue and, indeed, a quasi-Senecan chorus preceding Act II. We have noted, moreover, a tendency for prologues and epilogues not to occur in the years immediately following the dramatic activities of the University Wits. From these years, too, few tragedies have survived.

Just before the end of the century, however, two closely related phenomena show themselves. One is the new popularity of the children's companies in the private theaters; the other is the growth of a new form of satiric comedy. In the private theater the audience was comparatively small, and it was homogeneous. The dramatists had the feeling of addressing a group of people with similar outlooks, similar stations in society. This led to the development of a more informal and intimate style of writing, and a readiness to address the audience directly, not in the unbending terms of the old prologue but in the casual and sometimes ironic manner of one who was both preceptor and suitor. The tone, in fact, is very much that of the *Parnassus* plays performed at Cambridge. The new satiric comedy first shows itself in a well-developed form in *Every Man out of his Humour,* acted by the Chamberlain's men, but Jonson's two subsequent comedies of this type were for the children, as of course also were Marston's. The informal talk of prologues and epilogues written for these plays extends itself also to the inductions that they also brought back into favor, as in *1 Antonio and Mellida* (which, in contrast to *Antonio's Revenge,* is more of a satiric comedy than a tragedy), *Every Man out of his Humour, Cynthia's Revels, What You Will,* and *The Malcontent* (where, however, the induction was added for later performance by the King's men). At this time the prologues,

[13] Each of the two Parts of this play is prefaced by a set of verses headed "To the Gentlemen Readers." Those preceding Part I were clearly written with the prologue to *1 Tamburlaine* in mind, but their heading would suggest that no prologue to *The Troublesome Reign* was available to the printer.

epilogues, and inductions suggest, not the sense of the novelty of theater performances that seems to have motivated them earlier, but rather a sense that the theater has become a familiar thing which the authors and spectators are beginning to scrutinize with a sharper eye, so that they turn over in their minds its peculiarities and its purposes. But in the same years there was also a remarkable development of tragedy, of a specifically "Elizabethan" kind, and we find almost no prologues and epilogues in the plays that exemplify it. It will be instructive to list the extant tragedies written, as far as we can ascertain, between 1599 and 1610 and to note their apparent use or avoidance of prologues and epilogues. It may also be worth indicating the instances where the play was first acted in a private theater. Closet dramas and plays written for university performance will be omitted.

	Prologue	*Epilogue*	
Julius Caesar	–	–	
1 Antonio and Mellida	1	1	Private
2 Antonio and Mellida (Antonio's Revenge)	1	1	Private
Hamlet	–	–	
Charlemagne	–	–	
A Woman Killed with Kindness	1	1	
Sejanus	–	–	
Hoffman	–	–	
Othello	–	–	
Bussy d'Ambois	1	1	Private; prologue added for late revival, first published in edition of 1641
King Lear	–	–	
Macbeth	–	–	
Antony and Cleopatra	–	–	
The Rape of Lucrece	–	–	
Sophonisba	1	1	Private
The Devil's Charter	1	1	
Coriolanus	–	–	
Timon of Athens	–	–	
The Revenger's Tragedy	–	–	
The Turk	1	1	Private
1 Biron	1	–	Private
2 Biron	–	–	Private
The Revenge of Bussy d'Ambois	–	–	Private
The Insatiate Countess	–	–	Private
The White Devil	–	–	
The Atheist's Tragedy	–	–	
The Maid's Tragedy	–	–	Private[14]

[14] A rough count of nontragic plays in these twelve years indicates an appreciably

1 Antonio and Mellida, as we have seen, belonged to the satiric rather than the tragic kind, and the use of prologue and epilogue in its sequel can be seen as a mere carrying-over of the practice from the first Part. In writing *A Woman Killed with Kindness,* Heywood was conscious of departing from the normal tragic manner, and his prologue exhibits a certain diffidence, a need for preparing the audience. *Sophonisba* continues Marston's already established habit of using prologues and epilogues. *Biron,* an unusual play in every regard, is the only instance of the use of a prologue for a tragedy written by a major writer in these years where we cannot easily see special circumstances operating; this prologue does, in fact, take us back to the manner of early tragedies, concluding:

> *see in his reuolt,* how honors flood
> Ebbes into ayre, when men are Great, not Good.

The general avoidance of prologue and epilogue provides an important indication that the writers of tragedy in the early seventeenth century were conscious of a difference between their work and that of a decade earlier. Wilhelm Creizenach observed that it was no longer the dramatists' habit to plunge *in medias res* and to need a prologue, as in *The Spanish Tragedy,* to provide a résumé of anterior events,[15] but this is an insufficient explanation of the almost total abandonment of the device. A tragedy might still depend on previous happenings (notably in *Hamlet, Julius Caesar, The Revenger's Tragedy, Hoffman*), but the dramatist in each case has utilized other means of conveying the necessary information to the audience. In *Hamlet,* for example, we become aware of what has happened from the speeches of Horatio in I.i and later from the Ghost's speeches in I.v. Lüders suggested that Shakespeare did not use prologues and epilogues in his major tragedies because he realized that an ideal play should be complete in itself,[16] but the insufficiency of this explanation is demonstrated by Shakespeare's return to the device in some of his final plays. The root of the change seems to lie, rather, in the spirit of the new tragedy. It was no longer, even on the most superficial level, the demonstration of a moral thesis: there was no simple generalization to offer in the prologue and to come back to in the epilogue. The plays exhibit a series of events which show the working out of a process of destruction, usually dependent on the commission of an evil act but also upon the nature of the existing situation. The destruction is no simple

---

larger proportion of prologues, a slightly larger proportion of epilogues. But the non-tragic plays are of so many differing types that some investigation of incidence in each type is needed.

[15] *The English Drama in the Age of Shakespeare* (London, 1916), p. 275.

[16] *Op. cit.,* pp. 290-91.

retribution, for those involved may be innocent or may have offended to only a minor degree. It would be idle to deny a resemblance between some of these plays and the morality dramas — *Macbeth,* for example, has some relation to *Richard III* and *Faustus* and, through them, to the morality itself — but it is shortsighted to see this relationship as dominant in the total effect. We have difficulty today in finding words to represent the "meaning" of an early seventeenth-century tragedy, and the dramatist himself would feel it inappropriate to provide one explicitly in prologue or epilogue. Nor was a bridge generally needed to link the worlds of audience and play, for the new tragic manner was, in comparison with that of the University Wits, realistic in character and event and speech, cultivating something of the informality of satiric comedy. Where the world of the play, however, was more apart than usual from the world of everyday, as in *Macbeth* and *Lear,* the dramatist used opening scenes (the witches, the conversation between Gloucester and Kent) which acted as a bridge but without the explicitness that a prologue would almost inevitably have entailed. The witches symbolize the play's world without making a direct statement on its nature; the talk of Kent and Gloucester makes Lear's world appear for a moment to be reasonably close to ours. On the other hand, if the audience was to be caught up in the world of the play, as in tragedy it must, there was no room for the kind of toying with theatrical purposes and conditions that made prologue, epilogue, and induction common in the other most notable dramatic form of these years.[17] The world of early seventeenth-century tragedy is an image of the cosmos in its variety and its mystery: because of the very inclusiveness of the picture, it was as well that explicit utterance on the play should be avoided. When, however, Shakespeare was inserting in *Hamlet* a mock tragedy on an antique model, it was appropriate that he should employ the old prologue device. As it was a miniature tragedy, however, and the moral could hardly be given to Claudius in express terms, the briefest of prologues had to serve.

When Shakespeare's tragic period was over, he returned to prologue and epilogue with *Pericles.* This may have arisen through his taking over an existing or partly existing play, yet there is no doubt that the use of a commentator at beginning and end, and at intervals during the play, is fitting for this more relaxed dramatic kind. He apparently abandoned the device again in *Cymbeline* and *The Winter's Tale,* but he remembered the prece-

[17] *Hamlet* is, of course, an exception here. It belongs to some extent to the world of satiric comedy: even so, however, it puts the comment on theatrical matters into the body of the play and thus avoids the heavy emphasis that is given when it occurs in an induction. See J. M. Nosworthy, "The Structural Experiment in *Hamlet,*" *RES,* XXII (1946), 281-86.

dent of *Pericles* when he wished to indicate in *The Winter's Tale* the passing of sixteen years between the third and fourth acts. To *The Tempest* he added an epilogue, and the effect is appropriate enough there: the final insistence on prayer (for Prospero links the request for applause with the general reference to "prayer,/Which pierces so that it assaults/Mercy itself, and frees all faults") is in keeping with the brooding air of much of this play. Though Shakespeare's practice is not a uniform one in these final romances, the fact that to some extent he makes use of prologue and epilogue does serve as a pointer to the different approach that characterizes them. Beaumont and Fletcher, who would not be so conscious of a difference between tragedy and romantic tragicomedy, apparently used neither prologue nor epilogue for *Philaster* and *A King and No King.*

In the Caroline years, as we have noted, there is a more persistent use of the devices than ever before. By this time, in the private theaters now used by the adult players, we have in a more stable form conditions very similar to those that obtained for the children's performances at the turn of the century. The audience was a homogeneous one, its tastes were for comedy rather than tragedy, and its occasional tragedies (Ford's almost alone excepted) were derivative and patently contrived. The group-feeling, moreover, was doubtless increased through the growing division in the country, with the actors and audience of the private London theaters being, with few exceptions, on the side of royalty. Within the group, however, there was plenty of room for debate and critical complaint. Prologues and epilogues could make fun of the audience's tastes, as in the epilogue to *The Broken Heart* and in Theophilus Bird's prologue to *The Lady's Trial;* they could complain that with greater sophistication had come excessive demands on the playwright, as in the prologue to Davenant's *The Unfortunate Lovers;* they could assert critical principles, as in Shirley's insistence on the virtues of plain language in his prologue to *The Brothers.* All this is close to what Jonson and Marston were doing for the children's performances a quarter of a century before. Yet the tone is not quite the same. The Caroline prologues and epilogues are on the whole rather more relaxed and assured; there is less in them of a sense of novelty, of the eccentric. This was in part due to a general difference in temper between the dramatic writing around 1600 and that of Charles's years, for the plays differ in these respects at least as much as the prologues and epilogues, and partly also it may have come from the fact that in the earlier private theaters it was the children who acted, giving to the whole performance a sense of oddity and extravagance, and thus easily occasioning the note of challenge. Nothing, however, could be further from the prologues and epilogues around 1590, and earlier, than these that we find in the Caroline theater. The relation between prologue and epilogue on the one hand and play on the other was now often barely existent, and, as we have seen, a prologue or epilogue could be used for more than one play. They normally functioned as a means of arousing the audience's attention by means of witty observation, making people feel once again at home in their playhouse: what followed or preceded might be tragedy or comedy or pastoral, but little clue would be given through the speaker's words.

I should add a few comments on certain Shakespearean prologues and epilogues that have so far been rapidly passed over. The prologue to *Romeo and Juliet,* together with the chorus passage preceding Act II, associates the play with the earlier, more Senecan tragic type. In the prologue we have a general sketch of the action, with an indication of the moral lesson. Lüders suggested that the omission of this prologue in the Folio text was due to its having been dropped in performance,[18] but this would depend on the Folio editor having access to a playhouse manuscript: there appears to be no evidence of this.[19] In any event, the Folio retained the chorus passage between Acts I and II, which would surely have been dropped along with the prologue if any omission were made.

According to G. L. Kittredge, Puck's epilogue to *A Midsummer Night's Dream* may have been added when the text was revised for public performance, the original version having been planned for a wedding festivity.[20] Professor Dover Wilson, on the other hand, thinks it was part of the play as originally written for public performance, the rest of the Fairies' speeches in the last scene constituting an addition for a private occasion.[21] We might, however, expect the epilogue in the socially homogeneous gathering rather than in the public theater: no certainty is here possible, but this is the only extant Shakespearean epilogue before *2 Henry IV* and special circumstances of performance may provide the more likely explanation.

This brings us to the group of plays in which Shakespeare most frequently used the prologue and, more particularly, the epilogue. The earliest in date is probably *2 Henry IV,* which is certainly the earliest Shakespeare history for which prologue or epilogue is extant. One function of the prologue is immediately obvious: the audience is to be reminded of the events of Part I,

[18] *Op. cit.*, p. 285, n.2.

[19] Cf. *Romeo and Juliet,* ed. Richard Hosley, *The Yale Shakespeare* (New Haven, 1954), p. 162; *Romeo and Juliet,* ed. J. Dover Wilson and George Ian Duthie, *New Cambridge Shakespeare* (Cambridge, Eng., 1955), p. 112.

[20] *Sixteen Plays of Shakespeare,* ed. George Lyman Kittredge (Boston, 1946), p. 146.

[21] *A Midsummer Night's Dream,* ed. Sir Arthur Quiller-Couch and J. Dover Wilson, *New Cambridge Shakespeare* (Cambridge, Eng., 1924), p. 88.

and must be made aware of the falsity of the favorable news brought to Northumberland at the beginning of I.i. Yet we would as readily have expected a prologue before *3 Henry VI.* This prologue, moreover, is no bare recital of fact. It is spoken by Rumour, and the tone is markedly satiric: those who vent rumours form "the blunt monster with uncounted heads"; the audience in the theater is Rumour's "household"; the source of rumours is "surmises, jealousies, conjectures," and their common nature is "continual slanders." Here indeed we have moved into the world of satiric comedy, and the play that follows has itself affiliations with that dramatic kind. We can date the writing of *2 Henry IV* not later than February 25, 1598,[22] but we cannot be sure that this prologue, whose Folio-heading "Induction" may reinforce the link with the satiric comedies, was written along with the play: its date of publication was 1600, while *Every Man out of his Humour* and *1 Antonio and Mellida* were first acted in 1599. In any event, it fittingly introduces the kind of critical comment that Shakespeare was not infrequently to make on human affairs in the years that followed. The epilogue is in prose; although no name is given to the speaker, the fact that he is a dancer is insisted upon, and in this way the author remains again remote. Its most apparent dramatic function is to link the play with its sequel; its tone is light and relaxed, rather in contrast to the high seriousness of the rejection scene and the accompanying promise of martial glory. In the Quarto of 1600 the reference to praying for the Queen comes at the end of the first of the three paragraphs, but the rearrangement in the Folio brings it to a more probable position at the end of the epilogue. It seems likely that in its original form there was only the first paragraph, bringing this very complex play to a relaxed ending: Shakespeare then aimed at increasing this effect of relaxation by inserting the references to the dance and the French campaign ("with Sir John in it"), but the insertion was taken by the printer as a simple addition.[23] The tone is indeed different from that of the prologue: together they point to opposing impulses within the play.

As far as our evidence indicates, *2 Henry IV* was the first play in which Shakespeare used both prologue and epilogue. In its sequel he went much further than this, using chorus speeches between the acts as well as at the beginning and end. This, presumably, was what had been at first intended for *Romeo and Juliet,* and indeed it is in line with the early practice that we see in *The Spanish Tragedy* and *The Battle of Alcazar,* and with the neo-

[22] Chambers, *William Shakespeare: A Study of Facts and Problems,* I, 248.

[23] Other possibilities have been suggested: see *2 Henry IV,* ed. Matthias A. Shaaber, *New Variorum Shakespeare* (1940), pp. 459-60.

classic tradition generally. Here Shakespeare appears to have sought the kind of framework which would most heavily underline the basic impulse in this play, producing indeed the effect that we have associated with the earlier prologues and epilogues. *Henry V* has certain elements (such as the King's debate with his private soldiers, the references to savagery in battle, the satiric presentation of some of Henry's soldiers, an occasional discomforting word of the King) which run counter to the theme of glory. It is, however, that theme that is dominant, and the chorus speeches insure that it is safely so. They have, too, a dramatic function in holding together what might otherwise seem a loose chronicle, and in making us duly impressed by the Agincourt battle that Shakespeare knew was not easy to make impressive on his stage. The effect is enhanced through the use of an impersonal Chorus, who speaks for the author in a way unusual in Shakespeare. We should, however, be on dangerous ground if we suggested that this is, without qualification, the author's voice. We might say, rather, that it is the explicit assertion of an attitude that, in this play of respite from civil strife, Shakespeare wanted us to take up: he did not want here the manifest complexity of feeling that he doubtless realized had developed in his previous history play. The use of the sonnet form for the epilogue, as for the prologue to *Romeo and Juliet,* also underlines the return to the more formal style and gives a sense of completion to the play.

At about the same time Shakespeare wrote epilogues for *As You Like It* and *Twelfth Night,* using prose for the first and song for the second, and in each case assigning the speech to a prominent character in the play. Rosalind's epilogue is light in tone, a little like that to *2 Henry IV,* and brings a character from the Forest of Arden into close touch with the spectators' world: "If I were a woman, I would kiss as many of you as had beards that pleas'd me"; Feste's concluding song does in a sense function in the reverse fashion, emphasizing the merely playhouse character of the comedy and leaving Feste a rather forlorn figure in his offstage existence. In both instances, however, Shakespeare was using the epilogue to place the comedy in relation to the everyday world. And the variation in form and in approach shows that he was experimenting with the revived practice.

But perhaps the most interesting of all plays in relation to the use of prologue and epilogue is *Troilus and Cressida.* Here we have "A Prologue arm'd" and an epilogue spoken by an important character. The nearest Shakespearean analogue to the prologue is that for *2 Henry IV;* the epilogue is partly in prose, thus associating itself with those for *2 Henry IV* and *As You Like It,* and there is also a snatch of song which takes it in the direction of *Twelfth Night.* The note of challenge is strong in both prologue and epilogue. The prologue takes up a position of impartiality in the struggle at Troy: "The ravish'd Helen, Menelaus' queen,/With wanton Paris sleeps; and that's the quarrel"; "Now expectation, tickling skittish spirits,/On one and other side." It makes a learned reference to Horace, and ends with an unaccommodating suggestion that the audience's tastes are as haphazard as the chance of war:

> Like or find fault; do as your pleasures are;
> Now good or bad, 'tis but the chance of war.

The reason why there is no reference to Troilus and Cressida here may be that any mention of an affectionate love would have had a softening effect on this opening. The epilogue brings Pandarus very much into the audience's world, and he suggests that the less agreeable of the things that the play has presented are not foreign to that world. He is, of course, more hostile in his comments than Feste is in the *Twelfth Night* epilogue, but a resemblance exists.[24] Professor Harold S. Wilson, in arguing that we must take *Troilus* as a tragedy, has confessed that this epilogue will not fit into his picture of the play's design.[25] Indeed, the mere presence of prologue and epilogue in this play associates it with the satiric comedies of the time, and Shakespeare seems to have taken trouble to underline the play's satiric impulse through the special tone of his introduction and conclusion.

There is a singularly brief and poor epilogue to *All's Well,* spoken by the King of France. This, of course, is a play that has been associated with *Troilus, Measure for Measure,* and the satiric comedies of Jonson and Marston. Shakespeare may have included an epilogue here because he was aware of this connection, though *Measure for Measure,* where indeed there is a far greater complexity in the design, has no epilogue, or he may have felt that the rather uneasy ending of *All's Well* needed the word of tidying that an epilogue could roughly provide. As far as our knowledge goes, this is the last epilogue that he wrote before *Pericles.*

In the group of last plays, we find Gower as prologue-, epilogue-, and chorus-speaker, using for the most part the octosyllabic couplets of the *Confessio Amantis:* a near-parallel is provided by the use of Skelton and Skeltonics in Munday and Chettle's *Robin Hood* plays. We have already noticed the way in which Shakespeare's return to the use of prologue and epilogue reflects his turning to a new kind of drama. Apart from the prologue and epilogue to *Henry VIII,* however, he avoids, as usual, the impersonal speech.

[24] Leslie Hotson, *The First Night of Twelfth Night* (London, 1954), pp. 167-71, has emphasized the bluntness of Feste's observations.

[25] *On the Design of Shakespearian Tragedy* (Toronto, 1957), p. 136.

It need not be emphasized that this discussion of Shakespeare's use of prologues and epilogues, and its relation to current practices in his time, is merely exploratory of ground that has hitherto been little considered. We need a fuller compilation of statistics than has yet been attempted, and a thorough consideration of the differences in function and tone among prologues and epilogues from *Gorboduc* to the closing of the theaters, and it would also be useful to trace their varying employment of blank verse, rhymed couplets and other rhymed forms, and prose. What does perhaps emerge now is that Shakespeare's practice was rarely haphazard, that, to some extent at least, he reflects current fashions but does so in a way that helps us to comprehend his approach to his varying dramatic task. In particular, the consideration of their prologues and epilogues should further our understanding of *2 Henry IV* and *Troilus and Cressida,* and the almost total absence of the device in the earliest seventeenth-century tragedy should help us to recognize the special character of that dramatic kind.

University of Durham, England

GILES FLETCHER AND THE CATHOLICS

Allan Holaday

After the English Reformation, the Fletchers became almost as notable for extreme anti-Catholicism as for poetry. Their antagonism began, apparently, with the elder Richard Fletcher, grandfather of Phineas, Giles, and John, who, after standing with John Fox for ordination by Nicholas Ridley,[1] suffered imprisonment and near-martyrdom in the Marian persecutions. "Hatred of the papacy became the family heritage," notes Abram Langdale;[2] "it seems to have cost the vicar's [i.e., Richard's] eldest son his life, and to have led the second son, Giles, perilously close to the execution block." Phineas carried the family bitterness undiminished into the third generation, letting it affect in one way or another nearly everything he wrote. As Langdale continues, hatred of Romanism, "tempered his [i.e., Richard's] spirit, making of it a sword which he handed on to his sons and their sons, and the blade kept all its sharpness for one hundred years."[3]

A modification of the family's extreme attitude finally appeared in the younger Giles Fletcher, Phineas' brother. Langdale, who properly concerns himself with Phineas, offers no comment on Giles' less elaborate antagonism. But finding an explanation for the younger poet's point of view becomes a matter of some interest, since the bitterness burned so fiercely in Phineas, and since, during the years in which each produced his principal works, the brothers shared ideas with extraordinary thoroughness.[4] If Giles had not

[1] Strype's *Ecclesiastical Memorials* (Oxford, 1922), II, 402.

[2] *Phineas Fletcher, Man of Letters, Science, and Divinity* (New York, 1937), pp. 5 f.

[3] *Ibid.*

[4] As Phineas remarked in *The Purple Island,* I, 3:

> Their souls self-same in nearer love did grow:
> So seem'd two joyn'd in one, or one disjoyn'd in two.

Such remarks as this, of which several appear in the works of both poets, only cor-

mentioned the Catholic issue, or, if he had avoided provocative attacks generally, we might assume that he shared the family hatred without expressing it. But on several occasions he discussed the Catholic problem, and in belaboring lay parsons, nonresident clergymen, and false prophets, he laid about him with all the vigor that Phineas had turned on the Papists. Apparently the explanation is less simple than at first seems likely.

Since Giles' attitude chiefly resulted, I think, from his response to a changing intellectual climate, its explanation has significance beyond that of the usual biographical detail. To say, simply, that he feared the new philosophy as the ultimate destroyer of faith and therefore looked with friendly eye upon the conservative Church would oversimplify to the point of error. Yet he undoubtedly sensed in the incipient skepticism of his age, one cause for the many "euill heartes of vnbeliefe, all standing ready to depart from the liuing God."[5] And since from early youth he had dedicated himself to awakening in men an unequivocal acceptance of Christ as the essential to salvation, he would, with severe reservations, accept the Catholic church as an ally — wrong in theological details and politically dangerous, but still an ally. One characteristic of the Catholic Counter-Reformation, as Professor Coffin notes,[6] was resistance to the new philosophy. And although Giles, like many an intellectual, occasionally manifested the new influences, and although he pointedly criticized the Catholic church for failure to apply methods of biblical interpretation in harmony with the new point of view, he still sensed that in the basic struggle for the Christian essentials — the Living and the written Word — the Church and he were on the same side.

During a youth passed in Jacobean Cambridge, where he heard Anglican, all shades of Puritan, and even Catholic doctrine vigorously debated, Giles, like Donne, Phineas' friend Edward Benlowes, and many others sensed an incipient splintering of truth. Implicit not only in the new astronomy and physiology, but also in the new geography and the new concern for various non-Christian religions lay disturbing implications. In his reference to "a threatened philosophy and a dimly threatened religion,"[7] S. L. Bethell accurately suggests the dawning conception among some intellectuals of what lay ahead; for others besides Donne, the new philosophy had called

---

roborate the evidence of interdependence apparent in dozens of correspondences readily noticed in their poetry.

[5] *The Reward of the Faithfull,* sig. A4^v — hereafter cited as *RF.*

[6] Charles Monroe Coffin, *John Donne and the New Philosophy* (New York, 1937), p. 75.

[7] *The Cultural Revolution of the Seventeenth Century* (London, 1951), p. 88.

all in doubt. As Bethell implics, the impact first shook the old philosophy: either the stars moved or they did not; either the earth stood at the center, or it did not. But less quickly did men urge the religious implications in a new discovery, the champions of religion, in fact, usually supporting the exponents of the new science. Fletcher, for example, has only warm praise for Bacon;[8] Herbert apparently assisted in making a Latin translation of the *Advancement;* and even Hobbes managed to sound orthodox. Yet for an increasing number of men, a realization that all could not be well when such books as Kepler's *De Stella Nova* and Galileo's *Sidereus Nuncius* continued to appear manifested itself in an energetic concern for religion. The widespread dedication after the turn of the century to intensely original religious poetry; the fashion of scorning all except divine topics as unworthy of verse; and the increased interest in problems involving natural theology and grace, all of which Fletcher manifested, arose in part, at least, from a growing concern for faith. Men accept complacently an established tenet; only when challenged does it inspire its hosts of defenders.

What evidence have we that Fletcher responded to the threat? As he tells us again and again in *The Reward of the Faithfull,* he found his age indifferent to religion. In *Christs Victorie and Triumph* he sought by decorating the familiar scriptural account with paradox, baroque figures, and other trappings of theological wit to startle his readers from complacency. His theme, announced in a gloss to the first stanza, is man's salvation through Christ. In dealing with the crucial problem of natural and revealed religion, he accepted, in Anglican tradition, the importance of reason; in fact, man learns about God through his "eye of reason, guided (like the wise men in search of our Sauiour) by the heauenly starres of light that shine euery where in Gods word"; but Fletcher insisted that by reason we come only to "the out-side of Gods Temple"; we but reach "the Porch dore";[9] the essential addition must come through Christ and the Scriptures.

For our purposes, however, the important thing to notice is that Fletcher here uses *reason* in an early sense, the sense employed by Jewel, Hooker, and Andrewes. Yet what he fears is the developing tendency, which he already detects, to identify as *reasonable* and *logical* only what may be demonstrated to the senses, a connotation fostered by the new empiricism, and one that grew increasingly apparent in the Age of Reason. "And what might the reason be of so much infidelitie among so many beleeuers of vs?" he asks. "Is it not because they liue neither as iust men by Faith, nor as

[8] *RF,* sigs. A3^{v} ff. Since Bacon had granted Fletcher the living at Helmingham and had later helped him exchange it for that at Alderton, Fletcher had reason to be grateful.

[9] *RF,* sigs. D5^{r-v}; P1^{r}.

wise men, by reason, but wholy by sence? so ignorant are they, & like bruit Beasts before God, beleeuing only what they see, *& quae sunt ante pedes,* as the Oratour speakes, what they must needes stumble vpon with their eyes, and no more? Well: hast thou both thine eyes out of Faith, and Reason?" (***RF,*** sigs. $R6^{v}$-$R7^{v}$). Clearly Fletcher, ahead of his age, has sensed a significant change in what some men were willing to call reasonable.

He clearly anticipated also another result of the new empiricism in his appeal to self-interest. Long before Tillotson, Giles exploited a prudential motivation for virtue, urging the practical utility, even the expediency, of Christianity. In *Christs Victorie and Triumph,* III, 10, he remarked:

> . . . and yet the creature hasts to runne
> From his Creator, and self-good doth shunne . . . .

And in *The Reward of the Faithfull* he observed that "wee are all naturally engrossers of goods for our selues, but wee are loth, though iustly, to diuide or part them, with any other; and therefore with more reason the religious man, who is the most ambitious creature vnder heauen, may whet and edge his flaming desires to goe through all the sweat and labour of righteousnesse. . . . " And a little later he noted "that Religion should bee thought good husbandrie, and should enrich the man, that is a faithfull practiser of it" (***RF,*** sigs. $F1^{r-v}$; $I3^{r}$; $I6^{r}$; $I9^{v}$-$I10^{r}$). In such remarks one can almost hear the clergymen of the next age or even that epitome of the age, Ben Franklin, observing that nothing is so likely to make a man's fortune as virtue.

And he shared sufficiently in the new learning to understand its implications. Because of his intellectual intimacy with Phineas, he could hardly have escaped the new ideas. About 1608 or 1609, during the composition of their masterpieces, *Christs Victorie and Triumph* and *The Purple Island,* the brothers' intellectual interdependence reached its height.[10] But as early as 1604 Phineas in a Latin poem had evidenced his scientific interests,[11] revealing a taste that became emphatically apparent later. From his study of Phineas' scientific knowledge, Langdale decided that "in physiology, in all science, as we shall find, he was a Baconian and was in advance of the average contemporary writer."[12] And Giles, who knew so well his brother's work and his brother's mind, also understood the new point of view.

In *Christs Victorie and Triumph,* Giles readily mentioned various planets, stars, and constellations (a feat by no means extraordinary, of course), expressed some interest in celestial geography, and accurately interpreted a

[10] Each refers in his poem to his brother's work, and each freely borrows imagery and phraseology from the other. I note well over three dozen clearly recognizable correspondences in language or idea between the two poems.

[11] I accept Langdale's dating of the work, *op. cit.*, p. 39.

[12] *Ibid.*, p. 107.

solar eclipse (I, 41). But, most significant of all, even though, like Milton, he constructed a Ptolemaic stage for his action, he conceded the reality of a newer arrangement. In describing Mercy, Fletcher drew an elaborate analogy with the solar system, noting that among the stars that require a sun "to giue their tapers light," (i.e., among the planets) "where the Sunne centers himselfe by right" shone Mercy's face. In other words, he placed the sun at the center. In *The Reward of the Faithfull* one notes also his reference to "wandring Starres" (sig. F2^{v}); the impossibility, as "Phylosophy teaches us" of instantaneous motion (sig. K5^{r}); and to a scientific demonstration, which he described accurately, performed by "those who are skilfull in the Opticks" (sigs. D9^{r-v}).

Often his thinking indirectly reflected attitudes associated with the new empiricism. Interest in primary authorities and texts, in philology and linguistics characterized the new thought, and Fletcher revealed such interests more than once.[13] Even his strenuous emphasis upon the Scriptures, freed from all "rotten and vnwritten Traditions" reflects the "definite search for fundamental sources, the causes and grounds of truth"[14] that Professor Coffin associates with the new learning. The impact of geographical accounts, particularly those involving religious information, affected his thinking. Of them all, Fletcher knew best that by Edward Brerewood, professor of astronomy in Gresham College, London, whose *Enqviries Tovching the Diversity of Langvages and Religions Through the Chiefe Parts of the World* (1614) he closely followed. After noting that Christians occupy but five parts in thirty in this world, rapidly expanded by the new science, he proceeded, following Brerewood, to discuss various faiths (*RF,* sigs. P6^{v} ff.). And, quite aware of his method in all such argument, he paused to note, "But some perhaps will thinke this discourse . . . to be fetch'd rather out of the schools of Reason, then of Gods Word, and to haue more ground in Philosophy then Faith" (sigs. E5^{v}-E6^{r}).

Since for Fletcher, then, the central issue was the establishing of Christ and Scripture as religious essentials, he, like Donne, could look with some tolerance upon Catholics. Like Donne, too, who wrote "The channels of God's mercies run through both fields; they are sister teats of his graces, yet both diseased and infected, but not both alike,"[15] Fletcher also saw the faults in both churches. And, like a man of the new age, he charged the Catholics

[13] *E.g., RF,* sigs. P5^{v} ff.; Q2^{r} ff.; R2^{r} ff.; S6^{r}.

[14] *John Donne,* p. 291.

[15] From a letter given by Edmund Wilson Gosse, *The Life and Letters of John Donne* (New York and London, 1899), II, 78. I have taken the above excerpt from R. C. Bald's edition of Southwell's *An Humble Supplication* (Cambridge, Eng., 1953), p. 80.

with failure to employ methods that had risen to dignity with the new learning:

Well, when wee heare say, hee [i.e., the pope] is better able to make good his Interpretations by the Lights of Art, & helpe of Tongues, and authoritie of Scriptures, rightly inferred from the Collation of places, the significancy of phrases, the light of circumstances, the Ayme of the words, and the Analogie of Faith, and hath ioyned to all these a sincere loue of the Trueth, without any siding, and part-taking for gainefull and honourable respects, and an vnwearied search for it without praeiudicating affections (all which together make vp, not an infallible, but the least fallible Interpretour,

why then, perhaps, we can accept his interpretation. But in the meantime, "It is best therefore to keep on this side of the seas" from the whore of Babylon "and to consider those Ecclesiasticall home-Droanes . . . which hiue themselues vnder the shadow of our Church" (*RF,* sigs. S6^r-S7^r).

University of Illinois

CONJECTURES ON *THE LONDON PRODIGAL*

Baldwin Maxwell

The only surviving quarto of *The London Prodigal,* which appears to have been printed without entry upon the Stationers' Register, bears the date 1605, and there seems to be no reason to suspect that there may have been an earlier issue. The title page presents the thoroughly unambiguous claim that the play was "By *William Shakespeare*" and had been "plaide by the Kings Maiesties seruants." The argument and the setting are obviously unlike those of any play known to have been by Shakespeare; and, though the text may well be rather badly mangled, there are not to be found, as there are perhaps in *A Yorkshire Tragedy,* occasional lines which may be thought not unworthy of Shakespeare's pen. Wholly lacking are passages which may be pronounced bold or original in language or characterized by any depth of thought. The abundant moralizing is in every respect conventional.

The Argument

I.i. Father (Old Flowerdale), just returned from Venice, explains to Uncle (his brother) that he has disguised himself that he may the better inquire into the behavior of Flowerdale (his son). Uncle's account of Flowerdale's prodigality is interrupted by the latter's entrance after Father has instructed Uncle to report to Flowerdale that his father has died and has intrusted his will to a sailor Christopher, the disguise Father has assumed. Flowerdale has come to borrow more money to enable him, he says, to marry Luce, daughter of Sir Lancelot Spurrock. Learning that his father's ship has returned, he claims to have received a letter from his father, dated in October, telling of rich cloth sent him, but Uncle, supported by Father (i.e., Christopher), announces that his father had died in June. Father produces the will, from which Flowerdale discovers that he has been bequeathed only "two bayle of false dyce" and certain precepts. He thereupon renews his request for a loan, which Uncle grants upon Father's entreaty. Father's offer to become Flowerdale's manservant is accepted.

I.ii. Sir Lancelot, traveling toward his home with two of his daughters, discusses with Master Weathercock, a parasite, the matrimonial prospects of his three daughters: Delia has resolved to remain a maid; Frank, a "sillie girle, a foole," has as yet no suitor; Luce's hand is sought by Sir Arthur Greenshield, a gallant soldier but poor, by Oliver, the Devonshire lad, a wary fellow, rich and full of wit, and by young Flowerdale, "all aire, Light as a feather, changing as the wind." Master Civet, much enamored of Frank, has followed Sir Lancelot's party to learn her identity. After the boastful Flowerdale has joined the group, wine is brought in, ordered for them by Civet, who is sent for and invited to Lewsome, Sir Lancelot's home in Kent.

II.i. At Lewsome Sir Arthur, impressing soldiers, is on the point of impressing Oliver when Sir Lancelot, returning with the others, intercedes. With Luce's three suitors present, Sir Lancelot expresses his preference for the rich Oliver, but Luce in an aside tells Sir Arthur she loves only him. It is announced that Civet has arrived to seek the hand of Frank. After the others have left, Flowerdale at Father's suggestion advises Oliver that he shall "hear from him." Oliver gone, Father suggests that they draw Flowerdale a will, naming Luce and Sir Lancelot his heirs, "Where weele set downe land that we neuer sawe," and promises that Weathercock, told of it in confidence, will quickly report to Sir Lancelot, who shall "intreat you take his daughter."

II.ii. The servant Daffidill, also in love with Luce, when repulsed by her, snatches her bracelet. Sir Lancelot, recognizing it on his arm, dismisses him from his service.

II.iii. Luce tells Sir Arthur that if she may choose, she shall be his wife.

II.iv. After Sir Lancelot has promised Oliver that he shall marry Luce with all speed, Father brings Flowerdale's challenge to Oliver, who over Sir Lancelot's protest declares he will be at the appointed place. To Sir Lancelot, now alone, Weathercock hastily enters to tell of Flowerdale's great wealth as revealed in his will, and the two of them hurry off to forestall the duel, Sir Lancelot promising an immediate double wedding: "*Luce* shall be *Flowerdales*."

III.i. The third sister, Delia, offers good advice on husbandry to the silly Frank and the almost equally silly Civet.

III.ii. Upon Sir Lancelot's arrival at his lodgings, Flowerdale, protesting first that he is too busy to see him, then that he has no quarrel with Oliver, agrees with feigned reluctance to fail the meeting with Oliver and proceed to marriage with Luce. Once Sir Lancelot has gone, Flowerdale declares he cares nothing for Luce but will merrily spend her dowry. When Uncle enters after Flowerdale's exit, Father instructs him to have Flowerdale arrested for debt immediately upon his marriage; by such means he hopes to test Luce's love and to reform his son.

III.iii. Oliver arrives at the place appointed for the duel, followed by Sir Arthur, who wishes to see fair play. Daffidill, entering to report that Luce has been married to Flowerdale, is followed by Uncle and sheriff's officers. As the wedding party comes from the church, Flowerdale is arrested and the fraudulence of the will revealed. Sir Lancelot, refusing to supply bail, seeks to take Luce home with him, but she, though married against her wishes, will, she says, remain with her husband. After the others have left, Uncle at Luce's entreaty releases Flowerdale, and to provide for Luce's care gives one hundred angels to Father, which he, again at her entreaty, hands over to Flowerdale. When her husband leaves, ordering her not to follow, Father promises to help her to a disguise and to place her in service in the town.

IV.i. Leaving for their home, Frank and Civet extract promises from the others to attend their wedding feast. Sir Arthur and Oliver go to seek and succor Luce.

IV.ii. Having lost the one hundred angels at dice, Flowerdale wishes he could take a purse. As he is about to rob Delia and her servant, he is thwarted by the entrance of Sir Arthur and Oliver.

IV.iii. As Civet and Frank talk with Father and Luce, who, disguised as a "Dutch frow," has entered their service, Delia arrives to help her silly sister with her new house, and her servant tells of Flowerdale's effort to rob them.

V.i. Refused a loan by those to whom he had lost the one hundred angels, Flowerdale with varying success begs aid from a prostitute, an ancient citizen, a citizen's wife, Oliver, Sir Arthur, and finally his uncle, who enters with Father. Father calls to Tanikin (Luce in her Dutch disguise) to open the door. As she does so she recognizes Flowerdale, questions him, and is told that his wife, having brought him to beggary, has died. He seeks to persuade her to steal Civet's plate for him. Tanikin called within, Father upbraids Flowerdale, urges him to leave if he would escape hanging, but Flowerdale declares he will await Tanikin's return. When, all but the servants having entered, Sir Lancelot orders Flowerdale arrested for the murder of his wife, Luce reveals herself and again declares her love and duty to her husband. Flowerdale repents, but is further accused by Sir Lancelot of having caused the death of his father. Father, thereupon, reveals himself, and all ends happily, though Delia again refuses to marry either Sir Arthur or Oliver.

Although *The London Prodigal* was included in the third and fourth folios of Shakespeare, 1664 and 1685, and was several times reprinted in the first half of the eighteenth century as a play by Shakespeare,[1] during the past two hundred years only a few of the earlier German critics[2] and still fewer of the English have been so bold as to urge Shakespeare's authorship. Fleay, impressed by the evidence of the title page, suggested that Shakespeare may have "plotted" the play, but he denied him any of its lines. Shakespeare's authorship was, however, argued in 1875 by Richard Simpson,[3] who saw the play as an attack by Shakespeare upon his old belittler, Robert Greene. To support the ascription of the title page, Simpson advanced only the identification, long since discarded, of Shakespeare as the poet Posthaste in the old play *Histriomastix,* to whom is attributed a dramatization of the story of the prodigal son. To Simpson the young prodigal Flowerdale was intended as a portrait of Greene, to whose pamphlet *Never too late* he saw a mocking

[1] Not only in editions of Shakespeare but separately by Tonson and Walker, both in 1734.

[2] By Tieck and Schlegel, who says that Lessing "pronounced this piece to be Shakespeare's, and wished to bring it on the German stage." *A Course of Lectures on Dramatic Art and Literature,* trans. John Black (London, 1846), p. 444.

[3] "On Some Plays attributed to Shakspere," *Transactions of the New Shakspere Society,* 1875-76. Part I. Reprinted in *The School of Shakespeare,* II, ed. Richard Simpson (London, 1878).

allusion in Father's line "If e'er his heart doth turn, 'tis ne'er too late." Simpson rendered favorable consideration of his views the more unlikely by arguing that Shakespeare wrote both *The Puritan* and *A Yorkshire Tragedy;* the former he thought an attack upon George Peele and the latter an attack upon Thomas Nashe merely because some penitent verses from *Pierce Penniless* are put into the murderer's mouth.

Although rejecting Simpson's interpretation and ascription of *The Puritan* and *A Yorkshire Tragedy,* A. F. Hopkinson enthusiastically accepted his views on *The London Prodigal* and attempted to equate Flowerdale, Luce, and Sir Lancelot with characters in *Never too late.*[4] He noted an interesting parallel in *The Prodigal* and Greene's *James IV,* in both of which characters speak of having made notes on their reading of Machiavelli,[5] but neither this nor anything else which Hopkinson added serves in the least to strengthen the case for Shakespeare's authorship — whether or not it be thought to suggest that the author recalled Greene's works. Midway in his essay Hopkinson declared that "the internal evidence seems to me as strong and as pertinent to the conclusion that Shakespeare wrote the play, as the external. The whole tone, style, and method of the piece, on the face of it, is Shakespeare's. . . ." Yet just fourteen pages later, with surprising readiness to cast aside what he claimed to be the tone, style, and method of Shakespeare, he adds "If it could be proved that this drama was not written till 1603 — which I much doubt — that circumstance would be sufficient to exonerate the great dramatist from being the author of it."[6]

Toward determining the date at which *The Prodigal* was written, little evidence has been found. It has been generally assumed, but certainly on meager grounds, that the composition of the play should be assigned to the early years of James I, 1603 to 1605. Although there are within the play a great many allusions to London places, the play is singularly free of topical allusions which might help in determining its date, and equally free of such satire as might be expected during the early years of the reign of James I. There is, for instance, no reference to the Puritans, the Scots, or the numerous knights created by King James, no satire directed upon lawyers or moneylenders, so frequent in early Jacobean drama. The only attack in the play is directed against swaggerers

> That beare the name and shape of souldiers,
> Yet God knowes very seldom saw the war —

[4] *Essays on Shakespeare's Doubtful Plays* (1900).

[5] *The London Prodigal,* III.ii.44-50; *James IV,* ll. 1302-3 (Malone Society Reprint). All references to *The Prodigal* are to the text in *The Shakespeare Apocrypha* (Oxford, 1908), ed. C. F. Tucker Brooke.

[6] *Op. cit.,* pp. 23, 37.

an object of attack no less characteristic of Elizabethan than of Jacobean comedy.

The title page, as has been noted, claims that the play had been acted by his Majesty's Servants, a designation which of course the company acquired only in 1603; but as the title page also claims the authorship of Shakespeare, it may be felt that no more credence need be given the one claim than is accorded the other and that its publisher, the notorious pirate Nathaniel Butter, deliberately falsified the acting company in order to encourage belief that the play was by Shakespeare. The company which had presented a play, however, not only could have been more easily identified but, on title pages, seems even to have been considered of more interest and importance than the identity of the dramatist. Moreover, on a play first printed in 1605, even though it had been acted by Shakespeare's company before James came to the throne, the company's Jacobean title would certainly have been given if the play had continued in its repertory after 1603.

Only two arguments for Jacobean composition have been advanced, both by Fleay.[7] One which has perhaps been thought conclusive, and which certainly urges Jacobean performance, is the declaration by Sir Arthur Greenshield in II.i.16: "I am a commander, syr, vnder the King" (where, of course, *King* might easily have been substituted for *Queen*). The other Fleay recognized in the dialogue between the disguised Luce and Flowerdale in V.i. When the latter declares himself "a poor gentleman that would desire of you, if it stand with your liking, the bountie of your purse," we have:

LUCE: O here, God, so young an armine.
FLOW: Armine, sweetheart? I know not what you meane by that, but I am almost a beggar. (74-77)

In *armine* Fleay saw an allusion to the actor Robert Armin, who he declared "took the part of Matthew Flowerdale" and who he thought joined the Chamberlain's-King's men only in 1603.[8] Not only is the role of young Flowerdale, the juvenile lead and much the longest part in the play, one we should hardly expect to be taken by a famous clown, but there is certainly no need to see in Luce's use of the word *armine* a punning allusion to the actor. In her Dutch disguise Luce speaks a broken English, *v* for *w*, *d* for *th;* just as she in the same scene uses *yonker* (i.e., *jonker*) and *scone* (i.e., *schoon*) as Dutch words, so in *armine* she uses a word obviously formed from the Dutch adjective *arm,* "poor, wretched."

Convinced that *The Prodigal* was an attack by Shakespeare upon Greene

[7] *Biographical Chronicle of the English Drama* (London, 1891), I, 152.

[8] E. K. Chambers, *Elizabethan Stage* (Oxford, 1923), II, 300, shows that Armin had joined the Chamberlain's Men by 1599.

but unwilling to admit that Shakespeare would have attacked Greene after his death, Hopkinson argued that the play was written in 1591 by urging (1) that a reference to Spenser's *Faerie Queene* in III.ii[9] was more likely to have been made immediately after its publication in 1590 than some twelve or more years later, and (2) that as there was frequent pressing of troops in 1591-92 and none in 1603, there would, if the play were written later, be less point to the opening lines of II.i, in which Sir Arthur is engaged in pressing unwilling men into the king's service. Hopkinson's statement, however, is in error. Not only was there pressing in 1603, but the pressing of that year was remarkably similar in one respect to that described in the play. Scene i of Act II, which takes place before the house of Sir Lancelot in Kent, opens with the following dialogue:

AUR: Lieuftenant, leade your Souldiers to the ships . . .
SOL: I, we are now sent away, and cannot so much as speake with our friends.
OLY: No, man; what, ere you vsed a zutch a fashion, thicke you cannot take your leaue of your vreens? . . .
AUR: Fellow, no more. Lieuftenant, lead them off. . . .
OLY: Bin you a presser, syr.
AUR: I am a commander, syr, vnder the King.

In February, 1603, before Elizabeth's death, the Venetian secretary in London wrote the Doge and Senate that "the Queen's ships are being manned, but not without using the violence of the press-gang in seizing men in the streets of London to send them on board, whether they like it or no";[10] and five months later he reported that "the King has ordered a levy of two thousand seamen in Kent to complete the armament of the ten ships and two pinnaces, about which I have already written."[11] The play's presenting a press gang in Kent may be a pure coincidence; there is no indication that those being pressed in the play are to serve as mariners. Indeed the pressing of men to serve in the army or aboard ship had been sufficiently frequent and no doubt sufficiently resented to make it unnecessary to seek in the incident in *The Prodigal* a reference to any particular instance. Certainly it is unnecessary to choose between 1591-92 and 1603. Of the press of mariners for the expedition to Cadiz in 1596, Sir Walter Raleigh wrote, "As fast as we press men one day they run away another, and say they will not serve";[12]

[9] Lines 99-103 of III.ii have been taken as a reference to Abessa's slander of Una in the third canto of Book I of *The Faerie Queene:*

LANCE: Slanders are more common then troathes, maister *Flowerdale:* but proofe is the rule for both.
FLOW: You say true; what doe you call him hath it there in his third canton.

[10] *Calendar of State Papers, Venetian,* 1592-1603, IX (1897), 534.

[11] *Ibid.,* X (1900), 67.

[12] Quoted by E. P. Cheyney, *A History of England,* etc., (New York, 1926), II, 52.

and in April, 1602, the Council authorized a press of 3,000 soldiers to serve in the Netherlands, "but of these a quarter ran away before they reached a port of embarcation."[13] Presumably it was to this impressment of 1602 that Philip Gaudy referred in a letter which, though undated, is assigned by its editor to that year: "All the playe howses wer besett in one daye and very many pressed from thence, so that in all ther ar pressed ffowre thowsand besydes fyve hundred volyntaryes, and all for fflaunders."[14] After such a raid upon the playhouses, the portrayal of the despotic power of the press gang would obviously not be untimely in a play of 1602.

Though many *ifs* must be taken into consideration, it may be possible to set a date earlier than which our text of *The Prodigal* cannot have been prepared, for there is in the closing scene what I think may be an hitherto unnoted echo of *Romeo and Juliet.* Before urging the disguised Luce to rob her sister's house for him, Flowerdale declares that his present penury had been brought upon him by the extravagance of his wife. "But," he adds,

> . . . but she is dead
> And in her grave my cares are buried —

lines strikingly similar to the closing lines of Capulet's lament for the supposedly dead Juliet (IV.v.63-64):

> Alack! my child is dead,
> And with my child my joyes are buried.

Neither these lines nor any lines approximating them are to be found in Q1 of *Romeo and Juliet,* 1597; they first appear in Q2 printed in 1599 as "Newly corrected, augmented, and amended." Yet even though one be convinced that Q2 contains revisions and additions, he can hardly argue that these particular lines were among the additions, for not only does Q1 present an obviously pirated and badly mangled text but the lines themselves seem hardly such as we should expect Shakespeare to insert at any date after 1596. If, however, the lines given Flowerdale be accepted as an echo or parody of the lines spoken by Capulet, we may say that the author of *The Prodigal* could not have found Capulet's lines in print before 1599 and was not likely to have heard them on the stage before the date *Romeo and Juliet* was first presented, be that date 1591, as earlier critics suggested, or 1595, as most modern critics prefer.[15]

As the later limit for the composition of *The Prodigal* we have, of course, the date of its publication, 1605. That the play was in all probability written before the end of 1604 and acted not later than the early months of 1605 is

[13] Cheyney, II, 564.

[14] Quoted from Chambers, *Elizabethan Stage,* IV, 18.

[15] See E. K. Chambers, *William Shakespeare: A Study of Facts and Problems* (Oxford, 1930), I, 345.

indicated, I believe, by what I take to be a reference to the elderly, foolish-prating Mr. Weathercock in Peter Woodhouse's *The Flea,* which was entered upon the Stationers' Register on March 22, 1605. In his dedicatory epistle Woodhouse wrote: "And when thou sittest to consult about any weighty matter, let either Iustice *Shallowe,* or his Cousen, Mr. *Weathercocke,* be foreman of the Iurie."[16] Surely there can be little doubt that the reference is to Mr. Weathercock of *The Prodigal,* who is gulled by the absurd claims of Flowerdale's will into advising Sir Lancelot to reverse his plans for Luce's marriage. Although Woodhouse's wording may suggest that Mr. Weathercock is a more recent creation than Justice Shallow, it hardly requires a Jacobean date for *The Prodigal.* To urge such a date there remain only the title page identification of the actors as "the Kings Maiesties seruants" and Sir Arthur's declaring himself "a commander under the King," both of which we might expect if the play, although written earlier, remained in the company's repertory after May, 1603.

Perhaps some help in determining the date of *The Prodigal* could be found in a fuller knowledge of the physical characteristics of the actors of the day, for although the play is singularly free of allusions to contemporary events or to topics then under discussion, it contains so many references to the physical peculiarities of the actors as to suggest that the dramatist when writing the play had a particular company in mind and had at least some idea of which actors would take certain parts. The physical characteristics of Sir Lancelot's three daughters are hardly distinguished, though Luce, who has much the largest part of the three, is by her father spoken of as "black-browes" (I.i.41). Civet, although he is clearly English, is twice referred to as Monsieur, possibly because he was intended to be somewhat nice and dainty. When Artichoke announces Civet's arrival in II.i, there occurs the following dialogue:

LANCE: O, I remember, a little man.
ARTY: I, a very little man.
LANCE: And yet a proper man.
ARTY: A very proper, very little man.
LANCE: His name is Mounsier *Civet.* (134-38)

For one of a very different physique was intended the role of Oliver, the Devonshire lad, who by his wit and his hotheaded determination not to be imposed upon, as well as by his dialect, supplies most of the comedy of the play. Sir Lancelot in II.i, urges Luce to

looke on the Deuen-shyre lad:
Fat, faire, and louely, both in purse and person.

[16] Quoted from John Munro, *The Shakspere Allusion Book* (London, 1909), I, 145.

And after Oliver has interrupted Flowerdale's robbery of Delia and prevented her making him a gift of her purse, the prodigal soliloquizes:

> This Deuenshyre man, I think, is made all of porke,
> His hands made onely for to heaue vp packs:
> His hart as fat and big as [is] his face. (IV.ii.57-59)

The strangely limited role of Daffidill was obviously intended for one of a large and strong physique. When, after dismissing him, Sir Lancelot orders his servants to scour their swords preparatory to defending the Devonshire lad against the plots of Flowerdale, he wishes for Daffidill again: "O for that knaue, that Vyllaine *Daffidill* would haue done good service" (II.iv.97-99); and Artichoke, taking up the cry, declares, "But Ile not fight if Daffidill bee a tother side, that's flat." Earlier Weathercock had called him "an honest fellow and a tall," and when Daffidill had said to Lancelot "I know my strength," Weathercock had added, "A, by the matkins, good syr *Lancelot,* I saw him the other day hold vp the bucklers, like an *Hercules*" (II.ii.13-16).

As indicated in the chart below,[17] Oliver's is the fourth most important role in the play — indeed the principal comic role unless it be that of Sir Lancelot, the credulous victim of his own over-scheming. Civet's part in importance stands exactly midway in the cast; that of Daffidill is remarkably slight.

Except for those who are either mute or upon the stage briefly in but one scene, *The London Prodigal* required a cast of ten men and three boys —

17

	Flowerdale	Sir Lancelot	Father	Oliver	Uncle	Luce	Civet	Weathercock	Delia	Arthur	Frank	Artichoke	Daffidill
I.i	50		88		97								
ii	25	49				4	19	18			5	5	16
II.i	21	33	15	36		3		11		12		5	
ii		19				4		13					10
iii						11				16			
iv		75	14	38				19				24	
III.i							31		26		10		
ii	58	59	61		10								
iii	48	43	33	26	46	51	2	9	4	18	4		4
IV.i		31		15			20	11	3	6	12		
ii	39			12					13	2		4	
iii			10			18	19		12		13	10	
V.i	148	53	45	42	12	34	5	11	12	9	8	5	
Total	389	342	266	169	165	125	96	92	70	63	52	53	30

or perhaps nine men and four boys if the part of Civet, "a very little man," were taken by a boy. Nor could the cast have been further reduced by any of the actors taking more than one part. It appears rather odd, therefore, that greater use was not made of Sir Lancelot's two servants, Daffidill and Artichoke. Except for a few lines at the beginning of I.ii, they never appear on the stage together; indeed the dramatist seems to have resorted to rather obvious shifts to keep them apart and to prevent either's part much outdistancing the other's. When they both appear at the beginning of I.ii, Artichoke is at once dispatched to drive home calves, and when Daffidill next appears, he is dismissed from Sir Lancelot's service because of his love for Luce. The parts of both servingmen are surprisingly small; Artichoke is assigned twenty-three speeches, a total of fifty-three lines, Daffidill but seventeen speeches totaling only thirty lines, although there are at least twenty-one lines by others commenting upon him. Indeed, from the many references to him in the early scenes, it would appear that Daffidill was originally intended to be a much more important figure than he turns out to be. The only comedy he furnishes is in his brief conversation with Master Civet in I.ii; elsewhere he is merely surly. The only thing gained by the introduction of both Artichoke and Daffidill rather than a composite of the two, is the latter's love for Luce; yet his love for Luce is not developed, it provides no comedy and leads nowhere, and except for his serving as a messenger in III.iii, Daffidill never reappears after his dismissal in II.ii. Possibly the personnel of the dramatic company may have dictated the introduction of two servingmen where one could easily have been made to suffice. Or possibly scenes in which one or both originally appeared were for some reason dropped.

In spite of the general agreement that the title page is in error in ascribing the play to Shakespeare, there is, as has been noted, no reason to question its statement that *The Prodigal* had been acted by the company to which Shakespeare belonged. If one might indulge in speculation and were encouraged to name the member of Shakespeare's company for whom the dramatist in most likelihood wrote the comic role of Oliver, large, fat, and ham-handed, one could, I suspect, most reasonably nominate Thomas Pope. Both Samuel Rowlands in 1600 and John Taylor, the Water poet, refer to Pope as an actor of comic parts.[18] Professor T. W. Baldwin, who has pioneered in efforts to discover the actors of different roles, has given reason to believe that it was to Pope that Ben Jonson in *The Poetaster* (1601) refers as "your fat fool," and he, as had others, assigned to Pope the original roles

[18] In passages quoted by Baldwin, p. 231. See following note.

of Armado, Falstaff, and Sir Toby Belch.[19] Pope's usual roles, he claimed, were the comedian and the gruff soldier, real or pretended — roles which would demand much the same qualities as would that of Oliver. Although Pope had been one of the original members of the company, the date at which he ceased to act is uncertain. The latest play he is definitely known to have acted in is Jonson's *Every Man out of His Humour,* but there is no reason to believe that he did not continue to act for some time after 1599. Rowlands in *Letting of Humours Blood in the Headvaine* wrote as though Pope were still active in 1600,

> What meanes *Singer* then?
> And *Pope* the clowne, to speake so Boorish, when
> They counterfaite the clownes vpon the stage?[20]

And if Pope is correctly identified as the fat fool referred to in Jonson's attack upon the players in *The Poetaster,* he must have been acting as late as 1601. He was not, however, listed in the patent granted the company on May 19, 1603; he was alive on July 22, 1603, the date of his will, but dead before February 13, 1604, when his will was proved.[21] There is, therefore, every reason to believe that Pope had ceased to act by the time James came to the throne and before the company was nominated his Majesty's Servants. Yet surely the company would have been so named on the title page if the play, though first acted one or two years before, was still or again acted after the company's change in title.

The description of Oliver as one "made all of porke," "His hart as fat and big as [is] his face" — suggesting that the effect of corpulence was not produced by mere padding — seems not to agree with what is known of any other member of the company. Although Burbage may have grown "fat and scant of breath," the comic and comparatively minor role of Oliver is hardly one the company's leading actor would be expected to take. John Lowin, whom the company hired in 1603 after Pope's withdrawal and who seems to have inherited the role of Falstaff, was certainly potbellied by the time of the later Beaumont and Fletcher plays, but references which seem to be to him in plays before 1610 emphasize rather his height and strength. If, though the part of Oliver were originally intended for Pope, the play was finished or revived after his withdrawal, another actor would have had to take over the role. The only other part referred to in the play as acted by a man of large stature is that of Daffidill. If such a transfer were made, perhaps the com-

[19] *The Organization and Personnel of the Shakespearean Company* (Princeton, 1927), p. 232.

[20] Quoted by Chambers, *Elizabethan Stage,* II, 334.

[21] Chambers, *William Shakespeare,* II, 78.

pany, having no other outsize comedian, was forced to excise the comedy in Daffidill which the early scenes of the play seem clearly to promise.

The suspicion that the part of Daffidill may have been shortened is strengthened by evidence that something has clearly been added to the original draft of the play. Although the confusion is hardly sufficient to justify a suggestion of any extensive revision or the participation by a second author, Act III, scene ii, presents several surprises. It is surprising, but perhaps of no significance, that in this scene the parasite Weathercock, who on every other appearance is eager to aid, abet, and agree, remains on stage for 140 lines — the entire time he is present — without uttering a word. Of greater significance are not only what I take to be superior writing in this scene but both a confusion of the time element and a conception of the wit and ingenuity of young Flowerdale entirely different from that met with elsewhere in the play. In the earlier scenes it is clear that Flowerdale has in the past lived only on what he had got from his uncle or had been able to borrow on his bond or his friends' bonds; later, after he has lost the guidance of his disguised father, he resorts to nothing more subtle or witty than begging and robbery. The suggestions of the challenge and the false will are, of course, Father's. But after these have been inaugurated, not only does Flowerdale in III.ii, play his part with skill, but in his opening speech, "Syrrha *Kyt,* tarrie thou there, I haue spied syr *Lancelot,* and old *Weathercocke* comming this way; they are hard at hand. I will by no meanes be spoken withall . . ." he appears to be the director of the scheme. So, later in the scene Father declares him to be "one that doth nothing but inuent deceits," although the invention of the deceits — at least of those in which we are then interested — had been wholly Father's own.

Insignificant or perhaps even fanciful as this change within the role may seem, it deserves mention because of the confusing statements within this same scene concerning the day on which Luce and Flowerdale were to be married. In II.iv, Oliver, while with Sir Lancelot, is by Father handed the challenge which "showes both the time and place" of the proposed duel. After Oliver has departed without revealing them, Weathercock hurries in to report to Sir Lancelot the unexpected wealth revealed in Flowerdale's will, and the two of them at once set forth to insure that no duel prevents Sir Lancelot's securing so rich a son-in-law. After an interlude of Civet, Frank, and Delia (III.i), Sir Lancelot and Weathercock at the opening of III.ii, arrive at Flowerdale's lodgings. To them Flowerdale says, "I am to ride forth to morrow" to meet Oliver; and that the morrow is the day which had been set for their duel is indicated in the following scene by Oliver's arrival at the appointed place and by Sir Arthur's saying, "I had an inckling

. . . yesternight That *Flowerdale* and he should meet this morning." And as Sir Arthur and Oliver await the arrival of the challenger, Daffidill enters to announce that

> Your loue, and yours, and mine, sweet mistress *Luce,*
> This morne is married to young *Flowerdale.*

Thirteen lines later the wedding party enters, coming from the church, and Flowerdale is taken into custody. It is, therefore, quite clear that the wedding was to take place, as it does, at about the same hour of the same day as that appointed for the duel. Agreeing with that is Father's declaring (III.ii.175-76), ". . . but one thing comforts me: Brother, to morrow hee's to be married To beautious *Luce.*" However, in the lines which immediately follow it would appear that the wedding is to take place not on the morrow but on the very day on which they are speaking—that on which Sir Lancelot called on Flowerdale. Shortly after Sir Lancelot leaves Flowerdale's lodgings, Father first announces to Uncle, as noted above, that the wedding will be tomorrow and then continues:

> . . . thus I meane to curbe him.
> This day, brother, I will you shall arrest him (179-80).
> VNCK: What, arrest him on his wedding day? . . .
> *Forbeare him then to day, doe it to morrow,*
> *And this day mingle not his ioy with sorrow.*
> FATH: Brother, ile haue it done this very day,
> And in the viewe of all, as he comes from Church: . . .
> Good brother, let [it] be done immediately.
> VNCK: Well, seeing you will haue it so,
> Brother, ile doot, and straite prouide the Sheriffe (184-98).

If Father's *this day* and *this very day* may be taken in the sense of "that day," as meaning the day of the wedding, i.e., tomorrow, perhaps the only confusion is in the couplet I have italicized. The date of the wedding as given in the couplet, however, is in obvious disagreement with that given elsewhere in III.ii and III.iii, and so presumably is it in all the lines from 180 to 198. That these closing lines of III.ii, do indeed represent a revision or an addition written over or appended to earlier lines is urged not alone by this obvious confusion but as well by the fact that, though the play was printed without act and scene divisions, the following scene (III.iii) is the only scene in the play which opens without a stage direction noting the entrance of the characters.

If the omission of the opening stage direction of III.iii was due to a revision of the close of III.ii, the printer obviously must have worked from the manuscript in which the addition was originally made, not from a theater copy made afterwards and presumably not from a reported text. The quarto furnishes abundant evidence that the printer's copy was a poor one. Many words are omitted; there is occasional mislineation; verse is at times printed as prose and, much more often, prose as verse. Numerous extra-metrical verses (e.g., "*In the* meane time, take heed of cutting *Flowerdale,*" II.ii.23), suggest that deletion marks have been ignored. As no other text of the play is available for comparison, however, it is impossible to know how corrupt the text we have may be.

I need not remind my reader that I have indulged in a good deal of speculation, but if what I suspect to be true is acceptable — that the part of Daffidill was originally designed to provide much more comedy than it now offers and that there is in III.ii, evidence that some addition was made to the original text of the play — there seems to be no reason to insist that *The Prodigal* was written after King James came to the throne. It may well have been written when Thomas Pope was still one of the principal actors, and later modified to meet the needs of the new company when the theaters, after being closed for more than a year, were reopened in 1604.

As to who was the author of *The Prodigal* I can offer no evidence at all. Fleay suggested that the play was by the same author as *Thomas Lord Cromwell,* which he (erroneously, I think) ascribed to Drayton, but no reason for his belief is discernible other than his desire to discover some work by Michael Drayton to fit into the years in which he thought him strangely inactive. Properly discarding Drayton, Tucker Brooke thought that *The Prodigal,* "so full of the intimate details of domestic life, shows as much affinity perhaps to the early works of Dekker and those of Marston as to the writings of any other well-known dramatist of the period." He presumably preferred Marston, as he added that "Dekker's authorship would become plausible only if he could be shown to have written for the King's Players just before 1605. We know that Marston's *Malcontent,* 1607 [for 1604], was acted by the King's Majesty's Servants."[22]

My own belief is that *The Prodigal* is most unlike what we might expect Marston to write just before 1605 or earlier. The complete absence of bitterness, or even of a wish to ridicule, renders Marston's authorship of the play, to me, hardly conceivable. Dekker's authorship would not be difficult to accept were it possible to assign to the play a date near the brief period in 1601, during which he (and Marston as well) is known to have had, through *Satiromastix,* at least some connection with Shakespeare's company. Presumably, he could have written it at no other date.

[22] *The Shakespeare Apocrypha,* p. xxx.

State University of Iowa

IZAAK WALTON AND *THE ARTE OF ANGLING*, 1577

Marcus Selden Goldman

The Rev. Dr. George Washington Bethune, its first American editor, was, beyond question, one of the wisest and most learned of the many wise and learned men who, in the course of three centuries, have provided Walton's masterpiece with appreciative commentary and elucidative notes. Everywhere evident, his wisdom and learning are nowhere more impressive than in those pages of the "Bibliographical Preface" to the first American Edition[1] in which he deals with the sources, known, putative, and merely possible, of the *The Compleat Angler*. Equipped as he was with a perfect command of the classical languages and a knowledge of philosophy and theology which included remarkable familiarity with the speculative, dogmatic, devotional, and controversial writings of the sixteenth and seventeenth centuries, he was ideally suited for the task which he undertook.

It is plain that Bethune in his editorial work, as Walton in his creative, "made a recreation of a recreation" and, inviting the reader to share his joy in "this darling book," took pains that his commentary should "not read dull and tediously."[2] In short, except for the circumstance that Bethune was in

[1] *The Complete Angler; or The Contemplative Man's Recreation* by Isaac Walton. And *Instructions How to Angle for a Trout or Grayling in a Clear Stream* by Charles Cotton. Parts I & II. (New York and London, 1847.) Some of the copies present the two parts in a single volume and some in two volumes. In all copies Part II has a separate title page and separate pagination. Hereafter cited as *Bethune*.

[2] Bethune, p. xc. In the First Edition, A5v, the phrasing and punctuation are slightly different. References in the present study to the First Edition are based upon use of an undated facsimile, evidently a copy of the edition called "The Griggs Facsimile" published in 1882 — hereafter cited as *Walton, 1653*. See No. 106 in Peter Oliver's *A New Chronicle of the Compleat Angler: 1653-1936* (New York and London, 1936), p. 141.

Dutch Reformed, not Anglican, orders,[3] he was exactly the sort of editor that Walton would have most rejoiced in, the learned clerical angler *par excellence* who would not have been beyond his depth in the company of Dean Nowell or Dr. Donne. Despite the lack of enthusiasm for clergymen and anglers as editors recently expressed by an Australian scholar,[4] it is

[3] Walton and Bethune would never have quarreled over matters of religion, for Bethune made no objection to the Anglican turn that Walton gave the piety which some later editors, e.g., Le Gallienne and Keynes, seem to have found obtrusive; and Walton, though he could not hit it off with Richard Franck, was full of good will toward Colonel Robert Venables, a much more militant Calvinist than Bethune. One wonders, however, whether Walton could have resisted the temptation to tease his learned editor regarding that puritanic strictness of his flock which prevented him from openly acknowledging his labor of learning and love. Certainly he could have pointed out that those in Anglican orders suffered no such inconvenience and that even one of them so hospitable to Calvinistic theology as Alexander Nowell "was well content, if not desirous, that posterity should know he was an angler, as may appear by his picture, now to be seen, and carefully kept in Brazen-nose College, to which he was a liberal benefactor, in which picture he is drawn leaning on a desk with his Bible before him, and on one hand of him his lines, hooks, and other tackling lying in a round; and on his other hand are his angle-rods of several sorts." Bethune, p. 40.

Peter Oliver, whose important bibliographical work is a constant aid to the student of Walton, makes this amusing comment on Bethune's editorial virtues and enforced anonymity:

"Of his edition of *The Compleat Angler* ('this darling book,' he fondly calls it), the *Dictionary of American Biography* says, 'owing to the public feeling against the propriety of such a book by a clergyman, it was published anonymously.' This tribute to the high standard of American 'public feeling' is partially borne out by the fact that G. W. Bethune's name nowhere appears in the book.

"It is one of the best editions of *The Compleat Angler,* and though it would doubtless not be popular if it were issued today, being too scholarly for an age that dedicates its scholarship to higher and more practical(!) things, it still should, and we believe does, command the affection of a few simple souls who have some little fondness for such pleasant futilities as 'quietnesse and vertue and angling.' " *A New Chronicle,* etc., pp. 98-99.

[4] "In spite of the amazing popularity of *The Compleat Angler* (the number of editions and reprints since Walton's lifetime must be about three hundred), it could hardly be said that the possibilities of critical investigation have been exhausted. Many of those who edited and commented on Walton's works have been fishermen or clergymen (or both) and their interests were not always literary; and many of the reputable critics who have written on Walton (for example Sir Leslie Stephen, Mr. Desmond McCarthy, and Sir Edmund Gosse) seem to have been caught off their guard, possibly because they have taken Walton's work too lightly. As a result, popular opinion still considers Walton an artist only by accident, and *The Compleat Angler* a miracle of ingenuousness. The truth would seem different." H. J. Oliver, "The Composition and Revisions of *The Compleat Angler,*" *MLR,* XLII (1947), 295.

H. J. Oliver's general thesis is that Walton might well have taken as his motto the *sententia* dear to literary critics: *Ars est celare artem.* Supported as it is by meticulous analysis of the changes which Walton made in the editions of *The Angler* which appeared in his lifetime, the thesis is not to be lightly rejected. It does not

difficult to see how a tincture of theology and a practical knowledge of fishing can be other than helpful to anyone who wishes to share fully Walton's thought and feeling. In fact, it might be maintained that a bit of both are nothing short of essential.

Bethune's survey of the literature of angling before Walton's time consti-

---

follow, however, that the interests of earlier students of Walton were less literary because they praised Walton's style instead of dissecting it or because they gave more attention to the tracing of Walton's sources than to minor textual emendations. Certainly the fact that some of these men were "fishermen or clergymen (or both)" did not make them less interested in literature than if they had been college professors. It is perhaps worth remarking that some of the professorial editors were scientists, not students of literature. Can one deny that the earliest of Walton's editors, the Rev. Moses Browne, who was both an angler and a clergyman — though he did not take orders until after his first edition of *The Angler* was printed — had literary interests? Both his poems and the story that Cave pointed him out to Samuel Johnson, then newly arrived in London, as one of the literary sights of the town testify to his status. Dr. Bethune, both fisherman and clergyman, though now chiefly remembered for his editing of Walton, was, in his day, a figure of some importance in American letters. James Russell Lowell, Henry Morley, Andrew Lang, Austin Dobson, Sir Arthur Quiller-Couch, Richard Le Gallienne, John Buchan, First Baron Tweedsmuir, and Bliss Perry, all of whom edited *The Compleat Angler,* were laymen. Some of them were great anglers, others rather indifferent ones, and a few, perhaps, not anglers at all. Without exception, however, they rank as "reputable critics," so it seems a bit rash to attribute, as H. J. Oliver does by implication, failure to emphasize the deliberate element in Walton's style either to lack of literary interest on the part of "fishermen or clergymen (or both)" or to some strangely repeated accident by which so many "reputable critics," some of them, most notably Andrew Lang, perhaps, celebrated for skill in literary detection, were caught off their guard. The fact is that they did not find, as H. J. Oliver apparently does, a contradiction between Walton's legendary simplicity and a love of language which made him strive for perfection of style. They were concerned with the man and the finished product of his effort, rather than with the details of his procedure. Thus, Andrew Lang, in the introduction to his edition of *The Angler* (London, 1896), p. xxviii, speaks of a notable example of Walton's preoccupation with style in another work: "He was busy with his Life of Richard Hooker (1665). The peroration, as it were, was altered and expanded in 1670, and this is but one example of Walton's care of his periods. One beautiful passage he is known to have rewritten several times, till his ear was satisfied with its cadences." The important thing to be borne in mind is that a man may be very simple and direct in his outlook on life, very modest, childlike in his attitude toward both spiritual and temporal authority, and yet extremely painstaking and meticulous in cultivation of one of the fine arts. History provides many examples, although, by the very nature of things, they are more numerous among painters, sculptors, and musicians than among men of letters. Society is always more aware of the self-assertive artist simply because he demands attention and is more likely to live in a manner which provides occasion for surprise and remembrance, but it is a mistake to assume that the Izaak Waltons and Richard Hookers are not only natural geniuses but naïve ones merely because they "study to be quiet." After all, that very effort may be a quite conscious part of their artistic dedication and concentration.

What has been said above is not intended as disparagement of studies like those

tutes a very considerable part of his preface. In it he displays great care and sound judgment in estimating the possible influence of each earlier angling work upon Walton and concludes his discussion of the several editions of the little book finally called *Barker's Delight*[5] with the remark:

Thus I have given some account of all the books on angling now known to have been published in England before Walton's Complete Angler. It is not, however, improbable that some treatises may have been lost. Walton, in his complimentary note to Col. Venables, says that he has read and practised by *many* books of this kind before made public;[6] and in his xviith chapter he quotes for "sport's sake an old rhyme out of an old fish book," which rhyme, it seems from their silence, the commentators on the Angler have been unable, like myself, to find in any treatise extant.[7] John Hockenhull, Esqr., in his *Pleasant Hexameter Verses in Praise of Mr. (Thomas) Barker's Book of Angling,* asks:

---

of H. J. Oliver, which are both interesting and useful. The first stage of Waltonian scholarship was largely biographical and genealogical, beginning with William Oldys and Sir John Hawkins and finding fullest expression in the work of Sir Harris Nicolas; the second was bibliographical and likewise owed much to Hawkins and Nicolas, but more to Bethune; the third is textual and stylistic, and, as H. J. Oliver suggests, offers opportunity for discoveries which may add something to our understanding of Walton as man and writer, and of his manner of handling his sources. It is most necessary, however, to avoid exaggerating the importance of recent work and to have a proper appreciation of the best in earlier scholarship. If it was a frequent fault of earlier critics to think Walton less intellectual, less shrewd, and less versed in the ways of the literary world than he really was, because of his reputation for simplicity, modesty, and honesty, there is now danger of going too far in the other direction and accepting too easily and completely the concept of him as delighting in "artifice for artifice's sake" which H. J. Oliver has presented in various places but most strikingly in "Izaak Walton as Author of 'Love and Truth' and 'Thealma and Clearchus,'" *RES,* XXV (1949), 24-37.

[5] In the first edition (London, 1651), and the reprint of 1653, it was entitled *The Art of Angling*. For a description of the various editions in the seventeenth century and later reprints, as well as a brief discussion of the book and its author, see *Bibliotheca Piscatoria* by T. Westwood and T. Satchell (London, 1883), pp. 21-23.

[6] The full text of Walton's note commending Venables' *Experienced Angler* — Walton refers to it by the subtitle *Angling Improved* — is given by Bethune, pp. xlix-l. It is also to be found in Dr. Geoffrey Keynes' beautifully produced single-volume edition of Walton's works (London, 1929), and in Horace Hutchinson's combined reprint of Gervase Markham's *Pleasures of Princes* and Venables' *Experienced Angler* (London, 1927).

[7] R. B. Marston remarked (*Walton and Some Earlier Writers on Fish and Fishing* [London, 1894], p. 220): "Difficult, indeed, would it be to find anything in *The Compleat Angler* which has not been 'annotated' in some form or other." It seems that only the phrase "in some form or other," which can be construed to include reference in a preface, keeps the verse from "an old fish book" from being an exception to the rule. Bethune does not refer by a footnote from the text to the remark in his preface, and the editors who have succeeded him seem to be as silent as those who went before. The present writer has not seen all editions of *The Compleat Angler* published since 1847, but in the very considerable number that he has had opportunity to examine, he has not found any comment on the "old rhyme."

"Markham, *Ward,* Lawson, dare you with Barker now compare?" but we have no trace of an angling book by any one of the second name. These unknown piscatorial treasures are hid in oblivion with the lost books of Livy.[8]

The lost books of Livy are still lost, as is the "old fish book" from which Walton quoted the six lines of verse on the equipment an angler must take with him to the streamside, but it seems probable that one of the "many books" to which Walton referred in his letter to Venables, one which he must have "practised by," even if he never held a copy in his hands, has recently been recovered.[9] It is possible too, though there may never be either proof or disproof of such a hypothesis, that this is the work by which the mysterious and elusive Ward won a place in John Hockenhull's brief list of angling authors. Certainly the writing of *The Arte of Angling, 1577* would constitute a better claim to such distinction than the translation of the *Secrets* of Master Alexis of Piedmont.[10]

The present study is not concerned, however, with identification of the author of the delightful dialogue so happily discovered by Carl Otto von Kienbusch and recently published in facsimile under the auspices of the Friends of the Princeton Library, but with the nature and extent of its influence on Walton and the manner in which that influence was exerted.

[8] Bethune, p. xlvii.

[9] *The Arte of Angling, 1577.* Edited by Gerald Eades Bentley, with an Introduction by Carl Otto v. Kienbusch, & Explanatory Notes by Henry L. Savage (Princeton, 1956) — hereafter cited as *The Arte.*

[10] Since the title page, if it ever existed, has disappeared from the now apparently unique copy of *The Arte of Angling,* 1577, it is impossible to know without the help of some happy additional discovery what author's name, if any, it bore. The mention of Ward and Lawson by Hockenhull has never been satisfactorily explained. Lawson has generally been identified as William Lawson (or Lauson), author of *A New Orchard and Garden* (London, 1617), and "augmenter" of the second edition of John Dennys' *Secrets of Angling.* The Rev. H. N. Ellacombe's suggestion that Ward was William Ward (1534-1604?), a physician who lectured on medicine at Cambridge, and that he was accorded a place among writers on angling because of his translation of the *Secrets* of Alexis of Piedmont, is discussed in *Bibliotheca Piscatoria,* p. 23. That Ellacombe could, when his heart was in the work, make a little evidence go a long way is amply proved by his *Shakespeare as an Angler* (London, 1883). Were he alive now, he might be tempted to put Ward forward as the probable author of *The Arte of Angling,* for the scholarly physician's flourishing time coincides nicely with that of the dialogue. Ward's translation was made from a French version and first published in 1558. See Lynn Thorndike, *A History of Magic and Experimental Science* (New York, 1941), VI, 215-16. It should be noted that the simple practicality of *The Arte of Angling,* especially in its treatment of baits, a subject on which some early writers elaborated wildly, and even horribly (see James Chetham's celebrated receipt beginning: "Take Man's Fat and Cat's Fat, of each half an Ounce, Mummy finely powdered three Drams, etc." in *The Angler's Vade Mecum,* 3rd ed. [London, 1700], p. 69) argues against the assumption that its author was a medical man willing to contribute to the diffusion of the type of ideas found in the *Secrets* of Alexis.

That there was such an influence, it is very difficult to doubt, for the more one reads and rereads *The Arte of Angling* and *The Compleat Angler* the more one is impressed by the frequency and clearness with which the later book echoes the earlier.

In bringing out their edition of *The Arte of Angling,* Mr. von Kienbusch, Professor Bentley, and Dr. Savage were careful not to make any excessive claims regarding its probable influence or to suggest that it raised any question regarding Walton's integrity as man and author. Despite the presence of two passages in the work of the unknown Elizabethan's dialogue which are reproduced almost verbatim in *The Compleat Angler,* the editors made no use of the ugly words "plagiarism" and "plagiarist," which occurred in some of the newspaper accounts of their discovery. Mr. von Kienbusch was at pains, both by implication in the bit of humorous verse set at the head of his introductory essay and by specific statement in it, to indicate his belief that there was nothing extraordinary or reprehensible about Walton's indebtedness to his predecessor.[11] In this course of procedure, the editors gave admirable proof of both integrity of spirit and soundness of judgment. By understatement of the case for the influence of *The Arte of Angling* they not only gained sympathetic consideration of it by admirers of Walton but established its right to claim attention on the strength of its intrinsic interest quite apart from that which it may derive from its relationship to *The Compleat Angler.*[12]

In his preface to *The Arte of Angling,* Professor Bentley presents his view of the principal elements of Walton's indebtedness to its author in a series of rhetorical questions followed by a very brief statement of his major conclusions:

> Can it be pure coincidence that Izaak Walton's famous *Compleat Angler* is written entirely in dialogue, begins with a chance encounter between a character named Viator and one named Piscator, continues in a series of episodes, some concerned with fishing, some with the eating of fish, in which the devoted Piscator instructs the uninformed Viator in the art of fishing, and concludes with allusions to a future meeting between the two — can it be mere coincidence that each of these hitherto unprecedented features in early English angling literature is now seen to have appeared in *The Arte of Angling* in 1577 before Izaak Walton

[11] See *The Arte,* pp. 1-2, especially the sentence: "He [i.e., Walton] took what he needed from the writings of his predecessors but, being an honest man and a pious one, he tried to give credit where credit was due."

[12] The present writer has already expressed in a review of *The Arte of Angling* (*JEGP,* LVI [1958], 136) his favorable opinion of the general policy of its editors in terms similar to those which he has employed above. In the review he has, however, registered objection to certain details of the editing, particularly some of the notes, and to the choice of an edition of *The Compleat Angler* for purposes of reference and comparison. This last point is discussed in Note 13 below.

was born? Is it coincidence that Walton's description of malt bait (p. 278)1[13] follows that in *The Arte of Angling* (Evi^{v}-Evii) point by point, using most of the same words and phrases? Or again coincidence that Walton's instructions for breeding and keeping gentles (p. 278) is that of *The Arte of Angling* (Eviii-Eviii^{v}) word for word except for a few substitutions and expansions? And there are other short passages in which the two texts are surprisingly similar.[14] Though I have made no exhaustive study of angling literature, it would appear to me likely that Izaak Walton had taken his idea for the general structure of *The Compleat Angler* from *The Arte of Angling*, and that he had had direct recourse to the text when he prepared his instructions for the preparation of malt bait and keeping of gentles.[15]

The evidence marshaled in the paragraph above is very impressive. In the face of it, only a very bold debater with something of the ancient sophist's love of maintaining an argument for its own sake would be inclined to deny that Walton was influenced by *The Arte of Angling* in a number of ways and in a very considerable degree. It must be added, however, that Professor Bentley's statement attains simplicity and succinctness only by ignoring a number of works in earlier literature and many important findings of his predecessors in Waltonian scholarship. A glance at some other possible influences may give a clearer idea of the background of literature and tradition regarding angling against which Walton should be viewed without in any way reducing the claim of his unidentified Elizabethan predecessor to a very high place among those whose work was of great assistance to him.

Professor Bentley's reference to the similarity in the use of the dialogue form and the identical names of the two chief interlocutors is repeated in its essentials but in different form and with different emphasis by Mr. von Kienbusch:

Returning to Mr. Rhodes' question "whether or not *The Arte of Angling* . . .

[13] "References to *The Compleat Angler* are to the edition of Edward Jesse, London, 1896." *The Arte,* p. 278, n.1.

In his review of *The Arte of Angling* referred to in Note 12 above, the present writer has expressed his conviction that it is both simpler and more profitable to compare *The Arte of Angling* with the first edition of Walton's *Compleat Angler* (London, 1653) than with the fifth edition of 1676, the text of which is reproduced in the several editions introduced and annotated by Jesse. The fifth edition, the last published in Walton's lifetime, is rightly the most popular, but the first is the shortest; and since there is apparently no additional evidence of indebtedness to *The Arte of Angling* in those which followed, it is the most convenient one with which to work. It has, of course, been necessary to make fairly frequent reference to various reprints of the fifth edition because of the commentary and notes of successive editors which they contain. Among these, as the reader will have already noted, the one most frequently cited is Bethune's of 1847.

[14] There will be occasion to refer to at least two such passages later in the present study. One of them, the present writer believes, may provide the key to better understanding of Walton's probable relationship to *The Arte of Angling.*

[15] *The Arte,* pp. ix-x.

was known to Walton and used by him as a source-book"[16] (a question to which no definite answer can be given) we are, nevertheless, in a fairly strong position if we assume that it was known to Walton and that he made some use of it. A startling bit of evidence is presented in the heading of the first page — "A Dialogue betweene Viator and Piscator." Dialogue is, to be sure, one of the earliest literary forms. But we have no record of its use in a book on angling until Walton invented (?) Piscator and Viator (the latter becomes Venator in the second and later editions), the same two whose conversations are set forth in *The Arte of Angling.* Why did Walton drop Viator? Can he have regretted following *The Arte* in this respect too closely?[17]

Mr. von Kienbusch's mention of the antiquity of the dialogue as a literary form makes it unnecessary to protest Professor Bentley's failure to allude to the fact. Still, it would appear that profitable reference might have been made by one or the other to a remark by Bethune which seems almost to have been written as an anticipatory caution against too heavy emphasis upon any one probable influence:

The method of treating a subject in a supposed conversation between two or more persons was, as the reader knows, common among the ancients, and readily adopted by writers after the revival of literature in the West; so that Walton may readily have adopted it without following any particular example. It is clear, however, that he had in his eye "A Treatise on the Nature of God," attributed to Bishop Morton, published in 1599. In both works the dialogue occurs between two persons travelling the same way, one of whom has overtaken the other, though the Bishop puts his characters on horseback; while Walton's, more appropriately, are on foot; and, in the former, the learner overtakes the teacher; in the later, Piscator "stretches his legs" to get company on the "fine, pleasant, May-day morning." The Bishop begins: "Well overtaken, Syr;" Walton: "You are well overtaken, Sir." Here, however, the particular resemblance ends, except in the inquiry about a lodging-place at the close of the day.

The probability that Walton took a hint from Plutarch's dialogue on the question "Whether Water or Land Animals are the most Crafty?" which was within his reach by the English translation of Dr. Holland from the French of Amyot (1602), has already been stated.[18] The spirit of the dispute is much the same in both, for it is mainly carried on between a hunter and a fisher. It must, however, be remembered, that in all treatises on fishing from the Halieutic fragment, called Ovid's, down to Gervase Markham, a comparison is run between other sports in favor of fishing, nor could it be more readily carried on than by a dialogue; so that all these conjectures as to the source from which Walton took his plan may be hypercritical.[19]

It is worth remarking, perhaps, with reference to Bethune's belief in the influence of *A Treatise on the Nature of God,* that Charles Cotton, in his Part II of *The Compleat Angler,* which was written as a supplement to

[16] See D. F. Rhodes, "A New Line for the *Angler,* 1577," *The Library,* 5th Series, X (1955), 123-25.

[17] *The Arte,* pp. 10-11. [18] Bethune, pp. xviii-xix. [19] Bethune, pp. lix-lx.

Walton's work for publication with the edition of 1676, names his characters Piscator and Viator in the manner of *The Arte of Angling* and Walton's first edition, puts them on horseback in the manner of *A Treatise on the Nature of God,* has Piscator overtake Viator and speak first as Walton did (in *The Arte* it is Viator who comes upon Piscator and has the first word), and varies the salutation slightly by making it: "You are happily overtaken, Sir." It seems futile to undertake to say what any one of these greetings owes to another, for all are natural, almost inevitable, in the situations in which they are spoken, and the variations are of the sort which would be likely to occur unless one writer copied another very carefully.

In *The Arte,* by contrast, Piscator is already engaged in fishing when Viator comes up and greets him. But a still greater difference in situation is to be remarked. In the other three works the greeting and subsequent conversation is between strangers, here the two characters are already well acquainted with each other. Viator's greeting is, "What, friend Piscator, are you even at it so early?" Moreover, the impression which the reader receives of long acquaintance, even friendship, between the two men is further emphasized by Piscator's manner of asking Viator to sup with him and bring a quart of sack, his casual reference to him as "my friend Viator" in informing his wife of the invitation, and his recognition of him by his voice before he sees him in the evening.[20]

As for Walton's naming of his characters, it can be explained by the logic of the situation quite as easily as by borrowing. It is difficult to think of any other designation which would have suited Viator so well as *Viator* in the first edition of *The Angler,* for his enthusiasm for hunting is emphasized in it less than in later editions. In *The Arte,* on the other hand, Viator is not on a journey but merely idling along the river near his own and Piscator's home. It would have been more logical had his creator anticipated Dr. John Davy[21] and indicated his relationship to Piscator by calling him *Amicus.*

Mr. von Kienbusch's questions regarding Walton's reasons for dropping Viator, or, more exactly, for making him over a bit and renaming him

[20] See *The Arte,* pp. 15, 24, and 28.

[21] Dr. John Davy not only shared the scientific interests of his celebrated older brother Sir Humphry but the piscatorial enthusiasm as well. In *The Angler in the Lake District* (London, 1857) he employed the dialogue method much as Sir Humphry had in *Salmonia* almost thirty years before, but in a less elaborate fashion. Sir Humphry presented four principal characters and gave them Greek names indicating their profession or chief interest. John Davy was content with two, Piscator and Amicus. In 1855 he had published a similar but slightly smaller book, *The Angler and His Friend.* This the present writer has not had opportunity to examine recently. The first two editions of *Salmonia,* 1828 and 1829, were published without Sir Humphry's name, but his authorship was probably known to many people. The fourth, that of 1851, was edited and augmented by Dr. John Davy.

Venator, can be answered without reference to *The Arte of Angling.* One of the traditional elements in early angling literature — and Walton was nothing if not a lover of tradition — was proof of the superiority of angling to other recreations, especially hunting and hawking. It constitutes an important, frequently the initial, element in what Mr. von Kienbusch aptly calls the "Berners pattern," a pattern from which, as he is at some pains to point out, *The Arte of Angling* departs in regard to the order in which ideas are presented.[22] The weight of critical opinion seems to be against the assumption that Walton was familiar with *The Treatyse of fysshynge with an Angle,* though the idea is generally accepted that he was acquainted with much of its matter which had been incorporated in other works.[23] Bethune, who was uncertain regarding Walton's knowledge of *The Treatyse,* pointed out that the comparison of the three principal field sports is as old as the *Halieuticon* attributed to Ovid, and believed, on the strength of Walton's evident familiarity with the dialogue *Terrestriane an aquitilia animalia sint callidora* in the *Moralia,* that the Plutarchan influence would account for much in the handling of the debate in *The Compleat Angler.*[24]

A passage in *The Arte of Angling* of which the possible importance was evidently overlooked by the editors is that in which Piscator alludes to the traditional argument among lovers of the three sports and refuses to engage in it. After a short digression on the Creation and the fallen state of humanity, Piscator returns in leisurely fashion to the subject of angling in the following speech:

Pi. To return yet, for all that, the same Almighty God hath not so avenged the fall and offence of man that he should be altogether over pressed with careful travail, but hath spiced man's pains with delight, pastime, and recreation, many ways: in the finding, winning, or ending of his labors, whereof the fisher, falconer, and hunter are well able to report. And, as the same Almighty hath not made all kind of living creatures upon earth to be but one, but divided them into beasts, fowls, fishes, and worms [reptiles],[25] and they of diverse sorts in every kind, so hath

[22] See *The Arte,* pp. 9-10. Demonstration of the superiority of angling to other sports occupies the first two sections of *The Treatyse of fysshynge wyth an Angle,* unnumbered leaves 1 and 2 of the text in the facsimile edited by the Rev. M. G. Watkins (London, 1880).

[23] For a well-documented discussion of Walton's probable relationship to *The Treatyse,* see H. J. Oliver, "The Composition and Revisions of 'The Compleat Angler,' " pp. 295-96.

[24] See p. 192 and note 18 above. Plutarch's dialogue is known by two other titles in Latin, *De Sollertia Animalium* and *De Industria Animalium.* Walton, 1653, p. 199, uses the last. In Greek the title is: *Πότερα τῶν ζῴων φρονιμώτερα, τὰ χερσαῖα ἢ τὰ ἔνυδρα.*

[25] For convenience in reference, quotations from *The Arte* are taken from the modernized version of the text immediately preceding the photographic facsimile. In this version, explanatory words and phrases have been introduced between brackets by the editors as an aid to readers unfamiliar with Elizabethan usage.

he given to sundry men, sundry minds; some in this, and some in that to have pleasure. For if all his living creatures should have been of one sort, as all fishes, all beasts, or all fowls, so had loathsomeness and waste hurt appetite and pleasure. But now to speak more particularly and to our purpose. As in fishing, fowling, and hunting there is degrees both of costs, pains, pleasures, and profits, so what cost, pain, pleasure, or profit the hunter or hawker hath, as I am not skillful in either of them, so do I leave such as would know to the sundry books set out by sundry men and in sundry tongues that doth write of them both at large. Neither do I purpose so to speak unto you of fishing as severally to tell of all the cost, pain, pleasure, or profit that is in that marvelous and wonderful science.[26]

Evidently the Elizabethan Piscator felt that comparison of the three sports was so traditional, so expected in a work on angling, that he could not pass over his omission of it silently but must make a definite statement of his adherence to the philosophy of *de gustibus et coloribus non disputandum*.

Walton, by contrast, either was swayed by tradition or permitted a certain evangelistic zeal for his favorite sport to overcome his natural dislike of disputation. Probably some tiresome and exasperating experiences with hunters and falconers were responsible for the vigor with which he made his Piscator assert the superiority of angling. At any rate, since Walton revived the debate which the Elizabethan had endeavored to adjourn, he had a better and more practical reason for the metamorphosis of Viator into Venator than regret for "having followed *The Arte* . . . too closely."

It must be admitted that there is a general resemblance between *The Arte* and *The Compleat Angler* in the discussions of the cooking and eating of fish.[27] It might be remarked, however, that one of the two chief reasons for angling has always been the eating of the catch, and that consequently a meal in which fish constitute a main dish is a most natural sequel to a good day by brook or river. It might also be noted that Thomas Barker's *Art of Angling*, which first appeared in 1651 and which Walton certainly knew, has in it rather more, proportionately, about the cooking and eating of fish than either *The Arte* or *The Angler*. Finally, one is sadly aware that the Elizabethan Piscator is one of those unfortunate men who do not have a gastro-

[26] *The Arte*, pp. 30-31.

[27] In *The Arte* one finds the cooking and eating of fish discussed intermittently from page 27 to page 46. In Walton's edition of 1653, these subjects are discussed in the following places: pp. 47-51, 71-74 (misnumbered 81, 72, 37, 84), and 157-60. The last of these is the elaborate recipe for cooking a large pike. There is a similar one in *Barker's Delight* (see the Hodgson reprint [1826] of "The Second Edition much enlarged" [London, 1657], p. 18). Since this recipe does not appear in Barker's *Art of Angling*, it would seem possible that Barker the cook owed something to Walton the gourmet, just as Walton the angler owed something to Barker the expert with a fly-rod. The debt may have been only for a jog of the memory, since Barker begins his recipe with a reference to the iron spits used in his native Shropshire.

nomic interest in fish equal to their enthusiasm for the sport of catching them. After discussion of the relative merits of different species for food, he remarks: "I do not much pass of [care for] any fish to eat, but that hunger forceth me sometimes and want of other things, and when I am weary (as it were) of flesh. And yet the chevin's head I do love very well, for next unto the carp's head it is the best and very sweet, if the mouth be clean washed."[28]

Far from sharing such distaste (or at best lukewarm enthusiasm) for fish, Walton is eloquent in praising both its delicious taste when properly cooked and its nutritive value. Walton's chub did not eat "flashly" as did the one served on the Elizabethan table, for the good reason that it was prepared according to art. Barker, who was half cook and half professional fisherman, was as proud of his culinary skill as of his piscatorial and not only succeeded in pleasing sundry noblemen and ambassadors by the exercise of both, but won the affection of Mr. von Kienbusch by his manner of recounting his prowess.[29] In the later editions of his work under the title of *Barker's Delight* he burst repeatedly into verse in which the cooking and eating of the catch are hailed as the end appropriately crowning the work.

The parallels and resemblances between *The Arte of Angling* and *The Compleat Angler* which have so far been discussed in this study can, the writer believes, be explained without assuming either direct or indirect influence of the earlier work upon the later, though assumption of such an influence cannot be rejected as demonstrably false. Explanation of the parallels and resemblances need not be based upon either of the opposite assumptions of influence of *The Arte* or accident, for the authors were clearly both men of much practical experience in the type of angling now generally referred to in England as "coarse fishing" and were working in the same literary tradition derived from late classical antiquity and the Middle Ages. Walton, quite obviously, might have derived an idea from the same source as the author of *The Arte* did, as easily as from him — rather more easily, it would seem, if we remember how much more readily available some of these other possible sources must have been than a book to which there is, as yet, no identified reference in later literature and of which apparently only a single copy has survived. Even in Walton's time *The Arte* must have been a very rare book, far rarer than *The Secrets of Angling* or Mascall's *Booke of Fishing with Hooke & Line,* which Walton is known to have read and which both have long been very rare. Otherwise, mention of it would almost certainly have been found somewhere before now.

In regard to the directions for the preparation of malt bait and the breed-

[28] *The Arte,* pp. 45-46. [29] See *The Arte,* pp. 4-5.

ing and keeping of gentles, matters stand in an entirely different light.[30] Nobody, it would seem, has serious doubt that the various compilers of post-Waltonian angling manuals who offered their readers useful instructions regarding baits in almost the same words in which they appear in *The Compleat Angler*[31] got them from it, so, when passages in *The Angler* turn up, now, in *The Arte of Angling,* it is practically impossible not to be convinced that Walton, either directly or indirectly, derived them from this earlier work.

Once Walton's indebtedness is admitted (and in the present writer's opinion no less than in those of the editors of *The Arte,* it must be admitted), the question arises as to why Walton, who, as Mr. von Kienbusch rightly avers, "being an honest man and a pious one . . . tried to give credit where credit was due," failed so notably in this instance to give credit where it was so notably due. Walton was very fond of naming his sources when he could, and though it may be maintained that he gave his work an air of authority by his references to Pliny and Plutarch, Du Bartas and Dubravius, Konrad Gesner, Randelet, and Sir Francis Bacon, and sought to cut a certain social figure by reminiscences of association with John Donne, with Sir Henry Wotton, and with one of the "chimical men" that "honest Sir George Hastings, an excellent Angler (and now with God)," he could scarcely have hoped to derive any benefit from his praise of Thomas Barker, or from his letter to Colonel Venables in the days of that once admired soldier's ill fortune and eclipse.[32]

[30] The instructions for the preparation of malt bait and for the breeding and preservation of gentles are to be found on pages 62-66 of *The Arte of Angling* with the corresponding passages from the fifth edition of *The Compleat Angler* printed in full in the footnotes. In the first edition of *The Angler* the corresponding passages are on pages 223-26. *The Arte* deals with malt bait first. Walton writes of the live bait first and by a neat transition comes to the malt. The differences between Walton's two versions are so slight as to be noticed only in very careful reading. The most striking difference between Walton's texts and that in *The Arte* is in Walton's occasional expansion of a sentence or phrase and in a somewhat more modest provision of carrion for the gentles' winter food. The author of *The Arte* would give the gentles "a cat, a buzzard, or a dead swan, full-blown and buried in the earth." Walton's maggots would be obliged to content themselves with "a dead *Cat* or a *Kite.*" Perhaps with the lapse of nearly a century, buzzards and swans had become scarce.

[31] For examples of such borrowing of the passage on gentles from Walton, see, e.g., Chetham, *The Angler's Vade Mecum,* pp. 47-48; *The Gentleman Angler* (London, 1726), p. 30, also 3rd ed. (London, n.d.), pp. 35-36; Thomas Best, *The Art of Angling,* 11th ed. (London, 1822), p. 24; Richard Brookes, M.D., *The Art of Angling,* 4th ed. (London, 1774), pp. 95-96. The recipe for malt bait does not seem to have been so popular.

[32] Walton refers to Bacon eleven times in the first edition of *The Angler* and to Gesner nineteen. He is sometimes careful to indicate that he is quoting an authority at second hand as in his reference to Randelet's account of the medical use of the

Walton, as everyone knows, frequently quoted from memory, as did most of his contemporaries, without verifying the quotation, and almost as frequently, misquoted. Since he was not only a stylist but something of a poet, he seldom greatly marred and occasionally somewhat improved upon the original. It is to be noted, also, that he sometimes disclaims credit for a piece of information, or for an idea or a phrase, without naming the person from whom he has derived it. In some instances there may have been reasons for withholding a name. In others, it seems safe to assume that he forgot the name or lost a note containing it. An example of the first sort is probably the suppression of the name of the person responsible for the recipe for the making of an odoriferous mixture to attract fish which Piscator delivers to his disciple "in the same words as it was by a friend given . . . in writing."[33] The apology offered to one unnamed at whom he laughed "for affirming that he knew *Carps* come to a certain place in a Pond to be fed at the ringing of a Bel"[34] may well be another. Still a third, though a more doubtful one, would be the reference to "a Gentleman of tryed honestie" who had told a strange story of the mysterious disappearance of carp from a pond.[35] One might remember a tale a bit difficult to believe, and also the circumstance that it had been told by a person in whose veracity one had great confidence, without being able to recall that person's name. Such examples of incomplete memory are common enough and sometimes very embarrassing when one is cross-examined.

More certain examples of forgetfulness (in these instances forgetfulness of the source of a good phrase) are: "and he [the salmon] recovers his strength, and comes next Summer to the same River, (if it be possible) to enjoy the former pleasures that there possest him; for (as one has wittily observed) he has (like some persons of Honour and Riches, which have both their winter and Summer houses) the fresh rivers for Summer, and the salt water for winter to spend his life in; which is not (as Sir *Francis Bacon* hath observed) above ten years:"[36] and "But bite the *Pearch* will, and that very boldly; and

tench (p. 176) and Bede's testimony in regard to eels and the Isle of Ely (p. 189), both of which he found in Gesner's *De Piscibus.* Evidently Walton did not discover Aldrovandus, whom he later quoted frequently, until after publication of the first edition of *The Angler.* A listing of the classical authors mentioned by Walton and a brief discussion of his use of some of them is to be found in Andrew Oliver's "Izaak Walton and the Classics," *Cl. Weekly,* XXXVIII (May 14, 1945), 179-80.

[33] *Walton, 1653,* p. 140. Another example is his failure to name the source of the recipe for a similar mixture, which he says was told him "as a secret." See pp. 156-57. It is worth remarking that Walton is careful to make clear that he has not tried these concoctions and cannot endorse them by reference to any practical experience. It is evident that he liked simplicity even in baits.

[34] *Ibid.,* p. 129. [35] *Ibid.,* pp. 163-64. [36] *Ibid.,* p. 134.

as one has wittily observed, if there be twentie or fortie in a hole, they may be at one standing all catch'd one after another; they being, as he saies, like the wicked of the world, not afraid, though their fellowes and companions perish in their sight."[37]

Walton evidently had forgotten, if he ever knew it, the name of the one who had "wittily observed" the similarity between hungry fish and wicked men, both heedless of warning and rushing on to destruction. He had even forgotten, if he had received the simile in its original form, the species of fish whose reckless rapacity had inspired it.

The one who "wittily observed" that the salmon had both summer and winter quarters is apparently still to be identified. The witty observer of the similarity between heedless fish and heedless men can now be known though not named. He was the author of *The Arte of Angling.*

At his instructor's table the Elizabethan Viator finds the great perch which he has helped to land in the morning served up with a garnish composed of its small kindred, ruffes. Piscator, in reply to questions, commends them as food, especially for invalids, and in speaking of the ease with which they can be caught says: "My master that taught me to angle could not abide to catch a ruffe; for if he took one, either he would remove or wind up and home for that time, he did know them so masterly among other fish. But for my part, I have been well content to deal with them, for this property they have, as is seen among the wicked: that though they see their fellows perish never so fast, yet will they not be warned, so that you shall have them so long as one is left, especially a little before a rain or in the bite time."[38]

When one has read these very similar and yet, in certain points, quite different comparisons between voracious fish and wicked men and reflects on them in connection with the almost identical instructions regarding baits[39]

[37] *Ibid.,* p. 181. [38] *The Arte,* p. 39.

[39] Although the editors of *The Arte of Angling* do not stress the point, Walton's discussions of other baits such as snails, congealed blood, and the caddis echo similar discussion in *The Arte* (see *The Arte,* pp. 48, 60-61, 65 and Walton, 1653, pp. 54, 226, and 230-34). It is to be remarked, however, that in recommending "a black snail, with his belly slit, to shew his white" as a bait for chub, Walton is much closer to Dennys' line, "Blacke snayles, their bellies slit to shew their white" (*Secrets of Angling* [London, 1883], p. 48) than he is to the corresponding passage in *The Arte.* Whether Dennys knew *The Arte,* as Professor Bentley seems to suggest (p. x) is not a question easy to answer. It is also to be noted that Walton's discussion of the caddis, which is much longer than that in *The Arte,* is largely a record of practical experience in collecting bait, and that the method he employed, though it might have been learned from a book, is more likely to have been derived from youthful observation of, and practice with, older anglers. It is plain that Walton had found the collection of caddis worms a pleasant prelude to their use in angling, exactly as many anglers today enjoy catching minnows, crayfish, or hellgrammites.

to be found in *The Arte* and *The Angler,* one begins to get a better understanding of Walton's indebtedness to his Elizabethan forerunner.

Walton was unwilling to be thought an expert in fly-fishing when he was none and caused his Piscator to begin a lecture to Viator on the subject with the preamble: "because you shall not think yourself more engaged to me then indeed you really are, therefore I will tell you freely, I find Mr. *Thomas Barker* (a Gentleman that has spent much time and money in Angling) deal so judicially and freely in a little book of his of Angling, and especially of making and Angling with a *flye* for a *Trout,* that I will give you his very directions without much variation, which shal follow."[40] In like manner he was unwilling to claim credit for the rhyme from the "old Fishbook" or for the witticism about the ruffe, which he had, probably unconsciously, adapted to fit the perch to which it would apply with equal truth and felicity.

Since we do not know that the name of its author ever appeared in *The Arte of Angling,* it may be that "one hath wittily observed" is as definite a reference as Walton could have made to him, unless he had added some phrase such as "in an old book called *The Arte of Angling,*" an elaboration scarcely required by the literary practice of his time.[41] Also there is always the possibility that Walton's knowledge of *The Arte* came at second or even third hand.

This last point is of importance in relation to the almost verbatim reproduction in *The Compleat Angler* of so much of the discussion of baits found in *The Arte.* It seems beyond dispute that Walton either copied the instructions regarding malt bait and gentles from the Elizabethan book or received them from somebody who had. It must be remembered, however, that the preparation of malt bait and the breeding and preservation of gentles were not newly developed activities even in 1577, and that the achievement of the author of *The Arte* lay not in a discovery but in the succinctness and clarity with which he phrased instructions how to do what people had long been doing.

[40] *Walton, 1653,* p. 108.

[41] Even H. J. Oliver, who departs considerably from the traditional views of Walton's simplicity and directness, is careful to note that in the seventeenth century more latitude was allowed an author in regard to his use and acknowledgment of sources than is allowed in the twentieth. See "The Composition and Revisions of 'The Compleat Angler,'" p. 295. In this study, the table (pp. 303-9) of significant changes made by Walton between the first and fifth editions provides evidence of a desire to attain greater accuracy, provide more definite references, and support statements by citation of pronouncements by accepted authorities. For an examination of Walton's revisions in the interest of rhetorical effects, see Mr. Oliver's earlier article, "Izaak Walton's Prose Style," *RES,* XXI (1945), 280-88.

In the light of Walton's general care to give credit where credit was due, it seems reasonable to dissent from Professor Bentley's view that it is likely that Walton "had direct recourse to the text [of *The Arte*] when he prepared his instructions for the preparation of malt bait and for the breeding and keeping of gentles." In addition to the positive reason for such dissent arising from confidence in Walton's care to give credit where it was due, there is a negative one born of consideration of the ideas and passages which Walton could have taken from *The Arte* if he had had a copy at hand, and didn't. To anyone who has long walked with Father Izaak, it is difficult, almost impossible, to imagine him failing to put the delightful fishing grace said at the Elizabethan Piscator's table[42] into *The Compleat Angler* if he had known it. It is almost as difficult to imagine him failing to add to his discussion of the introduction of "the carp, a stately, a good, and a subtle fish," into England, the account of its abundance in the fens and of its spread from certain ponds in Bedfordshire and Buckinghamshire into other counties by way of the Great Ouse.[43]

If the idea of Walton writing *The Compleat Angler* with a copy of *The Arte of Angling* at hand for reference and borrowing is rejected, how is one to account for the almost verbatim reproduction of the instructions regarding bait, the changed but easily recognizable comparison of piscine and human folly, and certain other minor similarities between the two books which are not discussed in this study?[44]

There are two possible explanations of these matters, both of which are reasonable and between which, in the present state of knowledge of Walton's life, it is most difficult, if not impossible, to choose with assurance. In considering either, it must be remembered that Walton was sixty when the first edition of *The Compleat Angler* appeared and that many years of fishing, association with fellow fishermen, and reading about fishing, lay behind him. *The Arte of Angling* was published sixteen years before Walton was born, and if we accept the evidence of the battered and incomplete state of the sole surviving copy in support of the frequently iterated opinion that old angling books are very scarce because they usually received hard wear, it is plain that he would have had a better chance at sixteen than at sixty to

[42] *The Arte,* p. 35. [43] *Ibid.,* p. 51.

[44] One of the most interesting of these minor similarities, a not very minor one perhaps, is the almost identical manner of retelling the wonderful story of Frederick II's great pike, in the two books, with the same mistranslation of Gesner's "Haylprun imperialem Sueuiae vrbem." Since in view of his translation of other passages in the *Historiae Animalium Liber IV* which are not mentioned in *The Arte* there can be no doubt that Walton had direct knowledge of that great work, this matter can best be left for more extended treatment in a study of the great fish story and its analogues which the writer has in preparation.

make the acquaintance of the Elizabethan Piscator. It may well have been, then, that Walton read *The Arte* in his youth in Stafford, copied out the very plain and practical instructions about baits for use in his fishing, and kept them throughout life in some notebook from which he transcribed them later for *The Compleat Angler* without remembering where he originally got them. From such early reading, too, certain ideas and phrases would remain with him, though not exactly as they stood in the book, and, in the course of time, would receive new coloring from other reading and from his own direct experience and reflection. In such a manner, the simile concerning the ruffe might remain with him but with ruffe to perch. Everyone who has sought to trace the transmission of a tale of prowess or wonder, a moralizing fable, or a famous jest, through succeeding centuries or across geographic areas, is aware that such changes do occur and why. The tracing of such mutations has in recent years become one of the chief preoccupations of the historical and comparative folklorist.

It is worth remarking, perhaps, though the mere isolated fact will not take one very far, that the only previous owner of the surviving copy of *The Arte of Angling* who wrote his address in it lived at Stoke-on-Trent in Walton's native Staffordshire.[45] A truly daring student of the past, like those who continually find new reasons for maintaining that some other Elizabethan wrote the plays usually attributed to Shakespeare, might see in the battered copy of *The Arte of Angling* the very one from which Walton transcribed the instructions in regard to baits. From such precision in speculation, tempting though it may be, the present writer instinctively and decidedly draws back.

The other possible explanation of the appearance of elements from *The*

[45] This was Eli Baker, whose entry is dated "Septr. 1841." So far, the writer has not been able to discover any person of the name who flourished at the proper time and place. The two earlier names are more evocative. "Robert Stapleton His Booke Anno Domini 1646" brings to mind Sir Robert Stapleton or Staplyton, once a Benedictine monk of Douai, who being, according to Anthony à Wood "too gay and poetical to be confined within a cloyster," changed his religion, served Charles I in the Civil War, and has some slight claim to notice as a playwright. Unfortunately, he has no place in the annals of angling, and, since he was knighted at Nottingham, September 13, 1642, he might have been expected to use his title in inscribing a book. The third inscription is "Thomas Dale His Fishing Booke Anno Dom. 88 (i.e., 1788?)." Here again is a name which can be found in the *DNB* with a date to fit. There was a Thomas Dale (1729-1816) — his longevity would support the hypothesis that he was an angler, if one can trust the unknown author of *The Treatyse* — who took an M.D. degree at Edinburgh in 1775 and seems to have been a man of considerable standing. It would be interesting to know whether either Stapleton or Dale had any connection with Staffordshire, though it must be remembered that, although in the same county, Stoke-on-Trent and Stafford are not very close to each other.

Arte of Angling in *The Compleat Angler* is that, like the recipes for the two mixtures for attracting fish which Walton's Piscator communicates to Viator, one of which had been transmitted in writing and the other, however conveyed, offered as a secret, the instructions regarding baits were the gift of one angler to another. There is, as Walton never tired of reminding his readers, a true spirit of brotherhood among anglers, and therefore frequent communication from one to another of any information found useful, including even the most hard-won discoveries for the advancement of the art. Walton fished, talked, and corresponded with a great many of his angling brethren, from Donne, Wotton, and Sir George Hastings to "honest Nat. & R. Roe" whose names have come down to us only because of his love. Some of them had doubtless already begun to fish, or were soon to begin, when *The Arte of Angling* was first offered for sale by Henry Middleton as perhaps the first book in English on its subject since the ever-admirable *Treatyse*. They may have made its wisdom part of their piscatorial capital for life, a capital which could be drawn on for the benefit of friends such as Izaak without any fear of diminution.

In the foregoing pages an attempt has been made to determine the validity of the grounds for assuming that *The Compleat Angler* shows evidence of indebtedness to *The Arte of Angling, 1577,* to examine the nature of the indebtedness once the fact has been accepted, to account for it as far as is possible on the basis of existing information, and to decide whether knowledge of his borrowings from the work of his newly discovered predecessor makes necessary any change in the generally accepted concept of Walton as a writer of very great talent and as a notably honorable man.

It is the writer's belief that no reasonable doubt can be entertained regarding Walton's indebtedness to *The Arte of Angling,* but that the circumstances under which ideas, words, and phrases were transferred from the earlier work to *The Compleat Angler* are obscure and likely to remain so unless additional information becomes available. Any assumption that Walton copied the instructions regarding baits directly from *The Arte* to the pages of his own manuscript ought to be rejected in the light of both positive and negative evidence. Finally, there is occasion to emphasize the fact that, although the newly recovered dialogue is a precious addition to the twin treasuries of early angling lore and Elizabethan literature, it in no way endangers the position of *The Compleat Angler* as the supreme masterpiece among all books devoted to fishing. After a review of Walton's sources as they were known in 1896, Andrew Lang wrote: "So much for what Walton owed to others. For all the rest, for what has made him the favourite of schoolboys and sages, of poets and philosophers, he is indebted to none but his Maker and his genius."[46]

Despite the discovery of the debt that Walton owed to the unidentified author of *The Arte of Angling,* that judgment still stands.

[46] *The Compleat Angler* (London, 1896), p. xlvii.

University of Illinois

MILTON AND OLAUS MAGNUS

John E. Hankins

In the summer of 1954, I visited Milton's cottage at Chalfont St. Giles, now a museum which displays various items of Miltoniana. It was here that Milton composed a great part of *Paradise Lost.* Among the items displayed is a small book bearing Milton's monogram, Olaus Magnus' *Epitome de Gentibus Septentrionalibus* (Antwerp, 1558). I already possessed a copy of this entertaining little book (Amsterdam, 1669) and had observed several parallels between its text and the lines of *Paradise Lost.* With the discovery that Milton himself had owned a copy, these parallels assumed added significance, and further reading revealed more of them.

Olaus Magnus was Archbishop of Upsala, in Sweden, and in 1555 published his *History of the Northern Peoples (De Gentibus Septentrionalibus).* The *Epitome* is a condensation of this work into more compact form. The history is primarily concerned with the peoples of Scandinavia, Finland, Lapland, and Iceland, with occasional references to other countries. It abounds in lively descriptions of landscape, animals, plants, marine life, birds, minerals, and people, and in equally lively anecdotes of marvelous occurrences. There is a considerable admixture of the fabulous and some unacknowledged borrowing from earlier authors, yet we must place the good bishop with Herodotus and Marco Polo rather than with Sir John Mandeville or Baron Munchausen. He is credulous but not dishonest in using the materials which he has heard and now recounts to his readers.

The influence of the *Epitome* is particularly evident in the first two books of *Paradise Lost,* where it has supplemented descriptions drawn from other sources. We may take as a first example Milton's comparison of Satan in the fiery lake to the Leviathan:

> . . . or that sea-beast
> Leviathan, which God of all his works
> Created hugest that swim the ocean-stream.
> Him, haply slumbering on the Norway foam,

> The pilot of some small night-foundered skiff,
> Deeming some island, oft, as seamen tell,
> With fixèd anchor in his scaly rind,
> Moors by his side under the lee, while night
> Invests the sea, and wishèd morn delays.
> (I, 199-208)

Both Himes and Hughes, in their respective editions of *Paradise Lost,* have mentioned the appearance of this bit of folklore in Olaus' work. Modern readers know it as occurring in the First Voyage of Sindbad the Sailor in the *Arabian Nights,* a work not available to Milton. His location of the Leviathan "on the Norway foam" agrees with Olaus, whose account is part of a vivid description of the sea monsters found off the coasts of Norway. He here describes Physeter, the sperm whale:

> The whale also has over his skin a surface like the soil which is found on the seashore; whence often when his back is raised above the waves, it is believed by sailors to be nothing else than an island. Accordingly, the sailors steer toward it and land on it, after which they drive stakes, tie up the boats, and kindle fires for cooking food. After a while, however, the whale, feeling the fire, dives into the depths; and those remaining on his back are drowned unless they can save themselves by the lines extending from the boats. This whale (as was said above of Physeter and Prister) sometimes spouts such a flood of water that the downpour sinks a fleet of seafarers; and when a storm springs up at sea, he lifts himself above the water so that in these commotions and threshings-about he may overwhelm ships. Sometimes he carries sands upon his back, on which tempest-tossed sailors, rejoicing to have found land and having made fast the anchors, rest on this false *terra firma.* The beast *(belua),* suddenly excited by their kindled fires, sinks himself into the waters and, unless the anchors are broken, draws the men with their ships down into the depths. (XXI, 17)

Olaus' earlier reference to the sperm whale, here mentioned, is as follows:

> In the family of whales, Physeter, or Prister, of two hundred cubits length, is possessed of a harsh nature: for in hatred of sailors he often raises himself beyond the masts of ships, and the water-pipe on top of his head *(fistulus fluctus supra caput)* so spouts out the water he has taken in that the cloudy downpour often sinks the strongest ships or exposes the sailors to very great danger. (XXI, 6)

The language of this passage is substantially the same as that cited by Whiting from Pliny's *Natural History*[1] as a probable source for Raphael's lines on the creation:

> There Leviathan,
> Hugest of living creatures, on the deep
> Stretched like a promontory, sleeps or swims,
> And seems a moving land, and at his gills
> Draws in, and at his trunk spouts out, a sea.
> (VII, 412-16)

[1] George W. Whiting, *Milton's Literary Milieu* (Chapel Hill, N.C., 1939), p. 81 (citing Philemon Holland's *Pliny* [London, 1601], I, 235 ff.).

Here Milton's curious description of the Leviathan as spouting through his "trunk," in the manner of an elephant, was probably suggested by "the water-pipe on top of his head" in Olaus' account. Milton's term "sea-beast" may reflect Olaus' *belua;* in neither passage is the creature called a fish.

We need only add that the Leviathan's "scaly rind" is probably a verbal reminiscence of Job 41:15, "his scales are his pride" (Himes), though Milton is thinking of sand-encrusted skin in using the phrase.

Milton again mentions Norway in describing Satan's spear:

> His spear — to equal which the tallest pine
> Hewn on Norwegian hills, to be the mast
> Of some great ammiral, were but a wand.
> (I, 292-94)

Himes points out that Polyphemus' spear was likened by Homer to a ship's mast (*Odyssey,* IX, 322) and by Vergil to a pine (*Aeneid,* III, 659). "Ammiral" means an admiral's flagship. Perhaps the appearance of Norway in the quotation is indebted to Olaus:

> In the forests of the North there is very great abundance of firs and pines, of juniper and larch, and of so great height that they may equal high towers. And, because of this, those which are nearer the shore are used as the spars and masts of great ships; and principally pine trees which, because of their resin and pitch, are accustomed by their nature to resist the rains, and do not rot quickly but last a long time. (XII, 4)

Of course, pine trees grew in Norway in Milton's own day and his reference may reflect only a contemporary fact of commerce, but it is worth noting the possible source in Olaus' *Epitome.*

Milton's brief reference to "Lapland witches" (II, 665) may have some indebtedness to Olaus' chapter on witches and magicians in Finland and Lapland, though the contexts show no significant parallels (III, 15). The localization of witches in Lapland is also found in Purchas (III, 1).

Milton's Hell is divided into a region of fire and a region of ice, between which the inhabitants are dragged back and forth at intervals lest they become comfortably acclimated to one extreme of temperature. As I have elsewhere suggested,[2] Milton may be indebted for this arrangement to medieval visions of the other world, such as the Vision of Tundale. At the same time, the geography of his Hell is that of a volcanic region. Marjorie Nicolson has suggested that this description may proceed from personal observation of the Phlegraean Fields during his trip to Italy, possibly reinforced by references to these fields in the works of George Sandys and

[2] "The Pains of the Afterworld: Fire, Wind, and Ice in Milton and Shakespeare," *PMLA,* LXXI (1956), 482-95.

Athanasius Kircher.[3] We should note, however, that not merely Milton's Fiery Continent, but also his Frozen Continent, is a volcanic region, for in the latter is "many a frozen, many a fiery Alp" (II, 620). Consequently, we may check Olaus for details of volcanoes in the frozen lands of the North.

Book II of the *Epitome* deals primarily with the topography of northern lands, and the first three chapters are concerned with volcanic regions, especially those of Iceland. These are short chapters, less than a page each:

I. On the Veins of Sulphur and the Burning of the Waters

There are certain veins of sulphur near the banks of bodies of water, often widely kindled in the manner of flames, which spread over the whole circuit of an unpeopled area. In Iceland and Scotland, very cold countries, the inhabitants view that spectacle continually burning with increasing brilliance. Especially in the land of the Middle Goths, not far from the city of Vexionens, is a marshy and slimy lake with a fiery virtue so strong that whatever cookable is let down into it by a cord and withdrawn in a brief moment of time is sent back completely cooked or badly burned. . . .

II. On the Wonderful Nature of Certain Mountains

In Iceland are mountains of such a nature as is already known to the whole world, I suppose, since, beyond the narrative of the ancients, we have shown in our Gothic map supplementing Ptolemy's description that the situation and nature of these mountains are very singular. For on their peaks is almost perpetual snow, and in their bases is a sulphurous fire ever burning without being consumed *(ignem sulphureum continuo sine sui consumptione exardescentem)*. Those who approach too near are readily suffocated by the force of dust and whirling ashes, and particularly since in many places appear torrid chasms filled with ashes of the burning mountains and valleys. These, again, by the silent increase of the growing sulphur deposits, are disposed toward combustion in cyclical periods of time. . . .

III. Description of Iceland and its People

. . . The island is famous for unusual wonders. In it is a cliff or promontory which burns, in the manner of Aetna, with perpetual fire. And there is believed to be the place of pain and expiation for sin-soiled souls. . . .

Here are some highly suggestive details. Milton's lake of fire stems basically from the Bible (Rev. 20:10), but the burning waters fed from veins of sulphur and the volcanic region of sulphurous fire afford a parallelism of details. In particular, Milton's words, "a fiery deluge, fed/With ever-burning sulphur unconsumed," seem to be recalled rather closely from "ignem sulphureum continuo sine sui consumptione exardescentem." His "many a fiery Alp" in the Frozen Continent may likewise stem from the snow-capped

[3] "Milton's Hell and the Phlegraean Fields," *Univ. of Toronto Q.*, VII (1938), 500-513.

burning mountains of Iceland. Furthermore, the region is identified as the place of punishment for the sinful dead and would therefore be easily associated with the topography of Hell. In my edition of the *Epitome,* the Index refers to the fiery mountain as "mons ignivomus, qui creditur animarum purgatorium." This is presumably a reference to Mount Hecla.[4]

Other passages significantly resemble Milton's description of the Frozen Continent:

> Beyond this flood a frozen continent
> Lies dark and wild, beat with perpetual storms
> Of whirlwind and *dire hail,* which on firm land
> Thaws not, but gathers heap, and *ruin seems*
> *Of ancient pile*; all else deep snow and ice. . . .
> Through many a dark and dreary vale
> They passed, and many a region dolorous,
> O'er many a frozen, many a fiery Alp,
> Rocks, caves, lakes, fens, bogs, dens, and shades of death.
> . . . and Nature breeds,
> Perverse, all *monstrous,* all prodigious things,
> Abominable, inutterable . . . (II, 587-626)

In Olaus' *Epitome* (II, 8) occurs this passage describing the coast of the Norwegian Ocean:

> Here, indeed, are the longest nights, the most intense cold, rocks here and there like towers being raised, savage and formidable beasts, as is shown below concerning *monsters.* Moreover, *the crusted ice-heaps, like ruined walls of gigantic buildings overthrown by storms,* stand out from neighboring things as though victims of unavoidable shipwrecks.

Here is a close parallel to Milton's description of the ice heaped up in the semblance of a ruined castle, or "ancient pile." The Latin words are "crustatae glacies, quasi parietes ingentium domorum tempestatibus dirutarum." Other resemblances are not so close, yet the details of Milton's description appear repeatedly in the *Epitome.* The storms and darkness recur often, and the atmosphere of cold and dreariness "in vast solitudes" (II, 8; XVIII, 1) conveys an imaginative quality which may have influenced his lines. Rocks, caves, lakes, etc., are the staple materials of Olaus' descriptions; e.g., the loud noises from the caves along the banks of Lake Vener give rise to the belief that the area is inhabited by demons (II, 18). The great rocks look like steep city walls (II, 26). Horrible winds beat the Northland, picking up stones from the ground (I, 5). Blowing through caves along the coast, they make thunderous sounds which warn mariners to keep offshore (II, 4). Snow is omnipresent. Even Milton's fondness for the word "dire," as in

[4] For the tradition that Mount Hecla, in Iceland, was the abode of the dead, see James A. Mew, *Traditional Aspects of Hell* (London, 1903), p. 159.

"dire hail," may stem from Olaus' "dira tempestas" (II, 5; IV, 2) and "dira tormenta" (III, 20).

Milton's vague reference to "monstrous" creatures more hideous than those of Greek mythology may be in part a reminiscence of Olaus' chapter "On the Horrible Monsters of the Norwegian Coast" (XXI, 5). In particular, he describes a monstrous whale so ugly as to horrify and stupefy all beholders. This creature has enormous red-flaming eyes, which in the dark seasons appear through the mist to fishermen exactly like kindled fires. In a later chapter (XXI, 27) he describes great serpents in caves along the coast as having red-flaming eyes (*flammeos oculos rutilantes*). These descriptions may account for Satan's "baleful eyes" and eyes "that sparkling blazed" (I, 56, 194) as he floated on the fiery lake in the manner of the Leviathan.

Finally, Olaus' extended account of mining and smelting metallic ore among the northern mountains may have had some influence upon Mammon's activities in *Paradise Lost,* I, 670-709. Olaus devotes all of Book VI to this subject. He says that mineral-bearing mountains may be recognized by the fact that snow will not remain on them in winter, since it is melted by the sulphur fumes (ch. 1). He laments the "force of insatiable greed" (*ardorem inexplebilis avaritiae*) in men who ransack the soil for mineral wealth (ch. 1) and will sacrifice a good farm in the hope of finding a silver mine (ch. 4). They believe they must penetrate to the profoundest caverns and lowest abysses of the mountains to get the best silver and copper ore, already partially smelted by Nature (ch. 3). In mining, they bring up ore *ab antris infernis* (ch. 5), a phrase which can mean "from the lowest caves" or "from the caves of Hell." We immediately recall Milton's comment:

> Let none admire
> That riches grow in Hell; that soil may best
> Deserve the precious bane. (I, 690-93)

His dictum and Olaus' moralizing tone in discussing this subject are very much in harmony.[5]

These several parallels suggest that Olaus' *Epitome* had a considerable influence in providing the descriptive materials for Milton's account of Hell and in stimulating his poetic imagination.

[5] Cf. Ovid's *Metamorphoses,* I, 137-40.

University of Maine

THAT UNNECESSARY SHELL OF MILTON'S WORLD

Harry F. Robins

Though some aspects of the cosmos in *Paradise Lost* have not ceased to occasion differences of scholarly opinion, the broad outline of Milton's system has for some years received general editorial acceptance. No single passage offers a complete and graphic description of this system, and no reader can visualize it without the effort of synthesis. Still it is all there in the poem — the Heaven of Heavens, serenely poised above undisciplined Chaos and supporting by a golden chain the world of concentric spheres with the earth at its center, and Hell far below, joined to the world by an immense mole leading to Limbo on its convexity. The particulars of this cosmic landscape are not vague but rather delineated by the poet in such detail as to require little conjecture. It may be safely asserted, therefore, that the annotator of cosmological passages can reasonably hope for illumination from within the poem; and it would appear also that he should be reluctant to insert features which depend upon speculation as to Milton's intent, even when those features seem to accommodate the poet's cosmos as a whole. Such an insertion is the outside shell of Milton's world now credited as surrounding the ten concentric spheres which the poet lists (III, 481-83). In this paper I shall present my reasons for regarding the outside shell as an unnecessary and unjustified addition to the astronomy of *Paradise Lost*.

The idea of a surrounding shell was first put forward in 1913 by Dr. Thomas N. Orchard. In his *Milton's Astronomy* he urged that the *primum mobile,* which he understood to be an incorporeal, transparent, and swiftly moving zone of space, must have been conceived by Milton as enclosed in a motionless, solid, and opaque casing. The functions of this spherical envelope are summarized as follows: "(1) It served as a protection to the Universe against the storms of Chaos; (2) it supported the golden ladder when let down from Heaven; (3) it afforded a firm foundation upon which rested the terminal extremity of the Causeway from Hell; (4) it provided Milton with a locality for his Paradise of Fools."[1] The *primum mobile* which Dr. Orchard adduces could not, to be sure, operate in any of these capacities. Though convinced of the need for an orb beyond the *primum mobile,* he was nevertheless uneasy with the conception: "Milton vouchsafes to us no description of the formation of this opaque outer covering which enclosed the Universe, nor does he make any apology to his readers for the addition of this strange and improbable adjunct to the cosmos."[2]

It is not Dr. Orchard, however, but Professor Allan H. Gilbert who is responsible for the unquestioning acceptance by Miltonists of the exterior shell. In an article written in 1923, Gilbert argues its existence on much the same grounds as those which influenced Dr. Orchard; he strengthens his thesis, moreover, with the discovery of analogues from St. Basil and St. Thomas Aquinas.[3] Since Gilbert's article any number of alleged parallels have been found and cited as corroborative evidence. As an example Professor Grant McColley notes:

> Among the Hebrews it appeared as a curtain or solid firmament; and as reported by Eusebius and Diogenes Laertius, various ancient Greeks regarded the cosmos as bounded by a tunic, a membrane, or a crystal shell. Seneca wrote that Artemidorus described the sphere as a hollow globe formed by the flying up and accumulation of atoms. The medieval philosopher Richard of Middleton found it an enclosing surface, and as Mr. Allan H. Gilbert noted some years ago, both Basil and Thomas Aquinas believed the world surrounded by an encircling substance. During the Seventeenth Century, the conception was referred to by Thomas Tymme, Johannes Johnstonus, and John Swan, the last of whom declared, "The firmament is a vaulted roof," comparable to "a certain husk, shell, or box, inclusively containing all things within the heaven of heavens."[4]

The eclectic nature of this list demonstrates one thing merely: the adherence to the concept of a finite universe. Though as early as 1576, Leonard Digges posited an "orbe of starres fixed infinitely up,"[5] almost two centuries passed before the belief in an enclosure of some sort was finally abandoned. That Milton set bounds to his world is not, of course, in question. The only problem deserving inquiry from those interested in Milton's cosmology is that of identifying the limiting agent. Obviously, two possibilities exist: (1) as

[1] Thomas N. Orchard, M.D., *Milton's Astronomy* (London, 1913), p. 91.

[2] *Ibid.,* p. 74.

[3] Allan H. Gilbert, "The Outside Shell of Milton's World," *SP,* XX (1923), 446-47. Hereafter cited as *Gilbert.*

[4] Grant McColley, *Paradise Lost: An Account of its Growth and Major Origins, with a Discussion of Milton's Use of Sources and Literary Patterns* (Chicago, 1940), p. 129. Hereafter cited as *McColley.*

[5] Leonard Digges, *A Prognostication Everlasting* (London, 1576), Fol. 43.

Masson and all earlier commentators held, the *primum mobile* walls the universe; (2) as Orchard, Gilbert, and all later commentators have agreed, the frontier of the world is a shell exterior to the *primum mobile.* And the only kind of shell or boundary which can sensibly be proposed as analogous is one harmonious with the poet's system as a whole.

The passage cited by Gilbert from Basil's *Hexaemeron* does not, it seems to me, fulfill this requirement. Basil argues that the cosmos before the creation of the world was full of light. "When then, according to the order of God, the heaven appeared, enveloping all that its circumference included, a vast and unbroken body separating outer things from those which it enclosed, it necessarily kept the space inside in darkness for want of communication with the outer light. . . . The shadow of heaven forms the darkness of the world."[6] Basil clearly visualizes an opaque and material shell separating the world from Heaven, but Hell, Chaos, and Limbo, integral parts of Milton's universe, can have no place in this arrangement. Gilbert's inclusion of a quotation from Aquinas adds nothing to his case, since the passage is simply a paraphrase of Basil. Actually Aquinas differs with Basil — this Gilbert does not remark — in assigning transparency to the separating body.[7] At any rate, Basil and St. Thomas seem to be describing an empyrean heaven beyond the sphere of the fixed stars; they do not say that this heaven lies outside the *primum mobile.*

An analogue far superior to Basil or Aquinas exists in the *De Principiis* of Origen, where it was first discovered by Grant McColley.[8] Origen's statement of his beliefs about the nature of the cosmos is a curiously syncretic development from Greek philosophy and a sentence by Clement of Rome in *The Epistle to the Corinthians:*

. . . the whole universe of existing things, celestial and super-celestial, earthly and infernal, is generally called one perfect world, within which, or by which, other worlds, if any there are, must be supposed to be contained. For which reason he [Clement] wished the globe of the sun or moon, and of the other bodies called planets, to be each termed worlds. Nay, even that preeminent globe itself which they [the Greeks] call the non-wandering [the sphere of the fixed stars], they nevertheless desired to have properly called world. . . . above that sphere which they call non-wandering, they will have another sphere to exist, which they say, exactly as our heaven contains all things which are under it, comprehends by its immense size and indescribable extent the spaces of all the spheres together within its more magnificent circumference; so that all things are within it, as this earth

[6] Cited in *Gilbert,* pp. 446-47.

[7] *Basic Writings of Saint Thomas Aquinas,* ed. Anton C. Pegis (New York, 1944), I, 626 (*The Summa Theologica,* Q. 66, Art. 3, Reply Obj. 4). Hereafter cited as *Pegis.*

[8] *McColley,* pp. 131-32.

of ours is under heaven. And this also is believed to be called in the holy Scriptures the good land, and the land of the living, having its own heaven, which is higher, and in which the names of the saints are said to be written . . . by the Savior. . . .

[When from men] all corruption has been shaken off and cleansed away, and when the whole of the space occupied by this world, in which the spheres of the planets are said to be, has been left behind and beneath, then is reached the fixed abode of the pious and the good situated above that sphere, which is called non-wandering. . . .

. . . these [good men] after their apprehension and their chastisement for the offences which they have undergone by way of purgation, may, after having fulfilled and discharged every obligation, deserve a habitation in that land; while those who have been obedient to the word of God . . . are said to deserve the kingdom of that heaven. . . .

For it is called a descent to this earth, but an exaltation to that which is on high. In this way, therefore, does a sort of road seem to be opened up by the departure of the saints from that earth to those heavens; so that they do not so much appear to abide in that land, as to inhabit it with an intention, viz., to pass on to the inheritance of the kingdom of heaven, when they have reached that degree of perfection also.[9]

The correspondencies are striking indeed between this arrangement of the cosmos and that which is to be inferred from the section of *Paradise Lost,* Book III, in which Satan explores the newly created world. Both describe one cosmos containing Heaven, Hell, the earth, and all other worlds if any exist (III, 566-67). Both agree in a system of concentric spheres or heavens (III, 481-83), with one above the fixed stars pictured as firm and opaque, dividing the luminous interior spheres from their surroundings (III, 418-20). Both make the convexity of this orb a Limbo midway between earth and heaven (III, Headnote, 440-500, 494-96). Both depict disembodied souls passing through the lower spheres to Limbo, intending to proceed upward into Heaven (III, 481-86), and both allow the saints to bypass Limbo and enter Heaven directly (III, 519-22). In both, a specific road or passage connecting Heaven with earth and Limbo is mentioned (III, 501-15). The astronomical details in both accounts are incidental to the central subject, Limbo, and each system makes use of descriptive rather than scientific astronomy.

There are, to be sure, differences between Origen's conception and Milton's, and these differences are the more interesting because they demonstrate how Milton's diametrically opposed point of view transmutes the material. It has long been recognized that Satan's exploratory journey on the outside of the world constitutes an anti-Catholic digression as full of invective as the equally unexpected diatribe against a worldly clergy in

[9] Origen, *De Principiis,* trans. Frederick Crombie, in *Ante Nicene Christian Library,* ed. Alexander Roberts and James Donaldson (Edinburgh, 1849), X, 87-91.

Lycidas. Origen's purgatory is trenchantly satirized in the Miltonic passage, which was expressly designed to denigrate what the poet considered a religion of "painful Superstition and blind Zeal." Whereas Origen's Limbo is a land of peace, protected and illuminated by the empyrean heaven, a place in which the spirits of good men undergo their final preparation for entrance into the blessed Heaven above, Milton's Limbo is dark, starless, waste, wild, threatened by Chaos and Night, racked by windy storms, and, though empty when explored by Satan, later inhabited by idiots, hermits, friars, giants, and monsters. It is a place where vanities and vain men are hopelessly and eternally lost.

Origen's immobile, opaque, and solid Limbo is located just outside the sphere of the fixed stars; but it cannot be identified with the crystalline sphere or the *primum mobile* for the simple reason that neither of these additions to scientific astronomy was to be made for nine centuries. The invention of the crystalline sphere followed that of the *primum mobile,* itself a very late development in European astronomy; it was added in the thirteenth century to account for the precession of the equinoxes as described by Ptolemy, whose great work was not known in Europe until Sacrobosco produced his *Tractatus de sphaera* in 1256. Even the influence of Aristotle, who posited only eight major spheres, was not felt in medieval Europe until the early years of that century; for in 1209 and again in 1215 the reading and teaching of the philosopher were forbidden by the Church, and not until 1254 were official orders issued providing for the inclusion of Aristotle in the Paris University curriculum. Dante, a writer on astronomy as well as a poet, counts nine spheres in the *Divina Commedia* (*ca.* 1300), though St. Thomas Aquinas (1225-74) taught that there were ten. These facts being understood, it is plain that any writer prior to the middle of the thirteenth century who locates anything beyond the sphere of the fixed stars is placing it beyond the outermost sphere of the universe.[10]

Once the crystalline sphere and the *primum mobile* had been invented, however, theologians hastened to incorporate them into their own descriptive cosmologies, even though they understood little of the scientific astronomical functions for which the two orbs had been designed. The rotating *primum mobile* of the astronomers was married by theologians to Aristotle's unmoved mover, the Spirit of Good, which caused the diurnal motion of the sphere of the stars; the result was a composite creation part *primum mobile* and

[10] See my study, "The Crystalline Sphere and the 'Waters Above' in *Paradise Lost,*" *PMLA*, LXIX (1954), 903-14, where the subject of the development of the outermost spheres of the Miltonic universe is treated in more detail. Most of the material in this paragraph, however, may be readily checked in J. L. E. Dreyer, *A History of Astronomy from Thales to Kepler* (New York, 1953), Chs. V, X, and XII.

part empyrean heaven, an unmoved mover the outer surface of which served as a location for the home of God and the angelic host. In his commentary on Sacrobosco's *Tractatus de sphaera* (the little astronomical handbook known to have been used by Milton), Michael Scot remarks: "Et primum celum a theologis dicitur empyreum non ab ardore sed a splendore et est uniformiter plenum lumine et immobile, non uniformiter tamen influit lumen suum in inferioribus celis eo quod actio agentis non recipitur in passum per modum ipsius agentis sed etiam per modum patientis, ut dicitur in libro *De substantia orbis*."[11] The first heaven, then, is itself unmoved; but it makes possible the movement of the inferior orbs. Because Scot is counting from outside the world rather than from within, it is called the first heaven; but it can only be the tenth sphere, for further on Scot says: "Secundum celum dicitur nona sphera que a theologis dicitur crystalinum,"; and still further on he speaks of the "tertium vero celum quod est octava sphera."

The marriage brought about by Aristotle's laws of motion between the *primum mobile* and the empyrean heaven may be clearly seen in the following excerpt from Scot's commentary:

> . . . omne quod movetur mutat locum; sed spera [the first mover] non mutat locum, ergo spera non movetur. Probatio. Spera est in spatio sibi equali sed quod est in spatio sibi equali non movetur, igitur etc. Item nobiliori subiecto nobilior debetur dispositio. Sed celum est nobilissimum corpus, ergo ei debetur nobilior dispositio; sed quies nobilior est motu, ergo et magis debetur celo quiescere quam moveri. Item moveri est dissimiliter se haberi nunc et prius, sed celum non est dissimiliter nunc et prius, sic patet quod celum non movetur. Item motus est actus imperfecti; sed celum est corpus perfectum, ergo motus non est actus eius, igitur celum non mover [etur]. Sed in celo non est resistentia, quia ubi est resistentia ibi est violentia; sed in celo non est violentia, quia sic moveretur cum fatigatione et pena, et sic esset corporale, quod falsum est, ergo non movetur. Item dicit Aristoteles *in libro de celo et mundo*: Celum est locus dei et spirituum; sed deus est immobilis, igitur et locus eius erit immobile, sed locus eius est celum, ergo celum est immobile.[12]

Returning now to Professor Gilbert's case for the addition of an outside shell to Milton's world, I believe that I can show its basic weakness. After citing St. Thomas to the effect that the empyrean heaven was spherical, dense, and "sufficiently strong to separate what is outside it from what it encloses," Gilbert adds: "He [Aquinas] explains further that this is the heaven which causes the rapid motion of the *primum mobile*."[13] But here is what Aquinas actually says:

[11] Lynn Thorndike, *The Sphere of Sacrobosco and Its Commentators* (Chicago, 1949), p. 283.

[12] *Ibid.*, p. 279. [13] *Gilbert*, p. 447.

It is not improbable, as some assert, that the empyrean heaven, having the state of glory for its ordained end, does not influence bodies of another order — those, namely, that are directed only to natural ends. Yet it seems more probable to say that it does influence bodies that are moved, even though it remains motionless. . . . For this reason it may be said that the influence of the empyrean upon that which is called the first heaven, and is moved, produces therein not something that comes and goes as a result of movement, but something of a fixed and stable nature, e.g., the power of conserving and causing, or some other eminent thing of this sort.[14]

Certainly it is understandable that the heaven "which is called the first heaven, and is moved" should suggest the *primum mobile.* Aquinas himself is confusingly inconsistent in his use of the designation "first," which, of course, has only a relative meaning. The significant fact is the location of "that which is called the first heaven, and is moved" immediately beneath the empyrean heaven. In the following passage, the significant fact is that the sphere located immediately beneath the empyrean heaven is the crystalline: ". . . there are three heavens: the first is the empyrean, which is wholly luminous; the second is the aqueous or crystalline, wholly transparent; and the third is called the starry heaven. . . ."[15] These excerpts from Aquinas seem to me conclusively to demonstrate that his empyrean heaven is an unmoved mover, identical in location and in function with the *primum mobile* of the astronomers, acting upon the crystalline and impelling it to motion. I have found no evidence that astronomers placed a shell beyond the *primum mobile* or that theologians placed a shell beyond the empyrean. Without such evidence surely any argument that Milton intended the reader to imagine a sphere exterior to the first mover must be based entirely upon proof that it is needed to make sense of the poem.

If the *primum mobile* of *Paradise Lost* moves, if it is transparent and incorporeal, then admittedly it cannot serve as an anchorage for the bridge from Hell or the golden chain from Heaven. Excluding the astronomical dialogue of Book VIII — and it must be excluded[16] — only one phrase

[14] *Pegis,* p. 626 (*The Summa Theologica,* Q. 66, Art. 3, Reply Obj. 2).

[15] *Ibid.,* p. 645 (Q. 68, Art. 4, Obj. 3).

[16] The astronomical dialogue in Book VIII between Adam and the angel Raphael clearly demonstrates Milton's distrust of all man-made patterns for the universe. Adam asks the angel which of two basic astronomical systems, the Ptolemaic or the Copernican, is the one which truly explains the workings of the universe. The angel's response indicates that he does not know, that the answer is hidden by the Almighty from both men and angels, and that the subject is not important anyway — man is advised to cultivate his own garden. Neither system is the one developed in the body of *Paradise Lost,* for both are scientific, whereas Milton's is never more than a simple descriptive background for the poem carefully kept free from involvement in the scientific controversies of the day.

suggests that the *primum mobile* is in motion. When Milton depicts vain men on their way to Limbo,

> They pass the Planets seven, and pass the fixt,
> And that Crystalline Sphere whose balance weighs
> The Trepidation talkt, and that first moved.
> (III, 481-83)

"That first moved" is a translation of *"primum mobile."* Long before Milton's time the Latin words had become a generic term for the outermost sphere of the universe, and, as my quotations from Scot's commentary on Sacrobosco indicate, the question of whether it moved or did not move was a subject of lively debate. It could be presumed, I suppose, that Milton's choice of "moved" rather than "mover" shows that he took the affirmative side. In view of his cavalier disregard for celestial mechanics, however, this seems highly unlikely. The early annotators of *Paradise Lost,* separated by far fewer years than we are from the poet's intellectual milieu, unhesitatingly assumed that the phrase required explication. In 1734 the Richardsons comment: "This Crystalline is suppos'd to be Clear and Transparent; Beyond This is the *Primum Mobile,* or First Mover. . . ."[17] And James Paterson, in 1744, remarks: "He means the *Primum Mobile; Lat.* i.e. The *First Mover,* or the 11th Heaven, which puts all the inferior *Orbs* into Motion."[18]

As to whether Milton thought of his *primum mobile* as transparent or opaque, as incorporeal or solid, no textual evidence can be adduced one way or the other. The *primum mobile,* since it lies far above the sphere of the moon, must be an etherous body, and ether, in *Paradise Lost,* takes any form and may have any consistency. It may be animal (the ethereal angels eat earthly food "with keen dispatch of real hunger"); vegetable (immortal plants abound in Heaven); mineral (Satan mines the materials for cannon and gunpowder from the ethereal mould); liquid (the waters above, the streams of Heaven may be mentioned); solid, as the planets; gaseous, as the ethereal atmosphere; luminous, as the sun; invisible, as the inferior spheres. If I pursue this matter ad absurdum, my excuse is that I do not believe the physics of *Paradise Lost* deserving of solemn scientific inquiry.

The development of Milton's cosmos perhaps came about like this. Beginning with a general world system similar to that outlined by Origen

[17] J. Richardson, Father and Son, *Explanatory Notes and Remarks on Milton's Paradise Lost* (London, 1734), p. 122.

[18] James Paterson, *A Complete Commentary . . . on Milton's Paradise Lost* (London, 1744), p. 276. Paterson makes the *primum mobile* the eleventh rather than the tenth sphere because he includes two crystalline spheres in his discussion of astronomical matters useful to readers of the epic. See his note on III, 482.

in the *De Principiis,* Milton brought it into accord with later theological descriptive astronomy by the addition of the crystalline sphere and the unmoved mover as represented in Scot and Aquinas. Because he was militantly Protestant, he changed the "good men" who inhabit Origen's Limbo into the "vain men" who fill his own Paradise of Fools, satirizing by this alteration the Catholic purgatory. Origen's orbicular highest heaven, which contained, it will be remembered, "the whole universe of existing things, celestial and super celestial, earthly and infernal," and which was the home of the saints, was flattened out and opened up so that it allowed room for Chaos and Hell, and it became Milton's Heaven of Heavens. Minor touches from many sources were then incorporated into the whole — the golden chain linking Heaven and the world from Plato, the golden stair and the waters above from Genesis, and the methods by which souls enter Heaven from St. Luke and II Kings.

In this cosmological plan there is neither room nor need for an outside shell; and it becomes in truth what its inventor termed it, "an unnatural and incongruous addition to the system upon which Milton reared the fabric of his poem."

University of Illinois

"OUR VEGETABLE LOVE": MARVELL AND BURTON

Rufus Putney

Marvell's absolute charm and mastery of the "mighty line," even within the confines of the octosyllabic couplet, make his finest poems self-sufficing to a degree where discussion of them seems almost an impertinence. Preeminently among them all, "To His Coy Mistress" shines in the aura of its own clarity, strength, and beauty. Yet in the first section, the poem contains a phrase, "our vegetable love," that has at one time or another made most readers gulp and hurry on with visions of cabbages filling their heads. Nor have the editors of the poem done much to assist in exorcising the grotesque associations that continue to linger in the mind after frequent reading has homeopathically allayed the discomfort caused by first finding the noun "love" modified by the adjective "vegetable." Occasionally editors attempt to gloss the word, but most, like Margoliouth, tiptoe silently past it as though its homeliness made it self-explanatory.[1] In discussing the poem, I always hastened along with muttered references to sequoia trees and other giant forms of plant life until luck led me to find in Burton's *Anatomy of Melancholy* the far more psychological meaning and extensive implications of "vegetable" as Marvell probably used the word.

The information necessary to understand the term as Marvell must have

[1] An unusually imaginative, but still unsatisfactory, attempt was that of F. W. Bradbrook: " 'Vegetable' means 'having the power of sense-perception' as well as 'like a plant' (the Latin *vegetabilis* actually suggests speed and is equivalent to 'animating,' 'enlivening,' 'lively,' 'quickening'). The anticlimax is gained by the contrast between the size of the love and the time it takes to grow, and rhythmically this is given in the verse by the sudden pause in the middle of the second line, and the three dead, heavy monosyllables, emphasized by the long-drawn-out vowels. The reader taking 'vegetable' in its Latin sense would meet a sudden contradiction and reversal of meaning." "The Poetry of Andrew Marvell," *From Donne to Marvell,* ed. Boris Ford (Penguin Books, 1956), p. 196.

meant it and as contemporary readers would surely have understood it will be found in Burton's discussion "Of the Soul and her Faculties." There we are first informed that

The common division of the *soul* is into three principal faculties, *vegetal, sensitive,* and *rational,* which make three distinct kind of living creatures: *vegetal* plants, *sensible* beasts, and *rational* men. How these principal faculties are distinguished and connected, *humano ingenio inaccessum videtur,* is beyond human capacity, as *Taurellus, Philip, Flavius,* and others, suppose. The inferior may be alone, but the superior cannot subsist without the other; so *sensible* includes *vegetal, rational* both; which are contained in it (saith Aristotle) *ut trigonus in tetragono,* as a triangle in a quadrangle.[2]

Burton next proceeded to state the characteristics of the vegetable soul. My quotation omits his extended analysis of the details of nutrition, *"attraction, retention, digestion, expulsion":*

Vegetal, the first of the three distinct faculties, is defined to be a substantial act of an organical body, by which it is nourished, augmented, and begets another like unto itself; in which definition three several operations are specified, *altrix, auctrix, procreatrix.* The first is nutrition, whose object is nourishment, meat, drink, and the like; his organ the liver in sensible creatures, in plants the root or sap. His office is to turn the nutriment into the substance of the body nourished, which he performs by natural heat. . . .

As this *nutritive* faculty serves to nourish the body, so doth the *augmenting faculty* (the second operation or power of the *vegetal faculty*) to the increasing of it in quantity, according to all dimensions, long, broad, thick, and to make it grow till it come to his due proportion and perfect shape: which hath his period of augmentation, as of consumption: and that most certain, as the Poet observes:

Stat sua cuique dies breve irreparabile tempus
Omnibus est vitae.——————

A term of life is set to every man,
Which is but short, and pass it no man can.

The last of these three *vegetal* faculties is *generation,* which begets another by means of seed like unto itself, to the perpetual preservation of the *species.* To this faculty they ascribe three subordinate operations: the first to turn nourishment into seed, &c. (I, 178-79)

To dispel utterly any lingering associations with dormancy, vegetable marrow, or dried tubers, we ought to look at Burton's lyrical descriptions of love in the world of plants,[3] but his witty "&c." compels us back to Marvell's

[2] Robert Burton, *The Anatomy of Melancholy,* ed. Shilleto, 3 vols. (Bohn's Popular Library, 1926), I, 177. References will be to pages in this edition, but with one exception all quotations are taken from Part I, Sec. I, Mem. II, Subsections 5-11.

[3] "In vegetal creatures what sovereignty Love hath by many pregnant proofs and familiar examples may be proved, especially of palm trees, which are both he and she, and express not a sympathy but a love-passion, as by many observations have been confirmed.

(Footnote concluded on next page)

poem with heightened understanding of its meaning. The ultimate function of "vegetable love," we can now see, is not mere growth, but rather procreation, which, as we have always known, Marvell would cheerfully defer, if only time served, "till the conversion of the Jews." But the philosophical explanation of "our vegetable love" teaches us more about the first section of the poem. We understand now that his mistress was as amorous as he, that her love beneath her coyness had the same sexual orientation as his. We realize also that the specific details of the first division have to do with the nourishing and growth of love:

> A thousand years should go to praise
> Thine eyes and on thy forehead gaze,
> Two hundred to adore each breast,
> But thirty thousand to the rest;
> An age at least to every part,
> And the last age should show your heart.

With love so finely fed, consummation, in the ideal state of being with which this section deals, should be deferred until the ultimate and most rewarding moment when love has attained its fullest growth and supreme stature,

> For, lady, you deserve this state,
> Nor would I love at lower rate.

So far it seems to me undeniable that Marvell was expressing his feelings

---

> Vivunt in venerem frondes, omnisque vicissim
> Felix arbor amat, nutant ad mutua palmae
> Foedera populeo suspirat populus ictu,
> Et platani platanis, alnoque assibilat alnus.

Constantine, de Agric. lib. 10. *cap.* 4, gives an instance out of *Florentius* his Georgicks, of a Palm-tree that loved most fervently, *and would not be comforted until such time her Love applied himself unto her; you might see the two trees bend, and of their own accords stretch out their bows to embrace and kiss each other: they will give manifest signs of mutual love. Ammiannus Marcellinus, lib.* 24, [*cap.* 3,] reports that they marry one another, and fall in love if they grow in sight; and when the wind brings the smell to them, they are marvellously affected. *Philostratus, in Imaginibus,* observes as much, and *Galen, lib.* 6. *de locis affectis, cap* 5, they will be sick for love, ready to die and pine away, which the husbandmen perceiving, saith *Constantine, stroke many Palms that grow together, and so stroking again the Palm that is enamoured, they carry kisses from the one to the other:* or tying the leaves and branches of the one to the stem of the other, will make them both flourish and prosper a great deal better: *which are enamoured, they can perceive, by the bending of their boughs, and inclination of their bodies.* If any man think this which I say to be a tale, let him read that story of two palm trees in *Italy,* the male growing at *Brundisium,* the female at *Otranto* (related by *Jovianus Pontanus* in an excellent Poem, sometime Tutor to *Alphonso Junior,* King of *Naples,* his Secretary of State, and a great Philosopher) *which were barren and so continued a long time,* till they came to see one another growing up higher, though many *Stadiums* asunder" (Burton, III, 46-47, Part III, Sec. II, Mem. I, Subsec. 1).

in terms of the same psychological concepts Burton analyzed. Even though he may not have been directly thinking of Burton, I believe there can be no doubt that the qualities of the vegetable soul, nutrition, growth, and generation, are the characteristics of "our vegetable love." It is with less assurance — and far less conviction that our response to the poem is greatly enhanced — that I suggest that the other two sections of "To His Coy Mistress" are based on the concepts of the sensible and rational faculties of the soul, so that the three sections of the poem correspond to the three hypothetical divisions of the human soul. Such a proposal, however, affords new support for the tripartite structure of the poem — which has long been recognized — and maintains, as we shall see, its syllogistic organization without a premature appeal to the Hegelian form of thesis, antithesis, and synthesis. In addition to providing a better explanation of the structure of the poem, my proposition will add to the understanding of the intellectual milieu from which it emerged.

Supposing such an hypothesis correct, then Marvell in the second section of the poem would have alluded to the characteristics of "the sensible Soul." To see how the two match, it will be well to have the text of Marvell's lines before us:

> But at my back I always hear
> Time's wingèd chariot hurrying near;
> And yonder all before us lie
> Deserts of vast eternity.
> Thy beauty shall no more be found,
> Nor in the marble vault shall sound
> My echoing song; then worms shall try
> That long preserved virginity,
> And your quaint honour turn to dust,
> And into ashes all my lust.
> The grave's a fine and private place,
> But none I think do there embrace.

Before turning to the *Anatomy of Melancholy,* I would like to comment on these lines as reflections of common sense and fantasy, two terms we shall find Burton using. According to Burton, common sense distinguishes the presence or absence of sensory stimuli, but the entire passage in its true apprehension of the reality of their situation is also an expression of common sense in its modern meaning. In Burton's terminology that is a function of fantasy, but the supremely imaginative quality of the paragraph makes it for us also a tremendous fantasy in which the senses are intimately involved. Time's chariot is heard, in the mind's eye the deserts of eternity are seen, the trying worms imply touch, or possibly even "Scaliger's sixth sense of titillation" (I, 180). Her unfound beauty banishes sight, as his unsounded song negates hearing and speech, "which is the sixth external sense according to Lullius" (I, 180). Absence of lust is absence of appetite; to embrace would be to touch. The acrid mustiness of death shrouds the whole passage.

The psychological complexity of the harsh ironies that fill these lines are paralleled by the complexities Burton elaborated in his analysis of "the Sensible Soul." His discussion begins with this paragraph:

> Next in order is the *sensible faculty,* which is as far beyond the other in dignity, as a beast is preferred to a plant, having those vegetal powers included in it. 'Tis defined *an act of an organical body, by which it lives, hath sense, appetite, judgement, breath, and motion.* His object in general is a sensible or passible quality, because the sense is affected with it. The general organ is the brain, from which principally the sensible operations are derived. This *sensible soul* is divided into two parts, *apprehending or moving.* By the *apprehensive* power we perceive the species of sensible things, present or absent, and retain them as wax doth the print of a seal. By the *moving* the body is outwardly carried from one place to another, or inwardly moved by spirits & pulse. The *apprehensive* faculty is subdivided into two parts, *inward* or *outward; outward,* as the five senses, of *touching, hearing, seeing, smelling, tasting,* to which you may add *Scaliger's* sixth sense of *titillation,* if you please; or that of *speech,* which is the sixth external sense according to *Lullius; inward* are three, *common sense, phantasy, memory.* (I, 179-80)

Like Burton, for brevity I omit the "many delightsome questions" which are moved by him and other philosophers about the outward senses. When he came in the next subsection to write "Of the Inward Senses," he considered in some detail the characteristics of "common sense" and "phantasy:"

> *Inner senses* are three in number, so called, because they be within the brain pan, as *common sense, phantasy, memory.* Their objects are not only things present, but they perceive the sensible species of things to *come, past, absent,* such as were before in the sense. This *common sense* is the judge or moderator of the rest, by whom we discern all differences of objects; for by my eye I do not know that I see, or by mine ear that I hear, but by my *common sense,* who judgeth of sounds and colours: they are but the organs to bring the species to be censured; so that all their objects are his, and all their offices are his. (I, 182)

Common sense and fantasy combine in Burton's analysis, as in the poem, to foretell future probabilities. Proceeding to the second of these qualities, Burton wrote:

> *Phantasy,* or imagination, which some call *estimative,* or *cogitative,* (confirmed, saith *Fernelius,* by frequent meditation) is an inner sense which doth more fully examine the species perceived by *common sense,* of things present or absent, and keeps them longer, recalling them to mind again, or making new of his own. . . . His *organ* is the middle cell of the brain; his object all the species communicated to him by the *common sense,* by comparison of which he feigns infinite others unto himself. In *melancholy* men this faculty is most powerful and strong, and often hurts, producing many *monstruous* and prodigious things, especially if it

be stirred up by some terrible object, presented to it from the *common* sense or *memory*. . . . In men it is subject and governed by *reason,* or at least should be; but in brutes it hath no superior, and is *ratio brutorum,* all the reason they have. (I, 182)

Although common sense and fantasy, so defined, account sufficiently for the tone and the details of the second section of Marvell's poem, there should be added to them some of the concepts dealt with in the treatment "Of the Moving Faculty." This, said Burton, "is the other power of the *sensitive soul,* which causeth all those *inward and outward animal motions in the body.*" There are two faculties — appetite and the power of moving from place to place. Appetite is divided into three levels, natural, sensitive, and voluntary. Burton's comments on the voluntary appetite are not only relevant to the second and third divisions of "To His Coy Mistress," but are also fascinating in and for themselves:

For by this appetite the soul is led or inclined to follow that good which the senses shall approve, or avoid that which they hold evil. His object being good or evil, the one he embraceth, the other rejecteth: according to that Aphorism, *omnia appetunt bonum,* all things seek their own good, or at least seeming good. This power is inseparable from sense; for where sense is, there is likewise pleasure and pain. His *organ* is the same with the *common sense,* and is divided into two powers, or inclinations, *concupiscible* or *irascibile*: or (as one translates it) *coveting, anger invading,* or impugning. (I, 183-84)

Part of the contrast between the first and second sections of the poem is the shift from the serene and patient, though also whimsical and teasing, adoration of his mistress to the bitter ambivalences of the second paragraph, where her refusal fully to accept his love transmutes his love and admiration into anger and the wish to retaliate upon her the pain she causes him. Whether or not there was a direct relationship between Burton and Marvell, certainly there is a remarkable parallelism between the poet's expression of ambivalence and Burton's anticipations of hypotheses of Freudian psychology:

Concupiscible covets always pleasant and delightsome things, and abhors that which is distasteful, harsh, and unpleasant. *Irascible, quasi aversans per iram & odium,* as avoiding it with anger and indignation. All affections and perturbations arise out of these two fountains, which although the *Stoicks* make light of, we hold natural, and not to be resisted. The good affections are caused by some object of the same nature; and if present, they procure joy, which dilates the heart, & preserves the body; if absent, they cause hope, love, desire, and concupiscence. The *bad* are *simple* or *mixed*: *simple* for some bad object present, as sorrow, which contracts the heart, macerates the soul, subverts the good estate of the body, hindering all the operations of it, causing melancholy, and many times death itself: or future, as fear. Out of these two arise those mixed affections and passions of anger, which is a desire of revenge; hatred, which is inveterate anger; zeal, which is offended with him who hurts that he loves; and ἐπιχαιρεκακία, a compound affection of joy and hate, when we rejoice at other men's mischief, and are grieved at their prosperity; pride, self-love, emulation, envy, shame, &c., of which elsewhere. (I, 183-84)

Marvell's lines are a concrete expression of the abstractions Burton described.

Analyses that emphasize the logical structure of "To His Coy Mistress" usually define the final section as the synthesis of the syllogism. Synthesis, or the "conclusion" of a syllogism, as Burton and probably Marvell would have termed it, is a product of reason, which is, of course, the chief quality of the rational soul. Skipping subsection nine with its general commentary and its speculations on the immortality of this soul, we come to Burton's discussions "Of the Understanding" and "Of the Will," the principal faculties of the rational soul. These now become manifest in the poem. Hitherto common sense and fantasy had produced in the poet a true apprehension of the dilemma, but accompanied by an anger in which love could be expressed only in terms of its opposite, the bitterness and brutality of hatred, in which all consciousness of his mistress' charm and sweetness had evaporated. With the resurgence of reason, the awareness of her loveliness is recaptured in the opening lines of the third section, together with a reaffirmation of a love so strong that anger cannot really part them:

> Now therefore while the youthful hue
> Sits on thy skin like morning glew,
> And while thy willing soul transpires
> At every pore with instant fires,
> Now let us sport us while we may.

To feel and think like this, however, involves the understanding, concerning which Burton had written:

Understanding is a power of the soul, by which we perceive, know, remember, and judge, as well singulars as universals, having certain innate notices or beginnings of arts, a reflecting action, by which it judgeth of his own doings, and examines them. Out of this definition (besides his chief office, which is to apprehend, judge, all that he performs, without the help of any instruments or organs) three differences appear betwixt a man and a beast; as first, the sense only comprehends *singularities,* the understanding *universalities*; secondly, the sense hath no innate notions; thirdly, brutes cannot reflect upon themselves. Bees indeed make neat and curious works, and many other creatures besides; but when they have done, they cannot judge of them. His object is God, *Ens,* all nature, and whatsoever is to be understood: which successively it apprehends. (I, 188)

We are aware from other poems like "A Dialogue between the Soul and Body" and "The Mower against Gardens" how blithely the Puritan Marvell could espouse attitudes that are natural, pagan, and amoral. If he had been thinking in such terms as Burton used, his impassioned exhortation to his mistress to delay their joys no longer must have gained an added zest from its inversion of the right use of conscience, which is part of the understanding and should lead to ethical conduct:

> *Synteresis,* or the purer part of the conscience, is an innate habit, and doth signify *a conversation of the knowledge of the law of God and Nature, to know good or evil.* And (as our Divines hold) it is rather in the *understanding* than in the *will.* This makes the *major* proposition in a practick *syllogism.* The *dictamen rationis* is that which doth admonish us to do good or evil, and is the *minor* in the *syllogism.* The *conscience* is that which approves good or evil, justifying or condemning our actions, and is the conclusion of the *syllogism.* (I, 189-90)

To a considerable degree this quotation explains the structure of the poem, which in its entirety is seen to be a case of conscience, a syllogism by which his enlightened conscience attempts to persuade her obtuse reluctance to act as is natural and right by gratifying her own as well as his desires.

The final plea contains, however, elements of volition that Burton dealt with in his discussion "Of the Will":

> *Will* is the other power of the *rational soul, which covets or avoids such things as have been before judged and apprehended by the understanding.* If good, it approves; if evil, it abhors it: so that his object is either good or evil. *Aristotle* calls this our *rational appetite;* for as in the *sensitive* we are moved to good or bad by our *appetite,* ruled and directed by sense; so in this we are carried by *reason.* Besides, the *sensitive appetite* hath a particular object, good or bad: this an universal, immaterial; that respects only things delectable and pleasant, this honest. Again, they differ in liberty. The *sensual appetite* seeing an object, if it be a convenient good, cannot but desire it; if evil, avoid it: but this is free in his essence, *much now depraved, obscured, and fallen from his first perfection; yet in some of his operations still free,* as to go, walk, move at his pleasure, and to choose whether it will do or not do, steal or not steal. (I, 190)

Or love or not love. The final lines of the poem are an invitation to his mistress to join him in an exercise of the will to deal with the situation that the understanding has made clear:

> Now let us sport us while we may.
> And now like amorous birds of prey
> Rather at once our time devour
> Than languish in his slow-chapt power.
> Let us roll all our strength and all
> Our sweetness up into one ball,
> And tear our pleasures with rough strife
> Through the iron gates of life.
> Thus, though we cannot make our sun
> Stand still, yet we will make him run.

The poem has come full circle. Common sense and fantasy probed the unreality of the vegetable idyll with which the poem began. Since there is neither world enough nor time for such a love as was there envisioned, the rational mind was needed to dispel despair by suggesting that they do their best under the limitations with which men live. But the rational mind has also achieved the renewed understanding of their beauty, their sweetness, their strength, and of their ability to attain happiness despite the tragic ironies of life.

From Marvell's strange and fascinating mind the unpredictable and subtle may usually be expected. To realize this, one has only to recall other poems: "The Definition of Love," "The Nymph Complaining for the Death of her Faun," "The Coronet," "The Picture of Little T. C. in a Prospect of Flowers," "On a Drop of Dew," "A Dialogue between the Soul and Body," "The Garden," and "The Mower against Gardens." One can but speculate on the odd experiences and materials that went into the creation of such poems and observe the surprising perceptions and revelations of reality into which those strange materials were transformed. Some unrecoverable train of events in Marvell's mind gave "To His Coy Mistress" that somber power that makes it more impressive than such rivals as "O Mistress Mine" or even "Corinna's Going a-Maying." Can it be because the poem was conceived against the full range of psychological knowledge encompassed by *The Anatomy of Melancholy* that Marvell's vision of reality was so deep and ironic?

University of Colorado

THE PROBLEM OF BRUTUS: AN EIGHTEENTH-CENTURY SOLUTION

G. Blakemore Evans

I

The longstanding concern shown by critics and editors with the "problems" raised by Shakespeare's *Julius Caesar,* particularly in the character of Brutus, finds an early expression in some comments by a well-meaning "improver" of Shakespeare near the beginning of the eighteenth century. These comments, hitherto I believe unnoticed, are contained in the rough draft of a letter addressed to a lady, unfortunately anonymous, and signed "T Killigrew."[1]

One's first thought, of course, is to connect the letter with the well-known Restoration dramatist and manager of the King's Company, Thomas Killigrew (1612-83), but the evidence of handwriting and a single piece of internal evidence make such an identification impossible. The internal evidence appears in a comparison between Brutus and the Duke of Ormonde: ". . . there is a good natured weell meaning weakness not unlike the Duke of Ormonds, Brutus and Ormond were popular names, toolls that the Cassius's of all ages use to bring thier own Designs about with, . . ." If considered in relation to James Butler, the first Duke of Ormonde (1610-88), the comparison carries no meaning, but read in the light of the unhappy career of the second Duke, also James Butler (1665-1745), it takes on immediate significance and point. The second Duke of Ormonde, who had faithfully supported the crown during the reigns of William III and Queen Anne, had, nevertheless, strong Jacobite sympathies. With the coming of

[1] British Museum MS 22,629, foll. [238-39]; the letter is here reproduced with the permission of the Museum. It is a single sheet, folded, written on four sides. The existence of this MS is noticed in the *DNB* article on Thomas Killigrew (1612-83) and there mistakenly attributed to him. Alfred Harbage in his *Thomas Killigrew* (1930) makes no reference to it.

George I, however, although at first it seemed that he might be taken into favor, he was quickly stripped of his offices and impeached by Parliament for supposed traitorous dealings with Marshal Villars during the 1712 campaign. After fleeing to France, he took an open and leading part in the attempted Jacobite rising of 1715, led on by the false promises of the principal English Jacobites and by the regent Orléans. The rising was completely abortive and Ormonde once again left England never to return.[2] In both the affair of 1712 and that of 1715 Ormonde seems to have been used by politicians for their own ends, and the analogy drawn with Brutus might apply to either occasion, though the second seems a closer parallel, since, as in the case of Brutus, it entailed armed revolt against constituted authority. The Ormonde reference, therefore, may be taken to establish a period before which the letter cannot have been written, 1712 or 1715, with probability favoring 1715.

How much later the letter may have been written depends upon our identification of "T Killigrew," though it will, of course, be recognized that the reference to Ormonde must have been made while it would still carry weight, that is, while the Ormonde affair was still a *cause célèbre*. The only "T Killigrew" who seems at all likely and who fits into the time limitation imposed by the Ormonde reference is a Thomas Killigrew, author of a comedy called *Chit Chat* (1719), who died in July of 1719. Unfortunately, apart from the important fact of his interest in the theater, we know nothing of further significance about this Thomas Killigrew,[3] and his identity with "T Killigrew" must remain as not more than a fair likelihood. Having made this proviso, however, it still seems proper, in view of all the evidence, to suggest a date for the letter around 1716, possibly as early as 1712, probably not later than 1719.

II

It should be emphasized that Killigrew's letter is only a rough draft. Punctuation and capitalization are at best irregular and frequently lacking, though some attempt seems to have been made to substitute spacing for both. In the transcript which follows I have, for clarity's sake, inserted occasional pointing in square brackets and normalized the spacing, though

[2] See *DNB,* VIII, 63-64; see also Elizabeth Handasyde, *Granville the Polite* (Oxford, 1933), pp. 135-54, and Winston S. Churchill, *Marlborough, His Life and Times* (London, 1938), IV, 538-637.

[3] He was not, as the *DNB* makes him, the son of the Restoration dramatist (see Harbage, p. 125). This Killigrew, who may have been his grandson, however, served as gentleman of the bedchamber to George II while he was still Prince of Wales and enjoyed the patronage of the third Duke of Argyll (see *DNB,* XXXI, 115-16).

Killigrew's erratic punctuation has been allowed to stand unaltered. At times it has proved impossible to distinguish Killigrew's capitals from lower-case letters, particularly with *s* and *a*. Killigrew's first thoughts are given in angle brackets preceding his revision where the original reading has been deleted, or following his revision where the new reading has been written over the original.

Act the Second Brutus in his orchard

Bru: it must be by his death; ^ [4] (the rest of yᵉ speech tho beautifully ⟨b *written over an initial* w⟩ poetical) shoud be left out as a way of reasoning that will Iustefie my killing any man since there is no body so Inconsiderall as ⟨not⟩ some how or other has it not in his power to hurt his fellow) (& in the place of ⟨this⟩ it I woud haue Brutus conclud in this manner

^ if this Be wrong ye Immortal Gods who read the hearts of men Iudge not the Action, but the Intent[.] ⟨for⟩ Brutus might laugh; whilst his sad country groand if Brutus was a ⟨murderer or⟩ a [*sic*] Villain, yett I am strongly tempted by the repeated ⟨loud⟩ sharp complaints of Rome, Brutus thou sleepst[.] awake and see thy selfe[.] speak strike redress[.] I will. but first I'll prove this hauty man and try ⟨*written over an initial* a⟩ if he'll — be mov'd by reason, if not O Rome I make thee promise &c.

here I woud haue a scene betwixt Cesar & Brutus upon the Ill success of which Brutus shoud take his resolutions

Enter Brutus to Cesar & Calphunia [*sic*]

Cesar Brutus thour't well come[.] wrought on by Calphurnia's fears I think this day I will not mett [*sic*] the Senat[.] dark dreams haue frighten'd her and she perswaded me, (Cal: say out thy dream[.]
now Brutus tell me how shoud Cesar act[5]

Brut: a Roman Senator his Countrys friend, is by the gods protected; her dream protends no Ill but to the foe of Rome

Cesar ⟨Thy w⟩ Brutus thy words are dark as was Calp: dream, Lay by the Augur and asume yᵉ man

Brutus first tell me are we Romans both or must I kneel as speaking to a God

Cesar I every where am Cesar

Brutus and I am Brutus whom Cesar once bid live[.]
⟨heavens⟩ gods that you had then, for the first time been Cruel[;] for sure you did not know to give a Roman life, was to let Rome live free[.] if your Ambetion soars to Conqueor all thats great[,] him ⟨h *written over initial* w⟩ who non yett coud ere subdue, you must orecome yourselfe[.] the worlds a petty Victory[.] Scylla or Catiline coud yᵗ Inslave and what thier little ⟨geniuses⟩ souls coud act ⟨if sure⟩ Cesars superiour genius shoud disdain

[4] This caret mark, repeated several lines below, indicates where Killigrew's new lines are to be inserted as a continuation of Brutus's speech.

[5] It is not clear from the MS whether this line belongs to Calphurnia or to Caesar. Presumably it is meant to be the concluding line of Caesar's account of his dream.

Cesar ⟨Brutus⟩ no more[.] remember Cesar once again gives Brutus life, be wise and keep it

Exit Bru:

Act the Third florish

here I woud haue Brutus after the rest haue sued in vain for Mettlus's [*sic*] being recalled, say thus

Brut. peace ye unworthy of the name of Romans, how can you meanly think on privat wrongs, whilst Romes in Chains and murdred Liberty call's loud for Iustice[.] Brutus requiers of Cesar to recall the bannished Laws[;] to sett his Country free by Laying down his power userp'd

Cesar againt [*sic*] dast tempt me, know thou blind man and all the wandering herd that mutter Treasons in unwieldy Rome. Cesar is fix'd as Iove, & with a nod can turn your murmers into sighs and servil prayers to be forgiven (Caska. Speake[.] hands for me

Stabs

Brut thus Brutus pleads again his Countrys Cause, O t'was a dreadfull Conflict dreadfully decided

Cesar Et tu Brute — then fall Cesar

this I woud haue left out as it tends to reproach Brutus. by the seeming tenderness of the Expresions as if he coud not haue fell without him but that when he raisd his hand twas time for him to die[.] besides the words of a dying man make strongest Impressions & these last of Cesars blacken Brutus with Ingrate which Excits pity for the tyrant & Horror for the patriot, Contrary to the design of ye Author[.] tho it is very possible many understand the the [*sic*] beautys of Shakspeare better than me yett I dont think it Ease [*sic*] madam for any body to admire em more. this is by (way [*sic*] of preface to the ⟨t *written over initial* a⟩ following difficultys I allways find when ever I read this Excellent play[.] I ⟨a⟩ cant account for hating the historical Cesar and grieveing for the Poetical one, for my aversion to slavery and yett following the cause of the Tyrant with my best wishess thro all the fortunes of Anthony and Octavius, this is a contradiction I can solve no way but from disliking the Patriots whom I comprehend all under Brutus[;] for without him I Question withther [*sic*] it woud ever haue been attempted which at first sight seems to Iustife [*sic*] Brutus as finding him ⟨h *written over an illegible letter*⟩ self the only man able to free his Country, but if Im not mistaken Brutus had no Country atall[,] was no longer a Roman but a Cesarian[,] that is from a Citizen of Rome he became by the Mercy of ⟨Cesar⟩ the Conqueror a Creature of Cesars, he shoud Either haue refused his own life, as Cato did or not taken Cesars. since he ⟨Kn⟩ coud not but see after Pharsalia; what his benefactor aim'd at[,] it was in my opinion a Tacit agreement thou shallt live Brutus; but like the rest of the Vanquishd and accepting life, was consenting to the Contract[.] his Ingratitud is no where soften'd by Interduceing him moveing Cesar in behalfe of Rome[.] He Express [*sic*] no reluctance but in one ⟨o *written over initial* w⟩ word; to Entering into the Conspiricy nor shows the least sense of acknowledgment for life & fortune both which he derivd from Cesar[.] for his first right as I take it forfitted, it may be objected that touching Cesar upon so tender a point might haue alarmd him & prevented the success without remidieng the Evil by discovering the Conjuration, but for my part I dont see why a friend Cesar lovd so dear and a Brutus too, might not be suppos'd to say this thro an honnest open Zeal for the Countrys good & honour and safty of his Patron without being previously Ingag'd in a Conspiracy[.] I'm sure by the Charrecter of Brutus loaded with obligations to Cesar had he not appeard upon the Stage a Conspiritor I shoud never haue suspected ⟨em⟩ him — from any discontent he utters till Cassius works him to his purpose[;] nor Indeed is Cesar any where shown Iealouse of Brutus thro out ⟨y^e⟩ as he is of Cassius[;] nor to my mind shown Vicious Enough to Iustefi thier putting him to death no more than Brutus Vertuous Enough[.] there is a good natured weell meaning weakness not unlike the Duke of Ormonds, Brutus and Ormond were popular names, toolls that the Cassius's of all ages use to bring thier own Designs about with, (Cassius's hate to Cesar for prefering Brutus to him; not his love to Rome, works that very Brutus up to distroy his friend; on the ⟨the *written over* pr⟩ specious pretence of freeing his Country (who Else good man saw no Ills it sufferd, but of a sudden roused by the names of his ancestors without distinguishing ⟨betwixt⟩ the difference of thier Cases; or without ever as I said before trying his master & his father (for Conquest and kindness made ⟨Brutus⟩ Cesar both to Brutus) determins on a Plott with a sett of people whom he hardly knows but as Cassius declars em to him[;] ⟨some⟩ most of which appear actueted by privat Peke & even kill Cesar Interceeding for a perticular & a relation; ⟨that⟩ whom the Audience is no where told deserves the ffavor the [*sic*] beg; so that Cesar appears nither Cruel nor unjust in his refussal; as he woud have done, if they had mentiond his restoreing liberty & Law; and stabd him; ⟨demanding thier freedom or Gennerll, which the power he kept, deprived them of⟩ upon his denying to Lay down his power[.] these are as well as I coud degest my own thoughts; the obstacls I allways find to Brutus; the help I propose in the short scene; is no more than a ruled paper, for others to write on, ⟨[——] Certainly is a⟩ Brutus is Certainly a deffecttive Charrecter at best and therefore I thought wanted all the assistence poetical liberty woud allow him; very different from y^u m^d who need nothing but a faithfull historian to make you as much regreeted hereafter as y^r valued now ⟨now *written over* by⟩ by

T Killigrew

III

Killigrew's contemporaries were also critically exercised by *Julius Caesar*. Rymer spends several pages hooting at the character of Brutus for failing to preserve decorum and concludes that "every one must be content to wear a Fools Coat, who comes to be dressed by [Shakespeare]."[6] Criticism can

[6] *A Short View of Tragedy* (1692) in *Critical Works of Thomas Rymer,* ed. C. A. Zimansky (New Haven, 1956), pp. 164-70. The Furness Variorum *Julius Caesar* (Philadelphia, 1913) essentially ignores all the early criticism on the play. For this reason I have thought it worth while to bring together here other views of *Julius Caesar* more or less contemporary with Killigrew's.

scarcely fall lower. Dennis, ridden by the specter of poetic justice, objects to *Julius Caesar* on two grounds: it is "very Extravagant and Irregular" and it is "Irreligious." The killing of Caesar is "either a Murder, or a Lawful Action." If the second, then Shakespeare has failed in poetic justice by allowing the death of Brutus and Cassius; if the first, he has again failed in poetic justice by "introducing so many *Noble Romans,* committing, in the Face of an Audience, a very horrible Murder, and only punishing two of them."[7] In a somewhat later comment Dennis attacks Shakespeare's presentation of Caesar's character, whom he considers "but a Fourthrate Actor in his own Tragedy," objecting that he had failed to justify his actions or heighten his character by "showing that what he had done, he had done by Necessity." Dennis's solution is twofold: allow Brutus to enumerate to Cassius all Caesar's heroic qualities, a move which would have "heighten'd the Virtue and the Character of *Brutus*" if he had "resolv'd in spight of them all to sacrifice him [Caesar] to publick Liberty"; present a Caesar (based on the accounts of Sallust and Cicero) who secretly cherished the intent of restoring the Roman liberties, a secret which would be divulged (through Cicero) only after his murder. Such a handling of Caesar would produce "a Catastrophe the most dreadful and the most deplorable that ever was beheld upon the Tragick Stage" and show the "noblest of the Conspirators [Brutus and Cassius] cursing their temerarious Act."[8]

Charles Gildon, like Dennis an "improver" of Shakespeare, published his first serious "critique" of *Julius Caesar* in 1710. He felt strongly that the play should properly be two plays, the first ending with the death of Caesar and giving greater prominence to Caesar's character.[9] Even while Gildon was writing, as he observes, John Sheffield, Duke of Buckinghamshire, "a noble man of great Judgment in the *Drama,*" was engaged in preparing his alteration of Shakespeare's play, an alteration not published until 1723,

[7] *The Advancement and Reformation of Modern Poetry* (1701) in *Critical Works of John Dennis,* ed. E. N. Hooker (Baltimore, 1939), I, 200 — hereafter cited as *Works.* Mr. Hooker's notes were invaluable as a working bibliography.

[8] *Essay on the Genius and Writings of Shakespear* (1712) in *Works,* II, 10-12. The letter from which I have quoted is dated February 6, 1710/11. A year before, in *Tatler* No. 53 (August 11, 1709), Steele (? or Addison) had praised the effectiveness with which Shakespeare had presented his Caesar, though his point is confused by claiming II.ii as the moment of Caesar's first appearance in the play.

[9] Gildon's comments appear in "Remarks on the Plays of Shakespear" contained in Vol. VII, pp. 376-78, of Rowe's edition of Shakespeare (1710). In his earlier *Miscellaneous Letters and Essays* (1694) Gildon offers a defense (against Rymer) of Shakespeare's presentation of Brutus and Cassius in the "quarrel scene" (IV.iii; Gildon, p. 73). Dryden also, it will be remembered, praises the "quarrel scene" in the "Preface to *Troilus and Cressida,*" *Essays of John Dryden,* ed. W. P. Ker (Oxford, 1900), I, 205.

after Sheffield's death.[10] Sheffield breaks the original play into two parts, concluding the first part (called *Julius Caesar*) with the funeral oration of Marc Antony. He enlarges the role of Caesar, perhaps under Gildon's influence, and makes his expression of tyrannous intention much more obvious from the beginning. Using this second point as motivation, he makes Brutus in his first soliloquy comment on how "Ambition, like a mad tempestuous Sea, [has] Swell'd [Caesar] above the Bounds of wise dissembling." Brutus thereupon lists all Caesar's many virtues (shades perhaps of Dennis), but decides nevertheless that to "advise" Caesar would be more difficult than "to kill a Tyrant amidst all his Guards."[11]

The preceding paragraphs serve to bring out sharply the kind of critical climate which nourished Killigrew's reactions and suggestions. His main intentions seem clear. Brutus is not "good" enough; Caesar is not "bad" enough. To justify Brutus he will show him giving Caesar at least two opportunities to declare himself for the general good, in the process blackening the character of Caesar by allowing the audience to witness his tyrannical reception of Brutus's overtures. In this way we can admire Brutus with fewer reservations and hate the tyrant Caesar with more obvious cause. Killigrew's solution is typical of seventeenth- and early eighteenth-century

[10] Exactly when Sheffield began his alteration of *Julius Caesar* is not known. The evidence is confusing. In *Poems on Several Occasions* (1717), a volume which Pope is supposed to have edited, the choruses for Sheffield's *Julius Caesar* are printed with a headnote indicating that they were "written in the year 1692" (ed. Norman Ault [London, 1935], p. 141). Two choruses from the second part, *Marcus Brutus*, are also given and dated 1708. This suggests that the first part was probably completed by 1692, but that the second part was still only partly finished as late as 1717. How dependable Pope's dates here are may be judged from the fact that two of the choruses from *Julius Caesar* and the same two from *Marcus Brutus* had been earlier included in Lintot's *Miscellany* (1712) and there described as "Four Songs written in 1683" (see Ault, p. xciii). Dennis makes no reference to Sheffield's adaptation in his *Advancement and Reformation of Modern Poetry* (1701), a book dedicated to Sheffield, though he there discusses *Julius Caesar*. Writing some years later, however, in a letter dated February 6, 1710/11, Dennis speaks of Sheffield as one "who some Years ago, I hear, alter'd the *Julius Caesar*" (*Works*, II, 12). Gildon, on the other hand, in his "Remarks" (1710), is quite definite that Sheffield's version is only in progress ("[he] has been for some time altering this play"), but he shows that he has never seen Sheffield's version, in whatever state, by discussing Brutus's and Antony's orations as falling properly in the second part, whereas Sheffield concludes part one with Antony's oration. One point seems to emerge clearly: Sheffield was engaged on his project over a number of years and may well never have completed it himself. We know he asked Pope to write the first two choruses for *Marcus Brutus*, and Pope may, for all we now know, have had a final and substantial revising hand in the text of both parts.

[11] *The Tragedy of Julius Caesar*, II.i, in *Works of John Sheffield* (London, 1723), II, 248-50. The so-called D'Avenant-Dryden version of *Julius Caesar* published in 1719 makes no changes in the characters of Caesar or Brutus.

"improvers" of Shakespeare, who again and again reduced the complexities of Shakespearean character and motivation to an edifying but dull "simplicity." Indeed, the final effect of Sheffield's alteration is not at all unlike what would result from an application of Killigrew's "ruled paper." The ambiguities of Shakespeare's Brutus and Caesar struck no sympathetic chord in Killigrew's "committed" mind; but show us a Brutus activated by "reason" and a Caesar failing to "be mov'd by reason" and all might yet be well, even though "Brutus is Certainly a deffecttive Charrecter at best."

University of Illinois

MILTON'S CELESTIAL BATTLE AND THE THEOGONIES

Merritt Y. Hughes

Two recent studies of the sixth book of *Paradise Lost* — Arnold Stein's essay on "The War in Heaven"[1] and Dick Taylor's monograph on "The Battle in Heaven in *Paradise Lost*"[2] — begin by quoting Raphael's warning to Adam:

> . . . what surmounts the reach
> Of human sense, I shall delineate so,
> By lik'ning spiritual to corporal forms,
> As may express them best.
> (V, 571-74)

Then the studies go their different ways toward the common goal of refutation of Dr. Johnson's judgment that the "confusion of spirit and matter" weakens the narrative with "incongruity." Building on Arthur Barker's recognition of the sixth book as focal in the structure of the epic,[3] Taylor gives proper perspectives to its treatment of Obedience, Free Will, True Liberty, and the principle of Hierarchy in the emerging character of the Son of God and the degradation of Satan's character. In terms of structural logic, Milton could hardly hope for a better defense. In terms of poetic consistency Stein makes his case against the objection of "incongruity" and "confusion of spirit and matter" in Milton's celestial battle by reducing it to a single "complex metaphor."

Taylor and Stein face a severer critic of Milton than Johnson in Duncan Spaeth, who condemns him[4] for even trying to handle the subject of war,

[1] Arnold Stein, "Milton's War in Heaven: An Extended Metaphor," in *ELH,* XVIII (1951), 201-20; reprinted in *Answerable Style* (Minneapolis, 1953), pp. 17-37.

[2] In *Tulane Studies in English,* III (1952), 69-92.

[3] In "Structural Patterns in *Paradise Lost,*" *PQ,* XXVIII (1949), 17-30.

[4] "Epic Conventions in *Paradise Lost,*" in *Elizabethan Studies and Other Essays in Honor of George F. Reynolds* (Boulder, Colo., 1945), pp. 204-5.

which he said that he was not "sedulous to indite" and formally repudiated as an epic theme in favor of

the better fortitude
Of Patience and Heroic Martyrdom.
(IX, 31-32)

Echoing Johnson in Coleridge's language, Spaeth finds that "Milton's battle-scenes in heaven fail to induce that willing suspension of disbelief which constitutes poetic faith." He dislikes the "subtle disquisitions on the use of Force to make Reason prevail, which leave even Milton only half-convinced," and he is annoyed by divine meddling on battlefields either in heaven or on the windy plain of Troy. He is readier to excuse it in Homer's deities than to tolerate it in Milton's God. His objection is put in a way which nicely introduces the subject of the present study, when he declares that in Milton's choice of a myth for his narrative he blundered as Homer would have done if he had "made the *τιτανομαχία* the theme of his epic instead of the legendary but not mythical story of Troy."

The thesis of the present study is that Milton definitely conceived his celestial battle as representing events which were none the less actual for surmounting the reach of human sense, and that he found evidence for their occurrence and models for their likening to corporal forms in the classical accounts of the assaults of the Titans and giants on the gods of Olympus, of which the best example is in Hesiod's *Theogony*.

To say that Milton found proof of the actual occurrence of his celestial war in the ancient Titanomachies and gigantomachies amounts to saying that he regarded those accounts of war in heaven as substantially recording events which are less fully recorded in scriptural passages like the account of Michael leading the loyal angels against the legions of Satan in Revelation 12:7-9; the doom pronounced on the serpent in Genesis 3:15, that the seed of the woman should bruise its head; and the mysterious fall of Lucifer in Isaiah 14:12. Milton's acceptance of these passages as recording actual events is established by his opening statement in the chapter "On the Government of Angels" in *De Doctrina Christiana* (I, ix) that many of the angels revolted from God before the fall of man. As evidence he quoted Luke 9:26 and Luke 8:2, and among several passages from the epistles, II Peter 2:4: "God spared not the angels that sinned." Then, leaving no doubt of his adherence to the biblical record of the war in heaven, he went on to quote Revelation 12:7, and to explain that Michael, as leader of the embattled angels, must not be confused with Christ. The actual vanquisher of the devil, who singly tramples him under foot in the presence of the two exhausted armies of angels, is Christ.

In the *De Doctrina,* Satan's motives for revolting do not figure, yet Allan H. Gilbert is clearly right in thinking[5] that the exaltation of the Son over Satan and all other angels in Book V seemed to Milton to have the sanction of Psalms 2:6: "Yet have I set my king upon my holy hill of Zion." So it is the exaltation of the Son that provokes the revolt of the evil angels, all of whose rage, he says, as he goes toward his duel with Satan on the third day of the battle, is bent

> against mee . . .
> Because the Father, t'whom in Heav'n supreme
> Kingdom and Power and Glory appertains,
> Hath honour'd me according to his will.
> (VI, 813-16)

The Bible is chary of details about the celestial battle, but if Gilbert is right in his theory about the second Psalm as the basis of the exaltation of the Son to reign in heaven by right of merit, then he must also be right in interpreting its closing verse, "Thou shalt break them with a rod of iron," and the closing warning to "Kiss the Son lest he be angry," as parts of the historical record which is visualized in God's Decree:

> This day I have begot whom I declare
> My only Son, and on this holy Hill
> Him have anointed, whom ye now behold
> At my right hand; your Head I him appoint;
> And by my Self have sworn to him shall bow
> All knees in Heav'n. (VI, 603-8)

Protestant and Roman Catholic exegesis, as Gilbert shows, regularly treated Psalms 2:6, as parallelling Hebrews 1:6, "Let all the angels of God worship him"; and so Milton might regard the testimony of the Psalmist as corroborated by that of the apostle.

We may take still another step in the direction which Gilbert's theory points and see in the most famous verse in the psalm—"He that sitteth in the heavens shall laugh"—a glint of the element of true comedy in the ensuing situation. The verse is echoed in the Son's words on the eve of battle:

> Mighty Father, thou thy foes
> Justly hast in derision, and secure
> Laugh'st at thir vain designs and tumults vain.
> (V, 735-37)

[5] "The Theological Basis of Satan's Rebellion and the Function of Abdiel in *Paradise Lost,*" in *MP,* XL (1942), 19-42. The germ of Gilbert's thought is found in a connection between the second Psalm and *De Doctrina Christiana,* I, v, which is made by Sir Herbert Grierson in *Milton and Wordsworth* (New York, 1937), p. 99, on a hint drawn from Newton's note on *Paradise Lost,* VI, 603.

The prophecy is fulfilled when the Son routs the Satanic hosts without using half his strength,

for he meant
Not to destroy, but root them out of heav'n,
(VI, 854-55)

and so "as a Herd of Goats . . . Drove them before him Thunder-struck" (VI, 857-58).

In this scene Arnold Stein sees the capstone of Milton's entire "complex metaphor," since its whole purpose has been to leave the rebels "exposed to laughter." His conclusion harmonizes with C. S. Lewis' view of Milton's whole treatment of Satan as inevitably, to a great extent, comic and doomed to excite "the Divine laughter in *Paradise Lost* which has offended some readers."[6] Gilbert has frequently insisted on Milton's comic intention and talent, simply as a part of his gift for telling a many-sided story. Comedy is a part of all true epic, and recognition of it in *Paradise Lost* can help to support down-to-earth criticism like R. H. West's "Literal-Minded Defense of Milton's Battle in Heaven,"[7] and John E. Hardy's analysis of the merits of Book VI "as an epic battle."[8] Yet it is notorious that for irreverent readers Milton's battle scenes are absurd rather than comic. To A. J. A. Waldock[9] they all seem "rather nonsensical," like all his descriptions of the angels in action, because they have even more incongruities than Dr. Johnson saw in the attempt to accommodate "pure spirit" to the necessities of a narrative poem. Modern discovery of the "materialism" of Milton's view of the angels seems to Waldock only to complicate the incongruities. The worst of them, as E. M. W. Tillyard confesses,[10] is their use of artillery (which might not seem so incongruous if it were atomic), but he declares that it would not seem ludicrous if we were properly "impressed by the culminating emergence of the Son" in the heavenly battle.

We feel our modern difficulty in this matter acutely when we read a remark like Thyer's on *Paradise Lost*, VI, 746: "The description of the Messiah's going out against the rebel angels is a scene of the same sort with Hesiod's Jupiter against the Titans. They are both of them the most undoubted instances of the true sublime; but which has exceeded it is very difficult to determine." In spite of the reverence of the eighteenth-century editors for the classics, they were rather inclined to treat Milton as the

[6] C. S. Lewis, *A Preface to Paradise Lost* (London, 1942), p. 93.

[7] Unpublished address to SAMLA in 1952.

[8] In the *Sewanee Review* (1954), 32.

[9] In *Paradise Lost and its Critics* (Cambridge, Eng., 1947), p. 108. In *An Anatomy of Milton's Verse* (Baton Rouge, 1955), p. 17, W. B. C. Watkins briefly replied to Waldock in terms of seventeenth-century science.

[10] In *The Miltonic Setting Past and Present* (Cambridge, Eng., 1938), p. 170.

supreme master of sublimity, and they found it in some of the scenes which are most annoying to modern readers. Bishop Newton could annotate Milton's picture of the loyal and rebellious angels as having "vaulted either host with fire" (VI, 214) by observing that, "Our author," who "frequently had his eye upon Hesiod's giant-war, as well as upon Homer, . . . has imitated several passages, but commonly exceeds his original, as he has done in this particular . . . Milton has improved the horrour of the description; and a *shade of darts* (in *Theogony,* 716) is not near so grand and dreadful an image as a *fiery cope* or *vault of flaming darts.*"

But enthusiasm for Milton's battle scenes long antedated Newton and Thyer; it began with one of the first tributes to *Paradise Lost* on record, the Latin poem which was first published prefixed to the second edition, and which Masson confidently attributed to Dr. Samuel Barrow, who was eminent enough to be one of Charles II's physicians-in-ordinary.[11] To Barrow the celestial battle was clearly the most moving part of the whole work, and its peak was the moment of the appearance of the Son of God in the "Chariot of Paternal deity" with its convoying cherub shapes that come from Ezekiel's prophecy (I:4-27):

> At simul in coelis Messiae insignia fulgent,
> Et currus animes, armaque digna Deo,
> Horrendumque rotae strident, & saeva rotarum
> Erumpunt torvis fulgura luminibus
> (Lines 29-32)

The kindling of Barrow's imagination by Milton's passage is obvious, and his tribute in verses which were perhaps intended to suggest that Milton's style was worthy of its classical models, amounts to strong evidence that his first readers were far away from our danger of being insufficiently "impressed by the culminating emergence of the Son." By them, as Grant McColley pointed out,[12] the Son's emergence may have been expected in consequence of a tradition going back to Rupert of St. Heribert's Commentary on Ezekiel. For Rupert there was no doubt that "the likeness of the appearance of a man" on the sapphire throne above Ezekiel's terrible crystal firmament was Christ, or that the whole vision was a kind of apotheosis. So Milton regarded it, and he was irresistibly drawn to it because nowhere else among the many scriptural passages in which he found evidence of an actual war in heaven could he find one that was rich enough in imagery to furnish his picture of the Son mounted on

> The Chariot of Paternal Deity,

[11] David Masson, *The Life of John Milton* (New York, 1946), VI, 715.

[12] In "Milton's Battle in Heaven and Rupert of St. Heribert," *Speculum,* XVI (1941), 230-35.

Flashing thick flames, Wheel within Wheel, undrawn,
Itself instinct with Spirit, but convoy'd
By four Cherubic shapes, four Faces each
Had wondrous, as with Stars thir bodies all
And Wings were set with Eyes, with Eyes the wheels
Of Beryl, and careering Fires between;
Over thir heads a crystal Firmament,
Whereon a Sapphire Throne, . . .
(VI, 750-58)

Milton appropriated Ezekiel's vision both because he admired its poetry and because he regarded it as a supreme biblical example of "lik'ning spiritual to corporal forms." The evidence for interpreting it as a glimpse of the Son of God when he rode to battle against the rebel angels might not be conclusive, but it was as nearly so as that on which a great English angelologist, John Salkeld, had quoted "Aquinas and Valentin, with many other Schoole-Divines" as having interpreted Revelation 12, to mean that "Lucifer drew after him the third part of the Angels in his first combate with *Michael,* and fall from heaven."[13] Salkeld himself was inclined to regard the passage as a prophecy of a fight to come between Satan and Michael "a little before the day of Iudgement," and he was certain that the struggle between the two armies of angels should be understood as spiritual.[14] However Milton may have understood the passage in Revelation 12, he accepted Satan's past defeat in heaven as well as his future defeat at the end of the world, for both are implied by the prayer in the induction to the fourth book of *Paradise Lost* for

that warning voice, which he who saw
Th'Apocalypse, heard cry in Heav'n aloud,
Then when the Dragon, put to second rout,
Came furious down to be reveng'd on man . . .
(IV, 1-4)

Milton's confidence in his readers' acceptance of the celestial war with more than the suspense of disbelief which constitutes poetic faith is clear

[13] *A Treatise of Angels* (London, 1613), p. 345.

[14] Discussing "how the fore-said fight of the Divell was with the blessed Angels," Salkeld thought that Satan simply "declared (in the location of the Angels) his depraved minde and will: as on the contrary side, Michael, manifesting his constancie, affect, and minde to persevere in good, unto his part of Angels, was occasion of their persisting in good, by his good example, so that these two, as it were, armies of Angels, being contrary in manifest affections the one to the other, resisted mutually, as it is expressed in the Apocalypse Chap. 12 spiritually fought together." *A Treatise of Angels,* p. 347.

from his scenes in hell where Beelzebub grieves over the "foul defeat" which

> Hath lost us Heav'n, and all this mighty Host
> In horrible destruction laid thus low, . . .
> (I, 136-37)

And Belial reminds Moloch how they had so short a while ago

> fled amain, pursu'd and strook
> With Heav'n's afflicting Thunder.
> (II, 165-66)

II

The case for Milton's belief in a primordial celestial war may rest finally upon the chapter in *De Doctrina Christiana* (I, ix) which has already been quoted. Its evidence seems conclusive to Balachandra Rajan,[15] in contrast to the lack of evidence in the treatise to all else that he may have thought about events in heaven before the creation of the universe. Rajan is fully aware of a poet's right to mix facts with fiction in his story, and is quite ready to draw the inference that his "fable is misleading as a means of collecting and exhibiting a poet's beliefs." With that warning in mind, but fortified by Rajan's recognition of the fact that war in heaven was an important part in the construction and imagery of *Paradise Lost,* we may go on to the second of the two theses to which the present study is devoted.

It may seem less plausible than the first, and less important even if it can be accepted. It can be conveniently put in the form that Thyer gave to it in his note on the praise of the angel choruses for the Son of God in Milton's account of his return from the creation of the universe:

> what thought can measure thee or tongue
> Relate thee; greater now in thy return
> Than from the Giant Angels; thee that day
> Thy thunders magnifi'd; but to create
> Is greater than created to destroy.
> (VII, 603-7)

"Milton," said Thyer, "I doubt not, intended to allude to Hesiod's giant war; but I do not see with Dr. Bentley, that therefore he must insinuate that this relation is as fabulous as that. He probably designed, by this expression, to hint his opinion, that the fictions of the Greek poets owed their rise to some uncertain clouded tradition of this real event, and their giants were, if they had understood the story right, his fallen angels."

To take Thyer's suggestion seriously a reader needs a kind of classical education which has become obsolete. It may be acceptable, as R. J. Z.

[15] In *"Paradise Lost" and the Seventeenth Century Reader* (London, 1947), p. 31.

Werblowski has said,[16] only "in ages when the people could take it for granted that these myths (i.e., the myths of the hybristic protagonists of Greek tragedy), as well as those about the Giants and Titans warring with Zeus, were degenerate and paganized remains of the 'historical' Christian version." Writing as a disciple of Jung, Werblowski is mainly interested in identifying a common archetypal pattern in the *Prometheus* of Aeschylus and Milton's Satan — the hybris of the Titan and the *superbia* of the devil. He is not interested in Thyer's view of the matter except as it can be made to contribute to a psychological interpretation of the *Prometheus* of Aeschylus and *Paradise Lost* as embodiments of a common archetype.

Of course, Werblowski is right about the prevailing indifference of modern editors and scholars to Thyer's view of Milton's understanding of the relation of the ancient theogonies to the glimpses of a celestial war in the Bible. His point is proved by the modern editors and scholars who see nothing but casual literary allusions in the passages where Hesiod is clearly reflected. In the lines (VII, 603-5) which prompted Thyer's note, for example, Verity recognizes only a passing literary reference. To Arnold Stein all such passages in *Paradise Lost* seem to be simply "literary overtones."[17] In a careful study of Milton's angelology Robert H. West declares[18] that when he "has the warring angels pelt one another with hills and the rebels fall for nine days he has unmistakably borrowed from Hesiod imaginative items of titanic conflict and disaster, a purely literary debt distinct in kind from his debt to the speculative Psellus for the facts about angelic nature."

West regards Milton's "giant Angels" as an allusion to the giants of the Old Testament. Following a suggestion in a note on the passage by one of the most scholarly of the eighteenth-century editors, Zachary Pearce, West treats the word *giants* as meaning simply that the rebel angels had (in Pearce's language) "that disposition of mind, which is always ascribed to giants, namely a proud, fierce, and aspiring temper." Thyer found Pearce's

[16] R. J. Zwi Werblowski, *Lucifer and Satan* (London, 1952), p. 44. The "archetypal" theory is skeptically examined by Robert M. Adams in *Ikon: John Milton and the Modern Critics* (Ithaca, 1955), pp. 35-59. The editorial tradition of tracing many parallels to the *Prometheus* in *Paradise Lost* is attacked by J. C. Maxwell in "Milton's Knowledge of Aeschylus: The Argument from Parallel Passages," in *RES,* III (1952), 366-71.

[17] *Answerable Style,* p. 44.

[18] *Milton and the Angels* (Athens, Ga., 1955), p. 105. In *Paradise Lost: The Birth of an Epic* (Chicago, 1940), p. 40, Grant McColley found "a closer analogue than Hesiod's picture of the barrages of Hesiod's Titanomachy in 'the *Decay* of Du Bartas, a section of the *Divine Weeks.*'" But it is hard to find anything in Du Bartas which justifies McColley's statement, and we have the word of George Coffin Taylor in *Milton's Use of Du Bartas* (Cambridge, Mass., 1934), p. 85, that in the sixth book of *Paradise Lost* "there appear to be no borrowings from Du Bartas."

explanation "a little forced," even though it was supported by a reference to the fact that the Hebrew word *gibbor,* which means *fierce* or *proud,* "is always rendered a *giant* in Scripture." And then Thyer went on to declare his conviction that Milton "intended to allude to Hesiod's giant war."

If Thyer had wished to extend his note into a monograph, he might have reviewed the main coincidences between Hesiod's *Theogony* and Milton's battle in heaven: the crushing defeat of the attacking rebel powers and their nine-day fall from heaven into Tartarus (a parallel made prominent in *Paradise Lost,* I, 50, and again in VI, 871), the exchange of sky-darkening missiles which so impressed Newton, the reservation of the main might of the ruler of heaven until the stalemate of the struggle, and a final victory in both cases which is marked by something like apocalyptic fires and thunder. As detailed evidence Thyer might have quoted the passage which includes the Titans in the catalogue of fallen angels who assume the names of the various gods in the pagan pantheons so as to deceive the nations:

> Th' *Ionian* Gods, of *Javan's* Issue held
> Gods, yet confest later than Heav'n and Earth
> Thir boasted Parents; *Titan* Heav'n's first born
> With his enormous brood, and birthright seiz'd
> By younger *Saturn,* he from mightier *Jove,*
> His own and *Rhea's* Son, like measure found;
> So *Jove* usurping reign'd. (I, 508-14)

Milton puts the Titans and their usurping offspring, the Olympian deities, last in the list of rebel angels, whose leaders were to be the most powerfully realized actors in his story under the names of the devils of Hebrew or Christian tradition — Moloch, Beelzebub, Belial, and Mammon. All the demons in the list are treated alike as deceivers of the nations by the fraudulent[19] myths which they disseminated about themselves. But the fraud of their pretended generation by heaven and earth cast no doubt upon their myth as linking with the celestial battle of Scripture. Whatever fables might have been told about them by the erring Greeks, it was certain that they, like Mulciber, and all the rest of "this rebellious rout / Fell long before" (I, 747-48) the earliest tales had been told of the falls of deities from Olympus.

The fraud in the myths about the Titans might be obvious, yet they might contain recognizable fragments of biblical history. Many Renaissance scholars found evidence for the revolt of the angels in theogonies less familiar

[19] In *Classical Myth and Legend in Renaissance Dictionaries* (Chapel Hill, N. C., 1955), pp. 279-80, DeWitt T. Starnes and Ernest W. Talbert note the inconsistency of the Titan genealogies which the dictionaries took from various sources. In some, Rhea is identified with Ops, Vesta, and several other Titanesses, while in others she is made the daughter of one Vesta and the mother of another, the Vesta who appears as Saturn's daughter in *Il Penseroso,* I, 25.

than Hesiod's. Milton made a passing reference to one of them which, though lost, was supposed to have been written by "Blind Thamyris" (III, 35), with whom, as with Homer, he prayed that he might be "equall'd in renown." In a fragment of another such theogony, supposed to have been written by one of the "Seven Wise Men of Greece," Pherecydes of Syros, Milton knew of a passage suggesting identification of a Titan leader, the serpent-deity Ophion, with Satan. The appropriate place for an allusion to it was after the scene of the transformation of the devils into serpents in Pandaemonium after their celebration of Satan's seduction of Eve. The devils, he says, spread a tradition

> Among the Heathen of thir purchase got,
> And Fabl'd how the Serpent, whom they call'd
> *Ophion with Eurynome,* the wide-
> Encroaching *Eve* perhaps, had first the rule
> Of high Olympus, thence by Saturn driv'n
> And *Ops,* ere yet *Dictaean Jove* was born.
> (X, 579-84)

For confirmation of the belief that Saturn and Rhea stole the rule of Olympus from the serpent Titan Ophion, Milton might have referred his readers to the popular Mythology[20] of Natale Conti, but if challenged about his inference that Ophion could be identified with Satan he would have fallen back upon some authority like the famous demonologist Jean Bodin, who opened his *Daemonomanie des sorciers*[21] by relating the account of the casting out of "that old Serpent, called the devil and Satan, and . . . his angels with him," in Revelation 12:9, with the gigantomachy of the ancients. His primary authority was Pherecydes, and he went on, with doubtful justification, to appeal for support to Empedocles, "qui appelle les Daemones tombez du ciel οὐρομοπετές," to Hermes Trismegistus in the *Poimander,* and to St. Augustine in *The City of God* (VIII, xxii).

If further pressed, Milton might have quoted a remark of George Sandys on a passage in Ovid's *Metamorphoses* (I, 151-55), which has been used to illustrate his reference to Ophion by Douglas Bush.[22] Sandys wrote: "Pherecydes the Syrian writes how the Divels were throwne out of heaven by Jupiter (this fall of the Gyants, perhaps an allusion to that of the Angells) the chiefe called Opioneus, which signifies Serpentine: having after made use of that creature to poyson Eve with a false ambition."

[20] Natalis Comitis *Mythologiae, sive Explicationis Fabularum Libri decem* (Frankfurt, 1598), II, ii, p. 122.

[21] *De Magorum Daemonomania.* The French translation of 1580 is quoted.

[22] Bush quotes from Sandys' *Ovid's Metamorphosis Englished, mythologiz'd, and represented in figures* (London, 1627) in *Mythology and the Renaissance Tradition in English Poetry* (Minneapolis, 1932), pp. 273-74, n.65.

Like Milton, Sandys was thinking of the fall of the devils and the rout of the angels as a single event. Like Raleigh in the *History of the World* (I, vi), both Sandys and Milton regarded the classic myths as fabulous but venerable corroborations of Scripture. Milton may or may not have read Sandys, and he may not have known that Bodin identified Pherecydes' serpent-Titan with the "chef des Anges rebelles," or that in the *De Occulta Philosophia* (III, xviii), Cornelius Agrippa had identified the leader of the rebel angels with "that Ophis, i.e. the Devilish Serpent." Behind Agrippa and Bodin was Origen, in whose *Contra Celsum* (VI, xliii), Milton might read that the Titan Ophioneus was one and the same with "the serpent which was the cause of man's expulsion from the divine paradise, and deceived the male race with a promise of divine power of attaining greater things."

On a different level there is a more obvious hint at identification of another of the Titans with the leader of the rebel angels in Milton's portrait of Satan

> Prone on the Flood, extended long and large
> . . . floating many a rood, in bulk as huge
> As whom the Fables name of monstrous size,
> *Titanian,* or *Earth-born,* that warr'd on *Jove,*
> *Briareos* or *Typhon,* whom the Den
> By ancient *Tarsus* held, or that Sea-beast
> *Leviathan,* which God of all his works
> Created hugest that swim th' Ocean stream.
> (I, 195-202)

In Natale Conti's chapter on Typhon in the *Mythologia* (VI, xxii), aside from the monster's vast size, the outstanding topic is his part in the revolt of the earth-born giants against Zeus. Conti went on in a formal account of the allegorizations of his myth to recall that in the *Bellum Giganteum* of Theodore he had been made into a symbol of ruthless ambition, which had become traditional. As such he was familiar enough for Milton to use him in opening the Fourth Academic Exercise at Cambridge with a picture of Typhon as a symbol of rampant Error rebelling against Truth. In bracketing Satan "prone on the flood" with Typhon, Milton was not suggesting an identification like the seemingly literal one that he intended in the lines on Ophion. Satan and Typhon are compared in an epic simile like Satan's immediately following comparison with Leviathan. Nor is the literary character of the similes altered by the fact that they both come full circle. Typhon is a symbol of the Satanic sin of rebellious pride, and Leviathan, the whale which is called in Isaiah 27:1, "that dragon that is in the sea," was traditionally regarded as a type of Satan.

The Satan-Typhon simile is a special case on the edge of Milton's treatment of the Titanomachia, even though Milton's lines do recall Hesiod's description of Typhon in the *Theogony* (819-85) as the most frightful of the earth-born assailants of the Olympian gods. In the simile Typhon is distinct from the personages in the action of the poem. Milton's treatment of him is in striking contrast with his treatment in Odorico Valmarana's *Daemonomachia,*[23] one of the several Italian treatments of the war in heaven which it is probable that Milton may have known. At the outset of the *Daemonomachia,* after Lucifer has been challenged by Michael in a situation somewhat like that in which Milton's Satan is checked by Abdiel, as the rebel angels rally around their leader, a spokesman emerges from the mob:

> Unus (Graii dixere Typhoeum,
> Romano potuit dici sermone superbus)
> Lucifero accedens totius ab ore cohortis,
> Aerium quassans caput, inquit: Maxime princeps,
> Decretis his stare iuvat? privabere honore
> Tam merito? nulloque certamine tolli
> Munera tanta sines?

Valmarana's parenthetical words indicate that he thought of Typhoeus[24] as a tradition symbol of rebellious pride, but also as a demon who might play a part in his action analogous to that played by Beelzebub in *Paradise Lost.* Valmarana's Typhoeus goes on with his flattery of Lucifer until the latter breaks into an equally bombastic speech, and the die is cast, and a battle ensues in which the devils assume the names of Titans or giants as easily as Milton's devils assume names like Moloch or Mulciber.

Valmarana's treatment of Typhon and the Titans generally differs from Milton's somewhat as Spenser's does. For Spenser they were symbols which might casually enter into his narrative as personages in an allegory. In his final cantos, one of them, Mutability, whose name and myth are his invention, makes a new assault upon Olympus and moves Jove to exclaim:

> Will never mortall thoughts cease to aspire,
> In this bold sort, to heaven claime to make,
> And touch celestiall seates with earthly mire?
> I would have thought that bold Procrustes hire,
> Or Typhons fall, or proud Ixions paine,
> Or great Prometheus tasting of our ire,
> Would have suffiz'd the rest for to restraine,
> And warn'd all men, by their example, to refraine.
> (*The Faerie Queene,* VII, vi, 29)

[23] The edition which is quoted here (from its twenty-sixth page) was published in Bologna in 1623, under the title, *Daemonomachiae, sive de bello intelligentiarum Libri XV.*

[24] In *Classical Myth and Legend in Renaissance Dictionaries,* pp. 281-83, Starnes and Talbert suggest that Milton's Typhon is a conflation of accounts of Typhon (Typhoeus) and Tityus by several mythographers.

Against the Spenserian example we feel the force of C. M. Bowra's conviction that, in spite of Raphael's warning that he must delineate heavenly events "By lik'ning spiritual to corporal forms," Milton's war in heaven "need not be so allegorical as we think."[25] But admirers of G. Wilson Knight's interpretation of Milton's celestial war in *Chariot of Wrath* and of Arnold Stein's interpretation of it in *Answerable Style* are likely to qualify Bowra's faith that Milton's story "illustrates the universal truths which he proclaims and may be treated as something complete in itself." Stein's reading of the sixth book of *Paradise Lost* as a complex metaphor and "a kind of great scherzo, like some of Beethoven's — with more than human laughter,"[26] may be reconcilable with Bowra's doctrine, but Knight's attempt to establish his "equation of this main action in *Paradise Lost* with Milton's own prophetic nationalism"[27] certainly is not. Milton's celestial war shares its liability to allegorical and symbolic interpretation with Hesiod's myth of the Titans, but with this difference between Milton's time and ours: that they could alike be read as both history and allegory.

III

Even before Hesiod, as Werner Jaeger tells us,[28] the Orphic theogonies had overtones of cosmic or scientific allegory, and Pherecydes actually conceived of the "culprit deities" whom Zeus hurled into Tartarus and bound there as definitely representing "meteorological forces." Something like ethical overtones could easily be read into the first sculpture representing the repulse of the Titans at Apollo's great temple at Delphi, and they were still easier to read into the myth of the slaying of the earth-monster Python by the arrows of the sun-god. There is a hint of allegory in the story of Athene's helping Zeus to victory over the giants, which goes back to Callimachus' poem *On the Bath of Pallas,* and there is a note of moral victory in Pindar's prophecy of the share of Hercules in their defeat in the first Nemean Ode. The Titanomachies had assumed esoteric importance long before Plutarch wrote in *Isis and Osiris* (364, D) that some of the legends and rites pertaining to the Titans corresponded with the stories of the dismemberment and revivification of Osiris. In Alciati's *Emblemata*[29] the commentators on the myth of the Titans were quoted as agreeing upon its plain moral:

Huius figmenti rationem Mythologi adferunt, eamque traducunt ad homines

[25] *From Virgil to Milton* (London, 1948), p. 213.
[26] *Answerable Style,* p. 20.
[27] *Chariot of Wrath* (London, 1942), p. 155.
[28] *The Theology of the Early Greek Philosophers* (Oxford, 1947), p. 70.
[29] Andreae Alciati, *Emblemata* (Padua, 1661), p. 37.

quosdam impios, qui Deos negligerent, aut etiam negarent: quorum pedes in draconum volumina desisse aiunt, quod nihil superum, nihil rectum cogitarent, totius eorum vitae gressu ad inferna mergente. Macrobius, *Saturnalia,* . . . (I, xx)

The Titans had become a symbol of moral degeneracy — hence the half-human, half-serpentine form often attributed to them; and they had also become a symbol of the free-thinkers who despise or deny the gods. By the second century A.D., this interpretation had so long been taken seriously that Lucian mocked it in *Icaromenippus,* 33, with his picture of the assembled Olympian gods advising Zeus to throw the Epicurean philosophers into Tartarus with the Giants.

Milton, we may be sure, was familiar with the general development of the interpretation of the myths of the Titans and the Giants. He was enough interested in several other works of Philo to know something about his book on the giants of Genesis 6, the *De Gigantibus,* which insisted on regarding them as their counterparts in Greek mythology were regarded by the most rationalistic commentators — simply as depraved and materialistic men. Though Milton can hardly have been entirely sympathetic with the condemnation of matter as evil and hostile to spirit which ran through so much neo-Platonic thought from Philo to the school of Marsilio Ficino, he could hardly fail to sympathize with the conception of the ancient gigantomachy as a symbol of conscience (*sinderesi* or *sinteresi*) and the mastery of all human weakness by the "sun of the intelligence and the light of reason," as it was presented in the dedication of Giordano Bruno's *Spaccio de la Bestia Trionfante*[30] to Sir Philip Sidney, if he read it. He must have been very familiar with similar interpretations of the myth as they were to be found in Conti's *Mythologia* (VI, xxi), where the half-serpent, half-human form so often attributed to the giants by the poets was a mark of their depravity and rebellious pride. Though proof may be impossible, transference of these allegorical ideas about the mythological assailants of the Olympian gods to the revolt of the angels seems to have played a part in the treatment of the revolt by the Dutch poet Vondel in *Lucifer* (1654). In the moment of final defeat by Michael's loyal angels the Dutch poet had Lucifer transformed into a multiform beast: part lion (to symbolize pride), and then (to symbolize the six remaining deadly sins) part swine, part ass, part rhinoceros, part ape, part serpent, and part wolf. In *Paradise Lost* the only trace of such symbolism is in Satan's imbrutings of himself as a toad and as a serpent, and in the mass metamorphosis of his followers into hissing snakes in the welcoming scene in Pandaemonium.

The odor of allegory is faint indeed about Satan's imbrutings. In our

[30] *Opere Italiane,* ed. Giovanni Gentile (Bari, 1927), VI, 13.

prevailing tendency to treat them as part of his degradation we lose sight of what trace of the odor may actually remain; and in Arnold Stein's view of them as a part of Milton's plan to make Satan physically as well as morally ridiculous,[31] it vanishes altogether. More remarkable is Milton's deliberate intention to keep away from allegory in the main scene in his celestial battle. He will have none of the pious medieval efforts to interpret God's thunderbolts as "acts of the virtues" and "weapons of reason for the overthrow of the vices," or of his lightnings as "the light of reason, either ethical, economic, or political." By such ingenious hermeneutics Coluccio Salutati had expounded[32] the overthrow of the Titans, down to details like the head of the gorgon Medusa on the shield of Jupiter, which he regarded as a symbol of eloquence, or of "the consummate dialectic which the Titans dread."

But a part of Salutati's interpretation was the ancient idea which made the Titans symbols of atheism. His tone suggests intolerance of a kind which would have been offensive to the author of *Of True Religion, Heresy, Schism, Toleration.* He was anticipating the abuse of the myth in Reformation times, when the Ramists were attacked[33] for exposing theology to the giants, and when Bishop Jewel, writing his apology for Elizabethan Protestantism, protested against the charge that, "we are wicked men and make war after the manner of the giants (as the fable is) against God himself."[34]

Above all, Milton's rebel angels are atheists, for they accept Satan's plea that they have no creator. From that denial of God flows both the materialism and the anarchy which commentators are now stressing in Milton's revolt of the angels. He may have thought of the anarchy in the traditional way of Alciati's commentators, for whom all disorder (ἀταξία) was the work of evil men who hide their feral nature under human form. They saw the Titanomachy as an allegory of the Platonic view of anarchy as always ready to destroy liberty when

> upstart Passions catch the Government
> From Reason, and to servitude reduce
> Man till then free. (XII, 88-90)

Milton's ground for the doctrine was put in a sixain which was quoted by Alciati's commentators, and which is remarkable for making materialism the root of the Titan's revolt:

[31] In *Answerable Style,* p. 22.

[32] *De Laboribus Herculis,* ed. B. L. Ullman (Zurich, 1951), II, 385-413 *passim.*

[33] In P. Gallandi's *Pro Schola Parisiensi contra novam academiam P. Rami* (Paris, 1551).

[34] John Jewel, *An Apology or Answer in Defense of the Church of England concerning the State of Religion Used in the Same,* ed. Hyder Rollins and Herschel Baker in *The Renaissance in England* (Cambridge, Mass., 1954), p. 169.

Tale gigantaeum legitur genus, ut nihil altum
Cogitet, at spernat, vel neget esse Deum:
Et tantum, quantum sensu exteriore movetur,
Commodat at praesens se, vel ad id quod adest.
Hoc genus anguipedum mythici finxere Poetae,
Quorum affectus humi (segnis ad alta) repat.
(*Emblemata,* p. 37)

Materialism is hardly a word which Milton would have used of his rebel angels, but he would have sympathized with his modern interpreters who see their fall as a challenge to reason and consequently as a resort to violence. Modern criticism of his celestial war, when it is disapproving, deepens Dr. Johnson's objection to its "incongruities" and condemns the "double standard" which allows the loyal angels to stoop to wrath and lets the Son consciously "take over the Satanic standard of force."[35]

Lurking here is a charge against Milton's character — the charge that "Milton liked power." By most of us he will be judged by his thinking about truth and power, and J. B. Broadbent observes that in the last chapter of *Eikonoklastes* he discussed the clear verdict of King Darius "that truth of all things was strongest."[36] Milton corrects Darius by saying that "truth is properly no more than contemplation," while in action it becomes the justice which "in her very essence is all strength and activity: and hath a sword put into her hand, to use against all violence and oppression on the earth. . . . She never suffers falsehood to prevail, but when falsehood first prevails over truth; and that also is a kind of justice done on them who are so deluded."

Milton's most carefully considered statement about truth and power is his incarnation of truth in the Son of God who goes to war in a chariot which is all flames and wings set with eyes, and who wears the "radiant Urim" (VI, 761) of sure judgment in his breastplate. His violence against the devils is beyond any doubt, though it is exerted only because

by strength
They measure all, of other excellence
Not emulous, nor care who them excels.
(VI, 820-22)

Like the long-withheld might of Zeus in Hesiod's Titan war, the Son's power is used only after two days of drawn battle, which for Milton amounted to proof of the divine patience and of the self-deception of the rebel angels. The final step in that tragedy can come only after the uprooted hills have returned to their places "And with fresh Flow'rets Hill and Valley

[35] Milton Miller, "Paradise Lost: The Double Standard," in *UTQ,* XX (1951), 190.

[36] "Links between Poetry and Prose in Milton," in *English Studies,* XXXVII (1956), 54-55.

smil'd" (VI, 784). But the rebels are only "hard'n'd more by what might most reclaim" (VI, 791), and the outcome justifies G. Wilson Knight's suggestion of "an alliance of good and nature against the will to power and explosives"[37] of the devils. In Book VII, 605, in the passage which prompted Thyer to identify Milton's celestial battle with Hesiod's, the Son's creative power has the reverse effect on the loyal angels. In the celestial battle, however, the devils' will to power can be crushed only by violence and the Son's "wrath bent on his enemies" (VI, 826). To regret it is to regret Milton's life-long apocalyptic vision of the first and second routs of the Dragon. It was only in some mysterious, ultimate struggle of the Son with Satan — beyond any angel's power to adumbrate in corporal forms, that Milton could

Dream not of thir fight,
As of a Duel, or the local wounds
Of head or heel. (XII, 386-88)

[37] *Chariot of Wrath,* p. 149. Disregarding the hardening of the devil's will to evil, E. H. Emerson treats the prolongation of the battle as intended to teach the angels the virtue of patience. *MLN,* LXIX (1954), 399-402.

University of Wisconsin

GEORGE BERNARD SHAW AND SHAKESPEARE'S *CYMBELINE*

Rudolf Stamm

Bernard Shaw's career as a Shakespearean critic has been studied several times in recent years,[1] and was found to be of considerable interest and importance: an unexpected result for all those Shakespeareans who, disgusted by the outrageous statements with which Shaw peppered his important ones, had developed the habit of dismissing the whole subject as unworthy of serious consideration. In a lecture delivered before the members of the *Deutsche Shakespeare-Gesellschaft* in the spring of 1957[2] the present writer tried to define the extent and the limits of Shaw's understanding of Shakespeare's art, and came to the conclusion that, in some important respects, he was a precursor of the modern way of interpreting the plays, both in the study and on the stage. This achievement seems all the more remarkable if we remember that the Irish dramatist's own mind and art were akin to eighteenth-century classicism rather than to Shakespeare's manneristic or, in the last plays, baroque, style: a fact that is responsible for the most serious blind spots in an otherwise valuable body of criticism. There are other more superficial and more visible blemishes in it, springing from less fundamental causes. Many of the limitations and some of the virtues of Shaw's approach are strikingly exhibited by his treatment of one particular play of Shakespeare's, which fascinated him in the middle, and towards the close, of his

[1] Cf. E. J. West, "G.B.S., Music, and Shakespeare's Blank Verse," in *Elizabethan Studies and Other Essays in Honor of George F. Reynolds* (Boulder, Colo., 1945), pp. 344-56, and *G.B.S. on Shakespearean Production, SP,* XLV (1948), 216-35; Henning Krabbe, *Bernard Shaw on Shakespeare and English Shakespearian Acting, Acta Jutlandica,* XXVII, *Suppl.B, Humanistisk Serie 41* (Kopenhagen, 1955); P. A. W. Collins, "Shaw on Shakespeare," *Shakespeare Quarterly,* VIII (1957), 1-13. An important older study is "Shaw's 'Besser als Shakespeare' " by Wilhelm Rehbach, *Shakespeare-Jahrbuch,* LII (1916), 84-140.

[2] To be published in Vol. XCIV (1958) of the *Shakespeare-Jahrbuch.*

life: *Cymbeline*. It is the purpose of the present essay to concentrate attention on this test case, though it proves somewhat difficult to analyze correctly and evaluate justly, because Shaw's first major encounter with the play took place under very peculiar circumstances.

In the summer of 1896, when Sir Henry Irving was preparing the most famous nineteenth-century production of *Cymbeline,* Shaw had a unique opportunity of observing his preparations at close quarters through the medium of his correspondence with Ellen Terry,[3] and while he was pondering his article on the first performance for the *Saturday Review,*[4] he was in a strange quandary. Both the play and its production attracted and repelled him at one and the same time, and it was impossible for him to discuss them dispassionately, justly, or even consistently. Everything he put into his letters to Ellen Terry and into his article for the *Saturday Review* was written by an aspiring playwright with several axes to grind and, besides, by a middle-aged philanderer, who had half fallen in love with Ellen Terry and did his best, in the course of a curiously romantic letter flirtation, to impress her by his wit, artistic taste, understanding of the theatrical requirements of Shakespeare's play, and by his general helpfulness. The impulses of the aspiring playwright and the aspiring friend of Ellen Terry were frequently at odds with each other. The author of the early plays, from *Widowers' Houses* to *The Devil's Disciple,* was disgusted by his lack of theatrical success, by the fact that Henry Irving and Ellen Terry expended their genius and their resources on mediocre melodramas or on Shakespeare and, especially, by the great success of their policy. Many of the lines in his letters to Ellen Terry and whole paragraphs in his review are the outbursts of a modern artist, no longer so young, half-conscious of his own potential powers, oppressed by the reigning taste for a classic, and trying to make room for his own work. Many of these outbursts make bad reading nowadays by reason of their vulgar noisiness and manifest wrongheadedness. They should not be held against Shaw, because they are simply the journalistic counterpart of similar, though usually less outrageous, attacks on established art by growing artists trying to create their own style and the taste for it. We should remember here that a genuine dramatist, unlike a lyrical poet or a novelist, cannot possibly evade the problem of finding producers, actors, and an audience with a taste for his art. But, while Shaw was using his journalistic tricks for

[3] Published by Christopher St. John in *Ellen Terry and Bernard Shaw: a Correspondence* (London, 1931) — hereafter cited as *Terry-Shaw*.

[4] The first night of *Cymbeline* was on September 22, 1896, and Shaw's review, entitled "Blaming the Bard," appeared on September 26. It will be quoted from *Our Theatres in the Nineties,* Standard Edition of the Works of Bernard Shaw, 3 vols. (London, 1932), where it appears in II, 195-202.

the best of egotistical reasons to make Ellen Terry, Henry Irving, and everybody else, feel that they had outgrown Shakespeare and were just about mature for Shaw himself, he was in reality ill at ease because, being the artist that he was, he could not but love and revere the creations of Shakespeare, foreign and far away though they were from his own taste and artistic potentialities. For the time being he resolved the painful tensions in his attitude in a rather desperate way by frequently indulging in see-saw judgments according to the most approved classicist pattern. Formerly it had been "natural genius" versus "want of art"; now it was "miracles of expression" versus "intellectual sterility." Once more, we should not, and shall not, pay too much attention to this impossible separation of form from contents, of expression from thought, because it was merely a makeshift of Shaw's during those years of struggle and is at variance with his more considered statements on this fundamental problem of art.[5]

His awareness of the elementary fact that a work of art cannot be judged by its intellectual contents is already implied in the positive sentences, balancing the wild onslaught at the beginning of "Blaming the Bard," Shaw's public statement of his position, which we may consider briefly before examining the letters to Ellen Terry, although the most interesting among them were written before the review. Those sentences run as follows:

> But I am bound to add that I pity the man who cannot enjoy Shakespear. He has outlasted thousands of abler thinkers, and will outlast a thousand more. His gift of telling a story (provided some one else told it to him first); his enormous power over language, as conspicuous in his senseless and silly abuse of it as in his miracles of expression; his humor; his sense of idiosyncratic character; and his prodigious fund of that vital energy which is, it seems, the true differentiating property behind the faculties, good, bad, or indifferent, of the man of genius, enable him to entertain us so effectively that the imaginary scenes and people he has created become more real to us than our actual life — at least, until our knowledge and grip of actual life begins to deepen and glow beyond the common.[6]

This promising passage is followed, unfortunately, by a paragraph of slapdash character criticism. A number of characters are dismissed as "nothing": Cymbeline himself, the Queen (she is said to be nothing after Lady Macbeth), Posthumus ("most fortunately, as otherwise he would be an unendurably contemptible hound"), Belarius (seems nothing after Kent in *King Lear*). Iachimo is said to be "not much — only a *diabolus ex machina* made plausible; and Pisanio, less than Iachimo." Again this negative list is balanced by a positive one. It is opened by Cloten, "the prince of numbskulls, whose part, indecencies and all, is a literary masterpiece from the first line to the last." He is followed by the two princes ("fine presentments of that

[5] See the lecture mentioned in note 2.
[6] *Our Theatres,* II, 196.

impressive and generous myth, the noble savage"), by Caius Lucius ("urbane among the barbarians"), and, of course, by Imogen. In speaking of her the critic makes a further, particularly unhappy, use of his see-saw method of approach. He tries to convince his readers that there are, in reality, two Imogens, tied together "with ropes of blank verse (which can fortunately be cut)." One is "a solemn and elaborate example of what, in Shakespeare's opinion, a lady ought to be." She is characterized by chronic "virtuous indignation" and by "her fertility and spontaneity in nasty ideas." The other is "the Imogen of Shakespeare's genius, an enchanting person of the most delicate sensitiveness, full of sudden transitions from ecstasies of tenderness to transports of childish rage, and reckless of consequences in both, instantly hurt and instantly appeased, and of the highest breeding and courage."

In spite of some good remarks on several of the characters, the paragraph as a whole is disappointing, because Shaw neglects the meaning of the whole play in relation to which the single figures and their arrangement were viewed by the romantic critics and are viewed by the best modern ones, and chooses his place in the eighteenth-century tradition. In that position a plea for cutting and rearranging the play in order to make it fit for production becomes inevitable. We find a plea of this kind in Shaw's analysis of Imogen's character, but it is more solidly grounded than on an evaluation of the intellectual contents and the characters according to standards absolutely foreign to the Elizabethan drama: "The instinctive Imogen, like the real live part of the rest of the play, has to be disentangled from a mass of stuff which, though it might be recited with effect and appropriateness by young amateurs at a performance by the Elizabethan Stage Society, is absolutely unactable and unutterable in the modern theatre, where a direct illusion of reality is aimed at, and where the repugnance of the best actors to play false passages is practically insuperable. For the purposes of the Lyceum, therefore, Cymbeline had to be cut, and cut liberally."[7] We should not be discouraged here by the condescending way in which the Elizabethan Stage Society is mentioned. Shaw was in reality a friend and admirer of William Poel's work, as is shown by the following passage: "I welcome the advent of the Elizabethan Stage Society, founded 'to give practical effect to the principle that Shakespear should be accorded the build of stage for which he designed his plays' . . . It is only by such performances that people can be convinced that Shakespear's plays lose more than they gain by modern staging."[8] In "Blaming the Bard," however, Shaw's point of view is definitely that of the "modern" theater, proud of being able to create "direct illusion of reality," and his conclusion that Shakespeare's texts are

[7] *Our Theatres,* II, 197. [8] *Ibid.,* I, 188 f.

recalcitrant against its style, and vice versa, that this modern theater is no place for Shakespeare, is unimpeachable. If it insists on producing the plays, cutting and rearranging are inevitable. Here we touch the solid core of Shaw's many violent attacks against Shakespearean performances of the Lyceum type. The modern dramatist is crying: This is my own theater! Open it to my plays, and give Shakespeare another kind of theater, another type of performance, really adapted to his plays!

The praise of cutting we have quoted was meant for the paradoxical undertaking Shaw saw in Irving's production. In time he became a convinced opponent of the practice,[9] at least as long as the cutting was being done by other people. As to himself, he was far too imperialistic a personality to refrain from it; this is proved both by his letters to Ellen Terry and by his version of the last act of *Cymbeline.*

Having completed his defense of cutting in the *Cymbeline* review of 1896, he at once starts to belabor Henry Irving for the use he has made of the privilege so generously accorded him. The loss of the "antiphonal third verse of the famous dirge," of a great part of "the grotesque character tracery of Cloten's lines," "of the Queen's great speech about the natural bravery of our isle" is vehemently complained of. The rest of Shaw's review consists mainly of two careful appraisals of Henry Irving's and Ellen Terry's achievements in the parts of Iachimo and Imogen. Shaw writes admiringly of Irving's ability to create a fascinating character out of almost nothing: "the author's futility is the opportunity for the actor's masterpiece."[10] Passing briefly over the secondary actors, of whom we learn for instance that "Mr Gordon Craig and Mr Webster are desperate failures as the two noble savages. They are as spirited and picturesque as possible; but every pose, every flirt of their elfin locks, proclaims the wild freedom of Bedford Park,"[11] he extols Ellen Terry's Imogen, paying his pen-friend the compliment that she "had evidently cut her own part; at all events the odious Mrs Grundyish Imogen had been dissected out of it so skilfully that it went without a single jar."[12]

[9] An intermediary position between the passage before us and the unambiguous declaration of war against the cutters to be found in the *Fortnightly Review,* CVI (1919), 215-18, is held by an article contributed to the *Saturday Review* (February, 1905) and reprinted by the London Shakespeare League in 1920 in a pamphlet entitled *The Dying Tongue of Great Elizabeth.* Here he describes how Herbert Beerbohm Tree used the text of *Much Ado about Nothing* as the mere raw material for a fascinating stage creation of his own, and, half-seriously, defends the ingenious actor-manager on the ground that Elizabethan English is rapidly becoming a forgotten tongue for the average theatergoer — the Shavian way of approaching a very real and serious problem.

[10] *Our Theatres,* II, 199. [11] *Ibid.,* II, 200. [12] *Ibid.,* II, 201.

The fun of this compliment, both for its author and for its recipient, lay in the fact that there was an element of self-praise in it. It leads us to a consideration of the series of letters exchanged by the actress and the critic during the weeks and days before the first night of *Cymbeline*. They are half-professional, half-personal letters. Shaw wrote them because he was no less fascinated by the woman than by the actress, who replied so intelligently and wittily to his heresies about Shakespeare and Sir Henry, to his advice concerning the cutting of the text, and the acting of her part. His respect and his tender feelings for her made him realize — though he was a tactless man by nature and profession — that it would never do to run down the achievements of Shakespeare and Irving too insistently in his letters to an artist who was devoting all her time and energy to the study of Imogen. Therefore, the attacks on the master dramatist are not too frequent, though no opportunity is lost to offer a broad hint on the possibility of giving up the old plays for the sake of first-rate modern ones. Sir Henry receives an occasional thrashing for two somewhat contradictory reasons: because he has undertaken a Shakespearean, instead of a Shavian production and because his acting version of *Cymbeline* seems intolerable to Shaw, who cannot hide from Ellen Terry the fact that he is a very well-informed student, even a lover, of Shakespeare's art. Nor does he wish to hide it from her. He realizes that there is no better way to her esteem than by assisting her in the difficult work she is doing, and the idea that he can influence Sir Henry's production through her is far too extraordinary not to tickle his sense of the incongruous and, to a certain extent, his vanity.

He objects to Sir Henry's stage version because he thinks that the scissors have not been properly handled by the actor-manager. Ellen Terry is told that he has spoilt every part except his own; "and he has actually damaged his own by wantonly cutting off your white and azure eyelids laced with blue of heaven's own tinct."[13] Shaw raises this protest, and makes many of his other remarks, after having studied a playhouse text that is not identical with the printed version[14] of Irving's arrangement. In this version Iachimo's lines to which Shaw alludes are not omitted: perhaps a result of his timely intercession. According to Ellen Terry's statement[15] he seems to have saved, besides a few other good things, the famous simile "as small a drop of pity as a wren's eye," although it is not contained in the printed stage version.

[13] *Terry-Shaw,* p. 56.

[14] CYMBELINE. A Comedy in Five Acts by WILLIAM SHAKESPEARE, As Arranged for the Stage by *Henry Irving* and Presented at the *Lyceum Theatre* on Tuesday, 22nd September, 1896. Printed for Private Use Only, London, Printed at the Chiswick Press, 1896.

[15] *Terry-Shaw,* p. 58.

The accusation that Irving tried to increase the relative importance of his own part should not be pushed too far. It is certainly not entirely unfounded, but many of Irving's numerous and sometimes very extensive cuts have no other object than to shorten the play by about one-fourth of its original length without rendering any part of it incomprehensible. No part was completely spared, but Belarius and his foster sons, Cymbeline, the Queen, Cloten, and Lucius were, relatively speaking, deprived of more lines than Iachimo and Imogen. A few scenes were omitted entirely. Posthumus lost the whole of the vision scene, and the last act of the play was stripped of everything not absolutely indispensable. The trick of transposing speeches from one passage or scene to another was occasionally resorted to. On all these counts Shaw's judgment: "Generally speaking, the cutting of the play is stupid to the last extremity"[16] cannot be accepted. If there must be meddling with the text, Irving's solution would appear to be rather a good one, with the exception of its prudery. Shaw's strictures on this weakness are indeed well deserved. Irving had to undertake an incredible amount of pruning in order to make every single speech in the play "nice" and clean, and Shakespeare's diction became thin and pale in the process.

Shaw's own quite numerous proposals for cutting are no less dubious than Irving's, as will appear in the following survey of his theatrical advice to Ellen Terry. She is told, at the encouraging beginning of a letter entitled "The Intelligent Actress's Guide to Cymbeline," that the play "can be done delightfully in a village schoolroom, and cant be done at the Lyceum at all, on any terms."[17] In approaching the character of Imogen the critic introduces his theory of her double nature, and his advice consists, of course, in concentrating on the "natural aristocrat"[18] in her and extirpating everything belonging to the "Bishopess side of the part."[19] It is difficult to take seriously any of the negative results of this attempt at vivisecting a figure that was created whole and entire by Shakespeare.

On the other hand, we observe with interest how Shaw tried to develop his own idea of Imogen in Ellen Terry, who evidently found his letters stimulating, especially since she perused them critically, accepting some suggestions and rejecting others. He offers her, and us, a short-cut to his ideas when he states, rather provokingly, that "there are four good lines in the part."[20] The first is: — how far it is/To this same blessed Milford," a passage in which he seems to have appreciated the poignant note of tragic irony produced by the simplest of words. The second is: "Such a foe! Good heavens!", again an ironic remark, dear to Shaw because of "its touch of

[16] *Ibid.*, p. 56. [17] *Ibid.*, p. 46. [18] *Ibid.*
[19] *Ibid.*, p. 56. [20] *Ibid.*, pp. 46 f.

vernacular nature." Third, we find: "I'll hide my master from the flies," a line of drastic realism, one of those simple sayings which, no less than the passionate, imaginative, and highly metaphorical speeches, were part of Shakespeare's art in his maturity. Shaw's appreciation of such strokes of racy realism is also apparent in his defense of the "clouted brogues."[21] The last of his favorite lines is: "Fear not: I'm empty of all things but grief," called "the only good line of pure rhetoric in Mrs Siddons's style." He likes this line, but he is distressed by its complement: "Thy master is not there, who was, indeed,/The riches of it." He says of the first line: "Only, Shakespear, like an ass, spoils that line by adding, in words, all that the delivery of the line itself ought to convey," a piece of criticism that reminds us once more of Shaw's affinity with the classicist taste for simplicity and economy. The same affinity is more fully revealed in his discussion of the whole scene (III.iv) to which our last Shakespearean quotation belongs. One of its main topics is the letter handed by Pisanio to Imogen and read aloud by her. Using much wild rhetoric himself Shaw tries to dissuade Ellen Terry from following Shakespeare's arrangement: "And oh, my God, dont read the letter. You *cant* read it: no woman could read it out to a servant,"[22] a strangely snobbish argument, considering that Pisanio is the only friend and ally left to Imogen after her husband's banishment. In spite of the fervor with which he acts the part of the *avant-gardiste* in this correspondence and elsewhere, he cannot help occasionally being shocked by Shakespeare's lack of decorum not unlike any other middle-class Victorian. His opposition to the original arrangement has also a purely theatrical basis. He proposes to have the letter read out by Pisanio earlier in the play (III.ii), so that there should be no need for repeating it in the present scene. This would permit Ellen Terry to act the impact of the letter without reading it aloud. Knowing how well she could perform a task of this kind, Shaw wants to give her a splendid chance, although this proposal is out of harmony with his own important idea, that, in Shakespeare, one should not act between the lines, but to the lines and through the lines.[23] His advice was not accepted by the actress, who remained convinced that she could get through the reading of the letter successfully.

The cuts envisaged by Shaw in the following conversation between Pisanio and Imogen in III.iv are radical but there is a certain consistency in them. He wants to get rid of everything not directly connected with the events of the scene and the emotions of the characters. Everything of the nature of a commentary, of generalizing reflection, all the rhetorical height-

[21] *Ibid.*, p. 56. [22] *Ibid.*, p. 47. [23] See note 29 below.

ening and baroque rounding-off of the speeches must go. There is no room for Pisanio's

> No, 'tis slander,
> Whose edge is sharper than the sword, whose tongue
> Outvenoms all the worms of Nile, whose breath
> Rides on the posting winds, and doth belie
> All corners of the world. Kings, queens, and states,
> Maids, matrons, nay, the secrets of the grave
> This viperous slander enters,

nor for Imogen's

> Thou didst accuse him of incontinency;
> Thou then look'dst like a villain: now, methinks,
> Thy favour's good enough. Some jay of Italy
> (Whose mother was her painting) hath betray'd him:
> Poor I am stale, a garment out of fashion,
> And, for I am richer than to hang by th' walls,
> I must be ripp'd: — to pieces with me! — O,
> Men's vows are women's traitors! All good seeming,
> By thy revolt, O husband, shall be thought
> Put on for villainy; not born where't grows,
> But worn a bait for ladies.[24]

Instead of this whole speech Shaw recommends its introductory line only: "*I* false? Thy conscience witness: — Iachimo," adding that "everything can be conveyed in these four words." Evidently, the dramatic ideal he has in mind is very different from Shakespeare's. Shaw is on safer ground where he criticizes Irving's arrangement, or rather destruction, of the same speech, the actor-manager having retained no more than the four words "To pieces with me!", cutting them loose from their metaphorical context and thus giving them an incongruous meaning not intended by Shakespeare.

Another key passage of his advice to Ellen Terry deals with the scene between Imogen and Iachimo in Irving's second, Shakespeare's first act (I.vii). Here he combats the notion that the young woman could be capable of "half affections or half forgivenesses."[25] "It is quite easy for Iachimo to put her out of countenance by telling her that Posthumus has forgotten her; but the instant he makes the mistake of trying to gratify her by abusing him — 'that runagate' — he brings down the avalanche. . . . And Iachimo has nothing to do but praise Posthumus, and lay the butter on thick, and she is instantly as pleased as Punch, and void of all resentment."[26] This is an excellent elucidation of her character. Shaw has quite a number of similarly useful hints to give. His idea of how to perform Imogen's "O the gods!/

[24] *Cymbeline,* ed. J. M. Nosworthy, Arden Edition (London, 1955).
[25] *Terry-Shaw,* p. 54. [26] *Ibid.*

When shall we see again?" (I.ii) and his warning against making Pisanio's "and too much too" (III.ii) a comic aside, do honor to his dramatic and theatrical good sense. What he says on the words last quoted above is among those fine passages in his Shakespearean criticism that help us to forget and forgive many a wrongheaded remark on the great Elizabethan: "It is a perfectly serious, tender, *nurselike* thing to say. Any Irish peasant would say 'And too much too, darlint,' quite naturally."[27]

The scene that caused most trouble to Shaw, to Ellen Terry, and to Henry Irving himself, is Imogen's soliloquy in IV.ii, in the course of which she wakes up near the gory and headless trunk of Cloten, and mistakes it for the body of her husband. This is another event that strikes Shaw as brutal and foolish since he cannot accept it as a gruesome incident in a fairy tale should be accepted, but speaks of it with the ideals of realistic verisimilitude and classicist decorum somewhere in his mind. However, once he sets about the task of devising a way of speaking and acting the scene, he has many worthwhile remarks to make. It is in connection with this soliloquy that he offers his one severe criticism of Ellen Terry's interpretation in a letter written shortly after the successful first night of *Cymbeline:* "You made one AWFUL mistake. You actually bawled out the words 'a headless man!' before you had half seen him. Good heavens! you mustnt do that: it's ridiculous. You must simply start in horror, give the audience time to see in your face what is the matter, and then say 'a headless man' in a frozen whisper. If you must make a noise, screech like mad when you start. Then it will be all right."[28] This exhortation leads Shaw up to one of the best passages he ever wrote on Shakespearean acting. It reveals an awareness of the characteristic theatrical physiognomy of a Shakespearean play, an awareness that was not always his, but which came to him in his best moments as a critic:

> In playing Shakespear, play *to* the lines, *through* the lines, *on* the lines, but never between the lines. There simply isnt time for it. You would not stick five bars rest into a Beethoven symphony to pick up your drumsticks; and similarly you must not stop the Shakespear orchestra for business. Nothing short of a procession or a fight should make anything so extraordinary as a silence during a Shakespearean performance. All that cave business wants pulling together: from the line about "'tis some savage hold" to "Such a foe! Good Heavens!" You ought to get all the business of peeping and hesitating and so on packed into the duration of the speech, spoken without a single interval except a pause after the call. Otherwise it drags. Mind, I dont propose that you should omit or slur anything, but only that you should do it with the utmost economy of time.[29]

In looking over this critical effort as a whole we conclude that Shaw's

[27] *Ibid.,* p. 55. [28] *Ibid.,* p. 78. [29] *Ibid.,* pp. 78 f.

approach to Shakespeare was limited by a number of doctrinaire opinions, but much more by the nature of his mind and taste, which belonged in the classicist tradition. He was unable to conceive of the plays as organic wholes; he had hardly anything useful to say on their complete meaning and esthetic quality, but he was a shrewd interpreter of certain details, details of speeches, of characters, and of situations. Above all, he had the born dramatist's flair for the theatrical physiognomy of the plays. He understood the conditions in which they had been created; he saw how the theatrical potentialities of individual lines and situations could become effective on the stage. He knew about the proper speed for the speaking of Shakespeare's verse and about the proper relation between speech and action. All this made him a forerunner of present-day conceptions.

Late in his life, in 1945, Shaw returned to the subject of *Cymbeline*. At that time he did not resist the temptation to compose "A Variation on Shakespear's Ending" when somebody suggested this idea to him. After all we have said about his connection with the classicist tradition, there is nothing surprising in this. His foreword to *Cymbeline Refinished*[30] is a curious document. The improver on the Elizabethan plays justifies himself by saying that "Cymbeline, though one of the finest of Shakespear's later plays now on the stage, goes to pieces in the last act."[31] But he does not leave it at that. He confesses that, when he actually re-read the condemned act after many years, he found his former notion that it was "a cobbled-up *pasticcio* by other hands an unpardonable stupidity." He continues: "The act is genuine Shakespear to the last full stop, and late phase Shakespear in point of verbal workmanship."[32] He even accepts the masque as an appropriate device, characteristically judging it from the point of view of theatrical expediency. He does not think of relating it to the meaning of the whole play. What happens in the course of this foreword is almost the contrary of what he has set out to do: Instead of justifying his own version he comes near to justifying Shakespeare's original fifth act. Nevertheless, he has something to say for himself as well. Understandably and amusingly enough, he prefers to compare his own endeavor to "additions made by Mozart to the score of Handel's Messiah," to "trombone parts added by Wagner to Spontini's choruses," and similar highly respectable musical undertakings rather than to the operations performed on Shakespeare's texts by William Davenant, Nahum Tate, Colley Cibber, David Garrick, and his other English forerunners. In spite of these high aspirations he recom-

[30] *Geneva, Cymbeline Refinished, & Good King Charles,* Standard Edition of the Works of Bernard Shaw (London, 1946).

[31] *Ibid.,* p. 133. [32] *Ibid.,* p. 134.

mends his version, modestly enough, to such producers only as lack the good sense to present "the original word-for-word as Shakespear left it, and the means to do justice to the masque."[33]

Shaw's version of the fifth act is very short. It contains eighty-nine lines by Shakespeare and a little more than twice that number by himself. The whole text is an esthetic impossibility, as there is no connection between it and the all-pervading fairy tale quality of the play as a whole, the only quality justifying the leisurely unravelling of mysteries which have ceased to be mysteries for the audience before the beginning of the act. Shaw tries to give his act a new interest by making the most important characters react to the expected revelations in an unexpected post-Ibsen manner. Forgetting everything he wrote about the character of Imogen to Ellen Terry in the old days, he turns Shakespeare's heroine into a modern problem woman. She cannot forget and forgive her husband's cruel and impossible behavior, and leaves the stage with the resigned remark:

> "I must go home and make the best of it
> As other women must."[34]

The event of regeneration, the core and center of Shakespeare's ending, is unknown to Shaw and to his Imogen. His Posthumus behaves like an ass — if we may permit ourselves, for once, Shaw's own way of putting such things — after having discovered that his wife is alive and with him. Instead of repenting and looking with horror at his former self, he offers exasperatingly lame excuses:

> "Well, my dearest,
> What could I think? The fellow did describe
> The mole upon your breast."[35]

He even asks Iachimo to pay him ten thousand ducats, since he has lost the wager after all. Having to go on living with a Posthumus of this kind, Shaw's Imogen can hardly be expected to be overjoyed and generous. Another innovation consists in making Guiderius and Arviragus two angry young men, proudly refusing the conventional tasks connected with their new status as the King's sons. These tricks and some others characterize Shaw's version as a *jeu d'esprit,* which we should not judge too severely. We cannot help adding, however, that Shaw's blank verse, which, according to the foreword, came very easily to him, convinces us of his wisdom in having written in this style on very rare occasions only. It is unpretentious, but also flat: verse written by a clever imitator in a worn-out form. His imagery consists of similes in the conventional manner of the second-rate classicists. The following protestations of Posthumus are a good specimen:

[33] *Ibid.,* p. 138. [34] *Ibid.,* p. 149. [35] *Ibid.,* p. 145.

Sweet, I dare
Anything, everything. Mountains of mortal guilt
That crushed me are now lifted from my breast.
I am in heaven that was but now in hell.[36]

Occasionally, to be quite fair, he hits on a better line, e.g., when he makes Philario (a character quite forgotten in Shakespeare's last act, but benevolently given another chance in Shaw's) speak of

this witless savage Cymbeline,
Whose brains were ever in his consort's head.[37]

Nobody will deny that this dramatic exercise of Shaw's old age contains some amusing points, and is an elementary object lesson on the differences between Shakespeare's and his own style. And yet its main virtue consists in its sending us back to the original ending of *Cymbeline* with a sharpened sense for its beauty and vigor and a new appreciation of an art capable of telling the conclusion of a wonderful fairy tale the way it should be told to children, eager to hear all the details, including the long expected ones, and of making it, at the same time, a moving expression of faith in the possibility of human regeneration through the intervention of divine grace.

[36] *Ibid.,* p. 143.
[37] *Ibid.,* p. 140. It has also struck J. M. Nosworthy, who quotes it in the introduction to his edition of *Cymbeline,* p. lii.

University of Bern

A BIBLIOGRAPHY OF THE SCHOLARLY WRITINGS OF THOMAS WHITFIELD BALDWIN

Compiled by John Hazel Smith

Books

1927 *The Organization and Personnel of the Shakespearean Company.* Princeton. Pp. xii + 464.

1931 *William Shakespeare Adapts a Hanging.* Princeton. Pp. xii + 201.

1943 *William Shakspere's Petty School.* Urbana. Pp. 240.

1944 *William Shakspere's Small Latine and Lesse Greeke.* Urbana, 2 vols. Pp. xviii + 753; vi + 772. (Reprinted 1956.)

1947 *Shakspere's Five-Act Structure.* Urbana. Pp. xviii + 848.

1950 *On the Literary Genetics of Shakspere's Poems and Sonnets.* Urbana. Pp. xi + 399.

1951 *Shakspere at Illinois. Notes on an Exhibition of the Ernest Ingold Folios and Other Shakspereana in the University of Illinois Library May 15 Through July 15, 1951.* Written with Isabelle Grant. Urbana. Pp. 22.

1957 *William Shakspere's Love's Labor's Won.* Carbondale, Ill. Pp. viii + 42.

Ready for Press *On the Literary Genetics of Shakspere's Plays 1592-1594* (tentative title).

Editions

1918 Massinger, Philip. *Duke of Milan.* A Dissertation Presented to the Faculty of Princeton University. Lancaster, Pa. Pp. ix + 197.

1928 Shakespeare, William. *The Comedy of Errors.* The [American] Arden Shakespeare. Boston and New York. Pp. xxxv + 145.

1929 *Earlier English Drama from Robin Hood to Everyman.* Edited and arranged for acting. American edition revised by T. W. Baldwin. Nelson's English Series. New York. Pp. xx + 304.

1953 Shakespeare, William. *A New Variorum Edition of Shakespeare. Troilus and Cressida.* Edited by Harold N. Hillebrand; supplemental editor T. W. Baldwin. Philadelphia. Pp. xix + 613.

In Preparation Shakespeare, William. *A New Variorum Edition of Shakespeare. The Comedy of Errors.*

ARTICLES, NOTES, AND CORRESPONDENCE

1922 "On *King Lear,*" *MLN,* XXXVII (December), 504.

1923 "A Note on John Fletcher," *MLN,* XXXVIII (June), 377-78.

1924 "Shakespeare's Jester: The Dates of *Much Ado* and *As You Like It,*" *MLN,* XXXIX (December), 447-55.

"The Three Francis Beaumonts," *MLN,* XXXIX (December), 505-7.

1925 "On the Chronology of Thomas Kyd's Plays," *MLN,* XL (June), 343-49.

1926 "Nathaniel Field and Robert Wilson," *MLN,* XLI (January), 32-34.

"Nathaniel and Nathan Field," *TLS,* No. 1269 (May 27), 355.

1927 "Posting Henslowe's Accounts," *JEGP,* XXVI (January), 42-90.

"Nathan and Nathaniel Field," *TLS,* No. 1307 (February 17), 108.

"Thomas Kyd's Early Company Connections," *PQ,* VI (July), 311-13.

"The Date of *Ralph Roister Doister.*" Written with M. Channing Linthicum. *PQ,* VI (October), 379-95.

"Sir John Denham and *Paradise Lost,*" *MLN,* XLII (December), 508-9.

"Elizabethan Players as Tradesfolk," *MLN,* XLII (December), 509-10.

1928 "Texts and Prompt Copies," *TLS,* No. 1368 (April 19), 290.

1929 "The Revels Books of 1604-5, and 1611-12," *The Library,* Transactions of the Bibliographical Society, 4th Series, X (December), 327-38.

1930 "Normal Amount of Teaching and Research." [First Report of Committee T], read by Chairman T. W. Baldwin. *AAUP Bull.,* XVI (March), 206-14.

1931 "Normal Amount of Teaching and Research." Second Report of Committee T, read by Chairman T. W. Baldwin. *AAUP Bull.,* XVII (March), 213-19.

"William Kemp Not Falstaff," *MLR,* XXVI (April), 170-72.

"Shakespeare and Shallow," *TLS,* No. 1549 (October 8), 778.

1934 "Shakespeare's Company," *TLS,* No. 1671 (February 8), 92.

1935 "A Note upon William Shakespeare's Use of Pliny," *Essays in Dramatic Literature.* The Parrott Presentation Volume. Edited by Hardin Craig. Princeton, 157-82.

1936 "Parallels Between *Soliman and Perseda* and Garnier's *Bradamante,*" *MLN,* LI (April), 237-41.

1939 "Shakespeare Facsimiles," *TLS,* No. 1944 (May 6), 265.

1940 " 'Light on the Dark Lady.' " Written with Pauline K. Angell. *PMLA,* LV (June), 598-602.

1941 "A Line in Gabriel Harvey," *TLS,* No. 2033 (January 18), 31.

" 'A Double Janus.' " Written with Allan H. Gilbert and Thomas Ollive Mabbott, *PMLA,* LVI (June), 583-85.

"Phoenixities," *TLS,* No. 2054 (June 14), 287.

"Perseus Purloins Pegasus," *Renaissance Studies in Honor of Hardin Craig.* Edited by Baldwin Maxwell, W. D. Briggs, Francis R. Johnson, and E. N. S. Thompson. Stanford University, Calif., 169-78 (also in *PQ,* XX [July], 361-70).

1942 "The Genesis of Some Passages Which Spenser Borrowed from Marlowe," *ELH,* IX (September), 157-87.

1945 "The Genesis of Some Passages Which Spenser Borrowed from Marlowe," *ELH,* XII (June), 165.

1947 "Shakespeare's Bible," *TLS,* No. 2346 (January 18), 37.

"Gabriel Harvey," *TLS,* No. 2362 (May 10), 225.

1948 "Respice Finem: Respice Funem." *Joseph Quincy Adams Memorial Studies.* Edited by James G. McManaway, Giles E. Dawson, and Edwin E. Willoughby. Washington, 141-55.

1950 "Shakspere's Aphthonian Man," *MLN,* LXV (February), 111-12.

"Commentary on Dr. Pope's 'Shakespeare on Hell,' " *SQ,* I (October), 296.

1951 "Structural Analysis of 'Troilus and Cressida,' " *Shakespeare-Studien. Festschrift für Heinrich Mutschmann.* Edited by Walther Fischer and Karl Wentendorf. Marburg, 5-18.

1952 "Nature's Moulds," *SQ,* III (July), 237-41.

1955 "On Atomizing Shakspere," *Sh. Jbch.,* XCI, 136-44.

"Marlowe's Musaeus," *Studies by Members of the English De-*

partment University of Illinois in Memory of John Jay Parry. Urbana, 18-25 (also in *JEGP,* LIV [October], 478-85).

Reviews and Notices

1926 Tolman, Albert H. *Falstaff and Other Shakespearean Topics.* New York, 1925: *JEGP,* XXV (October), 588-90.

1927 Dunkel, Wilbur Dwight. *The Dramatic Technique of Thomas Middleton in His Comedies of London Life.* University of Chicago doctoral dissertation. Chicago, 1925: *JEGP,* XXVI (October), 601-2.

Oliphant, E. H. C. *The Plays of Beaumont and Fletcher. An Attempt To Determine Their Respective Shares and the Shares of Others.* New Haven, 1927: *SR,* IV (November 5), 282 (see also entry for 1930 below).

1928 Sprague, Arthur Colby. *Beaumont and Fletcher on the Restoration Stage.* Cambridge, Mass., 1926: *JEGP,* XXVII (January), 115-20.

Winslow, Ola Elizabeth. *Low Comedy as a Structural Element in English Drama. From the Beginnings to 1642.* Chicago, 1926: *JEGP,* XXVII (January), 139-40.

Tannenbaum, Samuel A. *The Booke of Sir Thomas Moore. A Bibliotic Study.* New York, 1927: *MLN,* XLIII (May), 327-32.

1929 *Eastward Hoe, by Chapman, Jonson, and Marston.* Edited with Introduction, Notes, and Glossary by Julia Hamlet Harris. Yale Studies in English. New Haven, 1926: *JEGP,* XXVIII (April), 299-303.

Silbermann, Abraham Moritz. *Untersuchungen über die Quellen des Dramas "The True Tragedy of Herod and Antipater with the Death of Faire Marriam," by Gervase Markham and William Sampson (1622).* Inaugural Dissertation, Würzburg. Wittenberg, n. d.: *JEGP,* XXVIII (July), 439-40.

Gaw, Allison. *The Origin and Development of 1 Henry VI in Relation to Shakespeare, Marlowe, Peele, and Greene.* Los Angeles, 1926; Second Edition, 1927: *JEGP,* XXVIII (October), 557-61.

1930 Oliphant, E. H. C. *The Plays of Beaumont and Fletcher. An Attempt To Determine Their Respective Shares and the Shares of Others.* New Haven, 1927: *JEGP,* XXIX (April), 280-85.

Boas, Frederick S. *Marlowe and His Circle. A Biographical Survey.* Oxford, 1929: *MLN,* XLV (May), 329-31.

Brandl, Alois. *Shakespeare, Leben-Umwelt-Kunst.* Vierte Auflage, Vermehrt um ein Vorwort: "Was ist uns Shakespeare heute?" Wittenberg, 1929: *JEGP,* XXIX (July), 446-47.

1931 *A Critical Edition of Massinger's* The Roman Actor. By W. L. Sandidge, Jr. Princeton, 1929: *JEGP,* XXX (July), 424-26.

The Life of Marlowe and The Tragedy of Dido Queen of Carthage. Edited by C. F. Tucker Brooke. New York, 1930; *Tamburlaine the Great.* Edited by U. M. Ellis-Fermor. New York, 1930: *MLN,* XLVI (December), 549-52.

1932 *The Taming of the Shrew. The Works of Shakespeare.* Edited for the Syndics of the Cambridge University Press by Sir Arthur Quiller-Couch and John Dover Wilson. Cambridge, 1928: *JEGP,* XXXI (January), 152-56.

1933 Neilson, William Allan, and Ashley Horace Thorndike. *The Facts about Shakespeare.* Revised Edition. New York, 1931: *JEGP,* XXXII (July), 415-16.

1934 *Shakespeare-Jahrbuch.* Herausgegeben im Auftrage der Deutschen Shakespeare-Gesellschaft von Wolfgang Keller. Band 68 (Neue Folge IX. Band). Leipzig, 1932: *MLN,* XLIX (December), 549-51.

Sibley, Gertrude Marian. *The Lost Plays and Masques 1500-1642.* Ithaca, 1933: *MLN,* XLIX (December), 552-53.

1935 Tiegs, Alexander. *Zur Zusammenarbeit Englischer Berufsdramatiker Unmittelbar Vor Neben und Nach Shakespeare.* Breslau, 1933: *JEGP,* XXXIV (January), 118-19.

Eccles, Mark. *Christopher Marlowe in London.* Harvard Studies in English, X. Cambridge, Mass., 1934: *JEGP,* XXXIV (April), 253-56.

Plimpton, George A. *The Education of Shakespeare. Illustrated from the Schoolbooks in Use in His Time.* Oxford, 1933: *JEGP,* XXXIV (July), 444-46.

Judge, Cyril Bathurst. *Elizabethan Book-Pirates.* Harvard Studies in English, VIII. Cambridge, Mass., 1934: *JEGP,* XXXIV (October), 595-97.

1936 Vollmann, Elisabeth. *Ursprung und Entwicklung des Monologs bis zu Seiner Entfaltung bei Shakespeare.* Mit einer Einführung von Gustav Hübener. Bonner Studien zur Englischen

Philologie, Heft XXII. Bonn, 1934: *JEGP,* XXXV (January), 150-51.

1937 Sharpe, Robert Boies. *The Real War of the Theaters. Shakespeare's Fellows in Rivalry with the Admiral's Men, 1594-1603. Repertories, Devices, and Types.* MLA Monograph. New York, 1935: *JEGP,* XXXVI (April), 272-75.

Sprague, Arthur Colby. *Shakespeare and the Audience. A Study in the Technique of Exposition.* Cambridge, Mass., 1935: *MLN,* LII (November), 530-32.

1940 Bernard, J. E., Jr. *The Prosody of the Tudor Interlude.* New Haven, 1939;

Greenewald, Gerard M. *Shakespeare's Attitude Towards the Catholic Church in "King John."* Washington, 1938 (see also entry for 1941 below);

The Warde. By Thomas Neale. Edited by John Arthur Mitchell. Philadelphia, 1937;

West, Robert Hunter. *The Invisible World. A Study of Pneumatology in Elizabethan Drama.* Athens, Ga., 1939;

Siebeck, Berta. *Das Bild Sir Philip Sidneys in der Englischen Renaissance.* Weimar, 1939;

Wollenberg, Robert. *Shakespeare Persönliches aus Welt und Werk.* Berlin, 1939;

Mair, John. *The Fourth Forger. William Ireland and the Shakespeare Papers.* New York, 1939;

Five Elizabethan Tragedies. Edited by A. K. McIlwraith. New York, 1938;

Coles, Blanche. *Shakespeare Studies. Macbeth.* New York, 1938;

Schücking, Levin L. *Die Zusätze zur "Spanish Tragedy."* Leipzig, 1938;

Schücking, Levin L. *The Baroque Character of the Elizabethan Tragic Hero.* New York, 1938;

Chambers, R. W. *The Jacobean Shakespeare and* Measure for Measure. New York, 1939;

Franz, Wilhelm. *Die Sprache Shakespeares in Vers und Prosa.* Halle, 1939;

Menon, C. Narayana. *Shakespeare Criticism. An Essay in Synthesis.* New York, 1938;

Van Doren, Mark. *Shakespeare.* New York, 1939;

Spencer, Theodore, and Mark Van Doren. *Studies in Metaphysical Poetry.* New York, 1939;

Wells, Henry W. *Elizabethan and Jacobean Playwrights.* New York, 1939: *MLN,* LV (June), 455-62.

Curry, Walter Clyde. *Shakespeare's Philosophical Patterns.* Baton Rouge, La., 1937: *JEGP,* XXXIX (July), 402-4.

McKeithan, Daniel Morley. *The Debt to Shakespeare in the Beaumont-and-Fletcher Plays.* Austin, Tex., 1938: *JEGP,* XXXIX (July), 407-8.

1941 Bowers, Fredson Thayer. *Elizabethan Revenge Tragedy 1587-1642.* Princeton, 1940: *JEGP,* XL (April), 285-90.

Greenewald, Gerard M. *Shakespeare's Attitude Towards the Catholic Church in "King John."* Washington, 1938: *JEGP,* XL (April), 292-95.

1942 Lewis, B. Roland. *The Shakespeare Documents, Facsimiles, Transliterations & Commentary.* 2 vols. Stanford University, Calif., 1940: *MLN,* LVII (May), 364-73.

1943 Clarkson, Paul S., and Clyde T. Warren. *The Law of Property in Shakespeare and the Elizabethan Drama.* Baltimore, 1942: *MLQ,* IV (June), 242-43.

Harbage, Alfred. *Shakespeare's Audience.* New York, 1941: *MLN,* LVIII (June), 481-83.

1946 Bentley, Gerald Eades. *Shakespeare & Jonson. Their Reputations in the Seventeenth Century Compared.* 2 vols. Chicago, 1945: *JEGP,* XLV (April), 232-34.

Woodward, Gertrude L., and James G. McManaway. *A Check List of English Plays 1641-1700.* Chicago, 1945: *JEGP,* XLV (October), 457-58.

1947 Chambers, E. K. *Sources for a Biography of Shakespeare.* Oxford, 1946: *JEGP,* XLVI (July), 310-12.

1948 Hudson, Hoyt Hopewell. *The Epigram in the English Renaissance.* Princeton, 1947: *JEGP,* XLVII (July), 296-99.

1949 Joseph, Sister Miriam. *Shakespeare's Use of the Arts of Language.* New York, 1947: *MLN,* LXIV (February), 120-22.

Reyher, Paul. *Essai sur Les Idées dans L'Oeuvre de Shakespeare.* Paris, 1947: *JEGP,* XLVIII (July), 400-4.

Armstrong, Edward A. *Shakespeare's Imagination: A Study of the Psychology of Association and Inspiration.* London, 1946: *JEGP,* XLVIII (July), 404-5.

Cleland, James. *The Institution of a Young Noble Man.* Vol. I,

Introduction and Text, Introduction by Max Molyneux. Scholars' Facsimiles and Reprints. New York, 1948: *JEGP,* XLVIII (July), 408-9.

Seven Satires (1598). By William Rankins. Edited by A. Davenport. Liverpool and London, 1948;

Faunus and Melliflora (1600). By John Weever. Edited by A. Davenport. Liverpool and London, 1948: *JEGP,* XLVIII (July), 409.

Hyde, Mary Crapo. *Playwriting for Elizabethans 1600-1605.* New York, 1949;

Rollo Duke of Normandy or The Bloody Brother. A Tragedy. Attributed to John Fletcher, George Chapman, Ben Jonson and Philip Massinger. Edited by J. D. Lump. Liverpool and London, 1948;

The Tragedy of Philotas. By Samuel Daniel. Edited, with Introduction and Notes, by Laurence Michel. New Haven, 1949;

Ten English Farces. Edited by Leo Hughes and A. H. Scouten. Austin, Tex., 1948: *JEGP,* XLVIII (July), 439-41.

1952 Fricker, Robert. *Kontrast und Polarität in den Charakterbildern Shakespeares.* Swiss Studies in English, XXII. Bern, 1951: *SQ,* III (April), 129-31.

1955 Stratman, Carl J. *Bibliography of Medieval Drama.* Los Angeles and Berkeley, 1954: *JEGP,* LIV (July), 405-7.

1957 *Edward II.* Edited by H. B. Charlton and R. D. Waller, Revised by F. N. Lees. London, 1955: *JEGP,* LVI (April), 268-69.

A New Variorum Edition of Shakespeare. The Life and Death of King Richard the Second. Edited by Matthew W. Black. Philadelphia and London, 1955: *MLN,* LXXII (May), 374-82.

A Census of the Doctoral Dissertations Prepared Under the Direction of Thomas Whitfield Baldwin

1931 Allen, Don Cameron. *Francis Meres's Treatise "Poetrie" A Critical Edition.*

Haswell, Richard Ellis. *The Heroic Couplet before Dryden (1550-1675).*

Hayde, Sister Mary Loyola. *The Source of the Latin Trope.*

1935 Brawner, James Paul. *The Warres of Cyrus, A Tragedy. Edited with an Introduction and Notes.*

Harris, Jesse W. *The Life and Works of John Bale 1495-1563.*

1936 Blair, Robert Lee. *An Edition of George Peele's* Old Wives' Tale.

1937 Henneberger, Olive Pauline. *Proximate Sources for the Italianate Elements in Shakespeare.*

1938 Roberts, Charles Walter. *An Edition of John Phillip's* Commodye of Pacient and Meeke Grissell.

1940 Peterson, Earl Herman. *Early English Chronicle and Biographical Antecedents of* I Henry VI.

1942 Larkin, James Francis. *Erasmus'* De Ratione Studii: *Its Relationship to Sixteenth Century English Literature A Critical Edition and Translation with Introduction and Notes.*

Sisson, Sarah Trumbull. The Coblers Prophesie *A Morality Edited with an Introduction and Notes.*

1945 Oliver, Earl Lester. *The Grammar School Background of Christopher Marlowe.*

1948 Robbins, Edwin Winslow. *Theories of Characterization in Commentaries on Terence before 1600.*

1949 Hunt, Effie Neva. *Ben Jonson's Five-Act Structure.*

Jackson, James Louis. *An Edition of Richard Edwardes'* Damon and Pithias *(1571 Printing).*

1950 Carpenter, Sister Mary Alphonsa. The Tragedy of King Richard II. *Its Background and Meaning.*

Lord, John Bigelow. *Certain Dramatic Devices Studied in the Comedies of Shakespeare and in Some of the Works of His Contemporaries and Predecessors.*

1951 Brooks, Robert Giles. *An Edition of W. W.'s 1595 Translation of Plautus'* Menaecmi.

Hegland, Leonard. *The* Colloquies *of Erasmus: A Study in the Humanistic Background of English Literature.*

1952 McAvoy, William Charles. *Shakespeare's Use of the* Laus *of Aphthonius.*

Owen, John Isaac. *An Edition of* The Rare Triumphs of Love and Fortune.

1953 Bale, John Christian. *The Place of Chaucer in Sixteenth Century English Literature.*

Brennan, Joseph Xavier. *The Epitome Troporum ac Schematum: Text, Translation, and Commentary.*

Soellner, Rolf. Anima *and* Affectus: *Theories of the Emotions in Sixteenth Century Grammar Schools and Their Reflections in the Works of Shakspere.*

1958 Smith, John Hazel. *Thomas Watson's* Absalom *An Edition, Translation, and Critical Study.*

In Progress[1] Pennell, Arthur Emmet. John a Kent and John a Cumber *by Anthony Munday An Edition.*

Sherwin, Wilma. *Rhetorical Structure of the English Sermon in the Sixteenth Century.*

[1] The titles of the two dissertations still in preparation are tentative.

Wayne State University